The Athenian Nation

✦ EDWARD E. COHEN ✦

The Athenian Nation

PRINCETON UNIVERSITY PRESS
PRINCETON, NEW JERSEY

Published by Princeton University Press, 41 William Street,
Princeton, New Jersey 08540
In the United Kingdom: Princeton University Press,
3 Market Place, Woodstock, Oxfordshire OX20 1SY

Second printing, and first paperback printing, 2003
Paperback ISBN 0-691-09490-X

The Library of Congress has cataloged the cloth edition of this book as follows

Cohen, Edward E.
The Athenian nation / Edward E. Cohen.
p. cm.
Includes bibliographical references and index.
ISBN 0-691-04842-8 (cl : acid-free paper)
1. Athens (Greece)—Social conditions. 2. Social classes—Greece—Athens—History. 3. Social stratification—Greece—Athens—History. 4. Greece—Social conditions—To 146 B.C. I. Title.

HN10.A74 C65 2000
306'.09495'12—dc21 99-054905

British Library Cataloging-in-Publication Data is available

This book has been composed in Times Roman

Printed on acid-free paper. ∞

www.pupress.princeton.edu

Printed in the United States of America

3 5 7 9 10 8 6 4 2

FOR

Abigail, Daniel, Emmanuelle, Jonathan, Julie, Solomon,
AND *Suzanne.*

יתן לך בנים ובנות צדיקים וצדקניות,

עוסקים בתורה ובמצוות כל־ימי חייהם.

✦ CONTENTS ✦

✦ PREFACE ✦

THIS BOOK presents a view of ancient Athens quite different from the prevailing paradigm. I focus on Athens as an *ethnos* (a "nation")—one of its ancient characterizations—rather than as a *polis*, the dominant modern denotation, and on slaves, foreigners, and women within this *ethnos* (rather than on *politai*, so-called male citizens).[1] The following observations are intended to clarify my approach:

THE TERM *POLIS*

Both modern and ancient authors often employ the word *polis* inexactly to cover a multitude of inconsistent meanings denoting a variety of physical, political, and social arrangements: "political community," "state," "urban center," "town," "society as a whole," "a physical territory and its inhabitants," or some combination of these properties. Herodotos's usage is instructive: in his *Histories*, *polis* seems to be used indiscriminately to denote towns, states, countries, territories, political communities, central urban areas, municipalities, and villages. "[In] 60 passages there is no way of deciding whether the principal meaning is 'town' or 'state' or 'country'" (Hansen 1996b: 39). Aristotle, the prime ancient authority on the *polis,*[2] explicitly notes the confusion resulting from the undifferentiated employment in the fourth century of this single word to denote multiple institutions.[3] But Aristotle himself "makes the mistake of conflating two concepts of the polis," the state and society, "two notions which are distinguished by modern political theorists."[4] The Greek analysts Lykophrōn and Hippodamos, by contrast, envisioned the *polis* as a mere libertarian guarantor of individual freedoms, an attenuated

[1] For the inappropriateness of the prevailing translation and conceptualization of *politai* (sing. *politēs*) as "citizen(s)," see Chapter 1, pp. 32–33; Chapter 2, esp. n. 1.

[2] Bertrand 1992: 3; Welwei [1983] 1998: 10; Sakellariou 1989: 27–57.

[3] πολλαχῶς γὰρ τῆς πόλεως λεγομένης (*Pol.* 1276a23–25; cf. Hansen 1996b: 25–34).

[4] F. Miller 1995: 365, 358. Cf. Irwin 1996; Hansen 1996a: 196–203; Runciman 1990: 348. For criticism of similar syncretism in modern studies, see Humphreys 1978: 256–64; Hansen 1991: 61–64.

form of political authority and nothing more.[5] Modern scholars do no better.[6] The Copenhagen Polis Centre, presently engaged in a massive study of the ancient polis, has emphasized the inconsistency of modern usage, and its frequent deviation from ancient practice.[7] But the Centre's initial publications, offering incompatible denotations of *polis* at different periods in antiquity, seem to perpetuate continuing discontinuities in the word's employment.[8]

Despite this confusion, complexity and inexactitude, my attention to Athens as an *ethnos* is not intended to suggest the invalidity, in appropriate context, of identifying "Athens" as a *polis*—whatever "Athens" or "*polis*" may mean in specific situations and aspects. The ancients certainly did speak of Athens, and Attika, as a *polis,* especially in political discourse, and modern writers will inevitably continue to do so. My hope is that *The Athenian Nation* will join other recent research in showing that the political dimension was only one of the manifold aspects of Athenian life, and that continual focus on the administrative organization of the *politai* obfuscates a more useful alternative conceptualization of Athens.

Status and Orders

Athens is renowned as the "birthplace of democracy." Yet for most scholars the discriminatory inequality of the Athenian democracy is chillingly clear:

> [T]he population of Athens, like that of every city-state, was divided into three clearly differentiated groups . . . ordered hierarchically. The citizens were the privileged order . . . the metics [resident foreigners] were the underprivileged order of free people . . . the slaves were the

[5] Aristot. *Pol.* 1267b37–39, 1280b10–11 (καὶ ὁ νόμος συνθήκη καί, καθάπερ ἔφη Λυκόφρων ὁ σοφιστής, ἐγγυητὴς ἀλλήλοις τῶν δικαίων, ἀλλ᾽ οὐχ οἷος ποιεῖν ἀγαθοὺς καὶ δικαίους τοὺς πολίτας). For comparable modern confusion between "nation" (a social construction relating to a culturally homogeneous group) and "state" (as a legal and political organization with coercive powers), see Seton-Watson 1977: 1; Connor 1978: 379.

[6] "The best that we can do is to say that a political entity was a *polis* if it was recognised as such" (Ste. Croix 1981: 9).

[7] Hansen 1996b: 7: "our sources often apply the term polis to a settlement that, according to modern orthodoxy, was not a polis."

[8] See Rhodes 1995: 96–97; Dreher 1995; Schuller 1995: 184–85; Perlman 1995: 135; Nielsen 1995: 94; Hansen 1995b: 38; 1996b, on the "distinction between the ancient concept of polis and the modern historical concept of city-state" (p. 8); and Chaniotis 1997: 2.

> unprivileged order, whose only right protected by law was that they could not be killed with impunity. (Hansen 1991: 86)[9]

Although the citizen "order" itself was a minority[10]—probably a small minority—of the inhabitants of Attika (see Chapter 1, p. 17), the group in dictatorial control was supposedly even smaller: adult males born of citizen parents held all power.[11] According to prevailing dogma, virtually every Athenian was a slave owner,[12] functioning in a patriarchal society more brutal and exploitative than modern repressive cultures,[13] a tyranny in which the vast majority of the population—slaves and women (including the mothers, wives, and daughters of *politai*)—were equally without rights and similarly victimized.[14] Exploitation of the noncitizen majority allegedly underlay the fabled stability of Athenian politics. "The success

[9] This tripartite division has not been seen as merely theoretical: "the three status groups . . . were sharply distinguished not simply as concepts but in actuality." Todd 1993: 173. Cf. Raaflaub 1980: 44–46; Meier 1984: 20–22; Pomeroy 1975: 78; Jameson 1997: 95. Even European neofascist politicians have embraced this hierarchical model: the National Front in France has cited "les premières démocraties, les démocraties authentiques" as characterized by "necessaire discrimination," claiming for modern racists "vingt-cinq siècles de tradition juridique et politique" (Stirbois 1990: 909–10).

[10] An "order"—at the heart of the prevailing tripartite analysis—is a term not of ancient (it has only etymological relationship to the Roman *ordo*) but of Weberian origin: it emphasizes a society's juridical arrangements by positing various groups who are assigned by law specified advantages or disadvantages, privileges or obligations. See Ste. Croix 1981: 42, 94; Finley 1985: 45–48. But when Aristotle seeks to isolate the constituent parts of the *polis* (*Pol.* 1274b38–41), his divisions are not juridical or tripartite. Rather they reflect such differentiations as residents' variant forms of military service, household arrangements (ἐξ οἰκιῶν), financial situation (εὔποροι, ἄποροι, μέσοι), or source of income (γεωργικόν, ἀγοραῖον, βάναυσον)—see *Pol.* 1289b27–1290a1—all of which distinctions transcend a tripartite hierarchical arrangement. The concept of "order" is entirely absent from Aristotle's formulation (Ober 1991: 116).

[11] For conceptualization and definition of "citizen parents," see Chapter 2.

[12] "In classical Athens, where the price of a slave was equivalent only to the cost of maintaining him for one to two years, all but the very poor could afford to own at least one slave." Garnsey 1980: 1. For the *opinio communis* stressing widespread dependence on slave labor, see, for example, Jameson 1977–78 and Ste. Croix 1981. Starr (1958) and Wood (1988) dissent, finding slavery less pervasive. R. Osborne argues for slaves' "limited employment in agriculture," in contrast to their prevalence in mines and in domestic labor (1995: 33).

[13] Athenian society was "an extremely patriarchal one in theory, not only legal theory but the generally accepted social understanding of the people" (Schaps 1979: 96; cf. Pomeroy 1975: 58). In practice, Athenian patriarchy was yet more "severe and crass" than that of modern "patriarchal industrial societies" (Keuls 1985: 12), although male-dominance in daily life might have been substantially modified by power yielded indirectly by women through personal and economic relationships (as Schaps argues [1979: 92–96]). Gallo 1984b similarly seeks to clarify possible differences between legal theory and social reality.

[14] See Wright [1923] 1969: 1; Vidal-Naquet 1986: 206–7; Cantarella 1987: 38; Schuller 1985. Keuls argues that "the two categories" (of slave and wife) are explicitly connected at Athens through "a considerable number of references and symbols"; for example, "the legal term for wife was *damar*, a word derived from a root meaning 'to subdue' or 'to tame' " (1985: 6). Just (1985) claims that ancient literature stereotypically attributes to women and slaves similar negative attributes. For the conjunction, anticipated in both Foucauldian descriptive and feminist ideological

of the democracy in securing the loyalty and devotion of the vast majority of citizens rested largely on its insistence on a marked distinction between citizens (whatever their social status) on the one hand, and all categories of non-citizens on the other."[15]

In my opinion, juridically based distinctions did have significance and, in overtly political contexts, overwhelming importance. But Athenian civilization, as I undertake to demonstrate in this book,[16] was far more complex and multifaceted than the prevailing tripartite oversimplification.

Modern Theory and Comparative Example

I have sought to derive themes and conclusions solely from Athenian evidence, and from sources contemporary with the matters described or interpreted. References to other periods and places, and to modern social research and theories, are intended essentially for clarification or suggestion or for their perceived intrinsic interest, sometimes as confirmation of conclusions drawn from Athenian material, but never as independent proof by analogy or as diktat concerning Athenian practices. For example, I note in Chapter 2 a prevailing modern approach to interpreting legal documents that is consonant with "the well-known Greek obsession with elaborate attention to choice, and even rhetorical placement, of specific words and phrases" (pp. 62–63). But modern practice, in my opinion, can never be evidence, ipso facto, for Athenian procedure, nor can modern theories of nationalism and ethnicity alone establish anything concerning Athenian behavior. To the contrary, the historian of Athenian institutions must pay close attention to the Athenians' organization and perception of their own unique reality. But a focus on culture-bound processes must be complemented by a recognition that the inhabitants of Attika necessarily lived their lives in accordance with fundamental human responses and motivations.[17]

---

models, of dependent individuals themselves interacting in a nonhierarchical relationship, see Foucault 1984: 381–82; Alcoff 1990; Dreyfus and Rabinow 1983: 233; Diamond and Quinby 1988.

[15] Raaflaub 1983: 532. In recent years, this alleged link between male citizen cohesion and exploitation of others living in Attika has been frequently advanced: see the examples in Roberts 1996, esp. 193–94; cf. Halperin 1990: 95–96.

[16] See Chapters 1 (pp. 30–48), 5, and 6.

[17] For a fuller exegesis of the interplay, in analysis of Athens, between a recognition of shared basic human similarities and a respect for the uniqueness of individual societies, see E. Cohen 1992: x–xi.

Chronology and Sources

Unless otherwise indicated or clear from the context, all chronological references in this book are "B.C.E." Our evidence, and my focus, relate primarily to the fourth century, for which relatively abundant but often chronologically undifferentiated data have sometimes required an essentially synchronic presentation. I have, however, attempted to make diachronic distinctions explicit wherever relevant.[18] Although material from the fourth century is often preserved only in collections compiled in later antiquity (commentaries on authors, lexicographical studies, and such), in using this material I have endeavored to note possible conflicts between these sources and information directly preserved from the fourth century, and to indicate suggestions made by others concerning the possible unreliability of later testimonia.

As a partial antidote to the absence of statistical evidence and archival material from ancient Athens,[19] I make considerable use of litigants' presentations in the lawcourts.[20] Although Athenian forensic speeches are rhetorical contrivances that virtually always present evidence tendentiously (and often dishonestly), the presuppositions underlying litigants' claims are generally reliable: since court presentations were made to panels composed of hundreds of jurors—with persuasion the speaker's dominant motive—the presence of a general phenomenon may be confirmed by a claim that presupposes such a phenomenon, even if we cannot establish (or strongly doubt) the truth of the speaker's specific factual assertion.[21] When the speaker in Isokratēs' *Trapezitikos* (17.4) claims that a slave acting without supervision legitimately provided him with six talents from bank funds, we may not be able to determine whether the transaction actually took place or was appropriate, but we *can* be sure that slaves engaged in banking at Athens did on occasion handle large sums of money without supervision. When Athenian public

[18] For the validity of such limited synchronicity, see Momigliano 1974: 68; E. Cohen 1992: xii. Cf. Golden 1992: esp. p. 13.

[19] On the lack of statistics, see E. Cohen 1992: 27. The Athenians did maintain an archive in the Mētroōn (Thomas 1989: 68–83), but none of its contents have survived in situ. Even in the fourth century the items on deposit were quite limited: there was no land register (Gabrielsen 1986: 113, n. 40; Christ 1990: 158), no list of *politai* (Davidson 1997: 215; Biscardi 1991: 140; 1970), only rudimentary financial accounts (Finley 1982).

[20] These speeches provide "the best image of contemporary society" (Garlan 1988: 16—cf. Mossé [1962] 1979: 179–215)—albeit a view fragmentary in content and chronologically largely limited to the fourth century.

[21] Cf. E. Cohen 1990: 178, 186–90; Millett 1991: 2; Todd 1990.

figures, in court presentations, challenge the civic status of opponents by attributing to them foreign or even slave origin, we need not accept as literal truth the specific charge (especially in the absence of corroborative evidence), but we *can* infer the likelihood that Athenian genealogy was porous enough for some politicians to be of misty antecedents.[22]

Of similar potential value are the factual patterns underlying the sarcasm, oxymoronic hyperbole, and humorous twistings of comic or sarcastic writers, even those passages sometimes peremptorily dismissed as implausible or impossible because they contradict today's Western preconceptions.[23] Consider the *Constitution of the Athenians*, included among the manuscripts of Xenophon—whose true but unknown author is often deprecatingly referred to, in anglophone scholarship, as the "Old Oligarch."[24] This work, to be sure, represents an extreme antidemocratic view and (yet more challengingly) is a caldron of irony. But, in my opinion, its explicit statements should be evaluated as part of the totality of surviving evidence, not automatically disregarded where they contradict prevailing modern opinion (especially on those points where no affirmative ancient testimonia support present-day assumptions). Thus, in Chapter 5, I offer the context and confirmatory passages justifying pseudo-Xenophon's indication that Athenian slaves were not obligated to show obeisance to free persons other than their own masters—a truth frequently dismissed because of its author's deficient *auctoritas* and its contradiction of the assumed self-abasing conduct of Athenian slaves.[25] Similarly, I have attempted to use to the fullest evidence from comic poets, not disregarding citations from Menander, for example, even those preserved only in Latin translation or paraphrase, and even those mandating fresh interpretations (as in the discussion of prostitutional contracts in Chapter 6, pp. 183–84).

[22] Cf. Chapter 2, pp. 76–77; Chapter 5, p. 138. For an approach to the problems inherent in using forensic material as evidence for political history, see Harris 1995: 7–16.

[23] Cultural historians are well aware of the need to focus on the seemingly inane: "when we cannot get a proverb, or a joke, or a ritual, or a poem, we know we are on to something" (Darnton 1984: 5).

[24] "The expression has no parallel in scholarship other than English" (Bowersock 1968: 463, n. 1). On the purpose and authorship of this work, see most recently Dimopoulou-Piliouni (forthcoming).

[25] The Old Oligarch avers that at Athens a slave will not yield to a free person on the street (§10: οὔτε ὑπεκστήσεταί σοι ὁ δοῦλος), a contention actually consonant with the conclusion recently reached by Jameson in a sensible and sensitive exegesis of the role of women and slaves in fourth-century Athens ("from a traditional point of view, things were turned upside down" in

Unless otherwise indicated, all translations and paraphrases of ancient sources are my own. Greek authors who are edited in Oxford Classical Text editions are generally quoted from that series; for other Greek authors, the text usually is that of the Budé edition. Unless the distinction is relevant to my discussion, I do not differentiate between speeches or other works properly bearing the name of an ancient author and those of doubtful attribution.[26]

My manuscript was delivered to Princeton University Press in May 1998, and it has accordingly been impossible to consider systematically secondary literature that has appeared thereafter.

---

many aspects of the relationship between free and enslaved [1997: 98]). Yet Jameson still disavows the Old Oligarch's actual testimony ("one need not suppose that the upper classes were, in fact, inhibited as they made their way through the streets of Athens" [1997: 97].

[26] Thus I generally cite as "Demosthenes" those speeches traditionally included in the Demosthenic corpus and as "Aristotle" those works similarly included in the Aristotelian corpus.

✦ ACKNOWLEDGMENTS ✦

I AM GRATEFUL for the help I have received in writing this book. At early stages I presented material ultimately included here to academic audiences in England at Oxford, Cambridge, and Keele Universities; in Greece at the European Cultural Center (Delphi) and at the University of the Ionian Islands; in Belgium at the Université Libre de Bruxelles; in Austria at the Josef-Krainer-Haus in Gratz; in Canada at the University of Toronto; and in the United States at Brown University. I gained much from lively discussions after each of these lectures, and from the stimulating contributions of my students at the University of Pennsylvania where I was a Visiting Professor in 1996. Early versions of parts of Chapters 2, 4, and 5 respectively have appeared in: *Symposion 1995* (Akten der Gesellschaft für Griechische und Hellenistische Rechtsgeschichte, 1997): 57–79; *Common Knowledge* 6 (1997): 97–124; and in *Le monde antique et les droits de l'homme* (1998): 105–29.

I owe special gratitude for helpful conversation to Sophie Adam-Magnisali, Eva Cantarella, Paul Cartledge, Robert Connor, Anthony Corakis, Athena Dimopoulou-Piliouni, Lin Foxhall, Virginia Hunter, Michael Jameson, William Loomis, Lene Rubinstein, Adele Scafuro, Gerhard Thür, Stephen Todd, Julie Vélissaropoulos-Karakostas, and Gayla Weng. I am indebted a fortiori to Robin Osborne who read Chapter 4 with his usual extraordinary insight, and to Josiah Ober and Ian Morris who read a draft of the entire manuscript and offered enormously helpful comments. None of these scholars necessarily endorses any of my views (and some have dissented most stimulatingly).

At Princeton University Press, Brigitta van Rheinberg has been a unique source of encouragement and good judgment. Brian MacDonald provided welcome skill and sense in editing this volume. In Philadelphia, Kimberly Touch, Susann Taylor, and Matt Waters have provided all manner of assistance, for which I am grateful. Above all, my deepest and ever continuing appreciation is to my wife, Betsy.

This book is dedicated to seven who have brought me unbroken joy.

ABBREVIATIONS

Aiskhyl.	Aiskhylos
Iket.	*Hiketides*
Prom.	*Promētheus*
Ail.	Ailianos
Poik. Hist.	*Poikilē Historia*
Aiskhin.	Aiskhinēs
Alkiphr.	Alkiphrōn
Andok.	Andokidēs
Alk.	*Against Alkibiadēs*
Antiph.	Antiphōn
App.	Appianos
Emph. Pol.	*Civil Wars*
Apollod.	Apollodōros
Bibl.	*Bibliothēkē*
Aristoph.	Aristophanes
Akh.	*Akharneis*
Batr.	*Batrakhoi*
Hipp.	*Hippeis*
Lys.	*Lysistrata*
Orn.	*Ornithes*
Plout.	*Ploutos*
Sphēk.	*Sphēkes*
Thes.	*Thesmophoriazousai*
Aristot.	Aristotle
Ath. Pol.	*Athēnaiōn Politeia*
EE	*Eudemian Ethics*
NE	*Nicomachean Ethics*
Oikon.	*Oikonomika*
Pol.	*Politics*
Athēn.	Athēnaios
Cic.	Cicero
Att.	*Epistulae ad Atticum*
Phil.	*Orationes Philippicae*
Dein.	Deinarkhos
Dem.	*Against Demosthenes*
Dēm. Phal.	Dēmētrios of Phaleron
Dem.	Demosthenes
Dio Cass.	Dio Cassius
Dio Khrys.	Dio Khrysostomos
Diod. Sik.	Diodōros of Sicily
Diog. Laert.	Diogenēs Laertios
Dion. Hal.	Dionysios of Halikarnassos
Epit. Ulp.	*Epitome Ulpiani*
Eur.	Euripides
Ēlek.	*Ēlektra*
Hērakleid.	*Hērakleidai*
Iket.	*Hiketides*
Mēd.	*Mēdeia*
Mel. Des.	*Melanippē Desmōtēs*
Ph.	*Phoinissai*
Harp.	Harpokratiōn
Hell. Oxyrh.	Hellēnika Oxyrhynkhia
Hdt.	Herodotos
Hesykh.	Hesykhios
Hom.	Homer
Il.	*Iliad*
Od.	*Odyssey*
Hyper.	Hypereidēs
Athēn.	*Against Athēnogenēs*
Epitaph.	*Epitaphios*
Euxen.	*For Euxenippos*
Lyk.	*For Lykophrōn*
Phil.	*Against Philippidēs*

Inst.	*Institutiones*
Isai.	Isaios
Isok.	Isokratēs
Panath.	*Panathēnaikos*
Plat.	*Plataikos*
Just.	Justinian
Dig.	*Digesta*
Inst.	*Institutiones*
Lykourg.	Lykourgos
Leōk.	*Against Leōkratēs*
Lys.	Lysias
Men.	Menander
Dys.	*Dyskolos*
Sam.	*Samia*
Paus.	Pausanias
Phōt.	Phōtios
Pind.	Pindar
Isthm.	*Isthmian Odes*
Ol.	*Olympian Odes*
Pl.	Plato
Alk.	*Alkibiadēs*
Euthd.	*Euthydēmos*
Gorg.	*Gorgias*
Khrm.	*Kharmidēs*
Men.	*Menexenos*
Polit.	*Politikos*
Prōtag.	*Prōtagoras*
Rep.	*Republic*
Symp.	*Symposion*
Theait.	*Theaitētos*
Tim.	*Timaios*
Plaut.	Plautus
Bacch.	*Bacchides*
Merc.	*Mercator*
Plut.	Plutarch
Bioi Rhēt.	*Bioi Rhētorōn*
Dem.	*Demosthenes*
Mor.	*Moralia* (*Êthika*)
Perikl.	*Periklēs*
Sol.	*Solōn*
Thēs.	*Thēseus*
Serv.	Servius
Aen.	*Aeneid*
Soph.	Sophoklēs
Ant.	*Antigonē*
Ēlek.	*Ēlektra*
Oid. Kol.	*Oidipous Kolōnos*
Oid. T.	*Oidipous Tyrannos*
Phil.	*Philoktētēs*
Theophr.	Theophrastos
Khar.	*Kharaktēres*
Thouk.	Thucydides
Xen.	Xenophon
Agēs.	*Agēsilaos*
Apom.	*Apomnēmoneumatōn*
Hell.	*Hellēnika*
Lak. Pol.	*Lakedaimoniōn Politeia*
Oik.	*Oikonomikos*
Por.	*Poroi*
Symp.	*Symposion*

The Athenian Nation

✦ INTRODUCTION ✦

Athens as Paradox—Athens as Nation

For contemporary scholarship, classical Athens is paradox and contradiction:

- Modern conceptualization of the ancient Greek political community, or *polis,* is based on the model of Athens, the only one of the hundreds of ancient Greek *poleis* for which detailed information on political and social institutions survives.[1] Yet, as the Greeks recognized, and as many modern authors have emphasized,[2] Athens differed fundamentally from the other *poleis*: among a multitude of incongruities, it was too large, too impersonal, too lacking in self-sufficiency to constitute a traditional Hellenic political unit; by Aristotle's criteria, it was not a *polis* at all.[3] Herodotos, "the Father of Ethnography no less than the Father of History," even terms Athens an *ethnos* (a "nation" or "people"), a word normally used in antithesis to *polis.*[4] Indeed, ancient Athens manifests to a high degree the characteristics now

[1] For the vast number of separate communities in Greek antiquity, see Ruschenbusch 1978: 3–17; 1984: 55–57; 1985: 257. Cf. Hansen 1994a: 14. Because very little information has survived about the political structure of these *poleis* (Whitehead 1993: 135–36), modern scholars have tended to appropriate Athens, relatively fully documented, as the "most typical example of the evolution of the Greek polis" (Pečirka 1976: 6; cf. Mossé [1962] 1979: 29).

[2] "An unusual polis" (Meyer 1993: 119); "cité atypique" (Migeotte 1995: 462); "peculiar" (Nixon and Price 1990: 137); "exceptional" (Arafat and Morgan 1994: 132; Morrow [1960] 1993: 141; Todd 1993: 3, n. 1; Sagan 1991: 1); "unique" (Whitehead 1984: 48; Will 1972: 680); "least typical" (Garnsey 1985: xi). Even its burial and commemorative patterns were distinctive: Morris 1992: 103–27; Kurtz and Boardman 1971: 244.

[3] See *Pol.* 7.4–7, discussed in Chapter 1, pp. 11–22. For Aristotle's inconsistent use of the term *polis,* see the Preface above, pp. ix–x.

[4] τὸ Ἀττικὸν ἔθνος: Hdt. 1.57.3. Cf. 1.59.1. Herodotos generally refers to Athens as "Athens" (1.60, 64, 98, 143, 147, 173; 2.7; 3.160; 5.66; and frequently in the later books). He does sometimes refer to Athens as a *polis,* but only in a political sense (1.30.4; 1.59.6; 5.91.2; 5.97.1; 6.99.2; 8.44.1). (He also refers to the central town of Attika as a *polis,* differentiated from the *khōra* at 7.133.2, and from the *akropolis* at 8.41.3.) His only other reference to the Athenian *polis* is in a (not surprisingly) ambiguous quotation from the Delphic oracle (7.140.2). For Herodotos as "Father of Ethnography": Jones 1996: 315. For *ethnos* as antithesis of *polis*: Chapter 1, pp. 22 ff. For the interchangeability of the names Attika and Athens, see n. 7.

utilized by modern ethnologists to identify a nation: the sharing, by the members of a culturally homogeneous social group, of a mutually conceptualized identity (see Chapter 2);[5] a scale of organization and existence that precludes personal contact among the majority of the members of this group, resulting in the creation of an "imagined community," *imagined* "because the members of even the smallest nation will never know most of their fellow-members, meet them, or even hear of them" (Anderson 1991: 15–16—see Chapter 4); the creation and perpetuation of "myths" set in historical fabrications that establish or reinforce this group's claims to cohesiveness, uniqueness, self-determination, and/or aggrandizement (Chapter 3); focus on a specific physical territory over which the group desires some form of autonomy (Chapter 2); and territorial mobility for members functioning through a common economy (Chapters 5 and 6).

- The largest of all Hellenic groupings, with a population and area greater than that of many modern nations, Athens is nevertheless, for some modern scholars, the "model of a face-to-face society" where people knew each other intimately and interacted closely on a societywide basis (see Chapter 4).
- Priding themselves on being the only Greek group autochthonous to their territory, the Athenians in fact did not restrict immigration, and newcomers (free and slave) came to outnumber the early inhabitants and their descendants.
- Although the indigenous residents supposedly formed "a closed group, inaccessible from outside" (Davies 1978: 73), the Atheni-

[5] Members' self-ascription through conceptualization of a shared culture is central to ethnological definition of a nation. See Barth 1969; Seton-Watson 1977: 1; Anderson 1991: 195; Greenfield 1992: 13. Such subjective construction explains the relatively common phenomenon of ethnic differentiation even in the absence of "objective" distinctions between groups. (See, for example, Danforth's study of modern "Macedonian" identification [1995: 56–78]; Keyes's discussions of "Tai" ascription outside Thailand [1992, 1995]; Uchendu on ethnicity in Africa [1995]. Cf. Royce 1982; Nash 1989.) Because of the current widespread transnational diffusion of diasporas containing individuals who identify with a national group with which they have limited objective relationship, theorists have posited even multiple "imagined" societies, "which are constituted by the historically situated imaginations of persons and groups spread around the globe" (Appadurai 1990: 7; cf. Dayal 1996: 129–44). Contemporary scholars have now largely abjured an earlier reifying tendency (exemplified by Deutsch 1966, ch. 1; Rustow 1967, ch. 1) to identify ethnic groups through essentialist characteristics such as common origin, history, and language. For discussion of "the complex and abstract nature of national identity," see now Smith 1991: esp. 8–18; de Vos and Romanucci-Ross 1995: 349–79; Hall 1997: 17–34. Chatterjee (1986: esp. ch. 1)

ans (according to Isokratēs and others) were actually quite liberal in accepting new citizens (see Chapter 2).

- A font of the high culture of Western civilization, celebrated throughout history for its cultural masterpieces, the achievements of Athens were to a considerable extent the accomplishment of outsiders. Although scholars frequently lament the exclusively "elite" origin of literary works and of social information surviving from antiquity, much of Athenian prose—especially court presentations—was written by or on behalf of foreigners, and sometimes by or for former slaves and their immediate families.[6]
- Although Athenian society and the Athenian economy were highly dependent on unfree labor, and Athens has therefore frequently been deemed one of the world's few true "slave societies," a number of enslaved businessmen and some unfree public servants amassed considerable wealth and significant authority. Communal values and economic circumstance mandated, as one contemporary observed, that "some slaves live magnificently, and properly so" (see Chaper 5).
- The birthplace and apogee of popular democracy, classical Attika[7] was supposedly controlled by a permanent dictatorship constituting a small minority of its inhabitants, "the Athenians," adult male citizens born from citizen stock (*politai*). The unanimity of male citizen support for Athenian democracy (free for decades from the internal strife rampant in many other ancient Greek

objects to the purported absence in Andersonian "imagination" of the "work of the imagination—the intellectual process of creation" (p. 21). Cf. Chatterjee 1993: 110–15.

[6] Of the thirty-three surviving "private" speeches attributed to Demosthenes, for example, seven relate directly or indirectly to the bank of Pasiōn, a business owned and operated over several generations by slaves or former slaves. At least seven (and possibly as many as nine) presentations included in the Demosthenic corpus are believed to have been written and delivered by Apollodōros, born to Pasiōn sometime before the likely date of his manumission from slavery (see Dem. 36.22, 46.13; Davies 1971: 429–30; E. Cohen 1992: 81, n. 101; 98, n. 182). For Apollodōros as the "eleventh Attic orator," see Trevett 1992: 62–70; Carey 1992: 17–20. Cf. Pearson 1966: 359 (= 1983: 223); 1969: 19, n. 8 (= 1983: 225, n. 8); McCabe 1981: 152–74; Gernet 1954–60: 3:11–13; Blass 1887–98: 3:514–43; Paley and Sandys [1896–98] 1979: 2:xxxix–xlvii; Sigg 1873. Resident foreigners could speak on their own behalf in Athenian courts: see Aristot. *Ath. Pol.* 58.2-3 (Rhodes 1981, ad loc.); Patterson forthcoming. Cf. Harrison 1968–71: 1:192, n. 1, 193–96; 1971: 10–11.

[7] Both in ancient and modern times, the territory of the Athenians has been referred to interchangeably as Attika or Athens. On the disputed etymology and implications underlying this dual nomenclature, see Patterson 1986: 50–53; Dittenberger 1906: 78–102, 161–219; 1907: 1–34; Chantraine 1956: 103–4; Loraux [1984] 1993: 116–19; Vidal-Naquet 1986: 206–7.

entities) was, at least partly, "a product of the oppression of noncitizen groups within the Polis."[8] Yet there is little indication of discontent among the disenfranchised majority,[9] and profuse evidence for the acquisition of power and full social, and even political, integration by "foreigners" (see Chapter 2).

- Because women lacked direct political rights, scholars generally deny the title "citizen" to the wives, daughters, and other female relatives of Athenian male citizens. But at Athens the feminine form "citizeness" (*politis*) was in general and meaningful use (see Chapter 1).
- Although a central tenet of contemporary political sociology holds that "political institutions are one of many clusters of social institutions,"[10] modern scholarship has sought to understand Athenian civilization through a singular focus on the political organization of the adult male citizens.[11] This group, and their political institution, have been seen as the exclusive incarnation of Athenian society and state.[12] "The polis did not comprise all who lived within its borders, but only the *politai,* i.e. the citizens"

[8] Ober 1989: 5. Vatin 1984: 27: "Au total, les citoyens de plein droit sont une petite minorité sur le territoire, et règnent en toute souveraineté sur une population majoritaire." Cf. Raaflaub 1983: 544, n. 93; 1980: 44–46; Schaps 1979: 96; Pomeroy 1975: 58; Keuls 1985: 12. On the ubiquity and genesis of violent conflict within ancient Greek political communities, see Gehrke 1985; Cohen 1995: 25–32.

[9] Although large numbers of unfree persons defected during the later stages of the Peloponnesian War (Thouk. 7.27.5), no form of slave insurrection is reported before the second century B.C.E. (and then only in the Laureion mines, "probably stimulated by reports of the Sicilian slave revolts" [Jameson 1997: 100, n. 5]). On the second-century rebellion, see Diod. Sik. 34.2.19; Athēn. 272e–f.

[10] Lipset 1959: 83. Cf. Washburn 1982.

[11] For the continuing identification of the male citizen as the exclusive avatar of Athens—despite the articulation in recent years of new sociological, anthropological, and ideological approaches to Athenian civilization—see the various articles in Boegehold and Scafuro: 1994, where "Athenian Identity and Civic Ideology" is equated with "the sorts of question asked about citizenship and the definition given by scholars to citizenship" (p. 2). Connor notes (1994: 34) that "the study of Athenian civic identity has to date largely been based on the understanding of Athenian citizenship." Manville even asserts (in an article entitled "Toward a New Paradigm of Athenian Citizenship") that "citizenship and the *polis* are one and the same. . . . 'the true citizens' are the adult Athenian males" (1994: 24–25), a view articulated in virtually the same terms for many decades (cf., e.g., Paoli 1936: 108). For the ubiquity of this interpretation, see Manville 1990: 35–54.

[12] This *opinio communis* divides between (1) a Weberian view that elevates the male citizens' political state (the *polis*) above the mundane activities of community life, which remain outside (and beneath) the *polis,* and (2) a Durkheimian approach that absorbs the entire Athenian society and civilization into the male citizens' *polis* (asserting the absence of any absolute boundary between public and private activities). See Lanza and Vegetti 1975: 25; Meier 1984: 30; Ober 1993: 129–30; Murray 1990a: 5–6; 1993: 197–98; Hansen 1993: 7–9, 13–18; Sakellariou 1989.

(M. H. Hansen 1989a: 19). "Those who count possess citizenship" (Canfora 1995: 124). Athens itself—territory, economy, disenfranchised majority—"never meant anything but a spot on the map" (Finley 1963: 35).[13] Yet Athenian writers frequently describe territorial toponyms, those alleged "spots on the map"—representing geographical unities rather than male kinship structures—as taking actions, making decisions, and exercising authority,[14] and significant archaeological and literary data place at the center of ancient Greek communities not male political organizations but religious cults and institutions,[15] in which women,[16] resident "foreigners" (metics), and slaves were often full participants (see Chapters 1, 5) and where women "enjoyed a kind of 'cultic citizenship'" (Parker 1996: 80). Under this religiocentric model of the *polis,* promulgated primarily by francophone scholars,[17] "the social unit established on a territory with a central inhabited area" is dominant, while political institutions

[13] "Athens, Corinth, Sparta" were merely "geographical place-names" (Finley 1984: 10)—a "highly influential orthodoxy" that has been "repeatedly uttered, echoed (and) taught to students" (Whitehead 1996: 3). In accord: Manville 1990: 6; Hornblower 1987: 81; Patterson 1986: 52; Hansen 1978: 15; 1991: 58; 1993: 7–8; Finley 1984: 10; Crawford and Whitehead 1983: 4. Cf. Ehrenberg 1969: 88–89; Bordes 1982: 17; Vernant 1986: 227–28; Morris 1987: 3ff.

[14] "Thousands of instances could be amassed" where Greek toponyms express "place and people" (Whitehead 1996: 2), where authors attribute action or function to a locational entity that encompasses a physical territory, its territorial residents and the intangible aspects and attributes connected with that toponym. See, for example, Xen. *Hell.* 5.1.31 (τὰς δὲ ἄλλας Ἑλληνίδας πόλεις καὶ μικρὰς καὶ μεγάλας αὐτονόμους ἀφεῖναι πλὴν Λήμνου καὶ Ἴμβρου καὶ Σκύρου); Hdt. 7.15 (οὐδεμίαν νομίζειν πόλιν Ἄργεος φιλιωτέρην); Isok. 15.109 (Κόρκυραν εἷλε, πόλιν ὀγδοήκοντα τριήρεις κεκτημένην); Xen. *Hell.* 5.1.36 (προσέλαβον μὲν σύμμαχον Κόρινθον). Often the text switches seamlessly between a group denomination and a toponym in the same sentence: see, for example, Xen. *Hell.* 2.2.9 (Λύσανδρος δὲ ἀφικόμενος εἰς Αἴγιναν ἀπέδωκε τὴν πόλιν Αἰγινήταις); Thouk. 2.2.1 (ἐσῆλθον . . . ἐς Πλάταιαν τῆς Βοιωτίας οὖσαν Ἀθηναίων ξυμμαχίδα).

[15] Sourvinou-Inwood 1990. Religious sanctuaries and cult activities appear largely to have predated the development of *poleis*, and to have been important factors in the eventual genesis of autonomous entities, which earlier, as inchoate urban centers, participated together in temple functions. Polignac (1995), for example, has demonstrated that many early religious sanctuaries were located not within but between or among centers that later emerged as *poleis*.

[16] See Eur. *Mel. Des.* fr. 660 Mette 1982–85, lines 12–13, 18–21 (P. Berl. 9772 and P. Oxy. 1176 fr. 39, col. 11) (fr. 13: Auffret 1987): "In regard to matters concerning the gods—which I judge to be of prime importance—we women hold the greatest portion. . . . Rites in honor of the Fates and the Nameless Goddesses are accomplished: these rites are not holy among men, but among women they prosper" (τὰ δ' ἐν θεοῖς αὖ—πρῶτα γὰρ κρίνω τάδε— | μέρος μέγιστον ἔχομεν. . . . ἃ δ' εἴς τε Μοίρας τάς τ' ἀνωνύμους θεὰς | ἱερὰ τελεῖται, ταῦτ' ἐν ἀνδράσιν μὲν οὐ<χ> | ὅσια καθέστηκ', ἐν γυναιξὶ δ' αὔξεται | ἅπαντα).

[17] The French appreciation of nonpolitical factors in the functioning of Greek institutions can be traced to Durkheim's early work (especially "The Elementary Forms of the Religious Life"), which emphasized social forms, and to the later anthropological insights of Louis Gernet. Cf. Mossé 1995: viii, xiv; Humphreys 1978: 76–106.

constitute only a "particular aspect of the civic organization," albeit one that "affects a number of the domains of collective life" (Polignac 1995: xv).

- In "simple societies," systems-theory sociology does posit a fusion of political and social functions that might provide a theoretical justification for the prevailing focus on the political organization of male citizens, the *polis,* as the sole embodiment of Athenian society and state.[18] But life in Attika was organized through complexly multiple, sometimes overlapping, sometimes distinct institutions and groupings (cult associations, self-help *eranoi,* political subdivisions, migrant social groups, business associations, groupings of messmates and funerary associates, religious congregations, "houses" and households, brotherhoods, kin groupings, family organizations and many others)—loci of significance and epicenters of authority often impacting, supplementing, superseding, negating the formalistic political organization of the male *politai.*[19]

THE anomalies adumbrated here are the subject of this book; their resolution, its objective—a topic and purpose important beyond the professional interests of classicists and ancient historians, and even beyond the daunting significance of Athens as cultural goddess of Western humanism. In various contemporary "discourses," Classical Athens is today invoked as alleged factual confirmation for numerous significant theses. Athenian sexual practices, for example—allegedly based not on heterosexual genitalia but on the abusive and exploitative dictatorial dominance of the male "citizen" (a thesis examined in Chapter 6)—shatter today's majoritarian assumptions while splintering feminist and homoerotic communities.[20] In Chapter 4, I challenge the historicity of Athens as a "face-to-face" society, a conceptualization to which a multitude of important

[18] For such "systems analysis," see Luhmann 1982: 140.

[19] For the ongoing importance of such groupings, see the "Solonian" law cited at Just. *Dig.* 47.22.4; Aristot. *EE* 1241b14–27, *NE* 1160a. Cf. Connor 1996b and the surveys in Scafuro 1994; Ogden 1996: 83–135. E. Hall emphasizes "the complex plurality of groups to which individuals simultaneously belong[ed] . . . even in the fifth century" (1989: 6–7).

[20] The contention that Athenian sexual protocols were based not on gender but on politicized dominance and submission "has generated great controversy, both as a historical topic of investigation and as an important issue of contemporary sexual politics" (Larmour, Miller, and Platter 1998: 28). David Halperin (1990: 10), for example, has found that "[in] the course of lecturing to different audiences around the United States," his espousal of sexual "constructionism," based

contemporary Western scholars and thinkers—from so-called communitarians through Kuhnians[21]—have appealed in citing Athens as historical exemplar of a hermeneutically sealed society in which the entire population knew one other intimately and interacted closely on a societywide basis, where a closed group of men, "a warrior band in Republican form" (Rahe [1992] 1994: 32), shared a mutuality of cultural coherence and individual responsibility, a "consensus based on the common outlook of citizens" (Millett 1991: 39). My Athens is quite different—a nation where "households" of varied origins and differing *mentalités,* functioning through societal structures that minimized the individual persona, created a culturally homogeneous world of intricate and multidimensional institutions and ideas, unified by a mutually conceptualized group identity forged partly through historical fabrication; where demographic mobility, civil mutability, cultural complexity, and a dynamic economy generated a society of relative anonymity; where membership in the *polis* (citizenship) was a fluid asset ultimately available (or deniable) to all segments of the local population, but where "power"—the manifold aspects of control, command, and influence in a society—transcended political arrangements and manifested social, economic, religious, and even sexual dimensions.

In my opinion, it is unnecessary, and indeed quite deleterious, to espouse the modern conceptualization of Greece as essentially a mosaic of *poleis*—a focus unknown to the ancients (and, in fact, introduced only in 1893 with Burkhardt's *Griechische Kulturgeschichte*).[22] It is this relatively recent obsession with the *polis* that underlies the obsession with the male "citizen" that has caused scholars largely to ignore the overwhelming majority of the permanent population resident in Attika. Study of Athens as an "*ethnos*"—an ancient characterization of Attika—mandates attention to the bulk of the population, the multitude of persons who were not *politai.* Accordingly, this book focuses on the many resi-

largely on Athenian evidence, has evoked "resistance" and "skepticism" among the large portion of gay and lesbian society committed to sexual "essentialism." Cf. Halperin 1990: 44, 47. See Butler 1990: 8–9, 147; Thornton 1997: 247. Cf. Calame 1996: ch. 5.

[21] See Chapter 4, n. 1. More generally, the communitarians—"four major political theorists" (Michael Sandel, Alasdair MacIntyre, Charles Taylor, and Michael Walzer)—have been charged with finding "their antidote to the supposed evils of modernity [in] a return to the Greek polis, religious revival, a socialist revolution or some combination of all three" (Rosen 1996).

[22] See Gawantka 1985; Hansen 1994b (*pace* Cartledge 1996: 182, n. 12).

dents registered as non-*politai* (so-called metics), and on the numerous other free non-*politai* (the *xenoi,* the *atimoi,* the *nothoi,* etc.), on the wives, daughters, and mothers of male "citizens," on enslaved public functionaries (*dēmosioi*) and "slaves living independently" (*khōris oikountes*), and on the nonpolitical sources of power rendered visible through the phenomena of successful businesswomen and wealthy slaves. The Attika that emerges from this study I call The Athenian Nation.

✦ 1 ✦

Anomalous Athens

An Anomalous *Polis*

By Aristotelian standards, Athens was not a *polis* at all. In the *Politics*, the only work surviving from antiquity dealing in detail with the realia of matters relating to the *polis* (hence the Greek title *Politika*),[1] Aristotle insists that a *polis*—"just like all other things: animals, plants, inanimate objects"—has an inherent limit to its size: it cannot encompass too many, or too few members (*politai*) and still be a *polis*.[2] Since autarky within an appropriate political arrangement defines the *polis* (for Aristotle, as for modern scholarship, "the *polis* is a self-sufficient [entity]," a "body of *politai* sufficing for the purposes of everyday life"),[3] a community too small to be self-sufficient is not a *polis*.[4] Yet a community self-sufficient through excessive numbers is also not a *polis*.[5] (Aristotle's emphasis on size and self-sufficiency is incorporated in "the

[1] Plato's two works, *Republic* and *Laws*, project utopian communities. Although the *Politics* sometimes assays the ideal (περὶ τῆς μελλούσης κατ' εὐχὴν συνεστάναι πόλεως: 1325b36–38), it is replete with historical and sociological data. Aristotle actually cites some 270 examples from more than 80 separate *poleis* (only about 30 from Athens) to support and clarify his various analyses.

[2] *Pol.* 1326a35–38: ἀλλ' ἔστι τι καὶ πόλεως μεγέθους μέτρον, ὥσπερ καὶ τῶν ἄλλων πάντων, ζῴων φυτῶν ὀργάνων· καὶ γὰρ τούτων ἕκαστον οὔτε λίαν μικρὸν οὔτε κατὰ μέγεθος ὑπερβάλλον ἕξει τὴν αὑτοῦ δύναμιν. Aristotle notes pointedly that his discussion of population and size limitations for *poleis* is based on factual information (τῶν γιγνομένων διὰ τῆς αἰσθήσεως) and not on theoretical argumentation (τῶν λόγων): *Pol.* 1328a17–21. (For the "preeminently practical" orientation of Aristotle's work in the social sciences [Lord 1991a: 2], see the essays by Salkever, Lord [1991a, 1991b], Shulsky, and Ober in Lord and O'Connor 1991; for the pragmatic orientation of Aristotle's ethical writings, see Ritter 1961; Höffe 1971; Bien 1973; Riedel 1975; Kullman 1983.)

[3] *Pol.* 1275b18–21: πόλιν δὲ τὸ τῶν τοιούτων πλῆθος ἱκανὸν πρὸς αὐτάρκειαν ζωῆς, ὡς ἁπλῶς εἰπεῖν; 1326b2–3: ἡ δὲ πόλις αὔταρκες. Modern scholars also emphasize self-sufficiency, especially economic autonomy (supplemented where necessary by bilateral trade in necessities), as critical to definition of a *polis*: see Finley 1985: 129–39; Nixon and Price 1990: 166.

[4] *Pol.* 1326b2–3: πόλις ἡ μὲν ἐξ ὀλίγων λίαν οὐκ αὐτάρκης (ἡ δὲ πόλις αὔταρκες). A *polis* becomes possible only when the mass of members of a political relationship reaches the point of effective self-sufficiency: διὸ πρώτην μὲν εἶναι πόλιν ἀναγκαῖον τὴν ἐκ τοσούτου πλήθους ὃ πρῶτον πλῆθος αὔταρκες πρὸς τὸ εὖ ζῆν ἐστι κατὰ τὴν πολιτικὴν κοινωνίαν (1326b7–9).

[5] *Pol.* 1326b3–5: ἡ δὲ ἐκ πολλῶν ἄγαν ἐν μὲν τοῖς ἀναγκαίοις αὐτάρκης ὥσπερ ἔθνος, ἀλλ' οὐ πόλις.

traditional modern definition of a *polis* as a small autonomous state" [Hansen 1993: abstract].) But what number of *politai* is excessive?[6] "The population must be easily cognizable at a glance," says Aristotle.[7] "It is necessary that the *politai* know one another," for if they do not, personal participation in decision making and office holding—the essence of the *polis*—is impossible.[8] Strikingly, this defining principle of the *polis*—members' personal familiarity with one another—is the precise opposite of an essential characteristic of a "nation" as identified in the late twentieth century by the emerging social science of ethnicity. For Benedict Anderson and his fellow theorists, a nation is an "imagined community," *imagined* "because the members of even the smallest nation will never know most of their fellow-members, meet them, or even hear of them" (Anderson 1991: 15–16). It is on exactly this criterion of members' mutual self-knowledge that Aristotle differentiates the *polis* from the *ethnos* ("nation" or "people"),[9] the "usual" (Hansen 1991: 59) ancient Greek term for any identifiable group larger than a *polis*: for Aristotle, "an (entity) self-sufficient as to necessities but excessively large in numbers, such as an *ethnos*, is not a *polis*."[10]

Attika was the incarnation of such an entity "excessively large in numbers." Far from the "face-to-face society" akin to a "university community" to which it is often likened by modern scholars,[11] Athens was larger in area and population than a number of modern nations. In

[6] *Pol.* 1326b11–12: τὶς δ' ἐστὶν ὁ τῆς ὑπερβολῆς ὅρος.

[7] *Pol.* 1327a1–2: τὸ πλῆθος τὸ τῶν ἀνθρώπων εὐσύνοπτον ἔφαμεν εἶναι δεῖν.

[8] *Pol.* 1326b12–17: εἰσὶ γὰρ αἱ πράξεις τῆς πόλεως τῶν μὲν ἀρχόντων τῶν δ' ἀρχομένων, ἄρχοντος δ' επίταξις καὶ κρίσις ἔργον· πρὸς δὲ τὸ κρίνειν περὶ τῶν δικαίων καὶ πρὸς τὸ τὰς ἀρχὰς διανέμειν κατ' ἀξίαν ἀναγκαῖον γνωρίζειν ἀλλήλους, ποῖοί τινές εἰσι, τοὺς πολίτας. Aristotle consistently focuses on the "right of sharing in deliberative or judicial office" as key to the functioning of the *polis*: ᾧ γὰρ ἐξουσία κοινωνεῖν ἀρχῆς βουλευτικῆς καὶ κριτικῆς, πολίτην ἤδη λέγομεν εἶναι ταύτης τῆς πόλεως (*Pol.* 1275b18–20). Cf. 1275a22–23: πολίτης δ' ἁπλῶς οὐδενὶ τῶν ἄλλων ὁρίζεται μᾶλλον ἢ τῷ μετέχειν κρίσεως καὶ ἀρχῆς. 1276a4: ὁ γὰρ κοινωνῶν τῆς τοιᾶσδε ἀρχῆς πολίτης ἐστίν, ὡς ἔφαμεν. 1275b31–33: ἔστω δὴ διορισμοῦ χάριν ἀόριστος ἀρχή. τίθεμεν δὴ πολίτας τοὺς οὕτω μετέχοντας.

[9] Modern lexicons agree on "nation," or "people," as the fundamental meaning of "ethnos." Chantraine, *Dictionnaire étymologique*: "nation, caste, classe" in the "ionique-attique" usage (1970: 315). LSJ: "nation," "people," "race," etc. and τὰ ἔθνη ("the nations"). Cf. Morris 1992: 6; Østergård 1992: 31–32. The word "recurs over and over in [Herodotos's] discussion of peoples," but in "practically every case can be translated 'people' or 'nation' " (Jones 1996: 315–16, citing documentation in Powell 1938).

[10] Aristot. *Pol.* 1326b3–5: ἡ δὲ ἐκ πολλῶν ἄγαν ἐν μὲν τοῖς ἀναγκαίοις αὐτάρκης ὥσπερ ἔθνος, ἀλλ' οὐ πόλις. Aristotle consistently applies the term to such larger groupings (Weil 1960: 367–415).

[11] See Chapter 4, pp. 104–5, 112–13.

absolute terms, its size (about 2,500 square kilometers)[12] and population (some 300,000 or more) were similar to that of modern Luxembourg (2,586 square kilometers and 373,000 inhabitants) and considerably greater, for example, than that of Barbados (430 square kilometers and 265,000 inhabitants) and a number of other nations.[13] Within this territory, primitive transportation and mountainous topography rendered travel challenging and time-consuming—and communication problematic—multiplying beyond modern comparisons the extensiveness of Attika's territory as perceived and experienced by its inhabitants (see Chapter 4, p. 106).

In fact, the Athenians at the beginning of the fourth century occupied in Attika the largest politically unified territory in the Hellenic world, a land mass colossal in comparison to the hundreds of Lilliputian *poleis*, which on average controlled a territory of less than 100 square kilometers—often far less—and generally had fewer than 800 members.[14] Massively larger than other Greek entities, in both territory and population, Athens was unique in the Greek heartland: the few other large Hellenic political groupings encompassed many individual *poleis*.[15] Sparta, for

[12] The area of Attika proper (excluding dependencies) has been calculated at 2,527 square kilometers (including Ōrōpos and Eleutherai, two border areas in Athenian possession for most of the sixth and parts of the fifth and fourth centuries), and at about 2,400 square kilometers without these two areas. See Garnsey 1988: 90; Beloch 1886: 56–57; Busolt and Swoboda 1920–26: 758.

[13] Some other modern nations comparable with Attika in demography and area (at mid-1991: *Economist Survey*): Brunei, 273,000 inhabitants and 5,765 square kilometers; Cape Verde, 382,000 and 4,033; Grenada, 84,000 and 344; Maldives, 223,000 and 298; Western Samoa 169,000 and 2,831. Compare Iceland, a nation of about 250,000 persons, which maintains a significant international diplomatic presence and supports extensive cultural and economic institutions within a harsh terrain much larger absolutely (103,000 square kilometers) but roughly comparable with ancient Attika in accessibility by contemporary transportation. In the last quarter of the nineteenth century, about a third of the U.S. states had fewer than 300,000 persons (1880 U.S. Census): Rhode Island, at some 3,000 square kilometers, comparable in size with Attika, counted only 276,532 inhabitants.

[14] A "Normalpolis" occupied 25 to 100 square kilometers, with an adult male population of 133 to 800: Ruschenbusch 1985: esp. 258, 263. Cf. Ruschenbusch 1978; Hansen 1991: 55; Raaflaub 1993: 567 (estimates of 50 to 100 square kilometers, 450 to 900 adult male citizens on average are "too high"). For the extent to which the territory of Attika dwarfed the typical Hellenic *polis*, see Stockton 1990: 4–6.

[15] Although scholars have generally assumed that *poleis* in their essence necessarily were autonomous (see, e.g., Murray and Price 1990: vii; Gaudemet 1967: 147; van Effenterre 1985: 24–25; Bruhns 1987–89: 323 [abstract]), there is ample ancient attestation of *poleis* that maintained independent domestic political institutions, albeit subject to hegemonic powers that controlled their regional and foreign relationships (see Hansen 1993: 18–20; 1995b; 1996d; cf. Hampl 1939: 16–17; Keen 1996; Lévy 1990: 55; Lotze 1990–92: 239). Rhodes 1993 surveys the several

example, controlled an area more than three times the size of Attika, but the communities within this territory were never politically united: the numerous local entities remained independent except in foreign affairs, and Greek authors explicitly refer to them as separate *poleis*.[16] Ēlis likewise encompassed a number of *poleis* subordinate to the eponymous *polis* that denominated the region.[17] In an area roughly equivalent in size to Attika,[18] Boiōtia was home to an alliance encompassing at least ten, and perhaps more than twenty-five, separate *poleis*.[19] Yet each of these *poleis* retained its own legislative body, maintained an armed force, and continued to deal separately with one another.[20] The Akarnanians similarly comprised thirty-four separate *poleis*.[21] Even the small island of Kea, with a territory of about 130 square kilometers, for much of its history was divided among four *poleis*, which still in the fourth century as members of the Second Athenian League maintained independent identities.[22] But the subdivisions of Attika, the demes,[23] totally subordi-

---

federations and leagues that offered alternative methods "of organizing units too large to function as a single polis" (p. 165). Such conglomerations were seen as inherently different from *poleis*: ἕτερον γὰρ συμμαχία καὶ πόλις . . . διοίσει δὲ τῷ τοιούτῳ καὶ πόλις ἔθνους (Aristot. *Pol.* 1261a24–28).

[16] See, for example, Hdt. 7.234.2; Thouk. 5.54.1; Xen. *Hell.* 6.4.15, 6.5.21, *Agēs.* 2.24, *Lak. Pol.* 15.3; Skylax 46; Isok. 12.179; Strabo 8.4.11; Paus. 3.6.2; Polemōn Περὶ τῶν ἐν Λακεδαίμονι πόλεων. Cf. Isager and Skydsgaard 1992: 131; Rhodes 1993: 163–64; Hansen 1995d: 25. On relations between Sparta and the various political units that ultimately joined in the Arkadian League, see Bergese 1995: 45–60.

[17] Xenophon (*Hell.* 3.2.23) refers to the other Elean communities as περιοικίδες πόλεις, a seeming parallel to the Spartan model (Hansen 1995c: 60). Cf. Xen. *Hell.* 3.30, 6.5.2, 7.1.26, 7.4.14.

[18] The modern nome of Boiōtia is actually somewhat smaller than Attika (Oikonomidēs 1981: 38, 40). On the topography, settlement patterns, and population of ancient Boiōtia, see Fossey 1988.

[19] This Boiotian confederation was termed an *ethnos* (*Hell. Oxyrh.* 19.4: τὸ μὲν οὖν ἔθνος ὅλον οὕτως ἐπολιτεύετο). Cf. Bakhuizen 1989. Ruschenbusch (1978, 1985) identifies at least thirteen and perhaps in excess of twenty-three *poleis* that are attested for Boiōtia during the period betwen 700 and 300 B.C.E. Hansen, with thorough documentation, posits at least twenty-five (1996c: 77). For the standard count of approximately ten *poleis* known for the fourth century alone, see Roesch 1965: 37–43; Salmon 1978: 101; 1985: 302; Bonner 1910: 406; Bruce 1967: 103–4; Moretti 1962: 140, 142.

[20] *Hell. Oxyrh.* 19.2–4. Cf. Hansen 1995a; 1995c: 47; 1996c; Dull 1985; Bruce 1967: 157–64, esp. 161, on the "sovereign cities in the federation." For the size and military strength of these *poleis*, see Beloch 1886: 161–72. Hansen argues persuasively that for much of this period only Thebes could be considered an "autonomous" *polis.*

[21] *I.G.* II^2 43.106. Cf. Thouk. 2.9.4. See Berktold et al. 1996. Until recently, scholars have largely ignored detailed exploration of the relationship between individual *poleis* and the geophysical areas and cultural subdivisions ("regions") in which they were located. See now Morgan 1991, Jameson, Runnels, and van Andel 1994: 73–101 (Halieis); Link 1994 (Crete); McInerney forthcoming a; forthcoming b. For an early exception, cf. Gschnitzer 1955, 1971.

[22] See *I.G.* II^2 43.82, 119–22; *I.G.* II^2 404 (= *S.E.G.* 19.50), lines 8 (αἱ πόλεις αἱ ἐγ Κέω[ι], 14 (πολιτεύεσθαι Κ[είου]ς κατὰ πόλεις); *I.G.* XII (5). 526ff. Cf. Cargill 1981: 134–40; Lewis 1962.

[23] In Attic Greek, a "village" was called a *dēmos*, elsewhere generally a *kōmē*. Hansen 1995c: 47–48. For the bifurcated nature of an Athenian *dēmos* (deme), see Chapter 4.

nate to central authority, were not *poleis*.[24] The political unification (*synoikismos*) of Attika produced a single huge entity of a size unparalleled in the Hellenic world[25]—but it was not, by relevant criteria, a *polis*.

Although the achievement of self-sufficiency required more than a minimal land area,[26] to Greek thinking an excessively large territory constituted an inherent barrier to contact and communication among the population and was incompatible with the limited defensive capacity imposed by a *polis*'s necessarily modest number of members.[27] Both the population of a *polis* and the territory occupied by that *polis*, according to Aristotle, "must be easily cognizable at a glance" (*eusynoptos*).[28] But Isokratēs notes explicitly that because of Athens's "great size and the large number of its inhabitants," the population was not "easily cognizable at a glance" (*eusynoptos*).[29] Similarly, Babylōn—although surrounded by a wall and thus urban in form—was so large in physical extent that three days after its capture portions of the population were supposedly not yet aware that it had fallen. All such conurbations, in Aristotle's opinion, were manifestations of an *ethnos*, not of a *polis*.[30]

Although self-sufficiency was an essential characteristic of a *polis* (see p. 11), Athens, despite its swollen land mass, was unable, from its

[24] Isokratēs (12.179) characterizes an Athenian deme's power as negligible. Over the demes "stood the laws and decrees of . . . the sovereign democracy itself, which not only determined how the Athenians should act as individuals but also delimited the areas within which the demes could make their own, lesser rules and regulations" (Whitehead 1986a: 256). Cf. Haussoullier 1884: 202–4. Prior to unification, Thucydides suggests, the Athenians did function on a basis similar to that of classical Boiōtia: ἐπὶ γὰρ Κέκροπος καὶ τῶν πρώτων βασιλέων ἡ Ἀττικὴ ἐς Θησέα αἰεὶ κατὰ πόλεις ᾠκεῖτο πρυτανεῖά τε ἐχούσας καὶ ἄρχοντας . . . αὐτοὶ ἕκαστοι ἐπολιτεύοντο καὶ ἐβουλεύοντο· καί τινες καὶ ἐπολέμησάν ποτε αὐτῶν, ὥσπερ καὶ Ἐλευσίνιοι μετ' Εὐμόλπου πρὸς Ἐρεχθέα (2.15.1). Sherk (1990: 278) notes that the so-called Marathonian *tetrapolis*—"a contradiction in terms" (Hansen 1996b: 66, n. 55) since composed of four demes—refers to a tetralogy of communities that were *poleis* long prior to their reformulation as demes by Kleisthenēs.

[25] Isok. 10.35: καὶ πρῶτον μὲν τὴν πόλιν σποράδην καὶ κατὰ κώμην οἰκοῦσαν εἰς ταὐτὸν συναγαγὼν τηλικαύτην ἐποίησεν [sc. ὁ Θησεύς] ὥστ' ἔτι καὶ νῦν ἀπ' ἐκείνου τοῦ χρόνου μεγίστην τῶν Ἑλληνίδων εἶναι.

[26] Aristot. *Pol.* 1326b26–31: Παραπλησίως δὲ καὶ τὰ περὶ τῆς χώρας ἔχει. Περὶ μὲν γὰρ τοῦ ποίαν τινά, δῆλον ὅτι τὴν αὐταρκεστάτην πᾶς τις ἂν ἐπαινέσειεν . . . πλήθει δὲ καὶ μεγέθει τοσαύτην ὥστε δύνασθαι τοὺς οἰκοῦντας ζῆν. . . .

[27] Aristot. *Pol.* 1326b39–1327a3: τὸ δ' εἶδος τῆς χώρας οὐ χαλεπὸν εἰπεῖν (δεῖ δ' ἔνια πείθεσθαι καὶ τοῖς περὶ τὴν στρατηγίαν ἐμπείροις) . . . τὸ δ' εὐσύνοπτον τὸ εὐβοήθητον εἶναι τὴν χώραν ἐστίν.

[28] *Pol.* 1327a1–2: ὥσπερ τὸ πλῆθος τὸ τῶν ἀνθρώπων εὐσύνοπτον ἔφαμεν εἶναι δεῖν, οὕτω καὶ τὴν χώραν.

[29] Isok. 15.172: διὰ γὰρ τὸ μέγεθος καὶ τὸ πλῆθος τῶν ἐνοικούνων οὐκ εὐσύνοπτός ἐστιν οὐδ' ἀκριβὴς, . . .καὶ δόξαν ἐνίοις τὴν ἐναντίαν τῆς προσηκούσης περιέθηκεν.

[30] Aristot. *Pol.* 1276a27–30: τοιαύτη δ' ἴσως ἐστὶ καὶ Βαβυλῶν καὶ πᾶσα ἥτις ἔχει περιγραφὴν μᾶλλον ἔθνους ἢ πόλεως· ἧς γέ φασιν ἑαλωκυίας τρίτην ἡμέραν οὐκ αἰσθέσθαι τι μέρος τῆς πόλεως. Cf. Hdt. 1.191; Aristot. *Pol.* 1265a13–17.

own resources, to feed more than a small portion of its population. Extensive imports—hundreds of thousands of medimnoi per year carried in hundreds of ships—were necessary to satisfy Athens's enormous need for grain, and for many other items.[31] While Attika's principal port, the magnificent Piraeus harbor, offered unparalleled access to the sea and to required commodities,[32] many Greeks deemed involvement with maritime trade inherently inconsistent with the proper organization and functioning of a *polis*: sea commerce brought into a community foreign merchants, men reared in alien ways, resulting in an enlarged and heterogeneous population destructive of the *polis*'s orderly way of life (*eunomia*).[33] Aristotle espoused a more liberal view, arguing that it was appropriate for a *polis* to achieve self-sufficiency through the exchange of local products for necessary imports, provided that such trade was limited to meeting the community's own needs and not directed toward the requirements of others.[34] But transshipment of cargo was an important aspect of Athens's central position as the dominant entrepôt for the entire eastern Mediterranean.[35] The Piraeus was a major redistribution center for goods destined ultimately for a further venue.[36] And so to the Piraeus

[31] Although the actual volume of food imports would have varied with the vagaries of local production (Jameson 1983: 6–16), in certain years Attika might have needed as many as 1 million medimnoi (Gomme 1933: 28–33), enough to feed more than 250,000 people. For similarly elevated projections, see Gallo 1984a: 48–57; Ste. Croix 1972: 46–49, 217–18, 1974: 44; Isager and Hansen 1975: 63; Gernet 1909: 273–93; Kocevalov 1932: 320–23. For a minimal estimate, see Garnsey 1985: 74 (at least 400,000 medimnoi in certain years). Cf. Segrè 1947; Scheidel 1998. Nongrain imports to Piraeus were probably similar in number of shiploads to those required for grain (Garland 1987: 85). For a summary list of the variety of goods imported to Athens by sea, see Hopper 1979: 92. For the organization of this trade, involving huge numbers of vessels and extensive (and complex) finance, see E. Cohen 1992: 140–50; Casson 1971: 183–84.

[32] The primitive nature and high cost of overland transportation resulted in the conduct of most long-distance trade in antiquity by sea: "le vrai commerce a toujours été, dans l'Antiquité grecque et romaine . . . le commerce en gros par voie de mer" (Biscardi 1982: 28). This was especially true at Athens in the fourth century: see Ste. Croix 1974: 42; Bleicken 1985: 73; Garland 1987: 85.

[33] Aristot. *Pol.* 1327a11–18: Περὶ δὲ τῆς πρὸς τὴν θάλατταν κοινωνίας, πότερον ὠφέλιμος ταῖς εὐνομουμέναις πόλεσιν ἢ βλαβερά, πολλὰ τυγχάνουσιν ἀμφισβητοῦντες· τό τε γὰρ ἐπιξενοῦσθαί τινας ἐν ἄλλοις τεθραμμένους νόμοις ἀσύμφορον εἶναι φασι πρὸς τὴν εὐνομίαν, καὶ τὴν πολυανθρωπίαν· γίνεσθαι μὲν γὰρ . . . ἐμπόρων πλῆθος, ὑπεναντίαν δ' εἶναι πρὸς τὸ πολιτεύεσθαι καλῶς. Cf. Pl. *Rep.* 704a–707d. See Roy 1998: 199–200.

[34] *Pol.* 1327a25–28: ὅσα τ' ἂν μὴ τυγχάνῃ παρ' αὐτοῖς ὄντα, δέχασθαι ταῦτα, καὶ τὰ πλεονάζοντα τῶν γιγνομένων ἐκπέμψασθαι τῶν ἀναγκαίων ἐστίν. αὑτῇ γὰρ ἐμπορικήν, ἀλλ' οὐ τοῖς ἄλλοις, δεῖ εἶναι τὴν πόλιν.

[35] Piraeus's position as the "leading commercial centre in the eastern Mediterranean" (Garland 1987: 95) continued until well beyond Athens's political eclipse by Macedonia, in fact until the rise of Rhodes beginning in the third century. See Burke 1990: 11; Adam 1989: 284; McKechnie 1989: 185–88.

[36] Isok. 4.42: ἐμπόριον ἐν μέσῳ τῆς Ἑλλάδος τὸν Πειραιᾶ . . . τοσαύτην ἔχονθ' ὑπερβολὴν ὥσθ' ἃ παρὰ τῶν ἄλλων ἓν παρ' ἑκάστων χαλεπόν ἐστιν λαβεῖν, ταῦθ' ἅπαντα παρ' αὐτῆς ῥᾴδιον εἶναι πορίσασθαι. Cf. Xen. *Por.* 5.3. Because of its need for food, Athens did make some limited efforts

and its burgeoning maritime trade, there came tens of thousands of foreigners—the very "men reared in alien ways" whose potentially destructive impact on the traditional *polis* was so feared.

The newcomers' influence on Athenian life and society *was* enormous, not least in their multitude. Although virtually every *polis* was likely to contain within its territory a number of nonmembers—slaves, free "resident aliens" (metics), and other foreigners[37]—the population of Attika appears to have encompassed an unusually large number of residents who were not *politai* (or related to *politai*). Although we have virtually no reliable demographic information for ancient Attika, a census reportedly conducted at Athens between 317 and 307 counted resident "foreigners" as about half the number of *politai* and a higher proportion (perhaps far higher) if unregistered alien residents and transients are added.[38] Because the metic population appears to have been more variable in number than that of the *politai*,[39] the percentage of free non-*politai* in the prior, and more prosperous, decades of the fourth century may have been even greater: Thür (1989: 118) has estimated the metic population during this earlier period at about 100,000. The number of slaves was also very large: the Athenians believed that the servile population of Attika exceeded that of the free.[40] From a male "citizen" body that he places at 30,000,[41] Hansen extrapolates for all of Attika a total population of 300,000 or more (1991: 93–94).

The impact and importance of these non-*politai* was enormous. Culturally, many of the renowned "Athenian" artistic masterpieces were the work of "foreigners"—of sculptors and painters like Zeuxis of Hēraklea and Parrhasios of Ephesos, of vase painters and pottery makers such as

---

to discourage transshipment of grain, including a prohibition on reexport of grain by residents of Attika and a requirement that at least two-thirds of the grain imported through the Athenian grain emporium be brought up to the city: Dem. 34.37, 35.51; Lykourg. *Leōk*. 27; Aristot. *Ath. Pol*. 51.4. See Garnsey 1988: 139–40; E. Cohen 1973: 68.

[37] Aristot. *Pol*. 1326a18–20: ἀναγκαῖον γὰρ ἐν ταῖς πόλεσιν ἴσως ὑπάρχειν καὶ δούλων ἀριθμὸν πολλῶν καὶ μετοίκων καὶ ξένων. Cf. Whitehead 1984: 49.

[38] Hansen 1991: 93. Cf. Hansen 1988: 10–11. The number of *politai* at this time, however, was limited by property requirements introduced after 322. This enumeration is known only from a late, and somewhat suspect, source (Athēn. 272c).

[39] Xen. *Por.* 2.1–7; Isok. 8.21; Lévy 1988: 54; Duncan-Jones 1980.

[40] Isager and Hansen 1975: 16–17. Canfora claims that "according to even the most conservative estimates, there were four slaves for every freeborn Athenian" (1995: 124). Cf. Hyper., fr. 33; Athen. 272c–d; Xen. *Por.* 4.4, 25, 28.

[41] Estimates of the number of adult male citizens during the second half of the fourth century vary greatly—from less than 20,000 to more than 35,000 (see Gomme 1933: 26, 29; Ehrenberg 1969: 31; Ruschenbusch 1979: 146; 1981: 112; Hansen 1985: 67–69; Oliver 1995: 9–38; Whitby forthcoming).

Amasis and Duris, and of non-Athenian workers in every form of metal.[42] Among a multitude of famous architects and builders, Hippodamos of Milētos rearranged the Piraeus harbors. Athens's vaunted intellectual life depended on foreign teachers, musicians, and physicians. The philosophers Aristotle and Theopompos (Plato's successors) dominated an intellectual tradition of alien metaphysicians that includes Anaxagoras, Zēnō, and innumerable other non-Athenian savants who made Athens "the School of Hellas." Legions of famous writers were settled in Attika. Even tragedy, the most Athenian of literary forms,[43] depended (at least in the fourth century) on outside dramatists like Alexis and Philemōn. The first local chronicler ("Atthidographer"), Hēllanikos, was not Athenian, nor was Herodotos, the historian of Athens's most significant victories. In the lawcourts, supposed domain par excellence of the "citizen," at least three of the canonical ten "orators" were resident foreigners (Lysias, Isaios, Deinarkhos), and the so-called eleventh orator (Apollodōros) was the son of a slave who had gained freedom and wealth.[44]

"Foreigners" suffused every dimension and manifestation of Athenian society. Although many non-*politai* lived in the Piraeus, the vast majority were scattered through Attika and were present in virtually every deme.[45] Their participation in social and religious activities, and their integration into communal life were so complete (see Chapter 4) that the great nineteenth-century savant Wilamowitz insisted that metics, as such, must have been accepted as full members of their demes.[46] In the armed forces, which were mobilized on a deme basis,[47] metics and slaves constituted a significant portion of total personnel, with metics sometimes occupying positions of high rank, contributing the manpower that permitted Athens to maintain the massive naval forces necessary to its hegemonic aspira-

[42] "The city was proud of its pottery, made from Attic clay, but often made by potters with flagrantly foreign names" (Connor 1996a: 120).

[43] See Sourvinou-Inwood 1994; Connor 1990: 7–32. Cf. Zeitlin's various articles on "the Dionysiac tragic theater of Athens" (1996: 338).

[44] For the cultural contribution of foreigners at Athens, see Glotz 1926: 182ff. On Apollodōros, see Introduction, n. 6. Both Lysias and Deinarkhos are known personally to have addressed Athenian juries (Lys. *Against Eratosthenēs*; Dein. *Against Proxenos*; Dion. Hal. *Dein.* 3). Isaios, who may have been born in Athens (Dion. Hal. *Isai.* 1; Edwards 1994: 31), is not known to have appeared before the Athenian courts. For the attraction to foreigners of forensic work in Attika, see Worthington 1994: 245–46.

[45] See Chapter 4, pp. 122–23.

[46] Wilamowitz 1887: 213–15. In accord: Hommel 1932: 1433.

[47] See Chapter 2, n. 165.

tions[48]—a reality inconsistent with the traditional military reliance of a *polis* on its own members.[49] Since modern scholars often conceive of thc *polis* in origin and in essence as a military force of kinsmen,[50] and thus inherently closed to nonkinsmen, Athens's integration of non-*politai* into the armed forces is monumentally inconsistent with the traditional scholarly model of the *polis*.

In commerce and trade, at Athens by the fourth century the impact of businessmen "reared in alien ways" had far transcended mere incompatibility with traditional *polis* values. Beyond the foreigners' importance, perhaps dominance, in Athenian business activity,[51] traders had recently introduced a new type of economic activity that functioned through the profit-seeking exchange of goods and services for money, replacing the prior system of household production-consumption augmented sporadically by barter within defined social relationships.[52] This new economic reality had created a new social reality: the rise of a "mixed" Athenian establishment, which added to the traditional upper classes a fresh infusion of wealthy resident forcigners, former slaves, naturalized citizens.[53] "Households"—*oikoi* or quasi *oikoi* analogous to the old dynasties, with their conspicuous consumption, pretensions and affectations, and concern for continuity—are organized and maintained by wealthy bankers of slave origin.[54] Metics and *politai* mix in the

[48] Aristot. *Pol.* 1327a40–b6: περὶ δὲ τῆς ναυτικῆς δυνάμεως . . . εἰ μὲν γὰρ ἡγεμονικὸν καὶ πολιτικὸν ζήσεται βίον, ἀναγκαῖον καὶ ταύτην τὴν δύναμιν ὑπάρχειν πρὸς τὰς πράξεις σύμμετρον. On metics' service, see Chapter 2, nn. 163–64. For slaves' contribution, see Chapter 2, n. 51.

[49] Even Aristotle recognized that by the fourth century military personnel need not be residential members of the community; see *Pol.* 1327b7–8: τὴν δὲ πολυανθρωπίαν τὴν γιγνομένην περὶ τὸν ναυτικὸν ὄχλον οὐκ ἀναγκαῖον ὑπάρχειν ταῖς πόλεσιν.

[50] Sagan 1991: 353: "To be a citizen, in fact, was almost synonymous with being a soldier." Cf. Rahe [1992] 1994: 32.

[51] Although scholars have long accepted the view that citizens functioned in business, if at all, as "rentiers" (Weber [1909] 1924: 32–33; Hasebroek [1933] 1978: 7–10, 22, 28, 35–37), the active involvement of Athenians in commerce has now been documented (Millett 1983: 52; Isager and Hansen 1975: 70–74)—although the relative importance of foreigners in trade and commerce is much disputed (see Millett 1983: 37–39; Hansen 1984).

[52] See Chapter 6, pp. 188–89. On the transition from an "embedded" to a "disembedded" economy, see E. Cohen 1992: 3–8; Morris 1994: 353–54. On premarket economies as embedded in society, see below Chapter 5, n. 4.

[53] A "striking transformation" (Davies 1981: 38) in sources of wealth occurred between the sixth and the fourth centuries. (Davies surveys this development at length [1981: 38–87]. Cf. Mossé 1973: 49.) Pečirka succinctly describes "a new social structure based on 'economic' wealth not bound to status and indifferent to the status monopolies of the citizens of Athens, a structure which cut across the status groups of the community of the citizens" (1976: 28). For analysis of these new relationships, see Mossé [1962] 1979: 133–215. For conservative objections to the new order, see Chapter 6, pp. 188–90.

[54] On banking *oikoi*, see E. Cohen 1992: 61–110.

aristocratic clubs of wealthy youth (the *hetaireiai*);[55] grand (and simple) gravestones of metics and *politai* stand together, indiscriminately, in the cemetery of the Kerameikos.[56] When Demosthenes, already a prominent political leader, and scion of a prominent Athenian family, prepared his important speech *Against Meidias*, he sought to equate his own financial contributions to the city with those of a trinity of "leading" citizens (*hēgemones*)—with Lysitheidēs and Kallaiskhros, high-pedigreed Athenians of aristocratic standing, and with Phormiōn, a former slave whose lack of fluency in Greek did not prevent Demosthenes from naming him first among the pace-setting trio.[57] Phormiōn was only one of many outsiders who now "moved in the highest social circles" (Finley [1973] 1985: 48), a fusion exemplified by the setting of Plato's *Republic* in the home of the metic Kephalos following Sōkratēs's visit to the inaugural festival honoring a Thracian goddess. Bendis was newly introduced into the Piraeus, a harbor area that was home to a vast polyglot community of traders and foreigners: of the 139 demes into which Attika had been divided,[58] the Piraeus has been most identified with foreign influence and foreign population (see Chapter 4, pp. 122–23). Yet Sōkratēs amalgamates the entire resident population of the Piraeus, denominating it by the single adjective *epikhōrios* (of the country), thus differentiating local persons—"citizen" or "noncitizen"—not from one another, but from the "Thracians" who had sent their own procession to the festivities celebrating Bendis.[59] The distinction reflects the Athenian practice of contrasting the entire residential population of Attika—"citizen" or "noncitizen"—with "foreigners," a recurrent and fundamental polarity in Athenian usage (see Chapter 2). (And in fact all elements of the local population—citizens, metics, and even slaves—are attested as partici-

[55] Andok. 1.15; Aurenche 1974: 111ff. Cf. Welwei 1992b.

[56] Garland 1982: 135–52; *I.G.* II[2] 6978, 7968.

[57] Dem. 21.157: ἡγεμὼν συμμορίας ὑμῖν ἐγενόμην ἐγὼ ἔτη δέκα, ἴσον Φορμίωνι καὶ Λυσιθείδῃ καὶ Καλλαίσχρῳ καὶ τοῖς πλουσιωτάτοις. For Phormiōn's unsuccessful attempt to speak in Greek to Athenian jurors, see Dem. 36.1 (cf. Apollodōros's mockery of Phormiōn's Greek at Dem. 45.30). But Phormiōn had performed enormous public and private benefactions for Athens (Dem. 36.55–57) and had attained incredible prosperity (Dem. 45.54 and 72) in the Piraeus both as a banker and as a maritime businessman (Dem. 45.64). Lysitheidēs is explicitly characterized as "kalos k'agathos" (Dem. 52.30): before 353, for his public benefactions, he had received the high honor of a crown from the state (Isok. 15.94). Kallaiskhros of Phegous was a kinsman of Plato: see E. Cohen 1992: 82–83, n. 104. For identification of the Phormiōn of Dem. 21.157 with his homonyme the banker, see Kirchner 1901–3: 2:392; Davies 1971: 436; MacDowell 1990: 376.

[58] On the number and nature of Athenian demes, see Chapter 4.

[59] καλὴ μὲν οὖν μοι καὶ ἡ τῶν ἐπιχωρίων πομπὴ ἔδοξεν εἶναι, οὐ μέντοι ἧττον ἐφαίνετο πρέπειν ἣν οἱ Θρᾷκες ἔπεμπον. Pl. *Rep.* 327a4–5.

pants in the worship of Bendis and in the maintenance of her shrine.)[60] At Kephalos's home, a potpourri of citizens and noncitizens is pictured interacting intimately in egalitarian fellowship.[61] The "alien" hosts are: the elderly Kephalos (of Syrakusan origin but already ensconced in Athens for at least half a century) and his adult sons Polymarkhos (portrayed as an intimate of Plato's own aristocratic family), Euthydēmos (best known to modern readers as the interlocutor of Sōkratēs in Plato's *Euthydēmos*), and Lysias (one of the canonical Athenian "orators" and a recurrently important figure in Athenian social, political, and legal history).[62] The guests constituted a cross section of Athenian aristocrats and outsiders: Plato's brothers, Adeimantos and Glaukōn, who were descendants of Solon the lawgiver, close relatives of the oligarchic political leaders Kharmidēs and Kritias, and stepsons of the Periklean democratic eminence, Pyrilampēs; Nikēratos (the son of Nikias, the highly respected and extremely wealthy political leader and general who lost his army and his life at Syrakuse); the impoverished stonemason, "philosopher," and Athenian "citizen," Sōkratēs, who was to lose his life at Athens; Thrasymakhos, a teacher of rhetoric originally from Khalkēdon on the Bosporos in distant northern Greece; Kharmantidēs of Paiania (one of the Athenian demes); and Kleitophōn son of Aristōnymos, usually identified as a supporter of the short-lived oligarchic regime of 411 (Aristotle *Constitution of the Athenians* 34). Far from confirming a sundered dichotomy of *politai* and foreigners, Plato portrays the metic hosts as "friends and virtually kinsmen" of their citizen guests,[63] an absence of social differentiation recurrent throughout Plato's dialogues. Indeed, in every aspect of Athenian life other than the political, our

[60] See the data set forth in Parker 1996: 170–75, esp. n. 74; Simms 1988. Cf. the recently published dedication to Bendis—Λαμπάδι νικήσας Δᾶος Βενδίδι ἀνέθηκεν—in Themelis 1990 = *SEG*. 39.210. "Daos" is "an archetypical slave name" (Parker 1996: 172, but see Osborne and Byrne 1994: 99, s.v.). The shrine appears to have been administered by a group of "Thracians" having Greek names.

[61] Plato's actual text, picturing the easy intermixture of persons of varied origin and present "status," is entirely inconsistent with academic assertions of rigid differentiation among the "orders" resident in Attika (Preface, "Status and Orders"): scholars accordingly posit Plato's "disapproval that doubtless underlies the text's infinitely urbane surface" (Parker 1996: 5, n. 14). Cf. Montepaone 1990: 105–9.

[62] The *Republic*, written in the 380s or later, is set in the late fifth century (see Grube 1974: ix, 2; Taylor 1952: 263–64); Kephalos was already resident in Attika in 459/8 when Lysias was born. The family was so identified with Athens that Lysias, who had moved at fifteen with one or both of his brothers to the Athenian colony of Thourioi, was ousted in anti-Athenian disturbances and thereupon returned to Attika. See Lys. 12; Dem. 59.22. Cf. Carey 1989: 1–2; Dover 1968: 28ff.; Blass [1887] 1962: 1:339ff.; Jebb 1893: 1:143ff.

[63] φίλους τε καὶ πάνυ οἰκείους (328d6).

sources chronicle a consistent rapport between *politai* and other free residents of Athens: "metics and citizens turn up on an equal footing without the slightest trace of social demarcation" (Hansen 1991: 87); "many citizens may have felt a greater affinity with wealthy (or poor) metics than with poor (or wealthy) citizens" (Sinclair 1988: 29); "rich Athenians and rich metics had much more in common than either group had with the citizen poor" (Parker 1996: 266–67). In my opinion, such phenomena of egalitarian comraderie and social assimilation reflect the fundamental sense of community and commonalty unifying the rooted residential population of Attika, the *astoi*. For these "local inhabitants" (the subject of Chapter 2), the political division between *politai* and non-*politai*—a demarcation that was far from eternal or unbreachable—did not obliterate the Athenian "imagined community" of group identity and cultural homogeneity, of shared mythology set in historical fabrication that marked the Athenian nation (Chapter 3).

An Anomalous *Ethnos*

> The Athenian nation, which was certainly Pelasgic, must have changed its language at the same time that it passed into the Hellenic body. . . . on inquiring into the condition of these nations, Croesus found that one, the Athenian . . .[64]
>
> Herodotos, *Histories* 1.57–59
> (adapted from the Rawlinson translation of 1860)

> Herodotos uses *ethnos* in a very restricted way, and practically every case can be translated 'people' or 'nation'.
>
> C. P. Jones (1996: 316)

For the Greeks, any grouping of people larger than a village (kōmē)[65] might be either a *polis* or an *ethnos*: there was no other alternative.[66] This limited choice resulted from the Greek tendency to understand and

[64] Τὸ Ἀττικὸν ἔθνος ἐὸν Πελασγικὸν ἅμα τῇ μεταβολῇ τῇ ἐς Ἕλληνας καὶ τὴν γλῶσσαν μετέμαθε. . . . Τούτων δὴ ὦν τῶν ἐθνέων τὸ μὲν Ἀττικὸν . . . ἐπυνθάνετο ὁ Κροῖσος . . .

[65] On the κώμη, see Lévy 1986; Hansen 1995c. Cf. the still useful, early studies by Kuhn 1878; Fougères 1900; Swoboda 1924.

[66] On the exclusivity of *polis-ethnos* as alternatives, see Larsen 1955: 23; Giovannini 1971: 14–16; Walbank 1985: 6, 22; Morgan 1996: 559.

to organize phenomena not through a definitional focus on a specific subject in isolation, but through contrast, preferably through antithesis.[67] Where modern Western thought generally posits a broad spectrum of possibilities and seeks to differentiate a multitude of slightly varying entities,[68] the Greek antithetical universe assumed not a medley of separate forms, but only a counterpoised opposition of *polis* and *ethnos*, complementary opposites occupying in mutual tension the entire relevant cognitive universe. Athens, differing so markedly from the prototypical *polis*, not surprisingly is identified in ancient literature (on occasion explicitly and more often implicitly) as an *ethnos*, a term generally defined in Greek and modern language lexica as "nation" or "people."[69] Yet—although Athens manifested to a high degree the characteristics now generally employed to identify a modern nation[70]—etymology, not shared meaning, is the closest linkage between ancient Greek *ethnos* and modern concepts of ethnicity,[71] and Athens as an *ethnos* must be comprehended in Hellenic, not in late-twentieth-century cognitive perception.

In the fourth century, numerous nouns were available to denote a farrago of differentiable sites smaller than a *polis*—*kōmion*, *khōrion*, *topos*, *epineion*, *amphodon*, *limēn*, *hieron*, *tonos*, *manteion*, *polikhnē*, and many others—but all were encompassed within the general term "village,"[72] itself a contrast to the "household" (*oikos* or *oikia*).[73] Simi-

[67] On this dualistic opposition so central to Hellenic culture that it has been said to have "dominated Greek thought" (Garner 1987: 76), see Lloyd [1966] 1987: 15–85; E. Cohen 1992: 46–52, 191–94.

[68] Thus, for example, Anglo-American law does contrast "real property" and "personal property" but still allows for items sharing certain characteristics of both ("fixtures"). The Greek antithetical universe permitted only two divisions: "disclosed property" (*phanera ousia*) and "undisclosed property" (*aphanēs ousia*). For modern frustration in seeking to analyze this Athenian binary division through non-Athenian categories, see Beauchet [1897] 1969: 3:13–21; Lipsius [1905–15] 1966: 677; Weiss 1923: 173, 464, 491; Gabrielsen 1986: 101. For the modern tendency "to divide each difficulty into as many parts as necessary the better to solve it," extolled by Descartes, see Lévi-Strauss and Eribon 1991: 112.

[69] See n. 9.

[70] See Introduction, pp. 2–3, and nn. 4–5; Chapter 3, pp. 79–80.

[71] The English word "ethnicity," first attested in 1953, was consciously derived from the Greek *ethnos*: see Glazer and Moynihan 1975: 1; Geary 1983: 16.

[72] "[I]t has become almost an orthodoxy, even in studies of archaic and classical Greece, to hold that a small settlement which was not a polis must have been a *kome*, except in Attica and some other regions where the preferred term was δῆμος" (Hansen 1995c: 50; Hansen believes that some of these *kōmai* "were considered *poleis* in so far as they were self-governing and had an urban centre," p. 81). On terminology, see Jones 1987: 387–88 (index).

[73] See, for example, Aristot. *Pol.* 1252b15–17: ἡ δ᾽ ἐκ πλειόνων οἰκιῶν κοινωνία πρώτη χρήσεως ἕνεκεν μὴ ἐφημέρου κώμη. μάλιστα δὲ κατὰ φύσιν ἔοικεν ἡ κώμη ἀποικία οἰκίας εἶναι. On the seminal importance of the Athenian οἶκος, see pp. 32–38.

larly, other terms were available to denominate and to differentiate the specialized attributes of groupings larger than a village—*koinon*, *sympoliteia*, *symmakhia*, *genos*, *syngeneia*, and others[74]—but *polis* and *ethnos* together encompassed all units larger than a *kōmē*. Thus the Amphiktyonic oath needed to refer only to *polis* and *ethnos* to achieve broad applicability ("if anyone—*polis* or *ethnos* or individual person—violates this").[75] Herodotos's universe is likewise binarily divided: without some prior ominous indication, disasters generally do not befall "*polis* or *ethnos*";[76] Xerxēs foresees complete hegemony for the Persians if they triumph over the Greeks—"no *polis* nor *ethnos* remains that will be able to withstand us."[77] In Aristotle's *Politics*, general political theses or inclusive observations are rendered universal through verbal phrasing that explicitly encompasses both *ethnē* and *poleis*. Most strikingly, in every paragraph in the *Politics* containing the word *ethnos*, its complementary opposite, *polis*, appears.[78] (*Ethnos* is found without *polis* only in the plural [*ethnē*], where it has the signification of "the nations," but even these references are sometimes accompanied by immediate complementary mention of *poleis*.)[79]

[74] *Koinon* (commonwealth, confederacy) emphasized that which was "common" to individuals or entities, "from the smallest club to the United Nations" (Larsen 1955: 24). *Sympoliteia* as "confederation" seems first to have appeared in literature in the late Hellenistic period (cf. Polybios 3.5.6, 4.3.6, 28.14.3). *Symmakhia* emphasized the military aspects of an alliance (βοηθείας γὰρ χάριν ἡ συμμαχία πέφυκεν, Aristot. *Pol.* 1261a26–27). Cf. Baltrusch 1994. *Syngeneia* was an often far-extended kin relationship based on mutual belief in common descent. Thus the Greek cities of Asia Minor appeal to Athens on the basis of their supposed mutual (Ionian) origin (Thouk. 1.95.1). Cf. Hall 1997: 36–37; Curty 1995; Roussel 1976: 29. On *genos*, see n. 85 and accompanying text. In late Hellenistic and Roman times, *ethnos* (equating to the Roman *natio*) was applied to unassimilated groups (like the Jews) who were accorded specified rights within an overall imperial arrangement.

[75] Aiskhin. 3.110: εἴ τις τάδε παραβαίνει ἢ πόλις ἢ ἰδιώτης ἢ ἔθνος.

[76] 6.27.1: φιλέει δέ κως προσημαίνειν, εὖτ' ἂν μέλλῃ μεγάλα κακὰ ἢ πόλι ἢ ἔθνεϊ.

[77] 7.8γ.3: οὔτε τινὰ πόλιν ἀνδρῶν οὐδεμίαν οὔτε ἔθνος οὐδὲν ἀνθρώπων ὑπολείπεσθαι, τὸ ἡμῖν οἷόν τε ἔσται ἐλθεῖν ἐς μάχην, τούτων τῶν κατέλεξα ὑπεξαραιρημένων.

[78] 1252b19–20: διὸ καὶ τὸ πρῶτον ἐβασιλεύοντο αἱ πόλεις, καὶ νῦν ἔτι τὰ ἔθνη. 1261a27–28: διοίσει δὲ τῷ τοιούτῳ καὶ πόλις ἔθνους. 1276a28–29: Βαβυλὼν καὶ πᾶσα ἥτις ἔχει περιγραφὴν μᾶλλον ἔθνους ἢ πόλεως. 1276a32–34: περὶ γὰρ μεγέθους τῆς πόλεως, τό τε πόσον καὶ πότερον ἔθνος ἓν ἢ πλείω συμφέρει, δεῖ μὴ λανθάνειν τὸν πολιτικόν. 1284a38–39: τὸ δ' αὐτὸ καὶ περὶ τὰς πόλεις καὶ τὰ ἔθνη ποιοῦσιν. 1285b30: ὥσπερ ἕκαστον ἔθνος καὶ πόλις ἑκάστη. 1285b32–33: οὕτως ἡ βασιλεία πόλεως καὶ ἔθνους ἑνὸς ἢ πλειόνων οἰκονομία. 1310b35: ἅπαντες γὰρ εὐεργετήσαντες ἢ δυνάμενοι τὰς πόλεις ἢ τὰ ἔθνη εὐεργετεῖν. 1326b4–5: αὐτάρκης ὥσπερ ἔθνος, ἀλλ' οὐ πόλις. 1327b21–23: βλέψας ἐπί τε τὰς πόλεις . . . ὡς διείληπται τοῖς ἔθνεσιν.

[79] 1257a24–25: καθάπερ ἔτι πολλὰ ποιεῖ καὶ τῶν βαρβαρικῶν ἐθνῶν. 1263a4–5: ὅπερ ἔνια ποιεῖ τῶν ἐθνῶν. 1324b9: ἐν τοῖς ἔθνεσι πᾶσι. 1336a11–12: χρῶνται καὶ νῦν ἔνια τῶν ἐθνῶν ὀργάνοις τισὶ μηχανικοῖς. 1338b17: οὔτε γὰρ ἐν τοῖς ἄλλοις ζῴοις οὔτε ἐπὶ τῶν ἐθνῶν ὁρῶμεν τὴν ἀνδρείαν ἀκολουθοῦσαν τοῖς ἀγριωτάτοις. For binary antithesis even in the plural (πόλεις and ἔθνη), see n. 78: 1252b19–20, 1284a38–39, 1310b35, 1327b21–23.

As with other Greek concepts that have frustrated academic efforts to identify a consistent underlying signification independent of the meaning derived from contrast with their cognitive complements,[80] *ethnos* has defied modern analysis: some scholars have even charged Greek authors with "idiolectic" usage that effectively prevents rational determination of the word's objective meaning.[81] But *ethnos*'s chameleon-like nature reflects Greek cognitive reality: since every entity not a *polis* must be an *ethnos* in any context where binary comparison is explicit (or implicit), *ethnē* encompassed the widest and, to us, amazingly disparate, even contradictory, potpourri of entities.[82] "Tribal states," "federal states," "ethnic states,"[83] genealogical groupings, kingdoms, Attika—all fall within this rubric, not because of any quality abstractly inherent in these entities, but because in the context of communal or political groupings larger than a village, the sole encompassing alternatives in a binary universe were *polis* and *ethnos*.[84] Thus a *genos* (a grouping in which membership is related to natal origins) can be characterized as an *ethnos*, often as an alternative to its potential identification as a *polis*.[85] Athens, federated in some aspects, incredibly large for a single *polis* but not a league of *poleis*, in certain contexts is characterized as a *polis*, in others as an *ethnos*—albeit a highly anomalous version of either. (Significantly, Athens as an ethnos appears almost invariably in the context of interaction with, or comparison with, other entities too large or complex to be characterized as *poleis* [see pp. 28–29].)

Modern scholars, working within a noncomplementary cognitive system, find Greek usage "inconsistent" (Jones 1996: 315). But for Greek

[80] On *eggeios ousia*, for example, see Cohen 1992: 131–33. On *phanera ousia*, see n. 68.

[81] Thus Weil (1960: 385) finds that Herodotos, in whose work *ethnos* recurs repeatedly, "définit mal l''ethnos.' " For C. Jones, Herodotos's "inconsistent" differentiation of *ethnos* from *genos* is attributable to the historian's "idiolect," which "does not use language with the precision of a philosopher" (1996: 315). J. Hall finds standard dictionary definitions of *ethnos* and *genos* "anachronistic" and "vitiated by Herodotos' use of the two terms as synonyms" (1997: 35–36).

[82] See generally Rocchi 1993; Beck 1997.

[83] On the *ethnos* as state, see Morgan 1991: 131; Roussel 1976: 5.

[84] Cf. J. Hall's "population groups" (1997: 35). In other contexts, especially before the fourth century, *ethnos* had wider significations. Homer applies the term to any identifiable collective grouping—birds, bees, insects, young men (see Donlan 1985: 295; Tonkin, McDonald, and Chapman 1989: 12). For Sophoklēs, bands of beasts are *ethnē* (*Phil.* 1147; *Ant.* 344). Pindar and Aiskhylos likewise use *ethnos* broadly (Chantraine 1968: 222).

[85] Athens as *genos*: Hdt. 5.91.1 (τὸ γένος τὸ Ἀττικόν). Cf. 5.62.2: γένος ἐόντες Ἀθηναῖοι. Analyzed independent of Greek orientation to binary cognition, the relationship between *genos* and *ethnos* seems impossibly muddled: LSJ defines *genos* as a tribal subdivision of an *ethnos*, J. Hall sees them as synonyms (1997: 36), and C. Jones suggests that the "distinction between

authors, working within an antithetical binary universe, an infinite spectrum of minutely differing choices would have seemed incomprehensibly anarchic. Thus, "the combining of separate *poleis* in a block of allies was the classical Greek way of organising units too large to function as a single polis" (Rhodes 1993: 165)—Boiotians, Arkadians, Akhaians[86]— —but no individual word existed in classical Greek exclusively and separately to delineate such federations.[87] Because they were composed of individual *poleis* and/or other entities and therefore could not themselves be termed *poleis,*[88] these groupings were commonly described as *ethnē*. Herodotos depicts the Peloponnese as divided among seven *ethnē*, including the Arkadians, Akhaians, and Aitolians, each incorporating various *poleis.*[89] Thucydides describes Greek Sicily—comprising numerous *poleis*—as divided between Khalkidian and Dorian *ethnē.*[90] The historian of the Oxyrhynchus Papyrus describes the constitutional interrelationship between the Boiotian *ethnos* and the several *poleis* encompassed therein.[91] Herodotos records the dedication on the Athenian Akropolis extolling the Athenian victory over the Boiotian and Khalkidian *ethnē.*[92] He similarly denominates as *ethnē* various groupings that clearly

the two words is not taxonomic, but instead is to be explained by linguistic 'intension' "—akin to the "distinction in English provided by the words 'house' and 'home' " (1996: 315).

[86] On the organization of these groups in archaic and classical Greece, see Morgan 1991: 146–48, Morgan and Hall 1996: 169 (Akhaia); Hansen 1995a, 1996c (Boiōtia); Bergese 1995, Nielsen 1996a, 1996b (Arkadia).

[87] "There is no ancient Greek term which precisely denotes a federal state" (Rhodes 1996: 591). Although innumerable modern books and articles have been written on Hellenic "federal states" and "hegemonic leagues," the nouns identifying these entities are invariably modern coinages. See Larsen 1945: 78, n. 72; 1955: 23.

[88] On the numerous *poleis* encompassed within Boiōtia, Akarnania, and Aitolia (Ēlis), see pp. 13–14. Fourth-century Akhaia encompassed numerous *poleis* lying between Sikyōn and Ēlis (Morgan and Hall 1996: 167–99). Cf. Larsen 1968: 83, 216. Nielsen sees the fourth-century Arkadian *ethnos* as a mixture of numerous major and minor *poleis*, even including some federations of *poleis* (1996a, esp. pp. 142–43 and fig. 2 [p. 149]). Cf. Nielsen 1996c.

[89] Hdt. 8.73.1–2: Οἰκέει δὲ τὴν Πελοπόννησον ἔθνεα ἑπτά. . . . Ἀρκάδες τε καὶ Κυνούριοι· ἓν δὲ ἔθνος τὸ Ἀχαιϊκὸν . . . τὰ δὲ λοιπὰ ἔθνεα. . . . Δωριέες τε καὶ Αἰτωλοὶ καὶ Δρύοπες καὶ Λήμνιοι. Δωριέων μὲν πολλαί τε καὶ δόκιμοι πόλιες, Αἰτωλῶν δὲ Ἦλις μούνη, Δρυόπων δὲ Ἑρμιών τε καὶ Ἀσίνη ἡ πρὸς Καρδαμύλῃ τῇ Λακωνικῇ, Λημνίων δὲ Παρωρεῆται πάντες. . . . τούτων ὦν τῶν ἑπτὰ ἐθνέων αἱ λοιπαὶ πόλιες, πάρεξ τῶν κατέλεξα, ἐκ τοῦ μέσου κατέατο. "Ēlis" in fact encompassed numerous other *poleis*: see p. 14, n. 17.

[90] Thouk. 4.61.2–3: ἃ χρὴ γνόντας καὶ ἰδιώτην ἰδιώτῃ καταλλαγῆναι καὶ πόλιν πόλει . . . παρεστάναι δὲ μηδενὶ ὡς οἱ μὲν Δωριῆς ἡμῶν πολέμιοι τοῖς Ἀθηναίοις, τὸ δὲ Χαλκιδικὸν τῇ Ἰάδι ξυγγενείᾳ ἀσφαλές. οὐ γὰρ τοῖς ἔθνεσιν, ὅτι δίχα πέφυκε, τοῦ ἑτέρου ἔχθει ἐπίασιν. Cf. 6.1.2–2.1: Σικελίας . . . ᾠκίσθη δὲ ὧδε τὸ ἀρχαῖον, καὶ τοσάδε ἔθνη ἔσχε τὰ ξύμπαντα.

[91] 19.2–4: εἶχεν δὲ τὰ πράγματα τότε κατὰ τ[ὴν] Βοιωτίαν οὕτως. ἦσαν καθεστηκυῖαι βουλαὶ τ[ό]τε τέττα[ρες παρ' ἑ]κάστῃ τῶν πόλεων . . . τὸ μὲν οὖν ἔθνος ὅλον οὕτως ἐπολιτεύετο. On the Boiotian confederation, see nn. 19, 20.

[92] Hdt. 5.77.4: ἔθνεα Βοιωτῶν καὶ Χαλκιδέων δαμάσαντες | παῖδες Ἀθηναίων ἔργμασιν ἐν πολέμου | δεσμῷ ἐν ἀχλυόεντι σιδηρέῳ ἔσβεσαν ὕβριν· | τῶν ἵππους δεκάτην Παλλάδι τάσδ' ἔθεσαν.

were not *poleis*: Medians, Libyans, Ethiopians, Phoenicians, Hellenes, Skythians, Lydians, Karians, the peoples of the Caucasus region.[93] For Aristotle, Spaniards, Persians, Thracians, Carthaginians, Makedonians are *ethnē* (*Pol.* 1324b10–19). But the term *ethnos* also encompassed substantial subdivisions of "barbarian" groups—the various peoples living west of the Halys River, tribal groupings of the Libyans, various Skythian groups[94]—as well as Hellenic *ethnē*. These Greek *ethnē* were almost always either affiliations that encompassed a number of *poleis*, such as the Boiotians, Arkadians, Khalkidians, and others enumerated here,[95] or identifiable groupings of supposed common kinship, again likely to incorporate a wide swath of individual *poleis*.[96] Thus the confederations that submitted to the Persians ("Medized") during their invasion of Greece—Boiōtia, Makedonia, Thessaly[97]—are denominated as *ethnē*.[98] The term *ethnos* could be applied to the Keans, comprising four *poleis*, and also to the Leukadians, likewise inhabitants of an island but one often integrated (politically and physically) with the Akarnanian confederation of thirty-four *poleis*.[99] But the prevailing binary classification, which divided every entity larger than a village exclusively between the categories of *polis* or *ethnos*, would not accommodate those

[93] τὸ Μηδικὸν ἔθνος (Hdt. 1.101); τέσσερα ἔθνεα νέμεται αὐτὴν . . . Λίβυες μὲν καὶ Αἰθίοπες αὐτόχθονες, οἱ μὲν τὰ πρὸς βορέω, οἱ δὲ τὰ πρὸς νότου τῆς Λιβύης οἰκέοντες, Φοίνικες δὲ καὶ Ἕλληνες ἐπήλυδες (4.197); Σκύθαι . . . νεώτατον ἁπάντων ἐθνέων (4.5.1; cf. 4.46.1); ἔθνος οὐδὲν . . . ἀλκιμώτερον τοῦ Λυδίου (1.79.3); τὸ Καρικὸν ἦν ἔθνος λογιμώτατον (1.171.3); ἔθνεα δὲ ἀνθρώπων πολλὰ καὶ παντοῖα ἐν ἑωυτῷ ἔχει ὁ Καύκασος (1.203.1). On the cultural dislocations likely in Greek authors' (frequent) delineation of non-Hellenic settlements as *poleis*, see Hansen 1996b: 33.

[94] Lydian ethnē: ἐθνέων τῶν ἐντὸς Ἅλυος ποταμοῦ (1.6.1); Thracian and Libyan: Βάκαλες, ὀλίγον ἔθνος, κατήκοντες ἐπὶ θάλασσαν κατὰ Ταύχειρα πόλιν τῆς Βαρκαίης . . . τὸ πρὸς ἑσπέρης ἔχονται Νασαμῶνες, ἔθνος ἐὸν πολλόν (4.171–72.1); Γαράμαντές, ἔθνος μέγα (4.183.1); Skythian: ἄλλο ἔθνος . . . Ἀλιζῶνες . . . ὑπὲρ δὲ Ἀλιζώνων οἰκέουσι Σκύθαι ἀροτῆρες . . . τούτων δὲ κατύπερθε οἰκέουσι Νευροί . . . ταῦτα μὲν παρὰ τὸν Ὕπανιν ποταμόν ἐστι ἔθνεα πρὸς ἑσπέρης τοῦ Βορυσθένεος (4.17) (cf. Aristot. *Pol.* 1324b11, 17); τὸ Ταυρικὸν ἔθνος (4.99); Βουδῖνοι δέ, ἔθνος ἐὸν μέγα καὶ πολλόν (4.108). Cf. Thucydides' Taulantioi, an Illyrian *ethnos* (1.24.1).

[95] Although Khalkis was the name of a *polis* in Euboia, τὸ Χαλκιδικὸν ἔθνος (Hdt. 5.77.4) would have encompassed the group of entities in the Lelantine Plain commanded by Khalkis (and in most contexts the "Khalkidian" *poleis* in western Greece and along the north Aigaian shore). Cf. 8.127 (τὸ Χαλκιδικὸν γένος). See Gomme, Andrewes, and Dover 1945–81: 1:203–8. For Thucydides, τὸ Χαλκιδικὸν ἔθνος explicitly included a number of the *poleis* in Sicily (see n. 90).

[96] Herodotos's "Dorians," for example, consist of πολλαί τε καὶ δόκιμοι πόλιες (8.73.2). On the often vast dimensions of *syngeneiai* and *genē*, see nn. 74, 82.

[97] Makedonia as *ethnos*: Hdt. 8.43 (Μακεδνὸν ἔθνος).

[98] Hdt. 9.106: ἐδόκεε τῶν μηδισάντων ἐθνέων τῶν Ἑλληνικῶν τὰ ἐμπόρια ἐξαναστήσαντας δοῦναι τὴν χώρην Ἴωσι ἐνοικῆσαι.

[99] Keans: ἔθνος ἐὸν Ἰωνικὸν (Hdt. 8.46.2). Leukadians: ἔθνος ἐόντες οὗτοι (Hdt. 8.45). On the Kean and Akarnanian confederations, see p. 14 and nn. 21, 22.

conurbations, Greek or "barbarian," that were of exceptionally large size and complexity but *polis*-like in political organization or origin.

Babylōn (see p. 15) and Athens were prime exemplars of this conceptual conundrum. Such colossal *poleis*, Aristotle reasoned, had the dimensions more of *ethnē* than *poleis*.[100] Similarly, Plato's ideal *polis* of the *Laws* is rejected by Aristotle as not realizable in the real world. Its vast size and scale—five thousand persons (and a much larger number of women and servants) requiring a territory as large as a Babylōn—would prevent such a "*polis*" from existing as a *polis*.[101] In chronicling Cyrus's entry into Babylōn, Herodotos notes that the invasion was similar to that which the Persian king had mounted against every *ethnos*—but he still denominates Babylōn itself as a *polis*.[102]

Similar ambivalence applied to Athens, the colossus of Hellenic *poleis*.[103] In addition to relatively frequent allusions to Athens as a *polis,* references to the Athenian (or to the Attic) *ethnos* also occur. The Athenians inform the Syrakousan dictator Gelōn that they are the oldest—and the sole autochthonous—Hellenic *ethnos*.[104] Herodotos explains a territorial arrangement in Skythia "as if another *ethnos* and not the Athenians inhabited the Sounian hill country." [105] Seeking the most powerful of the Greeks, the Lydian king Kroisos found the Spartans and Athenians preeminent: "these two were the most powerful, one originally a Pelasgic, the other a Hellenic *ethnos* . . . [but] the Athenian *ethnos*, which was certainly Pelasgic, must have changed its language at the same time that it passed into the Hellenic body. . . . on inquiring into the condition of these *ethnē*, Croesus found that one, the Athenian. . . ."[106]

[100] Aristot. *Pol.* 1276a27–30: τοιαύτη δ' ἴσως ἐστὶ καὶ Βαβυλῶν καὶ πᾶσα ἥτις ἔχει περιγραφὴν μᾶλλον ἔθνους ἢ πόλεως· ἧς γέ φασιν ἑαλωκυίας τρίτην ἡμέραν οὐκ αἰσθέσθαι τι μέρος τῆς πόλεως.

[101] Aristot. *Pol.* 1265a13–18: δεῖ μὴ λανθάνειν ὅτι χώρας δεήσει τοῖς τοσούτοις Βαβυλωνίας ἤ τινος ἄλλης ἀπεράντου τὸ πλῆθος, ἐξ ἧς ἀργοὶ πεντακισχίλιοι θρέψονται, καὶ περὶ τούτους γυναικῶν καὶ θεραπόντων ἕτερος ὄχλος πολλαπλάσιος. δεῖ μὲν οὖν ὑποτίθεσθαι κατ' εὐχήν, μηδὲν μέντοι ἀδύνατον.

[102] Hdt. 1.190–91: οἱ Βαβυλώνιοι . . . ὁρέοντες αὐτὸν παντὶ ἔθνεϊ ὁμοίως ἐπιχειρέοντα . . . Κῦρος δὲ . . . ἐς τὴν πόλιν ἐσβάλλει.

[103] For Athens's uniquely great scale, as a single Hellenic entity, see pp. 13–15.

[104] Hdt. 7.161.3: ἐόντες Ἀθηναῖοι . . . ἀρχαιότατον μὲν ἔθνος παρεχόμενοι, μοῦνοι δὲ ἐόντες οὐ μετανάσται Ἑλλήνων.

[105] Hdt. 4.99.4: ὡς εἰ τῆς Ἀττικῆς ἄλλο ἔθνος καὶ μὴ Ἀθηναῖοι νεμοίατο τὸν γουνὸν τὸν Σουνιακόν.

[106] Hdt. 1.56–59: ἱστορέων τοὺς ἂν Ἑλλήνων δυνατωτάτους ἐόντας . . . εὕρισκε Λακεδαιμονίους τε καὶ Ἀθηναίους προέχοντας . . . ταῦτα γὰρ ἦν τὰ προκεκριμένα, ἐόντα τὸ ἀρχαῖον τὸ μὲν Πελασγικόν, τὸ δὲ Ἑλληνικὸν ἔθνος. . . . Τὸ Ἀττικον ἔθνος ἐὸν Πελασγικὸν ἅμα τῇ μεταβολῇ τῇ ἐς

Like many other *ethnē*, the Athenians in turn had their own dependent *ethnē*: Athens is said by Aristotle to have treated Khios and Lesbos (both described by Thucydides as themselves *ethnē* encompassing *poleis*)[107] "in the same way" that the Persians dealt with Media and Babylōn.[108]

In short, the ancient sources make clear that "les Athéniens sont un 'ethnos' hellénique" (Weil 1960: 385), but an "anomalous" one. In contrast to virtually all other Hellenic entities identified as *ethnē*, the Athenians were neither a confederation of *poleis* nor a kin group encompassing a disparate *syngeneia* of far-flung *poleis*.[109] Attika instead, like many non-Hellenic *ethnē*, functioned politically as a single entity but was populated through villages,[110] for Aristotle a prime criterion in distinguishing *ethnos* from *polis*.[111] Indeed, through its stereotypical characteristic of bold and daring intellect, Athens was anomalous in the context of a further Aristotelian standard for *ethnē*. "Throughout the inhabited world," the philosopher observes, *ethnē* generally exhibited complementary shortcomings: the Europeans (along with other inhabitants of cold places) lacked intellect and skill, although possessing "spiritedness" (*thymos*); the Asians were skillful and intelligent, but their lack of spiritness rendered them servile and prone to being dominated.[112] Only the Greeks possessed both spirit and intellect. But even among the Hellenes, some Greek *ethnē* possess only one of the desired traits, although other *ethnē* possess both.[113] The Athenian *ethnos*—the Athenians "taking joy

---

Ἕλληνας καὶ τὴν γλῶσσαν μετέμαθε. . . . Τούτων δὴ ὦν τῶν ἐθνέων τὸ μὲν Ἀττικὸν . . . ἐπυνθάνετο ὁ Κροῖσος. Rawlinson translation. On the historicity of this report of the chief Greek entities, see Alty 1982; Gomme, Andrewes, and Dover 1945–81: 1:95–98.

[107] Thouk. 2.9.4: (ξυμμαχία) Ἀθηναίων δὲ Χῖοι, Λέσβιοι . . . καὶ ἄλλαι πόλεις αἱ ὑποτελεῖς οὖσαι ἐν ἔθνεσι τοσοῖσδε.

[108] Aristot. *Pol.* 1284a38: τὸ δ' αὐτὸ καὶ περὶ τὰς πόλεις καὶ τὰ ἔθνη ποιοῦσιν οἱ κύριοι τῆς δυνάμεως, οἷον Ἀθηναῖοι μὲν περὶ Σαμίους καὶ Χίους καὶ Λεσβίους . . . ὁ δὲ Περσῶν βασιλεὺς Μήδους καὶ Βαβυλωνίους. For the Persians as an *ethnos*, Hdt. 7.85.1 (ἔθνος Περσικόν); for Babylōn as *polis*, see n. 30.

[109] On such groupings, see pp. 24–25. For the relationship between the Athenian *ethnos* and the "Ionians," see Chapter 3, pp. 85–87.

[110] Athenians lived in *dēmoi*, a term supposedly current in Attika for *kōmē* (village), the word prevailing in other Hellenic areas. Cf. n. 23 with accompanying text, and Chapters 2, 4.

[111] Aristot. *Pol.* 1261a27–28: διοίσει δὲ τῷ τοιούτῳ καὶ πόλις ἔθνους, ὅταν μὴ κατὰ κώμας ὦσι κεχωρισμένοι τὸ πλῆθος, ἀλλ' οἷον Ἀρκάδες. For extended treatment of this passage, see Schütrumpf 1991: 2:163–66. The allusion to the Arkadians is unclear (cf. Saunders 1995: 109).

[112] *Pol.* 1327b21–28: βλέψας . . . πρὸς πᾶσαν τὴν οἰκουμένην. . . . τὰ μὲν γὰρ ἐν τοῖς ψυχροῖς τόποις ἔθνη καὶ τὰ περὶ τὴν Εὐρώπην θυμοῦ μέν ἐστι πλήρη, διανοίας δὲ ἐνδεέστερα καὶ τέχνης . . . τὰ δὲ περὶ τὴν Ἀσίαν διανοητικὰ μὲν καὶ τεχνικὰ τὴν ψυχήν, ἄθυμα δέ.

[113] *Pol.* 1327b29–36: τὸ δὲ τῶν Ἑλλήνων γένος . . . οὕτως ἀμφοῖν μετέχει. καὶ γὰρ ἔνθυμον καὶ διανοητικόν ἐστιν . . . τὴν αὐτὴν δ' ἔχει διαφορὰν καὶ τὰ τῶν Ἑλλήνων ἔθνη πρὸς ἄλληλα· τὰ μὲν γὰρ ἔχει τὴν φύσιν μονόκωλον, τὰ δὲ εὖ κέκραται πρὸς ἀμφοτέρας τὰς δυνάμεις ταύτας.

in innovation and sharp at conceptualizing and accomplishing whatever they conceive of . . . daring even beyond their power"[114]—manifested both attributes but paid dearly, in the hostility of its Hellenic contemporaries, for its vaunted dual excellence.[115] But in Attika the residents lived in relative concord and apparent harmony, a surprising phenomenon if the prevailing view of Attic communal arrangements is valid (see Chapters 2 and 4).

Women in an Anomalous Democracy

> The political process does not recognize a "citizeness." . . . there is no such thing as a "female citizen."
>
> Nicole Loraux, *The Children of Athena*

For many scholars, Athens is still seen as "the great example of democracy in operation which influenced political thought throughout antiquity and inspired the democratic revolutionists of the eighteenth and nineteenth centuries,"[116] the manifestation "of the idea of individual human autonomy, of the idea that all members of a political society were free and equal" (Forrest 1966: 44), the inspirational beacon for modern French and Anglo-American democracy.[117] Yet Athenian democracy debarred not only women, children, and slaves, "which is no surprise" (Finley 1981: 26), but further excluded "freed slaves or free men who migrated from other Greek states or from the 'barbarian' world, or even their children, born and raised in [an Athens] that labelled them aliens" [ibid.]. However, "to make too much" of such occlusions "is to be guilty of anachronism."[118] Athens, we are told, was not a modern nation-state, but an ancient city-state, where the dominant male citizen,

[114] Korinthian evaluation as rendered by Thucydides: οἱ μέν γε νεωτεροποιοὶ καὶ ἐπινοῆσαι ὀξεῖς καὶ ἐπιτελέσαι ἔργῳ ἃ ἂν γνῶσιν . . . οἱ μὲν καὶ παρὰ δύναμιν τολμηταὶ (1.70.2–3).

[115] They were both οἱ πρότεροι ἐπιόντες and ἐκεῖνοι ἐπιστήμῃ προύχουσι (Thouk. 1.23.2, 1.21.4). The result was that <ἐν> ὀργῇ εἶχον οἱ πλείους τοὺς Ἀθηναίους (2.8.5).

[116] Smith 1960: 63. French revolutionists: Vidal-Naquet 1990; Mossé 1989; Parker 1937; Palmer 1953. The American colonists recoiled, however, at what they perceived as Athens's unbridled egalitarianism—and fashioned instead a "representative democracy": see Wood 1996: 122–29.

[117] "Athènes-IIIe République à laquelle nous ont habitués nos manuels" (Mossé 1986: 119). Loraux criticizes the long-held French view of Athens as "the place where democracy once existed in its pure state" ([1981] 1986: 7). For Athens as a model proffered for emerging British democracy, see Grote [1859–65] 1907: 4.59–67; Anonymous 1828; Turner 1981: 187. Cf. Saxonhouse 1996: 1–29.

[118] Stockton 1990: 187. Similarly Loraux 1978; 1996: 194. Cf. Roberts 1996: 198.

by right of fortunate birth, alone was a "fully paid-up member of the club, (and) that club was virtually closed to [other] free, adult, male Greeks" (Cartledge 1993: 4). Even the minority of scholars who bestow the title "citizen" on Athenian women tend to trivialize the rubric, characterizing women as "passive" citizens or finding the essence of an Athenian woman's citizenship in the capacity to give birth to male citizens.[119] Yet because women lacked direct political rights, most modern scholars have closed the "club" even to the wives, daughters, and other female relatives of Athenian male citizens: "the political process does not recognize a 'citizeness,'" "there is no such thing as a 'female citizen.'"[120]

But significant evidence from Athenian sources offers a variant portrayal. Chapter 2 shows that for foreigners and their descendants Athenian political rights were not entirely beyond reach. Here I consider the implications of the presence in Attic Greek of the feminine *politis* ("citizeness," plural *politides*) in use parallel with the masculine *politēs* ("citizen," plural *politai*). In a speech of Demosthenes, for example, legislation is cited prohibiting criticism of "citizens or citizenesses" (*politai* or *politides*) who work in the central market.[121] In the same presentation, Euxitheos refers to his mother as a *politis*,[122] while Isaios defends another mother against the claim that she was *not* a *politis*,[123] and Isokratēs has a Plataian insist that his compatriots have been born from mothers who were Athenian *politides*.[124] In another speech attributed to Demosthenes, Apollodōros denies that the defendant, Neaira, was an Athenian *politis*: if such a woman were to be accepted as a *politis*, then Athenian *politides* would have no exclusive right to the benefits of being Athenian—the "sharing in" (*metekhein*, precisely the word used for male "citizenship") the rituals, sacred rites, and honors pertaining to the *polis*.[125] In a yet

[119] Birth of male citizens: Sealey 1990: 19; Just 1989: 24. "Passivity" of citizenship: Mossé [1962] 1979; Lotze 1981.

[120] Loraux [1984] 1993: 10, 119. For the prevalence of this view, see Davies 1977–78: 105; Vidal-Naquet 1986: 205; Wohl 1998: xvii; Ober 1993: 134–35; Carey 1992: 26; Saxonhouse 1991; Patterson 1994: 201 skeptically. Exclusion of women is often seen as "a structural element of democracy," at Athens and elsewhere: Fraisse 1989: 199; Loraux [1989] 1995: 3.

[121] 57.30: παρὰ τοὺς νόμους, οἳ κελεύουσιν ἔνοχον εἶναι τῇ κακηγορίᾳ τὸν τὴν ἐργασίαν τὴν ἐν τῇ ἀγορᾷ ἢ τῶν πολιτῶν ἢ τῶν πολιτίδων ὀνειδίζοντά τινι.

[122] 57.43: μαρτυρεῖ τοῖς ἔργοις ἀστήν τ' αὐτὴν καὶ πολῖτιν εἶναι.

[123] 8.43: Ἐὰν γὰρ ἐξαπατηθῆτε ὑμεῖς πεισθέντες ὡς ἡ μήτηρ ἡμῶν οὐκ ἦν πολῖτις, οὐδ' ἡμεῖς ἐσμεν· μετ' Εὐκλείδην γὰρ ἄρχοντα γεγόναμεν.

[124] Isok. 14.51: καὶ γὰρ οὐδ' ἀλλότριοι τυγχάνομεν ὑμῖν ὄντες . . . διὰ γὰρ τὰς ἐπιγαμίας τὰς δοθείσας ἐκ πολιτίδων ὑμετέρων γεγόναμεν·

[125] Dem. 59: (107) οὔθ' ὁ δῆμος πολῖτιν ἐποιήσατο; (112) ὥστε καὶ ὑπὲρ τῶν πολιτίδων σκοπεῖτε, τοῦ μὴ ἀνεκδότους γενέσθαι τὰς τῶν πενήτων θυγατέρας. (113) . . . προπηλακισθέντος δὲ τοῦ νόμου . . . ἡ μὲν τῶν πορνῶν ἐργασία ἥξει εἰς τὰς τῶν πολιτῶν θυγατέρας . . . τὸ δὲ τῶν ἐλευθέρων γυναικῶν

more explicitly political context, Aristotle observes that in certain *poleis*, in particular those functioning "democratically," citizenship is granted to an individual whose mother is a "citizeness" (even in cases where the father is an alien).[126] But Aristotle also points out that, "as a practical matter," a "citizen" (*politēs*) is generally defined as a person born from both a mother and a father who are "citizens":[127] it is not possible to fashion a requirement of birth from a "citizen" (*politēs*) or a "citizeness" (*politis*) over too extended a span of generations, because the founders of a city could not have been born to progenitors who were already "citizens."[128] The Athenian speaker in Plato's *Laws* envisions military training for both "citizens" and "citizenesses,"[129] and even the Athenian dramatists, Sophoklēs and Euripidēs, refer to women as *politides*.[130]

This recognition as *politides* of free female members of Athenian "households," relatives of *politai*, was a requisite consequence of Athenian social organization. Athens functioned through "households" (*oikoi*, singular *oikos*)—not on the basis of individuals or "families." Thus the term "citizen" is entirely inappropriate to describe communal relationships at Athens where membership in the *polis* (albeit often termed "citizenship" in modern works)[131] was conceptualized as a "sharing" or

---

ἀξίωμα εἰς τὰς ἑταίρας, ἂν ἄδειαν λάβωσι τοῦ ἐξεῖναι αὐταῖς παιδοποιεῖσθαι ὡς ἂν βούλωνται καὶ τελετῶν καὶ ἱερῶν καὶ τιμῶν μετέχειν τῶν ἐν τῇ πόλει. Mossé correctly notes: "les termes importants ici sont μετέχειν, qu'on retrouve dans toutes les expressions concernant l'exercise des droits politiques, τιμῶν bien entendu et enfin τῇ πόλει" ([1985] 1988: 79). Cf. Mossé and di Donato 1983.

[126] *Pol.* 1278a26–28: ἐν πολλαῖς δὲ πολιτείαις προσεφέλκει τινὰς καὶ τῶν ξένων ὁ νόμος· ὁ γὰρ ἐκ πολίτιδος ἔν τισι δημοκρατίαις πολίτης ἐστίν.

[127] *Pol.* 1275b22–23: Ὁρίζονται δὲ πρὸς τὴν χρῆσιν πολίτην τὸν ἐξ ἀμφοτέρων πολιτῶν καὶ μὴ θατέρου μόνον, οἷον πατρὸς ἢ μητρός.

[128] *Pol.* 1275b24–34: οἱ δὲ καὶ τοῦτ' ἐπὶ πλέον ζητοῦσιν, οἷον ἐπὶ πάππους δύο ἢ τρεῖς ἢ πλείους. οὕτω δὲ ὁριζομένων πολιτικῶς καὶ παχέως, ἀποροῦσί τινες τὸν τρίτον ἐκεῖνον ἢ τέταρτον, πῶς ἔσται πολίτης. . . . καὶ γὰρ οὐδὲ δυνατὸν ἐφαρμόττειν τὸ ἐκ πολίτου ἢ ἐκ πολίτιδος ἐπὶ τῶν πρώτων οἰκησάντων ἢ κτισάντων.

[129] Pl. *Laws* 814c2–4: Οὐκοῦν τιθῶμεν τὸν νόμον τοῦτον, μέχρι γε τοσούτου μὴ ἀμελεῖσθαι τὰ περὶ τὸν πόλεμον γυναιξὶν δεῖν, ἐπιμελεῖσθαι δὲ πάντας τοὺς πολίτας καὶ τὰς πολίτιδας;

[130] Eur. *Ēlek.* 1335: χαίρετε δ' ὑμεῖς πολλά, πολίτιδες. Soph. *Ēlek.* 1227: ὦ φίλταται γυναῖκες, ὦ πολίτιδες. Despite the frequent and relatively early appearance of *politis* in Athenian literature and litigation, the word is sometimes dismissed as "rare" and/or as a neologism. Patterson (1986: 49; 55; 66, n. 35), for example, points out that the word ἀστή, "by way of contrast," appears twenty times in Demosthenes 59. But the focus of that speech is a statutory prohibition explicitly relating to ἀσταί: accordingly, Demosthenes 59 contains the vast majority of Demosthenic references to ἀστή (which is found in only three other speeches attributed to Demosthenes [46, 48, 57]). For differentiation of πολῖται/πολίτιδες from ἀστοί/ἀσταί, see Chapter 2.

[131] "Citizenship" has even been considered a fundamental concept bequeathed to Western civilization by Hellenism (thus Cochrane 1944: 86–87). For the frequently inconsistent and confusing use of "citizenship" even in modern contexts to cover a variety of sometimes incompatible statuses and concepts, see Chapter 2, n. 1.

"participating" in the polis by free persons born of appropriate parentage,[132] a natal requirement necessarily imposed within the context of society's dominant institution, the "household":[133] "the Athenian citizen-to-be had to prove his legitimate birth into an Athenian *oikos*" (Strauss 1993: 42). Although the ancient Greeks did not even have a word for *family*, in the modern sense of a nuclear or extended grouping of people living together,[134] all persons of every status (both free and slave) were members of an *oikos*,[135] an associated entity encompassing the physical attributes of the group's house, the complement of members now (or in some cases previously) living in that house, and the property relating to those members.[136]

Although the paradigmatic "household" encompassed husband, wife, children, and slaves,[137] *oikoi* were multifaceted (and women's participation in the *polis*, derived from their position in such "households," accordingly multisourced). Numerous *oikoi* overlapped, many extending

[132] *Ath. Pol.* 42.1: μετέχουσιν μὲν τῆς πολιτείας οἱ ἐξ ἀμφοτέρων γεγονότες ἀστῶν, ἐγγράφονται δ' εἰς τοὺς δημότας ὀκτωκαίδεκα ἔτη γεγονότες. ὅταν δ' ἐγγράφωνται διαψηφίζονται περὶ αὐτῶν ὀμόσαντες οἱ δημόται, πρῶτον μὲν εἰ δοκοῦσι γεγονέναι τὴν ἡλικίαν τὴν ἐκ τοῦ νόμου . . . δεύτερον δ' εἰ ἐλεύθερός ἐστι καὶ γέγονε κατὰ τοὺς νόμους. Aristot. *Ath. Pol.* 55.3: ἐπερωτῶσιν δ', ὅταν δοκιμάζωσιν, πρῶτον μὲν 'τίς σοι πατὴρ καὶ πόθεν τῶν δήμων, καὶ τίς πατρὸς πατήρ, καὶ τίς μήτηρ, καὶ τίς μητρὸς πατὴρ καὶ πόθεν τῶν δήμων;' Scholiast to Aiskhin. 1.39 (Eumēlos fr. 2): μηδένα τῶν μετ' Εὐκλείδην ἄρχοντα μετέχειν τῆς πόλεως, ἂν μὴ ἄμφω τοὺς γονέας ἀστοὺς ἐπιδείξηται. Cf., for example, Lys. 16.3, 30.15; Dem. 39.31, 57.1–2, 59.105; Aristot. *Ath. Pol.* 26.4, 36.1, 40.2; *Pol.* 1268a24, 27–28; 1272a15–16; 1293a3–4, 8; 1294a12–14; 1297b4–6; 1302b26–27; 1306b10–11, 13–14; 1329b37; 1332a32–35; Athēn. 577b. Birth requirements for "participation" in the *polis* are discussed at length in Chapter 2, pp. 58–63. Ostwald (1996: 55–56; 60, n. 37) accurately differentiates the Athenian concept of participation from the modern "right of citizenship."

[133] *Oikos* as "household": Foxhall 1989; MacDowell 1989; Karabēlias 1984. For the relationship between *oikos* and *phratry*, and in particular the controversial Δεκελειῶν οἶκον, see Hedrick 1990, esp. 30–33, 75–77; Lambert 1993: 95–141; Ito 1988; Thompson 1968; Bourriot 1976: 639–48. For the significance of the household in other societies, see Netting, Wilk, and Arnould 1984: xxii. "The family" continues to be a dominant unit in modern Greece: see du Boulay 1974, ch. 1; Faubion 1993: 60–61.

[134] In explaining the importance of the *oikos*, Aristotle points out the lack of a descriptive term in Greek for the nuclear family (husband and wife): ἀνώνυμον γὰρ ἡ γυναικὸς καὶ ἀνδρὸς σύζευξις (*Pol.* 1253b9–10). Finley notes: "the necessity never made itself felt to provide a specific name for the restricted concept evoked by our word 'family' " (1985: 18–19). Cf. Humphreys [1983] 1993: 67; Shorter 1977 (who denies the existence prior to the Industrial Revolution of traits such as intimacy or privacy that supposedly are characteristic of the modern family).

[135] Slaves as members of the *oikos*: Chapter 5, pp. 145–46.

[136] Although "the different senses of the word" can be studied separately (as MacDowell [1989] does)—and in context a particular aspect may be emphasized (as with the physical premises in Antiph. 2d.8)—the unique signification of the term lies in its denotation of an *entity*. For each of the separate notations of physical place, the human beings associated with that place and assets of value belonging to those persons, Greek offers a plenitude of alternative terms, most particularly *oikia* for the physical house, *klēros* for the assets, and *agkhisteia* for a circle of related persons.

[137] Aristot. *Pol.* 1253b5–7: πρῶτα δὲ καὶ ἐλάχιστα μέρη οἰκίας δεσπότης καὶ δοῦλος, καὶ πόσις καὶ ἄλοχος, καὶ πατὴρ καὶ τέκνα. Cf. *Pol.* 1252a27–28: θῆλυ μὲν καὶ ἄρρεν τῆς γεννήσεως ἕνεκεν.

beyond a single generation,[138] others arising upon new marriages,[139] still others continuing after the death or departure of a prior member, or accommodating the affiliation of individual members with more than one *oikos*. Thus, as children matured or adults changed situation, they might be associated, for different purposes and in different contexts, with more than a single "household," as in the case of a married couple residing in a separate residence, and thus constituting with their own offspring and servants a "natural association for everyday purposes"[140] but still retaining an affinity, from a personal and property aspect, with their natal *oikoi*. Through dowry, a mother-in-law retained a financial relationship to her natal household, while a daughter-in-law was similarly joined to her own *oikos* of birth[141]—and both were connected through son and husband to their *oikos* of residence and to one another.[142] Similar

[138] Forensic evidence suggests that about three-quarters of newlywed couples resided with parents (Gallant 1991: 21). Limited longevity minimized the number of coexisting generations: in none of the eight families recorded on a phratry list from Paiania did grandfathers survive until their eldest grandsons reached their teens (*I.G.* II^2 2344; cf. Hedrick 1989: 131). Nevertheless, the potentially multigenerational and dual-gendered aspect of the *oikos* is shown most graphically at Dem. 43.48: Μακάρτατος, τίνος ὢν πατρός; Θεοπόμπου. μητρὸς δὲ τίνος; Ἀπολήξιδος θυγατρὸς Προσπαλτίου, ἀδελφῆς δὲ Μακαρτάτου Προσπαλτίου. ὁ δὲ Θεόπομπος τίνος ἦν πατρός; Χαριδήμου. ὁ δὲ Χαρίδημος τίνος; Στρατίου. ὁ δὲ Στρατίος τίνος; Βουσέλου. οὑτοσί . . . ἐστιν ὁ Στρατίου οἶκος. It is this dimension of the *oikos* that was the focus of the religiously oriented effort to avoid the expiration of a "House": see Isai. 7.30; cf. Asheri 1960; Rubinstein 1993, esp. 105–12.

[139] Children were not necessary: see Isai. 6.5 and 7.30, for example, where childless men are said to have their own *oikoi*. In speech 6, Philoktēmōn and his wife were childless (§5: τῷ Φιλοκτήμονι ἐκ μὲν τῆς γυναικὸς ᾗ συνῴκει οὐκ ἦν παιδίον οὐδέν), and in speech 7 Apollodoros's son had died (§14: Ἀπολλοδώρῳ γὰρ ἦν ὑός . . . ἐπειδὴ δὲ ἐτελεύτησε.)

[140] Aristot. *Pol.* 1252b12–14.

[141] Because Attic society did not function through modern Western concepts of ownership (Wolff 1944: 63; Harrison 1968–71: 1:201; Hunter 1994: 11), extensive scholarly efforts have failed to establish who "owned" a dowry: the female by or for whom the *proix* has been supplied; her natal *oikos,* which at all times retains a residual interest; her marital *oikos,* which controls the dowry; future *oikoi* of her offspring (which incipiently command at least an inchoate interest); or any or all of these under varying circumstances, definitions, and assumptions. But it is clear that the dowry did represent assets to which a female was entitled on marriage (subject to her natal household's continuing interest): see Foxhall 1989: 32–36 and forthcoming: n. 8. In his seminal work on the juridical aspects of dowry, Dimakis notes that, whatever the ultimate theoretical "ownership" of the *proix*, during the continuation of the marriage for which the dowry had been provided the wife was for all practical purposes in control of this household asset: κατὰ τὴν γενικῶς κρατήσασαν γνώμην, ἡ Ἀτθίς, διαρκοῦντος τοῦ γάμου, ἦτο κυρία τῆς προικός . . . ἡ κυριότης τῶν προικῴων πραγμάτων ἀνῆκεν εἰς τὴν γυναῖκα (n.d.: 186). Cf. Dem. 47.53, 57. Scholars do uniformly agree that a husband, although he might be referred to as *kyrios* (see n. 174), personally had no permanent property interest in the *proix*. See Dimakis n.d.: 189. Cf. Cox 1988: 382–84; 1998: 105–29; Petropoulos 1939: 211.

[142] If a marriage were terminated prior to birth of male offspring, the dowry returned to the natal *oikos*: Isai. 3.36, 78; Dem. 59.52. Where a marriage ended because of the husband's death after the birth of male offspring, the mother might continue to control the assets personally (as

bifurcated relationships affected a male who had established his own "household" while his natal *oikos* continued through his father[143] (or on the father's death or disability had been transmuted into that of another male relative, such as an older or younger brother).[144] Such duality or plurality also affected males who had been adopted into new households[145] and those who were married to, or were sons of, "heiresses" (*epiklēroi*).[146] Widowed mothers (numerous among a population of relatively low life expectancy in which men often married much younger women[147]) might continue to live in the family home, continuing a prior *oikos*, while a mature son—acclimated to respecting his mother's authority[148]—creates with his wife a new *oikos* within the same physical

in the case of Kleoboulē: Dem. 27–31; Hunter 1989a, 1989b) or the assets could come under the control of new *oikoi*—those formed by the widow's male offspring on reaching maturity (and sometimes including the widow as resident member: Dem. 42.27), or those formed by the widow on remarriage (Lys. 32.6).

[143] See, for example, Dem. 47: Theophēmos, having taken a portion of family property, lived on his own; his brother Euergos resided with their father (35: χωρὶς οἰκοίη ὁ Θεόφημος, αὐτὸς δὲ παρὰ τῷ πατρί). In Dem. 24, a father, son, and unmarried daughter maintain one home, while other sons live elsewhere (202–3). Cf. Philoktēmōn and his father Euktēmōn (the son made his own testamentary arrangements although his father was still alive and, in fact, survived the son by decades [Isai. 6.5]). For the dynamics of relations between Athenian "dyads" (father-son, brother-brother), see Cox 1998: 68–104.

[144] Cf. Dem. 43.19. These multiple relationships are reflected in the well-attested and relatively frequent challenges by agnatic kin to wills and adoptions instituted by male relatives: ancestral property rights often are intertwined with the property interests of several or more *oikoi*. To minimize possible friction (and presumably, in many cases, for reasons of economic "rationality"), siblings often left their elders' property undivided, or delayed partition for many years. See Aiskhin. 1.102; Dem. 44.10, 47.34; Isai. 2.28–29; Lys. 18.21, 32.4. Cf. Hunter 1993.

[145] Despite legislative efforts to assure the primacy of an adopted son's relationship to his new *oikos* (Isai. 9.33, 10.11; Dem. 44.64, 68; Ant. frag. 4 [Baiter and Sauppe] = Harp. 228.4–7), adoptees seem often to have continued to maintain a relationship with their natal *oikoi*. In fact, Makartatos II is accused at Dem. 43.77 of effectively controlling both his *oikoi* of adoption and of birth. A number of adoptees are known to have "returned" (ἐπανιέναι) to their natal *oikoi* and even perhaps to have been restored to their natal demes. See Dem. 43.77ff.; Dem. 44.21ff., 34–35, 39, 44, 46, 52; Isai. 10.11. Cf. Isai. 6.44. Where more than one generation was involved, affiliations were multiplied, and potential complications increased geometrically. For the theoretical and practical "difficulties" resulting from such multiple relationships, see Rubinstein 1993: 57–61; Harris 1996; Humphreys [1983] 1993: 7–8.

[146] See Just 1989: 95–98, 102–4; Fisher 1981; Harrison 1968–71: 10–12, 309–11, cf. 132–38; Todd 1993: 228–31.

[147] Men appear generally to have entered first marriages when in their late twenties or early thirties; women, to have married shortly after reaching puberty, perhaps generally at about fifteen. See Pomeroy 1997: 4–9; Foxhall 1994: 137; Humphreys [1983] 1993: 7; Golden 1981: 322. On the phenomenon of relatively low longevity at Athens, see n. 138.

[148] The young Demosthenes—destined to become the leader of the Athenian state—in his various speeches dealing with family property (Dem. 27–31) documents the familial authority of his mother, Kleoboulē, after the death of his father. See Hunter 1989a, 1989b; Foxhall 1996: 144–49; Chapter 2, pp. 76–77. Timarkhos's disposal of inherited property in defiance of his

boundaries (and the mother's other offspring might inhabit physically unrelated domiciles but retain an association with, and a property interest in, the assets of their original *oikos*). Or the widow might remarry, moving to a new physical domicile, but retaining relations with her old, now reformulated *oikos*—or she might even return to her natal *oikos*, however transformed it might have become during her absence![149]

Personal essence thus might be fragmented among, and in any case explicable only in the context of, these interrelated *oikoi*. This consideration underlies the frequent contention in court presentations that an entire group is threatened by an adversary's action that in modern Western context would seem directed only at a single individual. Consider, for example, the plea of the three sons in Lysias 20 that they and their father not be destroyed because of false charges against him alone,[150] or the assertion by young Theomnēstos in Demosthenes 59 that Stephanos's negative efforts against Apollodōros might destroy the entire group of interrelated persons clustered around Apollodōros.[151] Although modern scholars insist that in fact only Apollodōros was personally threatened,[152] the Athenians far better understood the potential negative impact: in Attic society individuality was negated by the mutual dependence, and interrelated empowerment, inherent in the *oikoi*.

And so, in contrast to modern Westernized societies with their focus on personal rights and obligations,[153] Athenian sources identify the *oikos*

---

mother's wishes is presented as remarkable—and deplorable: τὸ δ' Ἀλωπεκῆσι χωρίον ... ἱκετευούσης καὶ ἀντιβολούσης τῆς μητρός ... ἐᾶσαι καὶ μὴ ἀποδόσθαι, ἀλλ' εἰ μή τι ἄλλο, ἐνταφῆναί <γ'> ὑπολιπεῖν αὐτῇ, οὐκ ἀπέσχετο, ἀλλὰ καὶ τοῦτ' ἀπέδοτο δισχιλίων δραχμῶν (Aiskhin. 1.99).

[149] Hunter finds that "for the most part," younger widows immediately after their husband's death returned to their natal *oikoi,* which reclaimed the dowry (1989b: 296–98; 1994: 195, n. 9; cf. Thompson 1976). Of thirty older widows identified by Hunter, thirteen resided with adult sons (1994: 201, n. 46). These options are reflected in comedy. In Menander's *Dyskolos*, for example, a widow who had remarried left her new husband and went to live with her son (13–29). Cf. Myrrhinē, the mother of Gorgias in Menander's *Geōrgos*.

[150] (34) ἴστε ὅτι πρόθυμοι γεγενήμετθα εἰς ὑμᾶς, καὶ τὸν πατέρα οὐδὲν ἡμαρτηκότα.... (35) ἡμεῖς δὲ τὸν πατέρα τουτονὶ καὶ ἡμᾶς ἐξαιτούμεθα, μὴ ἡμᾶς ἀντὶ μὲν ἐπιτίμων ἀτίμους ποιήσητε, ἀντὶ δὲ πολιτῶν ἀπόλιδας. ... εἰ δὲ ἡμᾶς ἀδίκως ἀπολεῖτε, πῶς ἢ οὗτος ἡμῖν ἡδέως συνέσται ἢ ἡμεῖς ἀλλήλοις ἐν τῷ αὐτῷ.

[151] (1) ἠδικήμεθα ὑπὸ Στεφάνου μεγάλα, καὶ εἰς κινδύνους τοὺς ἐσχάτους κατέστημεν ὑπ' αὐτοῦ, ὅ τε κηδεστὴς καὶ ἐγὼ καὶ ἡ ἀδελφὴ καὶ ἡ γυνὴ ἡ ἐμή.... (7) πραθείσης δ' αὐτῆς εἰς τὴν ἐσχάτην ἀπορίαν καταστήσεσθαι καὶ αὐτὸς καὶ παῖδες οἱ ἐκείνου καὶ γυνὴ καὶ ἡμεῖς ἅπαντες.

[152] For example, Carey 1992: 85: "The [speech] effectively presents Theomnestos as Stephanos' victim; but in fact he faced neither exile nor disfranchisement, unlike Apollodōros."

[153] For the differing ancient and modern approaches to individual status and rights, see Ostwald 1996 and the essays in H. Jones 1998. Morris (1987: 3) notes that in ancient Greece "there were no natural rights of the individual" (but for a more nuanced view, see Miller 1974; 1995). Communitarians, as critics of the contemporary orientation toward individual rights, often insist

in its varied formations—and not the individual—as the basic constituent element of society. Juridically, "the polis was an aggregation of *oikoi,*"[154] with a legal system based on "the rights of families as corporate groups."[155] Materially, the *oikos* dominated "the economy of Greek city-states, since economic enterprises largely existed and were managed within the structure of households" (Foxhall 1994: 139). Practically, as the ancient sources demonstrate and modern scholars agree, the "household" occupied central position in Athenian life[156]—and women occupied a central position in the Athenian *oikos*. According to Xenophon, the wife bore primary responsibility for managing the household; her control of the domestic slaves made her a veritable queen.[157] In Euripides' words, "women order households . . . nor in the absence of a woman is even the prosperous household well provided for."[158] Aristotle derides as "absurd" Plato's suggestion that women and men, on the analogy of animal life, can

that the Hellenic "notion of the political community as a common project is alien to the modern liberal individualistic world" (MacIntyre 1981: 146–47). Cf. Sandel 1984: 87; Yack 1993: 30.

[154] Wolff 1944: 93. Some scholars have even suggested that individual *politai* attended the *ekklēsiai* and sat on the *dikastēria* as "representatives" of their respective *oikoi*. Clark, for example, has asserted that adult males were not expected to speak at assemblies or to hold office until they became heads of households (1982: 189). Similarly: Swanson 1992: 25. Although MacDowell (1989: 20) contends that there is "virtually no evidence" to support this claim, Aristotle tells of older men who have been "relieved" or "superannuated" (Robinson [1962] 1995: 4) as full "citizens," relegated to a position similar to that of adolescent males not yet enrolled as *politai*: καθάπερ καὶ παῖδας τοὺς μήπω δι' ἡλικίαν ἐγγεγραμμένους καὶ τοὺς γέροντας τοὺς ἀφειμένους φατέον εἶναι μέν πως πολίτας, οὐχ ἁπλῶς δὲ λίαν ἀλλὰ προστιθέντας τοὺς μὲν ἀτελεῖς τοὺς δὲ παρηκμακότας ἤ τι τοιοῦτον ἕτερον (*Pol.* 1275a14–18). Cf. Pl. *Rep.* 498c. Yet recognition of the seminal organizational role of the *oikos*—and of the derivation therefrom of male and female forms of "participation" in the *polis*—does not mandate its direct institutional intrusion into the political sphere, which was limited to males: "the basic unit of *political* organisation was the individual, more particularly the citizen male" (MacDowell 1989: 21) (emphasis added). It is on this political aspect that Aristotle focuses in book 3 of the *Politics* (in contrast to his emphasis on the *oikos* in book 1 which deals with society as a whole, transcending a merely political perspective; cf. Hansen 1996a: 196–205).

[155] Todd 1993: 206. The primacy of the *oikos* is the literal starting point for the two standard treatments of Athenian substantive law (Beauchet ([1897] 1969: 1:3; Harrison 1968–71: 1:1). (Todd sets out [1993: 208–11, 225–27] the substantial difficulties inherent in MacDowell's rejection [1989] of the *opinio communis*.)

[156] See Aristot. *Pol.* 1252; Xen. *Oik.*, esp. 1.5, 6.4; Lys. 1 and 32. Cf. Cox 1998: 13; Ogden 1996: 42; Strauss 1993: 35, 43; Todd 1993: 206; Patterson 1981: 9–10; 1990: 43–44, 51, 55–57, 59; Jameson 1990: 179; Foxhall 1989; 1994; 1996: 140–52; and forthcoming; Sissa 1986; Hallett 1984: 72–76; Sealey 1984: 112; Hunter 1981: 15; Lotze 1981: 169; Fisher 1976: 2: 5ff.; Lacey 1968: 88–90; Ledl 1907. Sourvinou-Inwood (1995: 113) notes the *oikos* to be "the basic economic unit of the polis" but finds "some ambiguity as to the extent to which the basic social unit is the oikos or the individual."

[157] *Oik.* 7.35–43, 9.14–17 (ὥσπερ βασίλισσαν: 9.15).

[158] Eur. *Mel. Des.* fr. 660 Mette 1982–85, lines 9–11 (P. Berl. 9772 and P. Oxy. 1176 fr. 39, col. 11) (fr. 13: Auffret 1987): νέμουσι δ' οἴκους καὶ τὰ ναυστολούμενα | ἔ [σω] δόμων σώιζουσιν, οὐδ' ἐρημίαι | γυναικὸς οἶκος εὐπινὴς ọ̔ γε ὄλβιọς· (οὐδ' ὄλβιọς· P. Oxy.). Cf. Todd 1993: 204–6.

do the same work: human females, unlike their biological counterparts in lower orders, have households to run![159] In fact, because so much of communal and personal life originated and functioned through the household, "the *oikos* [was] not simply 'the private sphere' to which women's activities were relegated,"[160] and women's involvement in the *oikos*, far from denying them a place in the *polis* (broadly conceived),[161] actually admitted them—just as male involvement in the *oikos* likewise admitted men—to participation in Athenian life.

For both female and male children, shortly after birth the *oikos* was the focus of significant recognition rites. In the *amphidromia* legitimation ceremony,[162] and in the *dekatē* naming feast and associated activities,[163] both male and female parents participated in introducing the newly born girl or boy into the *oikos* as a legitimate member.[164] The *amphidromia* itself was a "walking around" or "running around" the hearth, or around

[159] *Rep.* 451d ff. Aristot. *Pol.* 1264b4–6: ἄτοπον δὲ καὶ τὸ ἐκ τῶν θηρίων ποιεῖσθαι τὴν παραβολήν, ὅτι δεῖ τὰ αὐτὰ ἐπιτηδεύειν τὰς γυναῖκας τοῖς ἀνδράσιν, οἷς οἰκονομίας οὐδὲν μέτεστιν.

[160] Foxhall 1994: 138. Scholars sometimes deprecate the importance of women's role in the Athenian *oikos* by deprecating the significance of the *oikos* itself ("outside is the only really desirable place to be" [Murnaghan 1988: 13]), often on the fallacious assumption that the Athenian *oikos* somehow replicated recent American and European bourgeois household patterns. But see my subsequent discussion and Foxhall 1989; 1994: 138–45; 1996: 142–52; and forthcoming.

[161] For the various denotations of the term *polis,* often used imprecisely by both ancient and modern authors, see the Preface.

[162] *Amphidromia* for girls: Isai. 3.30; Aristoph. *Orn.* 922–23 (for the metaphorical birth of the feminine entity of Cloud-cuckoo-land: τὴν δεκάτην ταύτης ἐγώ, | καὶ τοὔνομ' ὥσπερ παιδίῳ νῦν δὴ 'θέμην); Hesykh., s.v. στέφανον ἐκφέρειν (different garlands on front door for male and female infants), and Ephippos, fr. 3 (K-A), garlanding of doors itself part of *amphidromia*. Deubner (1908–26: 2:649) suggests that the fifth and seventh days after birth, offered variantly in the ancient sources as the principal celebration of the *amphidromia*, were both utilized, one for boys and the other for girls. On the *amphidromia* generally, see Paradiso 1988; Golden 1990: 23, 30.

[163] See Eur. *Ēlek.* 561–66; Pl. *Theait.* 160e with schol.; Harp., Phōt., and Suda, s.v. *amphidromia*; Hesykh., s.vv. δρομιάμφιον ἦμαρ and δεκάτην θύομεν; Schol. Aristoph. *Lys.* 757; *Etym. mag.*, s.v. ἑβδομευομένου; *Anek. Bek.* 1.207.13, s.v. δεκάτην ἑστιᾶσαι. Hamilton 1984 describes how the ceremonies of the *amphidromia* extended over a period of days, from the initial "running around" the infant by the father and/or the mother, through the actual presentation of the child at the feast on the tenth day after birth, the *dekatē*. Cf. Stengel 1958: 1901–2.

[164] For explicit linkage of recognition formalities with entry into the *oikos*, see Isai. 6.22.6: ὡς ἐκ ταύτης παῖδας ἀποφαινῶν καὶ εἰσποιήσων εἰς τὸν οἶκον. Although some allusions to exposure do appear in Athenian drama, especially in late comedy with regard to *nothoi*, there is no Athenian evidence for the extent of abandonment, or for the process or nexus of decision making that might have led to exposure of infants (Patterson 1985: 116–17). In fact, it is doubtful whether the exposure of newborns "was widespread [or] even common at Athens" (Golden 1990: 87; cf. Golden 1988). Because she assumes that many infants were murdered and that the father in reality could actually make an autonomous and willful determination to eliminate (or "recognize") a child, Sourvinou-Inwood (1995: 113) sees the father's role as "central."

the child who lay in the hearth, which was the symbolic center of the *oikos*. "In being introduced to it the child was therefore welcomed into the *oikos* in both its physical and its abstract dimensions."[165] Because "marriage" for the Athenians was conceptualized as "a relationship between a man and woman which has the primary goal of producing children and maintaining the identity of the *oikos* unit (the household) within the social and political community" (Patterson 1991: 59), these ceremonies were inherent affirmation of the legitimacy of the marital cohabitation (which in Greek is termed, in verbal form, *syn-oik-ein*).[166] Once accepted into the *oikos* as infants, both boys and girls thereafter were entitled to participate in the sacred and holy rites of "*hiera* and *hosia*,"[167] a variety of ceremonies, of which some were performed at the "household" level and others as *polis*-wide rituals.[168] Significantly, the right to participate at the *polis* level—for example, in the rites of

[165] Ogden 1996: 90. Cf. Garland 1990: 94; Burkert 1985: 255. The *amphidromia* has been compared with the welcoming ceremony (καταχύσματα) for brides and slaves joining the *oikos* (Garland 1990: 94).

[166] For *synoikein* as "'living together' of a man and woman (which) was recognized and validated by classical Athenian law and custom, establishing what we can indeed call a marriage or marital relationship" (Patterson 1991: 48), see Dem. 59.122 (τὸ γὰρ συνοικεῖν τοῦτ' ἔστιν, ὃς ἂν παιδοποιῆται καὶ εἰσάγῃ εἴς τε τοὺς φράτερας καὶ δημότας τοὺς υἱεῖς, καὶ τὰς θυγατέρας ἐκδιδῷ ὡς αὑτοῦ οὔσας τοῖς ἀνδράσιν); Hdt. 2.92.1 (καὶ γυναικὶ μιῇ ἕκαστος αὐτῶν συνοικέει κατά περ Ἕλληνες); Dem. 59.16 (NOMOS: Ἐὰν δὲ ξένος ἀστῇ συνοικῇ τέχνῃ ἢ μηχανῇ ἡτινιοῦν); Dem. 59.62 (Στέφανόν τε τουτονὶ τὸν ἔχοντα ταύτην νυνὶ καὶ συνοικοῦντ' αὐτῇ).

[167] The law explicitly excluded both male and female *nothoi* from these rituals, thereby implying that women accepted into *oikoi* as legitimate offspring did have a right of participation. See Dem. 43.51: νόθῳ δὲ μηδὲ νόθῃ μὴ εἶναι ἀγχιστείαν μηθ' ἱερῶν μήθ' ὁσίων ἀπ' Εὐκλείδου ἄρχοντος. Cf. Isai. 6.47: Τοὐναντίον τοίνυν συμβέβηκεν ἢ ὡς ὁ νόμος γέγραπται· ἐκεῖ μὲν γὰρ ἔστι νόθῳ μηδὲ νόθῃ <μή> εἶναι ἀγχιστείαν μήθ' ἱερῶν μήθ' ὁσίων ἀπ' Εὐκλείδου ἄρχοντος. For participation by grandchildren, see Isai. 8.15. Some females might also have been presented to their fathers' phratry through the *meion* (or "lesser" sacrifice: the introduction of a child to the father's phratry on the first Apatouria following the infant's birth, presumably received by most but not all young boys). At 3.73, 75–76, and 79–80, Isaios insists that Phylē, if legitimate, should have received a *meion*; at 6.10 he implies the presentation of Euktēmōn's daughters to the phratry (Εὐκτήμονι . . . καὶ δύο θυγατέρας, καὶ τὴν μητέρα αὐτῶν . . . πάντες οἱ προσήκοντες ἴσασι καὶ οἱ φράτερες). Cf. Pollux 8.107. Ogden notes the absence of epigraphic evidence for a female *meion* and suggests that not all girls received such sacrifices under all circumstances, but that "all phratries would give *meions* to certain girls in certain circumstances—to heiresses, for example" (1996: 114). Cf. Scafuro 1994: 188, n. 50 (who cites early discussions); Lambert 1993: 38, 180; Sealey 1987: 18; Gould 1980: 40–42.

[168] Although "sacred and holy rites" conveys an appropriate general meaning, *hiera* and *hosia* are "idioms that defy translation" (Burkert 1985: 268). For the content and context of these ceremonies, and for their linguistic signification, see Rudhardt 1958: 22–36; Connor 1988. Many public rituals were both part of the *hiera kai hosia* and were open ("confusingly," says Ogden 1996: 100) to non-*politai*. For the resolution of this and similar anomalies arising from modern failure to differentiate the terms *politai* and *astoi*, see Chapter 2.

the Thesmophoria[169]—was often limited to those entitled to participate at the *oikos* level.[170]

Yet the centrality of the "household" at Athens extended far beyond the ceremonial, and impacted virtually every aspect of Athenian life. Ownership of property effectively came within the control, and production of income, within the activities, of the *oikos*. Although in practice both men and women might personally use or alienate individual items of property such as money in their possession[171] or jewelry, clothing, tools, or servants,[172] and individual men and women are sometimes referred to as though personally the owners of realty,[173] most wealth—

[169] Participation in these female rites (from which men were excluded) was based on household affiliation: Burkert 1985: 242 and nn. 7, 8 thereto. Some scholars (following Aristoph. *Thes.* 329–31: τελέως δ' ἐκκλησιάσαιμεν Ἀθηναίων εὐγενεῖς γυναῖκες) have concluded that participation was limited explicitly to *politides*: women "legitimately married to an Athenian citizen in full possession of his political rights" (Just 1989: 24). In accord: Detienne 1977: 78. Other scholars, following Isai. 6.49–50, see the festival as open to "women of the community" (Pomeroy 1975: 78; cf. Fantham et al. 1994: 87). The variant positions are reconcilable if the terms *astai* and *politides* are distinguished: see Chapter 2.

[170] See Vernant 1980: 50; Foxhall 1989: 22–25. For the restriction of certain *hiera* to free members of the *oikos*, see Isai. 8.15. But cf. Aristoph. *Thes.* 293–94 where a slave is present at the Thesmophoria (but is sent away either to perform an assigned task, or, according to a verse athetized by various editors, including Hall and Geldart in the Oxford Classical Text, is sent away "because slaves cannot hear the [secret] discourse").

[171] Arkhippē, for example, the wife successively of the Athenian banking tycoons (and former slaves) Pasiōn and Phormiōn, seems clearly to have had monetary assets fully recognized, in legal context, as her own: Apollodōros is accused in court of seeking 3,000 drachmas from her estate "in addition to the 2,000 drachmas that she had given to Phormiōn's children" (τρισχιλίας ἐγκαλέσας ἀργυρίου δραχμὰς πρὸς αἷς ἔδωκεν ἐκείνη δισχιλίαις τοῖς τούτου παιδίοις: Dem. 36.14). Cf. the four talents in cash attributed to Kleoboulē (Dem. 27.53, 55; 28.47–48), the substantial resources controlled by the wife of Polyeuktos (Dem. 41), and the loan transactions engaged in by Hyperbolos's mother (according to Aristoph. *Thes.* 839–45).

[172] Pasiōn in his will "gives to Archippē as dowry one talent from Peparēthos, another talent here at Athens, a *synoikia* (multiple dwelling house) worth 100 mnai, female slaves, gold jewelry, and the other items of hers that are inside [the house]" (Dem. 45.28: δίδωμι τὴν ἐμαυτοῦ γυναῖκα Ἀρχίππην Φορμίωνι, καὶ προῖκα ἐπιδίδωμι Ἀρχίππῃ, τάλαντον μὲν τὸ ἐκ Πεπαρήθου, τάλαντον δὲ τὸ αὐτόθεν, συνοικίαν ἑκατὸν μνῶν, θεραπαίνας καὶ τὰ χρυσία, καὶ τἄλλα ὅσα ἐστὶν αὐτῇ ἔνδον, ἅπαντα ταῦτα Ἀρχίππῃ δίδωμι). Cf. Dem. 36.8; Finley [1951] 1985: 192, no. 175A (house [*oikia*] in the center of Athens given to a woman as dowry). For the legal and economic issues relating to such dispositions, see E. Cohen 1992: 101–10; Carey 1991; Whitehead 1986b.

[173] For "ownership" by females, see *S.E.G* 12.100. 67–71 (field bordering on silver mine listed in fourth-century records of the *polētai* as belonging to "the wife of Kharmylos") and Finley [1951] 1985: 192 (175A [Fine 1951: no. 7]: ὅρος οἰκίας προικός Ἀρχίλλ[ηι], ("not a security transaction" according to Finley). Pasiōn leaves a multiple-residence building to Arkhippē (see note 172), and a woman is reported on a fragmentary *horos* inscription as one of the lenders in a real-estate financing (Fine 1951: no. 28; cf. Finley [1951] 1985: 188). Harris sees this arrangement as providing a mechanism for women in business effectively to own real property by foreclosing, through a male "straw party," on pledged real estate (1992a: 319). "This *horos* demonstrates that women's role in financial matters was potentially much more extensive than the evidence of Athenian law would lead us to assume" (ibid., 311).

especially ancestral property (*patrōia*)—belonged to the various *oikoi*.[174] Thus it is the *oikos* itself that Isaios characterizes as undertaking the daunting liturgical services required of the few who qualified, by primacy of visible wealth, to shoulder those oppressive burdens of taxation and civic honor of which wealthy Athenians often complained.[175] Likewise the *oikos* bears the significant imposts on capital (the *eisphora* and *proeisphora*), the extraordinary levies that were imposed at intervals to provide funds for a specific undertaking such as a naval campaign.[176]

Transfer of property through inheritance was effectuated exclusively through the *oikos*. Because men with legitimate children—probably the vast majority of adult males despite high infantile mortality[177]—could not make testamentary dispositions of assets by will,[178] decedents' successory arrangements were essentially only mechanisms by which the heirless *oikos* might arrange for the marriage of a female relative/household member, or adopt a male to serve as putative future *kyrios*.[179] Although some individuals might have made clandestine efforts to transfer property

[174] Foxhall (1989 and forthcoming) demonstrates that the senior male in an *oikos*, often referred to as the *kyrios* (a term for which "there is really no modern expression": Wolff 1944: 46–47, n. 22), was not the "owner" of family property but rather the household representative or "steward" (Hunter 1994: 12) in dealing publicly with household assets. Cf. Schaps 1998b: 163–67.

[175] οἶκον τριηραρχοῦντα: Isai. 7.32; cf. 42. For the functions of the *triērarkhoi* or the *lēitourgountes* as psychologically and financially equivalent to the payment of fiscal imposts by "taxpayers," see Aristot. *Pol.* 1291a33–34; Xen. *Ath. Pol.* 1.13; Dem. 21.151, 153, 208; Isok. 8.128; Lys. 27.9–10. Cf. Davies 1971: xx. These liturgies, imposed only on the rich, often amounted to "the major part of a man's income" (Davies 1981: 19–24). For this "bleeding of the wealthy" (Andreades [1933] 1979: 359), a "redistribuzione a favore delle masse popolari" (D'Albergho in Gera 1975: 13), see Dem. 1.8–9, 24.197–98, 38.26, 47.54, 50.8–9, 52.26; Isai. 4.27, 6.60–61, 7.40; Isok. 8.128, 12.145; Lys. 7.31–32, 12.20, 18.7, 18.21, 19.9, 19.29, 19.57–9, 20.23, 28.3, 29.4, 30.26; Xen. *Hell.* 6.2.1; *Symp.* 4.30–32; Hyper. fr. 134; Aristot. *Pol.* 1309a15ff.; Antiphanēs fr. 202 (K-A); Dēm. Phal. fr. 136 Wehrli = Plut. *Mor.* 349a; Diod. Sik. 13.47.7, 52.5, 64.4; Anaximenēs 2 [p. 22, lines 5ff. ed. Hammer], and cf. Davies 1981: 82–84; Christ 1990: 150–57; Wyse [1904] 1967: 396.

[176] On the *eisphora* system, see Thomsen 1964; Gabrielsen 1994, esp. 184ff.; Brun 1983: 3–73; Gera 1975: 31–84. For imposition of the tax on metics as well as "citizens," see *I.G.*² II–III 244.26 and the fragment from Hypereidēs preserved at Pollux 8.144. Cf. Whitehead 1977: 78–80; 1986a: 146. There is some evidence for annual imposition of the *eisphora* from 347/6 to 323/2 (Thomsen 1964: 239–43).

[177] Foxhall 1989: 29. Cf. Ogden 1996: 157–63.

[178] Men with legitimate sons (παῖδες γνήσιοι ἄρρενες) could make no arrangements whatsoever (Dem. 20.102, 44.49, 44.67, 46.14; Isai. 3.1, 6, 9, 29; cf. Lane-Fox 1985: 224–25; Ste. Croix 1970: 389–90). Complex legal regulations controlled dispositions by those whose only direct heirs were daughters (*epiklēroi*): see Harrison 1: 1968–71: 309–12; Todd 1993: 226–31.

[179] See Thompson 1981b; Hunter 1994: 9–13. On the signification of the term *kyrios*, see n. 174.

in defiance of legal proscriptions,[180] no Athenian examples survive of testamentary disposition of *oikos* assets permanently outside the household.[181] Conversely, those Athenians who were affiliated with more than one *oikos* might share in the enjoyment of the assets of more than one estate—a seeming inequity sometimes decried by disappointed would-be beneficiaries claiming close relationship to only a single estate.[182]

Property transmitted from an earlier generation (*patrōia*, quintessentially real estate)[183] was so interconnected with an *oikos* that its waste by the household's male representative (*kyrios*) was punishable by his full or partial loss of political rights.[184] Female members of the household might even object openly to the sale of assets felt to be integral to an *oikos*.[185] But even incremental assets—fresh wealth (*epiktēta*) augmenting inherited property—were generally produced not by individuals but by and through the household (which was the physical location of virtually all *tekhnai*,[186] the skilled activities of craft or trade that encompassed all professions, "manufacturing" activities, and even financial busineses and operations).[187] Aiskhinēs (1.124) describes how a single house might be used successively as both a business place and home by a doctor, a

[180] Formal estate procedures were utilized primarily to dispose of real estate: "in ancient Greece an inheritance was primarily real, rather than financial" (MacDowell 1978: 108). Public testamentary proceedings would not have reached "hidden assets" (ἀφανὴς οὐσία), a significant portion of total property (see E. Cohen 1992: 190–202).

[181] Thus Demosthenes' father grants Thērippidēs only the *use* (καρπώσασθαι) of a sum of money in gratitude for his anticipated services (Dem. 27.5), not the outright bequest that might have otherwise been expected (Thompson 1981b: 18). (At Lys. 19.39, Timotheos is said to have bequeathed some money for religious purposes, but the speaker emphasizes that this will was made in Cyprus, outside Athenian jurisdiction—αἳ διαθῆκαι, ἃς διέθετο ἐν Κύπρῳ.) Cf. Isai. 3.45–51; Men. *Dysk.* 729–39; Harp., s.v. νοθεῖα; Suda, s.v. ἐπίκληρος; Schol. Aristoph. *Orn.* 1655–56. See generally Gernet [1920] 1955; Paoli 1976: 559–70; Harrison 1968–71: 1:143–49.

[182] See, for example, Dem. 42.21, 43.77–78. Cf. Isai. 11.42. Kyrōnidēs (Isai. 10) demonstrates how an individual, through opportune adoption and/or marriage, might attain membership and property rights in multiple *oikoi*.

[183] Isai. 6.25. Cf. Lys. 19.37; Dem. 39.6, 35. See Harrison 1968–71: 1:233; Asheri 1963: 1–4.

[184] See Aiskhin. 1.154 (Chapter 6, p. 187 and n. 96). Transfer of assets into nonvisible (ἀφανής) form (to evade taxes or avoid creditors, for example) carried the risk of adversaries' charges of "waste" of an estate. Cf. Aiskhin. 1.101: ἐκέκτητο ὁ πατὴρ αὐτοῦ ἀργύριον οὐκ ὀλίγον, ὃ οὗτος ἠφάνικε. . . . φοβηθεὶς γὰρ τὰς λητουργίας ἀπέδοτο.

[185] Aiskhin. 1.99: τὸ δ' Ἀλωπεκῆσι χωρίον . . . ἱκετευούσης καὶ ἀντιβολούσης τῆς μητρός . . . ἐᾶσαι καὶ μὴ ἀποδόσθαι, ἀλλ' εἰ μή τι ἄλλο, ἐνταφῆναί <γ'> ὑπολιπεῖν αὑτῇ, οὐκ ἀπέσχετο.

[186] See, for example, Xen. *Oik.* 9; Aristoph. *Thes.* 415–20; Men. *Sam.* 234–36. Jameson (1990: 184–87) surveys both archaeological and literary evidence for work at home. Cf. Jones 1975: 68–71; Thompson and Wycherley 1972: 173–85.

[187] Thus *tekhnai* include pursuits as varied as medicine, food making and catering, architecture, metal working, production of beds and of swords, and banking. See Pollux's listing of τέχναι (esp. 7.170, 155, and 159: cf. 4.7, 22); Xen. *Oik.* 1.1; Dem. 27.9, 45.71.

smith, a fuller, a carpenter—and a brothel keeper. Even the permanent physical premises of banks, which required a secure venue for cash and other valuables, were generally coextensive with the residence of the proprietor (where the continual presence of members of the *oikos* presumably furnished additional protection).[188] Even in silver mining (where actual extraction was necessarily conducted on and within state-owned mineral-bearing properties), related business operations—ranging from those dependent on a single slave (as in Andokidēs 1.38) through enterprises commanding an entire ore washery (Demosthenes 37)—functioned on a household basis: to protect the silver often present in the washing rooms, homes at Thorikos (in the mining area of Attika) evidence special attention to security (Jones 1975: 121–22).

The economic primacy of the household, and the business importance of both its female and male members, also reflected a basic economic reality—the extreme difficulty at Athens of hiring free persons for the many commercial operations that required regular and repetitive service on an ongoing basis over an extended period. Although many free Athenians were self-employed in a great variety of occupations—unable or unwilling to attain the philosophically expressed ideal of leisurely dedication to cultural and social activities—Athenians abhorred extended labor for a single employer.[189] The resulting dependence of household-based businesses on household members as employees meant that effectively "[business] 'firm' and private household were one and the same."[190]

Merger of commerce and *oikos* was so complete that even the wealthiest entrepreneurs of fourth-century Attika—the bankers[191]—sought to assure continuation of their banks (*trapezai*) by providing, on their deaths, for marriage of their widows to their chief slaves (to whom

[188] For the bank of Pasiōn, see Dem. 49.22, 52.8, 52.14. Because residences even of persons having no connection with the banking business often encompassed substantial security features (Young 1956: 122–46; Osborne 1985a: 31–34, 63–67; Pečirka 1973: 123–28), valuables and documents were likely to have been no less secure in such private residences than in separate business edifices.

[189] See Chapter 6, pp. 186–87.

[190] Finley [1953] 1984: 69. Because business activity tended to be intensely personalized, frequently involving confidential (and sometimes even clandestine) arrangements, it was likely advantageous to operate through household members rather than with employees hired from outside. The use of related staff would have tended to increase customers' confidence, and to minimize the otherwise substantial risk of employees' usurpation of client relationships (see E. Cohen 1992: 62–66, 191–201).

[191] For the wealth of bankers (*trapezitai*), see, for example, Isok. 17.2; Dem. 36.4–6, 36.57 (regarding the banker Phormiōn), 45.72. Cf. E. Cohen 1992: 22, 65–66, 88–90; Thompson 1983.

control of the banking business often devolved).[192] Although marriage of a free member of a banking household to a slave or former slave was seen even by the Athenians as a special response to the business imperatives of financial operations,[193] the substantial involvement of wives in banking businesses was consonant with women's widespread involvement in business activities at Athens, in retailing, crafts, and various other callings—a commercial reality well documented in the ancient sources and long acknowledged by modern scholars.[194] As Foxhall has shown (1994), following pioneering studies by Hunter, the presence within many *oikoi* of more than a single generation often resulted in the senior female member's significant influence, sometimes even dominance. Late marriage for men (usually at about thirty) encouraged prolonged male adolescence and dependence; early marriage for women (often shortly after puberty) meant early maturation—and, most significantly, in many cases early widowhood (see n. 147). Hence, the Athenian phenomenon (described by Aiskhinēs) of numerous naive young men of wealth whose widowed mothers actively managed the family property.[195]

This phenomenon of the strong wife or widow is exemplified in the dominant familial influence of Kleoboulē, mother of the Athenian leader Demosthenes,[196] and in the mother and wife of the wealthy and influential Lysias, who did not dare to bring his girl friend, even chaperoned by her "mother," to his own house![197] The widow of the Athenian tycoon Pasiōn, Arkhippē, dominated her *oikos*: she was intimately conversant with all aspects of the family's banking business[198] and had such control

[192] Dem. 36. 28–29: οὐδ' αὐτὸν λέληθεν, οὐδ' ὑμῶν πολλούς ὅτι Σωκράτης ὁ τραπεζίτης ἐκεῖνος, παρὰ τῶν κυρίων ἀπαλλαγεὶς ὥσπερ ὁ τούτου πατήρ, ἔδωκε Σατύρῳ τὴν ἑαυτοῦ γυναῖκα, ἑαυτοῦ ποτὲ γενομένῳ. ἕτερος Σωκλῆς. . . . καὶ οὐ μόνον ἐνθάδε ταῦτα ποιοῦσιν οἱ περὶ τὰς ἐργασίας ὄντες ταύτας . . . ἀλλ' ἐν Αἰγίνῃ. . . . καὶ πολλοὺς ἂν ἔχοι τις εἰπεῖν τοιούτους. Many bankers were "citizens," either through birth (e.g., Aristolokhos, Arkhestratos, Antisthenēs, Antidōros) or through naturalization. See E. Cohen 1992: 70, n. 44.

[193] Dem. 36.30: ὑμῖν μὲν γάρ, ὦ ἄνδρες Ἀθηναῖοι, τοῖς γένει πολίταις, οὐδὲ ἓν πλῆθος χρημάτων ἀντὶ τοῦ γένους καλόν ἐστιν ἑλέσθαι· τοῖς δὲ . . . ἀπὸ τοῦ χρηματίσασθαι καὶ ἑτέρων πλείω κτήσασθαι καὶ αὐτῶν τούτων ἀξιωθεῖσιν, ταῦτ' ἐστὶν φυλακτέα.

[194] For some of the many examples of female commercial activity at Athens, see Herfst [1922] 1980; D. Cohen 1990: 156–57; Brock 1994.

[195] 1.170: Δημοσθένης . . . περιῄει τὴν πόλιν θηρεύων νέους πλουσίους ὀρφανούς, ὧν οἱ μὲν πατέρες ἐτετελευτήκεσαν, αἱ δὲ μητέρες διῴκουν τὰς οὐσίας. πολλοὺς δ' ὑπερβὰς κ.τ.λ.

[196] See Dem. 27 and related speeches. Cf. Hunter 1989a: 43–46; Foxhall 1996: 144–47.

[197] Dem. 59.22: ἀφικομένας δ' αὐτὰς ὁ Λυσίας εἰς μὲν τὴν αὑτοῦ οἰκίαν οὐκ εἰσάγει, αἰσχυνόμενος τήν τε γυναῖκα . . . καὶ τὴν μητέρα τὴν αὑτοῦ πρεσβυτέραν τε οὖσαν καὶ ἐν τῷ αὐτῷ διαιτωμένην·

[198] Dem. 36.14: ἡ πάντ' ἀκριβῶς ταῦτ' εἰδυῖα.

over the bank's records that she was even accused of having destroyed them to prevent development of legal claims against Pasiōn's successor, her second husband Phormiōn.[199] Menander's fictional Krōbylē likewise controls her *oikos*: mistress of land, building, "everything," she ejects from the house a servant girl who has annoyed her, leaving her husband to mutter his unhappiness at the power of his wealthy wife.[200]

And just as the *oikos* was the locus of initiation rites for infants of both sexes, the *oikos* was the focus of death rituals and memorials for its male and female members. Although many studies emphasize the dominant participation of women in funereal ritual,[201] in fact both women and men were involved with and interacted in the various rites relating to burial.[202] Funeral monuments of the fourth century often portray deceased men and women as members of a family group (Humphreys [1983] 1993: 104–11), and epitaphs of the classical period stress household unity. Memorials often attribute to both male and female members of the *oikos* comparable favorable traits, sometimes even expressed in identical language.[203] (One woman, however, is praised as "intelligent", a characteristic not attributed to any man on a tombstone from the fourth century.)[204] Another woman, Phanostratē, a midwife and doctor, is extolled as "missed by all."[205] Even *eukleia* ("favorable renown"), a phrase also applied to men, is sometimes attributed to women—a startling challenge to the modern orthodoxy that postulates anonymity as the only positive recognition available to a female resident of Attika.[206]

Denomination of Athenian women as *politides* is thus a natural reflection of the continuing and permanent importance of women within the

[199] Dem. 36.18: τὰ γράμμαθ' ἡ μήτηρ ἠφάνικε πεισθεῖσ' ὑπὸ τούτου, καὶ τούτων ἀπολωλότων οὐκ ἔχει τίνα χρὴ τρόπον ταῦτ' ἐξελέγχειν ἀκριβῶς.

[200] ἐκ τῆς οἰκίας | ἐξέβαλε τὴν λυποῦσαν ἣν ἐβούλετο | . . . οὖσ' ἐμὴ γυνὴ δέσποινα. . . . οἴμοι Κρωβύλην | λαβεῖν ἔμ', εἰ καὶ δέκα τάλαντ' <ἠνέγκατο>. . . . κυρίαν τῆς οἰκίας | καὶ τῶν ἀγρῶν καὶ πάντων (fr. 296–97 [K-A]).

[201] Sourvinou-Inwood (1987: 24–25, and forthcoming) argues that scholars have exaggerated the dominance of women in these rites.

[202] In the burial ceremony itself, a public proceeding (as distinguished from the πρόθεσις and other earlier activities that centered on the *oikos*), men's ritual role was dominant: see Foxhall 1989: 23–24.

[203] For women, for example, as χρηστή, ἀγαθή, σώφρων, and as possessing ἀρετή and σωφροσύνη, see P. Hansen 1989: *C.E.G.* 2.479, 486, 491, 493, 510, 526, 530, 539, 611.

[204] P. Hansen 1989: *C.E.G.* 2.516 (εὐσύνετος). A male *is* extolled as "intelligent" on an earlier epitaph: Hansen 1983: *C.E.G.* 1.67.

[205] P. Hansen 1989: *C.E.G.* 2.569. This formulation is more often applied to men.

[206] The modern shibboleth of normative anonymity for women is based, at least in part, on a misinterpretation of Thouk. 2.45.2 (where Periklēs' injunction that women are best not spoken

household and of the centrality of the household within the polis. Both men and women derived their right and their reality of participation in the *polis* not from personal attributes, but from their familial positions within the "household." Male participation in the *polis* was manifested primarily through the political process: on reaching maturity, men were enrolled in demes as members of an *oikos*, not on the basis of their individual qualities,[207] and thereafter participated in the decision-making and office-holding functions that Aristotle in the *Politics* repeatedly characterizes as the best definition of a male "citizen" (*politēs*)[208]—a dimension of civic life closed to women. But other aspects were open to and, in some cases, reserved exclusively for female "citizens" (*politides*), and female participation in these activities represented no less a "sharing" in the *polis* than men's political activities: "a citizen also shares in the social, economic and religious life of his community" (Ostwald 1996: 57). The speaker at Isaios 8.20, for example, insists that if his mother had not been a *politis*, she could not have been selected to preside at the Thesmophoria.[209] In Aristophanes' *Lysistrata*, the female chorus proudly enumerates Athenian women's sumptuous service in a number of the city's archetypically prominent religious functions.[210] A woman had from time immemorial held Athens's most sacred position, the priesthood of Athēna Polias,[211] and Lysistrata herself (who in the play installs her band of women on the Akropolis, "the place where the

of at all, for good or for bad, is better understood as pertaining only to war widows, not to Athenian women in general: Kallet-Marx 1993: 133–43).

[207] Lacey 1968: 129, 293–94, n. 21. The demes were hereditary subdivisions which, in their attenuated and bifurcated fourth-century form, should not be—but often are—equated with "villages"; see Chapter 4, pp. 112 ff.

[208] 1275a22–23: πολίτης δ᾽ ἁπλῶς οὐδενὶ τῶν ἄλλων ὁρίζεται μᾶλλον ἢ τῷ μετέχειν κρίσεως καὶ ἀρχῆς. 1275b18–20: ᾧ γὰρ ἐξουσία κοινωνεῖν ἀρχῆς βουλευτικῆς καὶ κριτικῆς, πολίτην ἤδη λέγομεν εἶναι ταύτης τῆς πόλεως. 1276a4: ὁ γὰρ κοινωνῶν τῆς τοιᾶσδε ἀρχῆς πολίτης ἐστίν, ὡς ἔφαμεν. 1275b31–33: ἔστω δὴ διορισμοῦ χάριν ἀόριστος ἀρχή. τίθεμεν δὴ πολίτας τοὺς οὕτω μετέχοντα.

[209] Isai. 8.20: μὴ οἴεσθ᾽ ἄν, εἰ τοιαύτη τις ἦν ἡ μήτηρ ἡμῶν οἵαν οὗτοι φασι . . . μήτε τὰς τῶν ἄλλων δημοτῶν γυναῖκας αἱρεῖσθαι ἂν αὐτὴν συνιεροποιεῖν τῇ Διοκλέους γυναικὶ καὶ κυρίαν ποιεῖν ἱερῶν; The son insists that his mother is a πολῖτις and not οἵαν οὗτοι φασι: "ἐὰν ἐξαπατηθῆτε πεισθέντες ὡς ἡ μήτηρ ἡμῶν οὐκ ἦν πολῖτις" (8.43).

[210]
ἡμεῖς γὰρ ὦ πάντες ἀστοὶ λόγων κατάρχομεν τῇ πόλει χρησίμων·
εἰκότως, ἐπεὶ χλιδῶσαν ἀγλαῶς ἔθρεψέ με.
ἑπτὰ μὲν ἔτη γεγῶσ᾽ εὐθυς ἠρρηφόρουν·
εἶτ᾽ ἀλετρὶς ἢ δεκέτις οὖσα τἀρχηγέτι·
κᾆτ᾽ ἔχουσα τὸν κροκωτὸν ἄρκτος ἦ Βραυρωνίοις·
κἀκανηφόρουν ποτ᾽ οὖσα παῖς καλὴ ᾽χουσ᾽ ἰσχάδων ὁρμαθόν·

Aristoph. *Lys*. 638–47.

[211] See Aleshire 1994; Gould 1980: 50–51; Schuller 1985: 52. Cf. Aristoph. *Lys*. 1049; Pl. *Gorg*. 502d; *Laws* 658d.

priestess of Athena has authority")[212] has been identified as the historical Lysimakhē, an actual high priestess.[213] (Aristophanes also gives prominence in *Lysistrata* to Myrrhinē, in life the first priestess of Athēna Nikē,[214] a position that, significantly, was filled exclusively from the ranks of female "citizens").[215] A protagonist in the Euripidean play *Melanippē Desmōtēs* even insists that "Now as for our dealings with the gods—and I judge these matters to be foremost—we women hold the greatest share,"[216] a claim confirmed at Athens by the many high religious offices and duties that could be exercised only by women: females are attested as priestesses in more than forty public cults, as holders of many additional subsacerdotal positions,[217] as performers of ritual roles, and as members of choruses, "a kind of 'cultic citizenship'" (Parker 1996: 80). In those instances where a shrine or cult had both male and female roles of importance, the status of the priestess was not inferior, and her authority could not be impinged upon.[218] Women offered sacrifices and dedications

[212] MacDowell 1995: 242. Sacral importance was transformative into substantive power: Herodotos (5.72.3) reports how the priestess of Athena Polias in the late sixth century imperiously ordered the Spartan king Kleomenēs to leave the Akropolis, which he had seized after the Athenians had capitulated to his demand that they send some seven hundred families into exile; within three days, Kleomenēs had evacuated Attika. See Parker 1998. Again in the fifth century, the Athenian decision to abandon Attika resulted "not least" (οὐκ ἥκιστα) from the priestess's proclamation that the goddess had already abandoned the Akropolis (Hdt. 8.41.3). (Herodotos often attributes importance to the pronouncements of Greek priestesses: see, for example, 2.53, 2.55, 5.63, 6.66, and cf. Dewald 1981.)

[213] For this identification, see Lewis 1955; Sommerstein 1990: 5–6; Wohl 1996: 64–65.

[214] Lines 916–47. Myrrhinē as priestess of Nikē: *I.G.* I³ 1330; Rahn 1986. Henderson 1987: xl–xli rejects this identification. Actual contemporary women possibly underlie other characters in *Lysistrata*: Lampito, for example, was a name used by one of the Spartan royal families (Hdt. 6.71.2).

[215] *I.G.* I³ 35, the sole surviving document that records the establishment of a priesthood at Athens: ἐχς Ἀθεναίον hαπα[σõ][v. . . . Cf. *I.G.* I³ 36, 1330. Election was probably by sortition (Parker 1996: 126), paralleling the usual mechanism for filling political offices that were restricted to Athenian male citizens. For the complex difficulties in determining the date of *I.G.* I³ 35, see Meiggs 1972: 497–503; Wesenberg 1981; Meiggs and Lewis 1988: addenda, p. 311.

[216] *Mel. Des.* fr. 660 Mette 1982–85, lines 12 and 13 (P. Berl. 9772 and P. Oxy. 1176 fr. 39, Col. 11) (fr. 13: Auffret 1987): τὰ δ' ἐν θεοῖς αὖ (πρῶτα γὰρ κρίνω τάδε) | μέρος μέγιστον ἔχομεν. For text, see Collard, Cropp, and Lee [1995] 1997: 273. Maurizio has demonstrated how modern scholars have disregarded the extensive evidence confirming the priestess of Apollo, the Pythia, as the sole source of Delphic oracles—and how they have arbitrarily attributed to her male attendants the dominant role of "reformulat(ing) her utterances and convert(ing) them into comprehensible prose or verse" (1995: 69).

[217] Turner 1983; McClees 1920: 5ff. This religious primacy parallels the situation at the Panhellenic shrines where positions of influence, power, and prestige were often occupied in their own names and personae by priestesses or divinely inspired female interlocutors.

[218] The hierophant Arkhias was punished for performing (on an occasion not customary) a sacrifice that belonged to the priestess. See Dem. 59.116: οὐδ' ἐκείνου οὔσης τῆς θυσίας ἀλλὰ τῆς ἱερείας.

not only as sacerdotal officials but quite commonly as individuals: they even founded shrines.[219] For "citizen women," "eligibility to hold important religious office . . . defined and articulated their identity" (Sourvinou-Inwood 1995: 116).

Yet it is women's position as *astai* ("local persons"), rather than as *politides*, that was requisite to their offspring's entry into the *polis*, providing a potential link (and sometimes an actual bridge) between Attika's large community of noncitizens and its hereditary grouping of *politai* and *politides*.

[219] See, for example, P. Hansen 1989: *C.E.G.* 2.744.

✦ 2 ✦

The Local Residents of Attika

IN THE fourth century, the residents of Attika shared a fundamental identification not as *politai* (citizens),[1] but as *astoi* (locals). As *astoi*, they stood in complementary polarity to *xenoi* (foreigners), a differentiation fortified by, and explanatory of, the wide participation of all elements of the resident population in the many communal activities (such as cult functions, *symposia*, military undertakings, religious festivals, and sexual dealings) that collectively defined Athenian society.[2] The *politai* were members of the *polis*, a portion of the *astoi* that monopolized not the totality of society but only (in Aristotle's words) the "right of sharing in deliberative or judicial office"[3]—that is, political power—and the economic and other benefits derived from that monopoly. When Athenian law provided for the selection of new *politai* only from among males who had been born to two *astoi*, it was not indulging in a redundant deployment of two synonyms of identical meaning, "citizen" (as scholars presently insist), but was providing a meaningful mechanism for the possible extension of political participation, and ancillary material benefits, to offspring of individuals who—even if they were not born to two *politai*—were, as *astoi*, recognizably "local" persons. Not an

[1] Modern conceptualizations of "citizen" and "citizenship" are problematic even when applied to contemporary phenomena (see Evans 1993: 2; Manville 1990: 4–5; Bulmer and Ress 1996). Although the demands of historical discourse may sometimes require the application to ancient institutions of terms inherently modern in connotation but familiar to contemporary readers (see Finley 1975: 63–64; Lauffer 1961: 380), "the modern Western notion of 'citizenship' is rooted in the experience of early modern Europe"—accordingly, in dealing with Athens "the best recourse is to avoid the terms 'citizen' and 'citizenship'" (Patterson 1986: 49). Although the Greek word *politeia* is often translated as "citizenship," its literal meaning is "regime" (see Lord 1984: 279).

[2] Cf. Schmitt-Pantel 1987; 1990. See the third section in this chapter.

[3] *Pol.* 1275b18–20: cf. *Pol.* 1275a22–23, 1275b31–33, 1276a4 (all cited in Greek at Chapter 1, n. 8). But the *polis* as a political community was only one, albeit for Aristotle in the *Politics* the preeminent, subdivision of the overall society: ἡ πασῶν κυριωτάτη καὶ πάσας περιέχουσα τὰς ἄλλας. αὕτη δ' ἐστὶν ἡ καλουμένη πόλις καὶ ἡ κοινωνία ἡ πολιτική, *Pol.* 1252a4–6. Cf. 1325b26–27: πολλαὶ γὰρ κοινωνίαι πρὸς ἄλληλα τοῖς μέρεσι τῆς πόλεώς εἰσιν. See Introduction, nn. 11, 12 for the prevailing equation of Athenian society and state with the political organization of the *politai*.

autochthonous society closed to new members under all but the most exceptional circumstances—as is now generally held[4]—Athens actually offered relatively easy access into political participation to the progeny of immigrants who had assimilated into Athenian life.

Astoi and *Politai*[5]

From earliest times, the Greek words *politai* (sing. *politēs*) and *astoi* (sing. *astos*)[6] carry sharply differentiated significations, contrary to the prevailing scholarly assumption that the two terms are synonyms meaning "citizen."[7] Reflecting a cognate differentiation found even in Linear B texts,[8] *astos* in Homer conveys the "intimate overtones" (Cole 1976: 28) inherent in its later notation of "insider," a shading absent from Homeric *politēs,* which signifies only an undifferentiated "community member."[9] In preclassical narrative and lyric, *astos* continues to carry the meaning of an "insider," often in explicit, otherwise in implicit contrast to its complementary opposite of *xenos* (a "local person" as against a "foreigner").[10] Thus, Pindar praises the champion who at home

See Preface, pp. ix–x for the ancient and modern use of the single term *polis* to cover a variety of conceptualizations.

[4] On the falsity of the present interpretation of the traditional Athenian claim to autochthony, see Chapter 3.

[5] Citations to these terms are conveniently gathered in Welskopf 1985, s.vv. Lévy ([1985] 1988), who surveys early usage, is properly insistent that the two terms "doivent être étudiés ensemble" (p. 53).

[6] Feminine forms are *astai* (sing. *astē*). For the feminine forms *politides* (sing. *politis*), see Chapter 1, pp. 31–32.

[7] Ogden 1996: 69: "*astos* (the common Attic term for 'citizen,' equivalent to *politēs*)." Mossé 1995: 40, n. 31: "*astos* parfois employé comme équivalent de *politès*, mais dans un sens plus général et moins étroitement politique, pour désigner le citoyen." Cf. Whitehead 1977: 60; Patterson 1986: 54. The standard works on Greek or Athenian law, without discussion, make the same assumption (e.g., Harrison 1968–72: 1:188: "the fully qualified citizen, the πολίτης or ἀστός"; MacDowell 1978: 67: "a citizen [*polites* or *astos*]"; Todd 1993: 178: "an *astos* is a [male] citizen").

[8] In Linear B, *asty* has a "residential character" and *polis,* a military "connection with the citadel," a distinction that also is found in late Bronze Age usage (Cole 1976: 7, 143–61).

[9] *Astos*: *Il.* 11.242; *Od.* 13.192. *Politēs*: *Il.* 2.806, 15.558, 22.429; *Od.* 7.131, 17.206. In Homer *astos* appears only in linkage with *alokhos*, "a result of the intimate overtones that *asty* carries . . . the five appearances of *politēs* show no special features" (Cole 1976: 28).

[10] Cole 1976: 247. "An *astos* is an insider, one of one's own while a *xenos* is an outsider" (Patterson 1981: 156). Cf. Lévy [1985] 1988: 61: "les *astoi* constituent le groupe auquel on appartient, les miens, par opposition aux *xénoi.*" The antithesis is present already in a sixth-century Attic funerary inscription urging the passerby to grieve, εἴτε ἀστό]ς εἴτε χσένος (Jeffery 1962: 133, n. 34; cf. Richter 1961: 158ff.).

is considerate of *astoi* and attentive to *xenoi*;[11] for an Olympic victor, the poet seeks veneration from contrasted *astoi* and *xenoi*.[12]

In classical literature, the same dichotomous opposition recurs frequently in dramatic works,[13] rhetorical presentations,[14] and historical writing. Sophoklēs' *Oidipous at Kolōnos,* a work poetically focused on the riddle of the outsider who is really an insider, seems fixated on the complementary opposition of *astoi* and *xenoi*. The Athenian chorus consistently views Oidipous and Antigonē as *xenoi* among *astoi*, a perception that both Antigonē and Oidipous reciprocate.[15] Oidipous, for example, assures his daughter that as *xenoi* they must learn from *astoi*;[16] Thēseus rebukes Kreōn for not acting as a *xenos* should among *astoi*.[17] Euripides' *Iōn*, a work poetically focused on the mystery of insiders who are really outsiders (Erikhthonios, Xouthos, Iōn himself), is likewise replete with *astos-xenos* antithetical contrast.[18]

Historians similarly exploit this antithesis with literary and interpretative efficacy. For example, Herodotos tells of the Egyptian criticism of Ēlis for opening the Olympic contests to both *astoi* and *xenoi*, but without precautions against favortism toward the local contestants.[19] And for Thucydides, the contrast of *astoi* and *xenoi* "has become almost a formula" (Cole 1976: 356), a frequent usage vividly employed in the historian's most dramatic depictions: the mass presence of foreigners (*xenoi*) and of the local population (*astoi*) for Periklēs' enunciation of Athenian values in the famed funeral oration and for the emotional departure of

[11] Pind. *Ol.* 13.1–3: Τρισολυμπιονίκαν | ἐπαινέων οἶκον ἅμερον ἀστοῖς, | ξένοισι δὲ θεράποντα.

[12] *Ol.* 7.89–91: . . . δίδοι τέ οἱ αἰδοίαν χάριν | καὶ ποτ' ἀστῶν καὶ ποτὶ ξεί | νων.

[13] In addition to the examples in the text, see Aristoph. *Akh.* 508; *Orn.* 32; Eur. *Hērakleid.* 411; *Iket.* 355, 843; *Mēd.* 222–23.

[14] For example, Anytos in Pl. *Men.* 92c (μήτε ἀστὸν μήτε ξένον).

[15] Lines 171, 184, 206, 214. Cf. 817.

[16] Lines 12–13: . . . μανθάνειν γὰρ ἥκομεν | ξένοι πρὸς ἀστῶν, ἃν δ' ἀκούσωμεν τελεῖν.

[17] Lines 926–28: χθονὸς | οὔθ' εἷλκον οὔτ' ἂν ἦγον, ἀλλ' ἠπιστάμην | ξένον παρ' ἀστοῖς ὡς διαιτᾶσθαι χρεών.

[18] For example, lines 290, 293: οὐκ ἀστὸς ἀλλ' ἐπακτὸς ἐξ ἄλλης χθονός | . . . καὶ πῶς ξένος σ' ὢν ἔσχεν οὖσαν ἐγγενῆ;); lines 673–74: καθαρὰν γὰρ ἤν τις ἐς πόλιν πέσῃ ξένος, | κἂν τοῖς λόγοισιν ἀστὸς ᾖ. The Athenians are inherently connected to the land of Attika (lines 589–92, 1000), and thus no *xenos* can be part of the *polis* (ξένος ἐπεισελθὼν πόλιν καὶ δῶμα καὶ σὴν παραλαβὼν παγκληρίαν [813–14]). Cf. lines 601, 607, 1058–60, 1069–73.

[19] 2.160.4: οὐδεμίαν γὰρ εἶναι μηχανὴν ὅκως οὐ τῷ ἀστῷ ἀγωνιζομένῳ προσθήσονται, ἀδικέοντες τὸν ξεῖνον. In discussing the giving of pledges among the Arabians, Herodotos similarly writes in the context of the *astos-xenos* polarity: ὁ τὰς πίστις ποιησάμενος τοῖσι φίλοισι παρεγγυᾷ τὸν ξεῖνον ἢ καὶ τὸν ἀστόν, ἢν πρὸς ἀστὸν ποιῆται (3.8.2).

the great fleet to Sicily.[20] That expedition's controversial proponent, Alkibiadēs, was attacked, in a speech attributed to Andokidēs, for having offended both *astoi* and *xenoi*;[21] in turn, he defended his extravagant expenditures on theatrical choruses as a cause of envy for the *astoi* but a manifestation of Athenian power to the *xenoi*—the foreigners who came to Attika in large numbers for the periodic festivals.[22] Defense measures were similarly conceived in terms of locals and foreigners: the Athenians offered rewards to both *astoi* and *xenoi* (and to slaves) for information about the desecration of the Herms;[23] in war, advises Aineias the Tactician, steps are to be taken to prevent both *astoi* and *xenoi* from defecting.[24]

In legal context, the *astoi-xenoi* dichotomy was fundamental. Fourth-century laws regulating marital arrangements, for example, are couched in local-foreign polarity:[25] "if a *xenos* should cohabit in marriage with an *astē* . . . let him and his goods be sold . . . and the same [sanction] shall be imposed if a *xenē* should cohabit in marriage with an *astos*."[26] For the provisions and processes of inheritance law, the universe of

[20] 2.34: (1) Ἀθηναῖοι . . . δημοσίᾳ ταφὰς ἐποιήσαντο. . . . (4) ξυνεκφέρει δὲ ὁ βουλόμενος καὶ ἀστῶν καὶ ξένων. . . . 2.36.4: τὸν πάντα ὅμιλον καὶ ἀστῶν καὶ ξένων ξύμφορον εἶναι ἐπακοῦσαι αὐτῶν. 6.30 .2: ξυγκατέβη δὲ καὶ ὁ ἄλλος ὅμιλος ἅπας ὡς εἰπεῖν ὁ ἐν τῇ πόλει καὶ ἀστῶν καὶ ξένων.

[21] Andok. 4.10: ἃ δὲ περὶ τὴν πόλιν εἴργασται καὶ τοὺς προσήκοντας καὶ τῶν ἄλλων ἀστῶν καὶ ξένων τοὺς ἐντυγχάνοντας, ἀποδείξω. On the authenticity and date of composition of this speech, see Raubitschek 1948; Hignett 1952: 395ff.; Kennedy 1963: 148–49.

[22] Thouk. 6.16.3: καὶ ὅσα αὖ ἐν τῇ πόλει χορηγίαις ἢ ἄλλῳ τῳ λαμπρύνομαι, τοῖς μὲν ἀστοῖς φθονεῖται φύσει, πρὸς δὲ τοὺς ξένους καὶ αὕτη ἰσχὺς φαίνεται. For the presence of foreigners at the City Dionysia, for example, see Isokratēs 8.82; at the Panathenaia, Wohl 1996: 25. Cf. Deubner [1932] 1966; Parke 1977; Parker 1996: 91.

[23] Thouk. 6.27.2: μηνύειν ἀδεῶς τὸν βουλόμενον καὶ ἀστῶν καὶ ξένων καὶ δούλων.

[24] 10.5: Ἐὰν δὲ ὦσιν φυγάδες, ἐπικηρύσσειν, ὃς ἂν ἀστῶν ἢ ξένων ἢ δούλων ἀποκινῇ, ἃ ἑκάστῳ τούτων ἔσται.

[25] This focus on insider-outsider (*astos-xenos*) marital criteria, rather than on the intrasocietal status of *politēs* or non-*politēs*, replicates a pattern often observed by ethnographers: "a good test of group membership for the purpose of assessing kin relatedness must meet the basic requirement of discriminating more reliably *between* groups than *within* groups" (Van den Berghe 1978: 410). Cf. Smith 1964. In fact, extensive efforts, based on the prevailing assumption that *astē* and *politis* are synonyms, have failed to provide a coherent explanation that reconciles the extant evidence with the supposed terms of the Athenian marital prohibition. See, for example, the multitudinous discussions of the marriage of the non-*politēs* Phormiōn with Arkhippē, widow of the (naturalized) *politēs* Pasiōn, a union impossible on the premise of synonymity (see Whitehead 1986b). Carey (1991: 88) is forced to suggest that Arkhippē ceased to be Pasiōn's wife after he became a *politēs*, although Pasiōn himself in his will terms her "my wife" (τὴν ἐμαυτοῦ γυναῖκα, Dem. 45.28; cf. Dem. 36.8, 30, 51; 45.33; 46.13, 17).

[26] Dem. 59.16: ΝΟΜΟΣ· Ἐὰν δὲ ξένος ἀστῇ συνοικῇ τέχνῃ ἢ μηχανῇ ἡτινιοῦν, γραφέσθω πρὸς τοὺς θεσμοθέτας Ἀθηναίων ὁ βουλόμενος . . . ἐὰν δὲ ἁλῷ, πεπράσθω καὶ αὐτὸς καὶ ἡ οὐσία αὐτοῦ, . . . ἔστω δὲ καὶ ἐὰν ἡ ξένη τῷ ἀστῷ συνοικῇ κατὰ ταὐτά. An *astos* cohabiting in marriage with a *xenē* was subject to a fine of one thousand drachmas. Ibid.: καὶ ὁ συνοικῶν τῇ ξένῃ τῇ ἁλούσῃ ὀφειλέτω χιλίας δραχμάς.

potential "heiresses" (*epiklēroi*) consisted of *xenai* and *astai*.[27] Even in the Cretan City expounded in Plato's *Laws*—although "no noncitizen can ordinarily be a permanent resident of the state" (Morrow [1960] 1993: 112, n. 51) and Plato in other contexts makes frequent use of the terms *politai* and *epikhōrioi* (natives)[28]—legal provisions that might affect both foreigners and local residents are enunciated within the *astoi-xenoi* dichotomy.[29] In delineating the characteristics of various tribunals, Aristotle posits a separate court for disputes between *xenoi* and *astoi*.[30] Physical presence and continuing contact is an essential element in conceptualization of the *astos*: Apollodōros ridicules the possibility that Neaira could be an *astē* since a woman of foreign origin who has whored "over all the Peloponnesos, in Thessaly and Magnesia, in Khios and through most of Ionia," one who has "worked the circuit of the entire Earth," could not possibly be an *astē* in Attika.[31]

In contrast, the word *politēs* by the classical period had eschewed all connotation of territoriality. Thus Aristotle, in book 3 of the *Politics*, defines a *politēs* as a person who participates in the decision-making and office-holding functions of the polis:[32] residence is entirely irrelevant—"a *politēs* is not a *politēs* because of his residing in a given place."[33] "A *Samios* may never have set foot on Samos in his life . . . an Athenian *citizen* was an Athenian citizen anywhere" (Whitehead 1977: 71–72). In fact, Aristotle insists, there is absolutely no relationship between *politai* and any specific territory: physical location can be entirely irrelevant to membership in the *polis*.[34] Accordingly, the *klērouchoi* who settled in Poteidaia and in the Thracian Khersonēsos (today the Gallipoli Peninsula), and on Lemnos, Imbros, and Skyros in the fourth century, had

[27] Dem. 46. 22: τὸν νόμον . . . ὃς κελεύει ἐπιδικασίαν εἶναι τῶν ἐπικλήρων ἁπασῶν, καὶ ξένων καὶ ἀστῶν. Confirming the applicability of the term *astoi* to both *politai* and at least some *metoikoi*, the reference to *astoi* is immediately followed by a further division: καὶ περὶ μὲν τῶν πολιτῶν τὸν ἄρχοντα εἰσάγειν καὶ ἐπιμελεῖσθαι, περὶ δὲ τῶν μετοίκων τὸν πολέμαρχον.

[28] For ἐπιχώριος, see, for example, 764b, 846d, 847a, 879d–e, 881c.

[29] See, for example, 849a–d, 866c, 872a, 882a, 938c.

[30] *Pol.* 1300b31–32: ἄλλο <δὲ> ξένοις πρὸς ἀστούς.

[31] Dem. 59.108: οὐκ ἐν Πελοποννήσῳ μὲν πάσῃ, ἐν Θετταλίᾳ δὲ καὶ Μαγνησίᾳ μετὰ Σίμου τοῦ Λαρισαίου καὶ Εὐρυδάμαντος τοῦ Μηδείου, ἐν Χίῳ δὲ καὶ ἐν Ἰωνίᾳ τῇ πλείστῃ μετὰ Σωτάδου τοῦ Κρητὸς ἀκολουθοῦσα, μισθωθεῖσα. . . . εἶτα τὴν τοιαύτην καὶ περιφανῶς ἐγνωσμένην ὑπὸ πάντων γῆς περίοδον εἰργασμένην ψηφιεῖσθε ἀστὴν εἶναι;

[32] See n. 3; Chapter 1, n. 8.

[33] *Pol.* 1275a7–8: ὁ δὲ πολίτης οὐ τῷ οἰκεῖν που πολίτης ἐστίν (καὶ γὰρ μέτοικοι καὶ δοῦλοι κοινωνοῦσι τῆς οἰκήσεως).

[34] Aristot. *Pol.* 1276a20–22: ἐνδέχεται γὰρ διαζευθῆναι τὸν τόπον καὶ τοὺς ἀνθρώπους, καὶ τοὺς μὲν ἕτερον τοὺς δ᾽ ἕτερον οἰκῆσαι τόπον.

no relationship with Attika—physical separation actually led them to establish in their own territories mechanisms of local self-government[35]—but they still remained Athenian *politai*, and retained a share in the Athenian *politeia*.[36] Conversely, Euripides envisions a *politēs* of one city whose origins are in another *polis*.[37]

Differentiation of the politically defined *politēs* from the territorially determined *astos* is clearest when the two terms are used proximately. Thus, Euripides has Medea condemn an *astos* who by headstrong boorishness has become disturbing to the *politai*.[38] Thucydides characterizes Aristogeitōn, assassin of the tyrant Peisistratos's son, as "one of the local people [*astōn*], a middling *politēs*."[39] When Aineias the Tactician insists that no one in a city anticipating attack should be allowed to depart without permission, he refers to the local population as *astoi*, but immediately thereafter in the political context of possible negotiation with outside emissaries he authorizes discussion only through the most reliable "*politai*."[40] In Demosthenes 57, Euxitheos differentiates his father's recognition as a local person from his possible standing as a

[35] These institutions appear to have been modeled largely on those of Athens proper. See Cargill 1995: 145–85; Cousin and Dürrbach 1885: 50. The fifth-century Athenian Tribute Lists even classify as separate *poleis* the *klērouchies* Hephaistia, Myrrhinē, and Imbros (*I.G.* I[3] 285 col. 1. 107–10). Cf. Hyper. *Lyk.* 18; Skylax 57, 66. See Hansen 1995c: 45.

[36] Dem. 23.103: τοῖς Χερρόνησον οἰκοῦσι τῶν πολιτῶν; Aiskhin. 2.72: ἐξέλειπον δὲ Χερρόνησον ἡμῶν οἱ πολῖται; Dem. 4.34: πολίτας ὑμετέρους; Hyper. *Phil.* 17: πολίτας ἄνδρας (with apparent reference to settlers on Lemnos); Dem. 7.18: Ἀθηναίων οἱ ἐν Ποτειδαίᾳ κατοικοῦντες; *I.G.* II[2] 228.15–16: μετὰ Ἀθηναί[ων ἐν Χ]ερρονήσωι; Aristot. *Oikon.* 1347a18: Ἀθηναῖοι δὲ ἐν Ποτειδαίᾳ οἰκοῦντες. For additional references, see Cargill 1995: 59–66. Cf. Figueira 1991: 48–53, table 1. Exemplars of *politai* returning to Attika and thereafter exercising political rights: Philōn (Lys. 31), Aphobos (Dem. 29), Leōkratēs (Lykourg. *Leōk.*). On the settlers' continuing status as *politai* at Athens, see Ehrenberg 1946: 129–43; Will 1954; Graham 1964: 166ff. On the large number of Athenian *politai* actually living abroad during much of the fourth century, see Chapter 4, pp. 118–19.

[37] *Erekhtheus,* fr. 360 (*TrGF*), lines 11–13: ὅστις δ' ἀπ' ἄλλης πόλεος οἰκήσηι πόλιν, | ἁρμὸς πονηρὸς ὥσπερ ἐν ξυλωι παγείς, | λόγωι πολίτης ἐστί, τοῖς δ' ἔργοισιν οὔ.

[38] Mention of the local individual (*astos*) is balanced by a preceding explicit reference to his complementary opposite, the foreigner (*xenos*). Eur. *Mēd.* 222–24: χρὴ δὲ ξένον μὲν κάρτα προσχωρεῖν πόλει· | οὐδ' ἀστὸν ᾔνεσ' ὅστις αὐθάδης γεγὼς | πικρὸς πολίταις ἐστὶν ἀμαθίας ὕπο.

[39] Thouk. 6.54.2: Ἀριστογείτων ἀνὴρ τῶν ἀστῶν, μέσος πολίτης . . . On the assumption that *politēs* and *astos* are synonyms, Thucydides' actual language is obfuscated in translations and ignored in scholarly commentary. (Warner renders ἀνὴρ τῶν ἀστῶν, μέσος πολίτης as "a citizen who belonged to the middle class.") Gomme, Andrewes, and Dover, in their magisterial commentary on Thucydides (1970, vol. 4), here are silent.

[40] 10: (8) ἐκπλεῖν μηδένα ἀστῶν μηδὲ μέτοικον ἄνευ συμβόλου. . . . (11) ταιξ δὲ δημοσίαις ἀφικνουμέναις πρεσβείαις ἀπὸ πόλεων ἢ τυράννων ἢ στρατοπέδων οὐ χρὴ ἐν αὐτοῖς τὸν εθέλοντα διαλέγεσθαι, ἀλλ' εἶναι τινας τῶν πολιτῶν τοὺς πιστοτάτους. For the position of metics—as individuals sometimes assimilated to *astoi* at Athens, as a group sometimes differentiated from, sometimes included with the *astoi*—see pp. 55ff., 72ff.

politēs. "Even if my father was an *astos* only on one side, he was entitled to be a *politēs*: for he was born before Eukleidēs."[41] The feminine forms of the two words are similarly distinguished: in an effort to prove that Neaira is a foreigner (*xenē*) and therefore a violator of the law prohibiting marriage between an *astos* and a *xenē*, the speaker carefully insists that Neaira is neither an *astē* nor a *politis*:[42] she was not a "local" (*astē*) by personal territorial attachment,[43] nor had she been naturalized as a *politis* by legislative decree.[44] In contrast to the frequent explicit antithesis between *astoi* and *xenoi*, *xenos* and *politēs* are seldom encountered even in juxtaposition,[45] and never in antithesis.[46]

Contradicting the prevailing scholarly assumption that the terms *astos* and *politēs* convey the identical meaning of "citizen," Athenian authors

[41] 57.30: τοῖς χρόνοις τοίνυν οὕτω φαίνεται γεγονὼς ὥστε, εἰ καὶ κατὰ θάτερ' ἀστὸς ἦν, εἶναι πολίτην προσήκειν αὐτόν· γέγονε γὰρ πρὸ Εὐκλείδου. On the decree forbidding further evaluation of those who had been accepted as *politai* "before Eukleidēs" (403/2), see n. 124 and accompanying text.

[42] Dem. 59.107: τὴν δὲ περιφανῶς ἐν ἁπάσῃ τῇ Ἑλλάδι πεπορνευμένην οὕτως αἰσχρῶς καὶ ὀλιγώρως ἐάσετε ὑβρίζουσαν εἰς τὴν πόλιν καὶ ἀσεβοῦσαν εἰς τοὺς θεοὺς ἀτιμώρητον, ἣν οὔτε οἱ πρόγονοι ἀστὴν κατέλιπον οὔθ' ὁ δῆμος πολῖτιν ἐποιήσατο; On women as *politides*, see Chapter 1, pp. 31–48.

[43] Allegedly having no prior ties to Athens—she had been purchased as a young girl by Nikaretē, the wife of a cook in Ēlis (Dem. 59.18, 49)—Neaira is assailed as a prostitute who had traveled throughout the Greek world copulating for pay before her first visit to Attica (22–23, 107). Having come to reside in Athens only as a mature woman with three children (38: cf. Patteson 1978: 70), supposedly violating in her deportment every cultural value and behavioral expectation of an Athenian *astē*, the Neaira of Apollodōros's description would have remained easily cognizable as a *xenē*.

[44] Such a *psēphisma*, although theoretically possible, would have been unique. Unlike certain other Greek states of the fourth century (see, e.g., *S.E.G.* 15.384, 18.264, 19.425, 23.470), Athens is not known to have enfranchised women in their own right. In contrast to their explicit grant of *politeia* to the descendants of male honorands, Athenian naturalization decrees ignore wives (Osborne 1972: 147, n. 75; 1981–83, 4:150).

[45] Whitehead (1977: 68, n. 129) claims that Plato "broke this rule four times." One example is irrelevant: the pseudo-Platonic Περὶ Ἀρετῆς at 376d refers to a wide variety of statuses (μαθητὴν ἢ τῶν ξένων τινὰ ἢ τῶν πολιτῶν ἢ ἄλλων, ἐλεύθερον ἢ δοῦλον), but "it is hard to doubt that we are dealing with late exercises in imitation of Plato's style, 'atticizing' copies of a classic" (Taylor 1952: 546). The other supposed deviations exemplify humorous or literary nuances of Platonic style: (1) *Gorg*. 473c3 where Pōlos ironically (in reference to "tyranny") joins *politai* with "the other" foreigners (ζηλωτὸς ὢν καὶ εὐδαιμονιζόμενος ὑπὸ τῶν πολιτῶν καὶ τῶν ἄλλων ξένων) in an idiomatic and abbreviated expression generally translated by ignoring ἄλλων; (2) *Men*. 91a, where reference to *politai* echoes the use of polis in the preceding line; (3) *Euthd*. 282b, where reference to *politai* is responsive to the erotic context and the attendant legal implications of being "enslaved" to "lovers, citizen and alien" (τῶν φασκόντων ἐραστῶν εἶναι, καὶ ξένων καὶ πολιτῶν, δεόμενον καὶ ἱκετεύοντα σοφίας μεταδιδόναι, οὐδὲν αἰσχρόν, ὦ Κλεινία, οὐδὲ νεμεσητὸν ἕνεκα τούτου ὑπηρετεῖν καὶ δουλεύειν καὶ ἐραστῇ καὶ παντὶ ἀνθρώπῳ). The actual legal irrelevance of lovers' political status underlies Plato's verbal wit here: cf. Chapter 6.

[46] Cf. Lys. 12.35 (καὶ τῶν ἀστῶν καὶ τῶν ξένων) with Lys. 14.28 (εἰς τοὺς πολίτας ἢ εἰς τοὺς ξένους ἢ περὶ τοὺς αὑτοῦ οἰκείους ἢ περὶ τοὺς ἄλλους) where "relatives" and "others" join *politai* as alternatives to *xenoi*. For this lack of opposition between *politai* and *xenoi*, Kalinka long ago

frequently include non-*politai* among the *astoi* (but never use the alleged synonym *astos* in referring to an individual or group participating in the decision-making or office-holding functions of the *polis*, the prerogatives definitive of a *politēs*).[47] Thus, in his report of the large Athenian military force that invaded Boiōtia in 424 after a general mobilization, Thucydides includes metics (as free non-*politai*) among the *astoi*, describing the expedition as consisting of *astoi* and of those *xenoi* who happened to be present in Attika. "Those who had joined in the invasion were many times greater in number than the enemy . . . inasmuch as there had been a general mobilization of *astoi* and of *xenoi* who were present."[48] This force had been previously described (4.90.1) as consisting of *politai*, metics, and "whichever *xenoi* were present."[49] More than a century ago, several commentators had already pointed out that the only possible inference from these two passages is the inclusion, for Thucydides, of metics as being among the *astoi*.[50]

But in a speech attacking Alkibiadēs, son of the prominent fifth-century politician, for his insistence on serving in the cavalry (which

---

(1913: 136) offered the explanation that *xenoi* were likely to be *politai* themselves—but in another state.

[47] Nor is *politēs* substituted for *astos* in discussions of laws referring to *astoi*. This is shown most strikingly in the many allusions in Demosthenes 59 to the law prohibiting marital arrangements between *astoi* and *xenoi* (text at 16): *politēs* is never substituted for its alleged synonym *astos*. The legislation is explained as that ὃς οὐκ ἐᾷ τὴν ξένην τῷ ἀστῷ συνοικεῖν οὐδὲ τὴν ἀστὴν τῷ ξένῳ (17); Phanō is alleged to be Stephanos's daughter ἐξ ἀστῆς γυναικὸς οὖσαν πρότερον πρὶν ταύτῃ συνοικῆσαι (51); when Phrastōr marries λαμβάνει γυναῖκα ἀστὴν κατὰ τοὺς νόμους (58), he considers his son to be ἐξ ἀστῆς γυναικὸς καὶ ἐγγυητῆς (60), later ἑτέραν γήμαντα γυναῖκα ἀστὴν κατὰ τὸν νόμον. A possible defense for Stephanos under this law is that πρότερον ἔγημεν γυναῖκα ἀστὴν (122). Neaira and Stephanos are not satisfied to claim that Phanō ἀστὴν εἶναι (72), while their opponent claims that οὐκ ἔστιν Νέαιρα αὑτηὶ ἀστή (64) and poses the issue as πότερον ὡς ἀστή ἐστιν Νέαιρα (118). Cf. Dem. 59.92, 106, 108, 110, 119, 121, 124, 126. Similar legislation consistently maintains the same differentiation of terms: the law governing service as religious *basilinna* explicitly requires the "queen" to be an *astē* (59.75); offspring of naturalized *politai* can serve as archons only ἐὰν ὦσιν ἐκ γυναικὸς ἀστῆς (92, 106). But when membership in the *polis* or *politeia*—directly or as a spouse of a *politēs*—is referred to, the speaker uses only the term *politēs*, never *astos*: see Dem. 59.13 (τὸν δῆμον . . . ἄν τινα βούληται πολίτην ποιήσασθαι κ.τ.λ.), 38 (πολίτας ποιήσων), 88 (ὁ δῆμος . . . νόμους ἔθετο αὑτῷ καθ' οὓς ποιεῖσθαι δεῖ πολίτην), 89 (εἰς τὸν δῆμον τὸν Ἀθηναίων ἄξιον ᾖ γενέσθαι πολίτην), 90 (κύριος ὢν . . . πρὸς ὅντινα μέλλει πολίτην ποιήσεσθαι), 106 (ὁ δῆμος πολῖτιν ἐποιήσατο), 112 (ὑπὲρ τῶν πολιτίδων σκοπεῖτε), 113 (τὰς τῶν πολιτῶν θυγατέρας), 117 (ἐκ γένους ὄντα τοῦ Εὐμολπιδῶν καὶ προγόνων καλῶν κἀγαθῶν καὶ πολίτην τῆς πόλεως). Similarly, 59.91, 92, 108.

[48] Thouk. 4.94.1: οἵπερ δὲ ξυνεσέβαλον ὄντες πολλαπλάσιοι τῶν ἐναντίων, ἄοπλοί τε πολλοὶ ἠκολούθησαν, ἅτε πανστρατιᾶς ξένων τῶν παρόντων καὶ ἀστῶν γενομένης.

[49] ὁ δὲ Ἱπποκράτης ἀναστήσας Ἀθηναίους πανδημεί, αὐτοὺς καὶ τοὺς μετοίκους καὶ ξένων ὅσοι παρῆσαν ὕστερος ἀφικνεῖται ἐπὶ τὸ Δήλιον. (For equation of *politai* with *Athēnaioi*, see Patterson 1986: 50–52.)

[50] See Schenkl 1880: 197, n. 86; Wilamowitz 1887: 224–25; Clerc 1893: 44, 259, n. 1.

was open only to *politai*) and not in the hoplite force (which was recruited from the entire male population of Attika),[51] Lysias does not use the term *astos* to refer to those eligible for the cavalry or to the Athenian jurors who would decide the case, alluding to both exclusively as *politai*, never offering *astos* as a synonym for *politēs*—even when stylistic considerations would favor variation in vocabulary.[52] In a presentation focused on the crimes of the Thirty against certain metics, Lysias appeals to his audience separately as *astoi* and *xenoi*, but differentiates the *politai* from the other *astoi*, and separates the metics long resident in Athens from the *xenoi*—implying that at least some of the metics should be included among the *astoi*.[53] Aristotle, Aristophanēs, and Aiskhinēs all distinguish metics as a group from the *xenoi*.[54] Xenophōn likewise subsumes the metics, as a group, within the *astoi* who were serving in the military as heavy infantry,[55] while in the context of freedom of speech

[51] For participation by *metics* in the Athenian armed forces, see pp. 73–74. For the possibly important role of slaves as active participants in Athenian forces in battle, especially in the navy, see Hunt 1998, esp. 87–101, 121–43, 177–78—*pace* Welwei 1974 and Garlan 1974.

[52] The task of a juror is πολίτου χρηστοῦ καὶ δικαστοῦ δικαίου ἔργον (Lys. 14.4). In choosing improperly to serve in the cavalry, open only to *politai*, Alkibiadēs *fils* was μόνον τῶν πολιτῶν (7). In subjecting himself to disenfranchisement (to becoming ἄτιμος), the defendant chose not to be μετὰ τῶν πολιτῶν (9). As a result of his punishment, βελτίους ἔσονται οἱ πολῖται (12). Cf. 14.1 (τοιοῦτον πολίτην); 23 (πολίτου χρηστοῦ γεγενημένου); 29 (ὅν ἔδει κοσμιώτατον εἶναι τῶν πολιτῶν); 30 (μετὰ τῶν πολιτῶν); 34 (τῶν δὲ πολιτῶν καὶ τοὺς βουλομένους δουλεύειν); 37 (τῶν πολιτῶν πρῶτος ἦν); 38 (ἐβούλετο πολίτης γενέσθαι). On 14.28 (εἰς τοὺς πολίτας), see n. 46.

[53] Lys. 12.35: καὶ μὲν δὴ πολλοὶ καὶ τῶν ἀστῶν καὶ τῶν ξένων ἥκουσιν εἰσόμενοι τίνα γνώμην περὶ τούτων ἕξετε. ὧν οἱ μὲν ὑμέτεροι ὄντες πολῖται . . . ὅσοι δὲ ξένοι ἐπιδημοῦσιν, εἴσονται πότερον ἀδίκως τοὺς τριάκοντα ἐκκηρύττουσιν ἐκ τῶν πόλεων ἢ δικαίως. Since the *xenoi* are described as having participated in the recent actions of foreign jurisdictions, those *metics* long resident in Attika could have had no involvement in these measures and hence could not be included among the *xenoi* referred to.

[54] Aiskhin. 1.195: τοὺς δὲ τῶν νέων, ὅσοι ῥαδίως ἁλίσκονται, θηρευτὰς ὄντας εἰς τοὺς ξένους καὶ τοὺς μετοίκους τρέπεσθαι κελεύετε. Aristoph. *Lys.* 579–80: ἅπαντας | καταμιγνύντας τούς τε μετοίκους κεἴ τις ξένος ἢ φίλος ὑμῖν. (MacDowell 1995: 237, noting the permanent nature of metic residence at Athens, concludes from this passage that "Aristophanes considers that there is no good reason to exclude [metics] from the status and rights of citizens.") Aristot. *Pol.* 1326a18–20: ἀναγκαῖον γὰρ ἐν ταῖς πόλεσιν ἴσως ὑπάρχειν καὶ δούλων ἀριθμὸν πολλῶν καὶ μετοίκων καὶ ξένων. Cf. Whitehead 1984: 49.

[55] *Por.* 2.2: τὸ συστρατεύεσθαι ὁπλίτας μετοίκους τοῖς ἀστοῖς. Because any foreigner who spent more than a brief period in Attika was required to become a metic (Gauthier 1972: 122, but cf. Lévy 1988: 53–61), not all metics could be considered "local" persons (*astoi*). See pp. 72–74 and n. 154. In seeking to attract a greater number of immigrants (οἱ ἀπόλιδες), Xenophon seeks their exemption from compulsory military service (lest immigration be dissuaded by danger and hardship—μέγας ὁ κίνδυνος ἀπόντι· μέγα δὲ καὶ τὸ ἀπὸ τῶν τέκνων καὶ τῶν οἰκιῶν ἀπιέναι: 2.2). But for the assimilated metic, he proposed the opening of certain elite units (such as the cavalry: 2.5; cf. Gauthier 1972: 125): the *polis* would benefit if the *politai* were seen to rely more on themselves for battles and were to serve with one another rather than being arrayed together with others "as at present" (ὥσπερ νῦν). Xenophon's proposal, however, "found no favour with his fellow-citizens" (Whitehead 1977: 129).

the Xenophonic *Ath. Pol.* equates the metics with the *astoi.*[56] Sophoklēs, in the *Oidipous Tyrannos*, refers to the individual Oidipous as both an *astos* (line 222) and as a *metoikos* (line 452).[57] And Aristophanes in the *Akharnians* calls the metics "the useless part of the *astoi.*"[58]

Precisely because *astos* is not a synonym for *politēs*, it is quite significant that in Athenian legislation the *astoi* (and not the *politai*) are explicitly denominated as the group from which *politai* may be chosen. In both the Periklean "citizenship" decree of the fifth century,[59] and in the arrangements set forth for the fourth century in the Aristotelian *Constitution of the Athenians (Ath. Pol.)*,[60] the Athenians mandated that an individual could be a *politēs* (literally "share in the *polis*" or "*politeia*")[61] only if he were born from two parents who each were *astoi.*[62] The provisions adopted in 403 under the restored democracy also explicitly restrict a "share in the polis" to those who could show that both of their

[56] 1.12: τοῖς μετοίκοις πρὸς τοὺς ἀστούς . . . εἰκότως τὴν ἰσηγορίαν ἐποιήσαμεν. On *isēgoria* at Athens, see Wallace 1994: 109–10; Bonner [1933] 1976: 70–71.

[57] Line 222: νῦν δ,᾿ ὕστερος γὰρ ἀστὸς εἰς ἀστοὺς τελῶ. Lines 451–53: οὗτος ἐστιν ἐνθάδε, | ξένος λόγῳ μέτοικος· εἶτα δ᾿ ἐγγενὴς | φανήσεται Θηβαῖος.

[58] Line 508: τοὺς γὰρ μετοίκους ἄχυρα τῶν ἀστῶν λέγω. Taillardat, in his study of Aristophanic style (1962: 391–93), interprets this passage as asserting the inclusion of the metics among the *astoi*.

[59] *Ath. Pol.* 26.4: Περικλέους εἰπόντος ἔγνωσαν μὴ μετέχειν τῆς πόλεως ὃς ἂν μὴ ἐξ ἀμφοῖν ἀστοῖν ᾖ γεγονώς. Scafuro translates it literally, and correctly: "whoever has not been born of two *astoi* parents has no share in the polis" (1994: 156). The only other ancient references to this legislation were written centuries later: Ail. *Poik. Hist.* 6.10 and Plut. *Perikl.* 37.2–5. Ailian too limits "a share in the city" to those born from parents who are both *astoi* (ἐξ ἀμφοῖν ἀστῶν). Although Plutarch refers to the law as providing that "only those born from two Athenians were Athenians" (μόνους Ἀθηναίους εἶναι τοὺς ἐκ δυεῖν Ἀθηναίων γεγονότας), his use of the anachronistic form δυεῖν, which is not found before 300 B.C.E., betrays his reliance on derivative material (in Chapot's opinion, "une source d'époque macédonienne" [1929:8]) rather than the actual text of the law. On this legislation, see generally Patterson 1981; Walters 1983; for the requirement of double endogamy, see Davies 1977–78; Boegehold 1994.

[60] *Ath. Pol.* 42.1: μετέχουσιν μὲν τῆς πολιτείας οἱ ἐξ ἀμφοτέρων γεγονότες ἀστῶν.

[61] Cf. Aristot. *Ath. Pol.* 36.1, 40.2; Lys. 16.3, 30.15; Dem. 59.105. For variant formulations, see Mossé [1962] 1979: 141–44.

[62] Participation in phratry activities in the mid-fifth century also is known to have focused on *astos* parentage. A father, on introducing a child to the phratry, had to swear that he was born from an *astē* mother. See Isai. 7.16, 8.19; Dem. 57.54. Cf. *I.G.* II^2 109–11. A fragmentary law prohibits an individual born to two *xenoi* from acting as a phratry member. *FGrHist* 342 F 4 (Krateros)(= Harp., Suda, s.v. ναυτοδίκαι): ἐάν δέ τις ἐξ ἀμφοῖν ξένοιν γεγονὼς φρατρίζῃ, διώκειν εἶναι τῷ βουλομένῳ Ἀθηναίων, οἷς δίκαι εἰσί. λαγχάνειν δὲ τῇ ἕνῃ καὶ νέα πρὸς τοὺς ναυτοδίκας. For the dating of the inscription, see Meritt, Wade-Gery, and McGregor 1939–53: 3:9–11; Meiggs 1972: 420–21; for its historical context, see Andrewes 1961: 61. There is, however, no evidence establishing any linkage between membership in a phratry and participation in the *politeia*. To the contrary, certain persons confirmed as *politai* by decree of the Assembly are known not to have been assigned to phratries. See Osborne 1981–83: 4:160, 182–83; Lambert 1993: 49–57.

parents were *astoi*.[63] The *Ath. Pol.* even sets forth the substantive and procedural requirements to be met by offspring of *astoi*. Demesmen may accept as *politai* "those males born from *astoi* on both sides" who are found to have attained eighteen years of age, to be free, and to have been born "in accordance with the laws."[64] (Parentage also was examined at the scrutinies of officials prior to their entry into office: significantly here too there is no suggestion of a requirement of birth from parents who were *politai*.)[65]

Among the Greek *poleis*, this Athenian requirement of *astoi* (rather than *politai*) as parents of new *politai*, is neither unique nor universal: the identification and definition of a *politēs* varied from community to community, and was frequently in dispute.[66] Certain states did explicitly require *politai* to be descended from other *politai*. Some jurisdictions even insisted on *politai* as antecedents for two, three, or even more generations.[67] But, according to Aristotle, many states accepted as a *politēs* an individual whose mother alone was a *politis* (even if the father were a *xenos*),[68] while some required ("as a practical matter") that both

[63] Scholiast to Aiskhin. 1.39 (Eumēlos fr. 2): μηδένα τῶν μετ' Εὐκλείδην ἄρχοντα μετέχειν τῆς πόλεως, ἂν μὴ ἄμφω τοὺς γονέας ἀστοὺς ἐπιδείξηται, τοὺς δὲ πρὸ Εὐκλείδου ἀνεξετάστους ἀφείσθαι. Cf. Athen. 577b.

[64] *Ath. Pol.* 42.1: μετέχουσιν μὲν τῆς πολιτείας οἱ ἐξ ἀμφοτέρων γεγονότες ἀστῶν, ἐγγράφονται δ' εἰς τοὺς δημότας ὀκτωκαίδεκα ἔτη γεγονότες. ὅταν δ' ἐγγράφωνται διαψηφίζονται περὶ αὐτῶν ὀμόσαντες οἱ δημόται, πρῶτον μὲν εἰ δοκοῦσι γεγονέναι τὴν ἡλικίαν τὴν ἐκ τοῦ νόμου, κἂν μὴ δόξωσι, ἀπέρχονται πάλιν εἰς παῖδας, δεύτερον δ' εἰ ἐλεύθερός ἐστι καὶ γέγονε κατὰ τοὺς νόμους.

[65] Aristot. *Ath. Pol.* 55.3: ἐπερωτῶσιν δ', ὅταν δοκιμάζωσιν, πρῶτον μὲν "τίς σοι πατὴρ καὶ πόθεν τῶν δήμων, καὶ τίς πατρὸς πατήρ, καὶ τίς μήτηρ, καὶ τίς μητρὸς πατὴρ καὶ πόθεν τῶν δήμων;" Because both *metics* and *politai* were affiliated with demes (see nn. 159 and 160), this inquiry could be answered satisfactorily by anyone whose parents—*politai* or not—had been registered in a deme. (Observe that there is no inquiry as to deme affiliation of grandparents: for jurisdictions that did inquire into the political standing of grandparents and even great-grandparents, see n. 67.) There were further inquiries concerning military service, payment of taxes, and participation in cult and shrine activities and such—all of which were open to metic participation (see pp. 72–74.) (μετὰ δὲ ταῦτα, εἰ ἔστιν αὐτῷ Ἀπόλλων πατρῷος καὶ Ζεὺς ἑρκεῖος, καὶ ποῦ ταῦτα τὰ ἱερά εστιν, εἶτα ἠρία εἰ ἔστιν καὶ ποῦ ταῦτα, ἔπειτα γονέας εἰ εὖ ποιεῖ καὶ τὰ τέλη <εἰ> τελεῖ, καὶ τὰς στρατείας εἰ ἐστράτευται. ταῦτα δ' ἀνερωτήσας "κάλει," φησίν, "τούτων τοὺς μάρτυρας"). Descendants of Plataians naturalized at Athens could serve as archons, ἂν ὦσιν ἐξ ἀστῆς γυναικὸς καὶ ἐγγυητῆς κατὰ τὸν νόμον (Dem. 59.106).

[66] Aristot. *Pol.* 1275a1–2: τίνα χρὴ καλεῖν πολίτην καὶ τίς ὁ πολίτης ἐστὶ σκεπτέον. καὶ γὰρ ὁ πολίτης ἀμφισβητεῖται πολλάκις·

[67] Aristot. *Pol.* 1275b23–24: οἱ δὲ καὶ τοῦτ' ἐπὶ πλέον ζητοῦσιν, οἷον ἐπὶ πάππους δύο ἢ τρεῖς ἢ πλείους. But Aristotle notes the practical implausibility of such genealogical investigation: οὕτω δὲ ὁριζομένων πολιτικῶς καὶ παχέως, ἀπορυοῦσί τινες τὸν τρίτον ἐκεῖνον ἢ τέταρτον, πῶς ἔσται πολίτης (ibid., lines 25–26).

[68] *Pol.* 1278a26–27: ἐν πολλαῖς δὲ πολιτείαις προσεφέλκει τινὰς καὶ τῶν ξένων ὁ νόμος· ὁ γὰρ ἐκ πολίτιδος ἔν τισι δημοκρατίαις πολίτης ἐστίν.

parents be *politai*.[69] But other jurisdictions accept as *politai* persons born from two parents who are only *astoi*,[70] a practice especially prevalent, Aristotle claims, in democracies that at one time—like Athens[71]—had extended *politeia* even to persons of slave or foreign background.[72]

The Athenians' clear differentiation of *politai* from *astoi* (and the importance of this distinction in determining access to a "share in the *politeia*") are confirmed by the only surviving court presentations dealing with implementation of the "citizenship" legislation, Demosthenes 57 and Isaios 12—unrelated appeals from the ousters of previously accepted *politai*.[73] Demosthenes 57 concerns Euxitheos, who is seeking reinstatement into the Halimous deme: the appellant repeatedly insists that his father, despite many years' absence from Athens,[74] was not a *xenos* but an *astos*; that his mother was an *astē*; and that he, Euxitheos, is therefore entitled to be accepted as a *politēs*. "It should be clear that my father was an *astos* and not a *xenos*."[75] "No one ever accused my father of being a *xenos*!"[76] "If my father were rich and could have suborned these [supportive] witnesses, there might be some basis for suspecting that he was not an *astos*!"[77] "My mother was an *astē*. How can I be a *xenos*?"[78] Isaios 12 likewise seeks reinstatement of Euphilētos as a *politēs* after

[69] *Pol.* 1275b22–23: Ὁρίζονται δὲ πρὸς τὴν χρῆσιν πολίτην τὸν ἐξ ἀμφοτέρων πολιτῶν καὶ μὴ θατέρου μόνον, οἷον πατρὸς ἢ μητρός.

[70] *Pol.* 1278a34: τέλος δὲ μόνον τοὺς ἐξ ἀμφοῖν ἀστῶν πολίτας ποιοῦσιν.

[71] *Pol.* 1275b35–37: Ἀθήνησιν ἐποίησε Κλεισθένης . . . πολλοὺς ξένους καὶ δούλους μετοίκους. See the next section.

[72] *Pol.* 1278a28–34: ἔν τισι δημοκρατίαις . . . δι' ἔνδειαν τῶν γνησίων πολιτῶν ποιοῦνται πολίτας τοὺς τοιούτους (διὰ γὰρ ὀλιγανθρωπίαν οὕτω χρῶνται τοῖς νόμοις), εὐποροῦντες δὴ ὄχλου κατὰ μικρὸν παραιροῦνται τοὺς ἐκ δούλου πρῶτον ἢ δούλης, εἶτα τοὺς ἀπὸ γυναικῶν, τέλος δὲ μόνον τοὺς ἐξ ἀμφοῖν ἀστῶν πολίτας ποιοῦσιν. *Telos* (finally) relates to the process by which the various jurisdictions tend over time to restrict acceptance of *nothoi* into *politeia*: liberality motivated by a lack of *gnēsioi* (i.e., non-*nothoi*) is eroded gradually as the number of *politai* increases.

[73] The two presentations arose from *polis*-wide *diapsēphismoi* (Dem. 57.2; Dion. Hal. *Isai.* 17): see n. 95 and related text.

[74] Dem. 57.18: πραθεὶς εἰς Λευκάδα . . . πρὸς τοὺς οἰκείους ἐσώθη δεῦρο πολλοστῷ χρόνῳ. Cf. n. 36.

[75] 57.24: ἐξ ὧν ἔστιν ὑμῖν εἰδέναι, πότερόν ποτ' ἀστὸς ἢ ξένος ἦν. Cf. 57.3: οἴομαι δεῖν ὑμᾶς τοῖς μὲν ἐξελεγχομένοις ξένοις οὖσιν χαλεπαίνειν; 18: διαβεβλήκασι γάρ μου τὸν πατέρα, ὡς ἐξένιζεν· . . . τὸ ξενίζειν αὐτοῦ κατηγορήκασιν. His father's acceptance as a *politēs* is seen as confirmatory of the elder man's not being a *xenos*: 26: οἴεταί τις οὖν ὑμῶν ἐᾶσαί ποτ' ἂν τοὺς δημότας ἐκεῖνον τὸν ξένον καὶ μὴ πολίτην ἄρχειν παρ' αὐτοῖς;

[76] 57.19: οὔτ' ἐν τοῖς δημόταις οὔτ' ἐν τοῖς φράτερσιν οὔτ' ἄλλοθι οὐδαμοῦ τὸν ξενίζοντ' οὐδεὶς πώποτ' ᾐτιάσαθ' ὡς εἴη ξένος.

[77] 57.25: εἰ μὲν τοίνυν εὔπορος ὢν ὁ πατὴρ χρήματα δοὺς τούτοις ἐφαίνετο . . . λόγον εἶχεν ἂν ὑποψίαν τιν' ἔχειν ὡς οὐκ ἦν ἀστός.

[78] 57.54: ἀλλὰ μὴν ὁ πατὴρ αὐτὸς ζῶν ὀμόσας τὸν νόμιμον τοῖς φράτερσιν ὅρκον εἰσήγαγέν με, ἀστὸν ἐξ ἀστῆς ἐγγυητῆς αὐτῷ γεγενημένον εἰδώς, καὶ ταῦτα μεμαρτύρηται. εἶτ' ἐγὼ ξένος;

his expulsion by the deme of the Erkhiëans. The appellant's argument focuses on the allegedly abundant proof that Euphilētos's mother was an *astē*, not a *xenē*, and that Euphilētos—born to two *astoi* in accordance with the laws[79]—was therefore "unjustly" ousted.[80]

Thus the Athenian procedure posits the existence in Attika of a recognizable group of free local persons (*astoi*)—including but not identical with the *politai* and including some but far from all of the metics[81]—whose sons the demes may accept (or reject) as new *politai* pursuant to the enunciated criteria of age, freedom, and lawful birth. In the absence of an appeal (available only if the applicant were found to be unfree), a rejected youth would not be entitled to participate in the decision-making and office-holding prerogatives and ancillary benefits reserved to *politai*. But his status as an *astos*, a resident of Attika, would not otherwise be affected.[82] This is precisely the arrangement postulated in the Liddell and Scott lexicon when it distinguishes *astos* "from *politēs*, *astos* being one who has civil rights only, *politēs* one who has political rights also," a usage observed "especially at Athens."[83]

[79] Isai. 12.7: ἡ μήτηρ ἀστή τέ ἐστι καὶ <γαμετὴ καὶ ἀστὸς> ὁ πατήρ. 9: ἡ τοῦ Εὐφιλήτου μήτηρ, ἣν οὗτοι ὁμολογοῦσιν ἀστὴν εἶναι. 9: Εὐφίλητον τουτονὶ ὑὸν εἶναι αὑτοῦ ἐξ ἀστῆς καὶ γαμετῆς γυναικός.

[80] 12.12: ὅτι μὲν οὖν ἀδελφὸς ἡμῶν ἐστιν οὑτοσὶ Εὐφίλητος καὶ πολίτης ὑμέτερος, καὶ ἀδίκως ὑβρίσθη ὑπὸ τῶν ἐν τῷ δήμῳ συστάντων, ἱκανῶς οἴομαι ὑμᾶς ἀκηκοέναι. The demesmen, however, apparently questioned Euphilētos's paternity (5: εἰ οὗτος ἐξ ἄλλου τινὸς ἀνδρὸς ἦν τῇ μητρυιᾷ καὶ οὐκ ἐκ τοῦ ἡμετέρου πατρός).

[81] See pp. 55–59, 72ff.

[82] *Ath. Pol.* 42.1–2: ἔπειτ᾽ ἂν μὲν ἀποψηφίσωνται μὴ εἶναι ἐλεύθερον, ὁ μὲν ἐφίησιν εἰς τὸ δικαστήριον, οἱ δὲ δημόται κατηγόρους αἱροῦνται, πέντε ἄνδρας ἐξ αὑτῶν, κἂν μὲν μὴ δόξῃ δικαίως ἐγγράφεσθαι, πωλεῖ τοῦτον ἡ πόλις· ἐὰν δὲ νικήσῃ, τοῖς δημόταις ἐπάναγκες ἐγγράφειν. μετὰ δὲ ταῦτα δοκιμάζει τοὺς ἐγγραφέντας ἡ βουλή, κἂν τις δόξῃ νεώτερος ὀκτωκαίδεκ᾽ ἐτῶν εἶναι, ζημιοῖ τοὺς δημότας τοὺς ἐγγράψαντας. The text explicitly limits appeal to cases where the demesmen have found the applicant not to be free (ἐλεύθερον), and explicitly provides for deprivation of rights only where such appeals are unsuccessful. Yet scholars either have rejected the plain language of the law as "improbably haphazard" (Rhodes 1981: 500), insisting that "we may guess that on all criteria a candidate rejected by the deme could appeal" (ibid.), or have suggested that ἐλεύθερος does not here carry its usual meaning of "free" but rather means "whether he is of citizen birth" (see Sandys [1912] 1966; Fritz and Kapp 1961; Moore 1986; Newman 1887–1902: 1:248, n. 1, 4:173–74; Wyse [1904] 1967: 281). The free status of applicants for the *politeia* should not be assumed. Because of the homogeneous appearance of the residents of Attika, and because numerous slaves actually lived "independently" (χωρὶς οἰκοῦντες), often maintaining their own households, and in some cases even owning their own slaves, it was difficult to identify slaves at Athens. See Chapter 4, pp. 106–9; Chapter 5. In any event, it would not be unreasonable to permit appeals only on the issue of free status: the candidate rejected on other criteria would suffer relatively benign consequences; he would not share in the political or economic benefits of the *politeia* (a temporary deprivation in the case of those rejected on age), but his freedom and other rights would be unaffected.

[83] Cf. the Bailly Greek-French lexicon, s.v. ἀστός, deuxième sens. But these definitions have been (generally) ignored, or denigrated as "eccentric" (Whitehead 1977: 60), "incertaine" (Chapot

Yet prevailing scholarship, with little discussion,[84] has insisted that the two words, *astos* and *politēs*, share an identical meaning—"citizen."[85] Beyond philological error, this assumption also violates a universal principle of statutory interpretation: legal texts should be construed on the premise that each word has significance, not on the assumption that differentiation of terms is inconsequential. "The reader of a statute or contract or other legal rule or instrument should assume that every meaning was placed there for a purpose."[86] If the Athenians had wanted to limit future *politai* to offspring of present *politai*, they could have so provided. Yet—despite the well-known Greek obsession with elaborate attention to choice, and even rhetorical placement, of specific words and phrases—the actual text of the Aristotelian *Constitution of the Athenians* is uniformly ignored in conventional translations and explanations, replaced by a paraphrase stating that "the right of citizenship belongs to those whose parents have been citizens."[87] The Periklean decree, on this interpretation, supposedly mandates that "those whose parents were not both citizens should not themselves be citizens" (Davies 1978: 104). Loraux departs even further from the Greek text and claims that acceptance as a *politēs* was limited to "a man who has nothing but citizen fathers on both sides: his own father, and his mother's father" (Loraux [1984] 1993: 119). (On this mutiliation of the evidence, Patterson is properly severe: "Loraux simply dismisses the actual language of this

---

1929: 8). The 1996 supplement to LSJ, without explanation, queries the definition provided in the lexicon's text proper.

[84] Although the meaning of *politēs* and *astos* "has not been extensively debated" (Patterson 1981: 171), the Italian scholar U. E. Paoli did seek to find a rationale for the use of the two words as synonyms: the *politēs, qua politēs*, held political rights ("diritti politici") supplementing the civil rights ("diritti civili") of the *astos* ([1930] 1974: 197). Paoli, however, identified these differentiated *astoi* as the dependents of the *politai*—the female and underage male relatives of *politai* ("i maschi prima dell'efebia sono ἀστοί—*spes* πολιτῶν, non πολῖται—ἀσταί le femmine," p. 198)—an impossible reading of the legal requirement that Athenian *politai* be born from two *astoi*. Indicative of the dearth of research on this issue, Paoli's brief treatment—noted at Biscardi 1991: 138–39 and Wolff 1944: 83—has been termed by Gould "still the best discussion of the two terms" (1980: 46, n. 57). Vatin (1984: 65–66), followed by Lévy ([1985] 1988: 53) accepts Paoli's distinction, differentiating between the *astoi* as a "corps civique" and the *politai* as a "corps politique." Commentators on the Aristotelian *Ath. Pol.* and on Athenian law have been silent: contrast, for example, the extended treatment by Rhodes and Sandys of other issues raised by 42.1.

[85] See n. 7.

[86] Posner 1995: 480. For the complex considerations that may affect the literal meaning (in American judicial rhetoric, the "plain meaning") of a legal document, see Bix 1993: 73–76. On the importance of language as the instrumentality through which law functions, see Hart 1994: 120–32; Dworkin 1986: 49–53; Marmor 1992: 36–39.

[87] Quoted from the standard English translation of 42.1 by Fritz and Kapp: 1961.

particular law. If Athenians intended the law to read as Loraux suggests, they could have written it that way" [1986: 54].)[88] Yet from such artificial readings—defiant of actual usage and of established standards of statutory interpretation—has arisen the shibboleth that Athenian *politai* constituted an impenetrable group of scions of *politai*, an autochthonous club sealed forever by doubly endogamous barriers, an unfounded interpretation in conflict with social, political, and historical realities.

New, Old, and Former Athenians: The Historical Context

From the beginnings of Athenian polity and throughout the classical period new *politai* were continually being accepted in massive numbers pursuant to mutable criteria, while numerous prior *politai* were removed under variantly ambiguous standards: a realpolitik of political and economic advantage sometimes masked by patriotic rhetoric.[89] Already in the sixth century, Solon had welcomed as *politai* "exiles" from other states and any persons who would come to Attika with their families to practice a trade.[90] Solon's successor, Peisistratos, provided a share in the *politeia* to "many" new *politai* of doubtful origin and/or diminished economic circumstance.[91] It was only after the ouster of the Peisistratids, however, in 510/9 that many of these new *politai* were branded "inappropriate"[92] and subjected to purge in the first of the numerous Athenian

[88] In fact, the report of the "reenactment" in 403 of Periklēs' law is explicitly contrary to Loraux's paraphrase: μηδένα μετέχειν τῆς πόλεως, ἂν μὴ ἄμφω τοὺς γονέας ἀστοὺς ἐπιδείξηται (see n. 59).

[89] Athenian claims of autochthony—οἵ τινες αὐτόχθονες μὲν εἶναι φαμεν (Isok. 8.49); cf. Lykourg. 1.41—did not necessarily imply genealogical purity: see Chapter 3.

[90] Plut. *Sol.* 24.4: τοῖς φεύγουσιν ἀειφυγίᾳ τὴν ἑαυτῶν ἢ πανεστίοις Ἀθήναζε μετοικιζομένοις ἐπὶ τέχνῃ. On the historicity of this report, see Davies 1977–78: 115. Although earlier scholars had interpreted Solon's program as liberalizing (see Clerc 1893: 332–35; Diller 1937: 101, 115; McGregor 1973: 53–55), recent commentators have argued that these policies actually represented a tightening of yet more open prior immigration standards (see Manville 1990: 122–23; Whitehead 1977: 141–42). On the artisans fleeing expansion of the Persian Empire at about this time, see Robertson 1975: 78 n. 78; cf. Andrewes 1982: 408–9.

[91] Aristot. *Ath. Pol.* 13.5: προσεκεκόσμηντο δὲ τούτοις οἵ τε ἀφῃρημένοι τὰ χρέα διὰ τὴν ἀπορίαν καὶ οἱ τῷ γένει μὴ καθαροὶ διὰ τὸν φόβον . . . πολλῶν κοινωνούντων τῆς πολιτείας οὐ προσῆκον. Manville has shown the significance in the overall population at this time of such "men of impure blood," who "had become assimilated in the Attica community" (1990: 176–185).

[92] Aristot. *Ath. Pol.* 13.5: σημεῖον δ' ὅτι μετὰ τὴν τῶν τυράννων κατάλυσιν ἐποίησαν διαψηφισμόν, ὡς πολλῶν κοινωνούντων τῆς πολιτείας οὐ προσῆκον. For the historicity and date of this first vote, see Hignett 1952: 132–33, Ostwald 1969: 141–42; for the historical context, see Welwei 1967; Luzzi 1980; David 1986: 8ff.

diapsēphismoi (exclusionary votes) that were to be a feature of the fifth and fourth centuries.[93] These former *politai*, however, were in turn reinstated by Kleisthenēs,[94] a precedent for the gyrating ousters and restorations that would recur frequently until the end of Athenian autonomy in the fourth century.[95] Kleisthenēs also massively expanded the total number of *politai*: among the new participants in the *politeia*, he included not only (in Davies's words) "all the free residents of Attika" but also (in Aristotle's words) "many foreigners and alien slaves."[96]

The gyrations (*metabolai* as they were termed by the Athenians)[97] continued through the fifth and fourth centuries: massive influxes of outsiders, expulsions of existing *politai*; construction of fresh barriers, removal of prior obstacles. Isokratēs claimed that Athens was more liberal than obscure foreign tribes in sharing its *politeia* with anyone

[93] The word διαψηφισμός means "voting by ballot" (LSJ, s.v.)—a term appropriate for a political process in which "they expelled some of themselves" (τινας ἀπήλασαν αὑτῶν [Dem. 57.26]). The broad scope of the *diapsēphisis* has apparently led to the prevailing translation—"scrutiny"—and the assumption that genealogy was a major focus. (Cf. the Scholion to Aiskhin. 1.77: Δημόφιλος δέ τις εἰσηγήσατο διαψηφίσεις γενέσθαι τῶν ἀστῶν ἐν τοῖς δήμοις, ὥστε τοὺς δημότας περὶ ἑκάστου τῶν ἀναγραφομένων διδόναι ψῆφον ὅτι ἐστὶν ἀστός, μηδενὸς κατηγοροῦντος μηδὲ ἀπολογουμένου ἀλλ' ἐκ τῆς συνιστορήσεως, καὶ ἴσχυον αἱ διαψηφίσεις τῶν δημοτῶν.) But votes in the demes appear to have been heavily influenced by local politics, resulting in arbitrary decisions that entirely ignored pedigree: see pp. 68ff.; Chapter 4, pp. 110–11.

[94] Aristot. *Ath. Pol.* 20.1: ὁ Κλεισθένης προσηγάγετο τὸν δῆμον, ἀποδιδοὺς τῷ πλήθει τὴν πολιτείαν. Scholars generally interpret *politeia* here to mean citizenship "in the narrow sense of restoring rights to those who lost them in the *diapsēphismos:* 'giving back the citizenship to those who had lost it' " (Manville 1990: 186). Cf. David 1986: 8–9. *Contra:* Wade-Gery (1958: 139, n. 2; 147–48), who interprets the phrase as "universo populo tribuens rempublicam."

[95] Dionysios of Halikarnassos alludes specifically to a law providing for "examination of *politai* throughout the demes" and ouster of *politai* after an adverse vote by a deme (*Isai.* 17). Wilamowitz felt that such referenda "without doubt must have occurred repeatedly" (1893: 1:31, n. 4). Jacoby found, in addition to the Attika-wide determinations of the fifth and fourth centuries, a number of other "scrutinies in some demes" between 403 and 346 ([1954] 1968: 3.b (Suppl.) 1:158; 2:144, n. 30). Other scholars, however, have denied that such *diapsēphismoi* were commonplace. For example, Wyse ([1904] 1967: 715–16) argues that the Isaios speech relates to the same "scrutiny" (of 346/45) described in Demosthenes 57 (although this premise would require Isaios, born about 420, still to be active in the late 340s, considerably beyond the latest date for which he is otherwise attested [c. 350]). Diller 1932 asserts that Dionysios was simply mistaken.

[96] Davies 1977–78: 116. Aristot. *Pol.* 1275b36–37: πολλοὺς ξένους καὶ δούλους μετοίκους. Cf. Aristot. *Ath. Pol.* 21.2 (ὅπως μετάσχωσι πλείους τῆς πολιτείας), 21.4; *Pol.* 1277b22–1278a2; Whitehead 1984: 54; Kagan 1963: 41–46. Although Aristotle's report is often rejected as inconsistent with modern concepts of Athenian practice (μετοίκους is commonly athetized), the term ξένος μέτοικος is well attested: see Aristoph. *Hipp.* 347; Soph. *Oid. T.* 452; Harrison 1968–71: 1:186. For the historical accuracy of *Pol.* 1275b36–37, see Davies 1977–78: 116–17.

[97] See Lykourg. 1.42: τοσαύτῃ δ' ἡ πόλις ἐκέχρητο μεταβολῇ. Cf. Aristot. *Pol.* 1275b35, 1292b18. According to Murray (1993: 207), the Aristotelian *Ath. Pol.* uses "radical [terms] like *metastasis*, *stasis*, *katalusis*, *katastasis*" in describing the "eleven" (actually twelve) *metabolai* enumerated in ch. 41. In the *Politics* (1275a33–b17), Aristotle explains that such variations in political regime will necessarily alter a society's determination and definition of *politai.* ὁ λεχθεὶς ἐν μὲν δημοκρατίᾳ μάλιστ' ἐστὶ πολίτης, ἐν δὲ ταῖς ἄλλαις ἐνδέχεται μέν, οὐ μὴν ἀναγκαῖον (1275b5–7).

wanting it: he decried the fifth-century acceptance as *politai* of multitudes "who had no claim upon the *polis*" but nonetheless filled its places of burial, social organizations, and military musterings.[98] Andokidēs, speaking in the late fifth century, complained to the Assembly about its continuing grants of *politeia* to large numbers of "slaves and foreigners from all over the world";[99] years later he was still decrying the acceptance of "Thessalians and Andrians as *politai* because of a shortage of manpower," and the ouster of others previously accepted.[100] Until the middle of the fifth century, no restrictions, or even guidelines, limited a deme's acceptance of new members, and hence the creation of new *politai*.[101] But in reaction to a huge increase in the number of *politai*,[102] the Periklean law of 451/0 purported to limit *politai* to those born through doubly endogamous marriages of *astoi*[103]—legislation followed in 445/4 by a large-scale ouster of persons who had previously been accepted as *politai*.[104] Almost five thousand individuals, a huge proportion of the total number of *politai*,[105] were deprived of participation in the *politeia*.[106]

[98] Isok. 8.50: ῥᾴδιον δὲ μεταδίδομεν τοῖς βουλομένοις ταύτης τῆς εὐγενείας ἢ Τριβαλλοὶ καὶ Λευκανοὶ τῆς αὑτῶν δυσγενείας. 8.88: τελευτῶντες δ' ἔλαθον σφᾶς αὑτοὺς τοὺς μὲν τάφους τοὺς δημοσίους τῶν πολιτῶν ἐμπλήσαντες, τὰς δὲ φρατρίας καὶ τὰ γραμματεῖα τὰ ληξιαρχικὰ τῶν οὐδὲν τῇ πόλει προσηκόντων.

[99] Andok. 2.23: ὁρῶ δὲ ὑμᾶς πολλάκις καὶ δούλοις ἀνθρώποις καὶ ξένοις παντοδαποῖς πολιτείαν διδόντας. On the context of Andokidēs' charge, see Missiou 1992: 40–43. It is uncertain how much time elapsed between the overthrow of the Four Hundred in September 411 and the delivery of this speech: every year between 410 and 406 has been suggested. See MacDowell 1962: 4–5, n. 9; Edwards 1995: 89.

[100] Andok. 1.149: καὶ μὴ βούλεσθε Θετταλοὺς καὶ Ἀνδρίους πολίτας ποιεῖσθαι δι' ἀπορίαν ἀνδρῶν, τοὺς δὲ ὄντας πολίτας ὁμολογουμένως . . . τούτους δὲ ἀπόλλυτε.

[101] "There was no polis law defining or controlling membership of the demes and phratries before Pericles set forth his requirement for 'having a share in the city'" (Patterson 1981: 3).

[102] Aristot. *Ath. Pol.* 26.4: διὰ τὸ πλῆθος τῶν πολιτῶν. This elliptical phrase was long wrongly assumed to refer to a natural increase in population (see, e.g., Gomme 1933: 12; Hignett 1952: 245), but recent demographic studies have demonstrated that through reproduction "the number of citizens living in Attica was doomed to be almost stationary and sometimes even declining" (Hansen 1985: 64). Accordingly, the substantial growth in numbers of *politai* "was most likely due in large part to the admission of foreigners into the demes and phratries" (Patterson 1981: 102).

[103] Aristot. *Ath. Pol.* 26.4: μὴ μετέχειν τῆς πόλεως ὃς ἂν μὴ ἐξ ἀμφοῖν ἀστῶν ᾖ γεγονώς. See n. 59.

[104] Plutarch (*Perikl.* 37.4) treats the Periklean law and the subsequent purge as related—a linkage rejected by some modern scholars (e.g., Hignett 1952: 345) because of the "unfairness" implicit in a retroactive change in standard. Patterson (1981: 95–97, 140) insists that the decree merely "applied to all future admissions." But, as sketched in the text, arbitrary reversals of policy, and politically motivated changes in the status of individuals, were recurrent throughout Athenian history.

[105] Gomme (1933: 26) estimates the total number of *politai* at about 35,000 in 480, and 43,000 in 431. Most other estimates are lower: see Patterson 1981: 40–81. For demographic estimates in the fourth century, see Chapter 1, pp. 16–17.

[106] Plut. *Perikl.* 37: πολλαὶ μὲν ἀνεφύοντο δίκαι τοῖς νόθοις . . . τέως διαλανθάνουσι καὶ παρορωμένοις, πολλοὶ δὲ καὶ συκοφαντήμασι περιέπιπτον. ἐπράθησαν οὖν ἁλόντες ὀλίγως

But Periklēs' restrictions appear to have been short-lived. Whether actually repealed within a few years, as suggested in our sources,[107] or simply allowed to lapse, as suggested by its reenactment after the Peloponnesian War,[108] within a few years of its adoption the Athenians were again making mass extensions of *politeia*. Although the best known are the grants to their Plataian allies (some time before 429)[109] and later to the entire population of the island of Samos,[110] at least a dozen collective grants are explicitly attested in our highly fragmentary sources[111]—about evenly split between the fifth and fourth centuries—including mass provisions for the Elaiousans in 341/0 (and probably for the Olynthians and Thebans and for considerable numbers of Akarnanians at about the same time),[112] and grants shortly thereafter to the Troizenians en masse.[113] Although such awards of *politeia* are often claimed to have been merely honorific—on the a priori assumption that "the Athenians are unlikely to have accorded citizenship to a very substantial set of

---

πεντακισχιλίων ἐλάττους. οἱ δὲ μείναντες ἐν τῇ πολιτείᾳ καὶ κριθέντες Ἀθηναῖοι μύριοι καὶ τετρακισχίλιοι καὶ τεσσαράκοντα τὸ πλῆθος ἐξητάσθησαν. Cf. Philokhoros (Scholia to Aristoph. *Sphēk.* 718 = *FGrHist* 328F 119): τετρακισχιλίους ἑπτακοσίους ξ ὀφθῆναι παρεγγράφους . . . τοὺς γὰρ λαβόντας (sc. τὴν δωρεὰν ἣν Ψαμμήτιχος ἔπεμψε τῷ δήμῳ) γενέσθαι μυρίους τετρακισχιλίους διακοσίους μ̃. The fullest treatment of this much discussed purge is found in Jacoby [1954] 1968: 3.b (suppl.) 1:462–70, 2:372–81. For the inconsistencies between the versions of Plutarch and Philokhoros, see E. Cohen 1973: 169–70.

107 Repeal by 429: see Beloch 1912–27: 3.1:14, n. 1, citing Aristoph. *Orn.* 1641ff.; Plut. *Perikl.* 37. Jacoby deems it "more likely" that it was annulled after the Sicilian disaster (1954 [1968]: 3.b (suppl.) 2:381 following Müller 1899: 786, 811). In accord: Wolff 1944: 85–86. Cf. Diog. Laert. 2.26: φασὶ γὰρ βουληθέντας Ἀθηναίους διὰ τὸ λειπανδρεῖν συναυξῆσαι τὸ πλῆθος, ψηφίσασθαι γαμεῖν μὲν ἀστὴν μίαν, παιδοποιεῖσθαι δὲ καὶ ἐξ ἑτέρας.

108 Walters (1983: 325–27) has argued that the "decree" of 403/2 was merely a codification of prior law.

109 Thouk. 3.55.3, 63.2, 68.5, 5.32.1; Dem. 59.104–6; Isok. 12.94. Cf. Amit 1973: 75–78; Gawantka 1975: 174–78.

110 *I.G.* II^{2}1; Meiggs and Lewis: no. 94. Although it is sometimes argued (e.g., Davies 1977/78: 107) that this grant was not intended to be implemented (since Samian autonomy on Samos was explicitly protected: lines 12–18), Samians present in Athens were allocated to tribes (and, under a likely restoration, to demes) (lines 33–34); their envoy Eumakhos is invited to *deipnon* as a *politēs* (line 37), not to *xenia,* the usual hospitality for foreign representatives. Cf. Gawantka 1975: 178–97.

111 Osborne 1981–83: 4:210–21.

112 Olynthians: see Suda, s.v. Karanos (Ἀθηναῖοι δὲ τοὺς περισωθέντας [from Olynthos] πολίτας ἐποιήσαντο). Thebans: Todd 1993: 175. Akarnanians: see n. 114. Elaiousans: *I.G.* II^2 228. Cf. *S.E.G.* 15.93. M. Osborne has suggested that "the decree is not so much a grant of citizenship as an assimilation of the status of the Elaiousians to that of kleruchs. Clearly there is no question of their coming to Athens" (1981–83: 2:83). But *klēroukhoi* did come to Athens: for example, shortly before this acceptance of the Elaiousans as *politai*, a large number of Athenian *klēroukhoi* had returned to Athens after being forced out of Thrace by Philip of Macedon (Dem. 6.20). Hansen (1982: 183) has suggested that this group may have included both *politai* and non-*politai.*

113 Hyper. *Athēn.* 32: ἐκπεσόντας αὐτοὺς ὑπεδέξασθε καὶ πολίτας ἐποιήσασθε καὶ τῶν ὑμετέρων ἀγαθῶν πάντων μετέδοτε.

refugees"[114]—the Plataians, for example, are known to have been present in Attika in such profusion that even well into the fourth century they gathered monthly as a recognizable ethnic community at the "cheese market."[115] But divided among the various demes spread throughout Attika,[116] they functioned fully and were recognized fully as *politai*, even in routine litigation.[117]

Massive numbers of new *politai* were admitted during and immediately after the Peloponnesian War, while many prior participants were ousted. After the ouster in 411 of the short-lived oligarchic regime which had limited participation in "public affairs" to "not more than five thousand,"[118] the democratic Assembly admitted many new "citizens," supposedly even some slaves (Andok. 2.23). By 406 the Athenians were accepting any individuals who would serve on board their warships, whereupon numerous men, including some slaves, gained a "share in the *polis*" by fighting at Arginousai.[119] In 405 the decree of Patrokleidēs purported to restore participation in the *politeia* to a complex grouping of persons who previously had been adversely treated, but did so in convoluted language that effectively would have proffered extensive discretion to Athenian jurors and demesmen in confirming *politiai*—and would have justified audacity among would-be claimants to Athenian *politeia.*[120] And after the war, participation in the *politeia* was granted to all who had participated in the advance from Phylē to Piraeus, a

[114] Osborne 1981–83: 3:72, dismissing the possibility of a grant of *politeia* to a number of Akarnanians who had come to Athens in 338/7—despite the clear text of *I.G.* II[2] 237 granting them "the right of *enktesis*, freedom from the metic tax, the judicial privileges and tax liabilities of Athenian citizens, and the *epimeleia* of the Boule and generals," "a status close to that of citizens" (Osborne 1981–83: 2:84).

[115] Lys. 23.6. Cf. Aristophanes (*Batr.* 694) and Hellanikos (*FGrHist* 323a F25).

[116] Dem. 59.104, 7–8: καταvεῖμαι δὲ τοὺς Πλαταιέας εἰς τοὺς δήμους καὶ τὰς φυλάς. Cf. Osborne 1981–83: 2:11–16; Lambert 1993: 115–16. Although MacDowell (1985) is skeptical about the authenticity of this decree, the text is compatible with *I.G.* I[3] 127.33–34 (Samians) and *I.G.* II[2] 10 (see n. 121).

[117] See Chapter 6, p. 170, esp. n. 78.

[118] Thouk. 8.65.3: οὔτε μεθεκτέον τῶν πραγμάτων πλέοσιν ἢ πεντακισχιλίοις. Cf. Thouk. 8.53.1, 3; Aristot. *Ath. Pol.* 29.5. See Rhodes 1972.

[119] Aristoph. *Batr.* 693–94: καὶ γὰρ αἰσχρόν ἐστι τοὺς μὲν ναυμαχήσαντας μίαν | καὶ Πλαταιᾶς εὐθὺς εἶναι κἀντὶ δούλων δεσπότας (cf. 33–34, 191). See Hellanikos, *FGrHist* 323a F25 (Schol. Aristoph. *Batr.* 694): τοὺς συνναυμαχήσαντας δούλους Ἑλλάνικός φησιν ἐλευθερωθῆναι καὶ ἐγγραφέντας ὡς Πλαταιεῖς συμπολιτεύσασθαι αὐτοῖς, διεξιὼν τὰ ἐπὶ Ἀντιγένους τοῦ <πρὸ> Καλλίου. Cf. Xen. *Hell.* 1.6.24; Diod. Sik. 13.97.1.

[120] Andok. 1.77–79. The decree, "usually accepted as a genuine transcript" (Edwards 1995: 177), restored rights as *politai* to a vast multitude, but explicitly excluded many others. "But the fact that only these are explicitly excluded does not prove that the decree covers all other persons who had lost any citizen-rights for any reason" (MacDowell 1962: 114).

critical stage in the restoration of the democracy.[121] Phormisios then made a motion to restrict participation in the *politeia* to landowners, which would (according to a late source) have disenfranchised about five thousand *politai*.[122] Instead of further restriction, however, the Assembly, on Thrasyboulos's motion, accepted as new *politai* all of the metics and slaves who had participated at any stage in the restoration of the democracy, a liberalization ultimately annulled by the courts on the technicality that it had not been previously considered by the Council.[123]

At about the same time, however, an equally extraordinary liberalization was effectuated when the "citizenship law" of Periklēs was renewed on Aristophōn's motion, again limiting participation in the *politeia* to offspring of *astoi*, but with a rider attached by Nikomenēs, specifically forbidding evaluation of the qualifications of those who had been accepted as *politai* before 403/2.[124] In a society lacking archival records of births, deaths, and marriages, and composed of demes where many if not most demesmen had only limited, if any, personal contact with applicants for membership,[125] this limitation on scrutiny insured, with the passage of time, increasingly arbitrary consideration of potential *politai*. By the mid-fourth century, fathers were being rejected as *politai*, while sons were allegedly retained; one brother supposedly might be ousted, while his sibling—a son born to the same mother and to the same father—would be confirmed.[126] Barred from examining relationships preceding the archonship of Eukleidēs, how could the demes knowledgeably resolve cases like that of the appellant in Demosthenes 57 whose

[121] *I.G.* II[2] 10+. 5–6: ἐψηφίσθαι Ἀθηναίοις ἔναι αὐτοῖς καὶ ἐκγόν[οις πολιτεί] | [αν καὶ νε͂μαι αὐτὸς αὐτίκα μάλα ἐς τὰς φυλὰς δέκαχα]. For the reconstruction of this text, see Osborne 1981–83: 2:26–43.

[122] Lys. 34 (Dionysios's introduction): Φορμίσιός τις τῶν συγκατελθόντων μετὰ τοῦ δήμου γνώμην εἰσηγήσατο, τοὺς μὲν φεύγοντας κατιέναι, τὴν δὲ πολιτείαν μὴ πᾶσιν ἀλλὰ τοῖς [τὴν] γῆν ἔχουσι παραδοῦναι. . . . ἔμελλον δὲ τοῦ ψηφίσματος τούτου κυρωθέντος πεντακισχίλιοι σχεδὸν Ἀθηναίων ἀπελαθήσεσθαι τῶν κοινῶν.

[123] The Aristotelian *Ath. Pol.* suggests that the rejection resulted only from the manifestly slavish appearance of some of Thrasyboulos's followers (40.2: ἔνιοι φανερῶς ἦσαν δοῦλοι: cf. Aiskhin. 3.195; Plut. *Mor.* 835f–836)—an anomaly in Attika where *politai*, metics, and slaves were often indistinguishable in appearance. On the homogeneous appearance of the residents of Attika, see Chapter 4, pp. 106–112.

[124] τοὺς δὲ πρὸ Εὐκλείδου ἀνεξετάστους ἀφεῖσθαι (Schol. Aiskhin. 1.39). Cf. Dem. 57.30.

[125] On the limited content of the Athenian state archive, see Preface, n. 19. On personal contact among demesmen, see Chapter 4.

[126] Dem. 57.58: οὗτοι γὰρ ἀδελφῶν ὁμομητρίων καὶ ὁμοπατρίων τῶν μέν εἰσιν ἀπεψηφισμένοι, τῶν δ' οὔ, καὶ πρεσβυτέρων ἀνθρώπων ἀπόρων, ὧν τοὺς υἱεῖς ἐγκαταλελοίπασιν. See Chapter 4, pp. 110–11.

status hinges on the contentious reconstruction of family relationships from almost a century earlier?

By the beginning of the fourth century, however, there was no need—even in appealing to Athenian juries—for ideological pretense that participation in Athenian *politeia* was a privilege reserved exclusively for autochthonous inhabitants of Attika. In court, the son of a woman from Selymbria avers his right to *polititeia* through witnesses testifying that his Athenian father introduced him into his phratry and that he had attended an appropriate school in Attika.[127] In Lysias 9, the Athenian *politēs* Polyainos acknowledges to the jurors his minimal ties to Attika, his alienation from his fellow citizens,[128] and even his contempt for Athenian *politeia.* He has come to Athens only recently[129] and seems to lack any prior familial or personal contact with Attika.[130] If the modest fine imposed on him by the authorities should be upheld, he will no longer be willing to continue as a *politēs* but will depart to a more appreciative land.[131]

But even for *politai* attached to Attika, the potential impermanence of a share in the *politeia*—and the chaotic reality of mid-fourth-century Athenian politics—is suggested by Halimous's balloting on its members: one-eighth of the entire deme membership ousted by vote of their fellows, all but one later restored by the courts.[132] And in 346/5 all 139 demes

[127] P. Oxy. 31.2538 (papyrus fragment written by an unidentified orator). The speaker's father was a merchant who came to Selymbria and became closely associated with a certain Antiphanēs, whose daughter he married and brought to Athens. The editor (J. R. Rea) dates the text to the period of Lysias. The context is unknown.

[128] Although "he is definitely a citizen," he speaks (Lys. 9.5) of consulting with "one of the *politai*"—"as if he were not a citizen himself" (MacDowell 1994: 154).

[129] Cf. 9.4: ἀφικόμενος προπέρυσιν εἰς τὴν πόλιν, οὔπω δύο μῆνας ἐπιδεδημηκὼς κατελέγην στρατιώτης. Cf. 9.8. Reiske's generally accepted emendation of προπέρυσιν for the manuscript's πρότερον reflects the length of time required between imposition of a fine and institution of an action for enforcement.

[130] He claims that his adversaries are relying in their sallies on the jurors' total ignorance of himself (9.2: εἰ μέντοι ὑμᾶς οἴονται δι᾽ ἄγνοιαν ὑπὸ τῶν διαβολῶν πεισθέντας καταψηφιεῖσθαί μου, τοῦτ᾽ ἂν θαυμάσαιμι). Although he asserts in his opening comments that he will respond to his opponents' ad hominem attacks (3: διαβαλλόντων δέ με τῶν ἀντιδίκων, ἀναγκαῖόν ἐστι περὶ πάντων <τὴν> ἀπολογίαν ποιήσασθαι), he actually avoids virtually all personal allusion, and provides no evidence of a prior relationship with Attika.

[131] 9.21: λόγῳ μὲν οὖν περὶ τῆς ἀπογραφῆς ἀγωνίζομαι, ἔργῳ δὲ περὶ πολιτείας. τυχὼν μὲν γὰρ τῶν δικαίων (πιστεύω δὲ τῇ ὑμετέρᾳ γνώμῃ) μείναιμαι ἂν <ἐν> τῇ πόλει· παραχθεὶς δὲ ὑπὸ τῶνδε εἰ ἀδίκως ἁλοίην, ἀποδραίην ἄν. Τίνι γὰρ ἐπαρθέντα ἐλπίδι δεῖ με συμπολιτεύεσθαι; The speech is usually dated to the end of the fifth or the early years of the fourth century (see Blass 1887–98 [1962]: 597–98). On the "small fine," see MacDowell 1994: 154.

[132] Dem. 57. 60: κατηγορῶν δέκα τῶν δημοτῶν ἐξέβαλεν, οὓς ἅπαντας πλὴν ἑνὸς κατεδέξατο τὸ δικαστήριον. Cf. 57.26, 58, 61. I assume here a total deme membership of eighty. But cf. Chapter 4, n. 78.

are known to have evaluated the entitlement of every *politēs*, voting on each individually. Numerous *politai* were ousted from every deme.[133] Yet a few years later, after military defeat at Khairōneia in 338, the Assembly, on Hypereidēs's motion, swiftly granted full rights as Athenians to all metics, and freedom to all slaves residing in Attika.[134] By explicitly restoring a share in the *politeia* to all of the so-called *apepsēphismenoi*[135]—the popular term for persons who had once been recognized as *politai* but subsequently ousted—the Assembly effectively reversed the massive reductions of only a few years earlier.[136] But another *metabolē* was to follow: the Assembly's action was reversed by the courts as "unconstitutional,"[137] but not before the new *politai* had "tasted" empowerment,[138] as the Athenian aphorism pithily put it.[139] Thus a fresh crop of former *politai* was created. But as *astoi* they retained, for themselves and for their offspring, a share in local society—and potential future participation in the *polis.*

Attikismos: Becoming Part of Attika[140]

Who then were the *astoi*? In a society almost entirely free of legalistic vocabulary and formalistic delineation,[141] where the absence of centralized registers resulted in "the functional incapacity of the Attic bureau-

[133] Dem. 57.2: πολλῶν γὰρ ἐξεληλαμένων δικαίως ἐκ πάντων τῶν δήμων.

[134] Hyper. fr. 27–39 (Kenyon). Lykourg. 1.41 (τὸν δῆμον ψηφισάμενον τοὺς μὲν δούλους ἐλευθέρους, τοὺς δὲ ξένους Ἀθηναίους); Dem. 26.11 (ὅτε γὰρ Ὑπερείδης ἔγραψε, τῶν περὶ Χαιρώνειαν ἀτυχημάτων τοῖς Ἕλλησι γενομένων . . . εἶναι τοὺς ἀτίμους ἐπιτίμους, ἵν᾽ ὁμονοοῦντες ἅπαντες ὑπὲρ τῆς ἐλευθερίας προθύμως ἀγωνίζωνται).

[135] On these *apepsēphismenoi*, see, for example, Isai. 12 (Hyp.): τὸν δὲ ἀποψηφισθέντα ὑπὸ τῶν δημοτῶν τῆς πολιτείας μὴ μετέχειν, τοῖς δὲ ἀδίκως ἀποψηφισθεῖσιν ἔφεσιν εἰς τὸ δικαστήριον εἶναι.

[136] The resolution was sweepingly inclusive: ὅπως πρῶτον μὲν μυριάδας πλείους ἢ δεκάπεντε τοὺς <δούλους τοὺς> ἐκ τῶν ἔργων τῶν ἀργυρείων καὶ τοὺς κατὰ τὴν ἄλλην χώραν, ἔπειτα τοὺς ὀφείλοντας τῷ δημοσίῳ καὶ τοὺς ἀτίμους καὶ τοὺς ἀπεψηφισμένους καὶ τοὺς μετοίκους. Hyper. fr. 29 (Kenyon), preserved in Suda.

[137] Dem. 26.10–11; Lykourg. 1.41; Dio Khrys. 15.21.

[138] For implementation of Hypereidēs's decree, see Mossé 1973: 72–74; Clerc 1893: 223. Diller argues—from the absence of reported protests against the repeal of the decree—that the reform never actually took effect (1937: 112; cf. 148), but the paucity of surviving evidence renders this argument *e silentio* unconvincing.

[139] ἄρτι μῦς πίττης γεύεται (Dem. 50.26).

[140] Ἀττικισμός: "an attachment to Athens." See Thouk. 3.64.5 (charged against the Plataians, who became Athenian *politai*); 4.133 (the Thespians). Cf. Alkiphr. 2.4; Cic. *Att.* 4.19.1. At least in its verbal form, the word appears to have been "in ordinary use" (Hornblower 1991: 1:455).

[141] In Athens "there was relatively little technical legal vocabulary and the language of the street was itself the language of the law" (Todd and Millett 1990: 17). Cf. Todd 1993: 61, n. 14.

cracy to identify its polis inhabitants,"[142] the *astoi* as a group were recognizable, in Athenian cognitive terms, not by crystalline technical definition, but by their antithesis to the *xenoi*, the outsiders.[143] As "insiders," the *astoi* could not include those foreigners who had resided in Attika only for a relatively brief period, or individuals whose activities—such as overt and continuing involvement with their land of origin—might be inconsistent with assimilation into Attic life.[144] "Many" metics, according to Xenophon, were blatantly non-Hellenic and, hence, necessarily outsiders—"Lydians and Phrygians and Syrians and every other sort of *barbaroi*."[145] But a great variety of persons permanently domiciled in Attika would be recognizable as *astoi*: most, if not all, of the *politai*;[146] some of those registered as metics; the offspring of *politai* who had not been born "in accordance with the laws" (e.g., the so-called *nothoi*);[147] the scions of *astoi* who had been rejected when evaluated by their demes (or not presented);[148] the *apepsēphismenoi* who had been, and might

Specialized business terminology was also limited: see E. Cohen 1992: 63–66, 111–12; Korver 1934: 28–39.

[142] Scafuro 1994: 182. Despite the "striking" profusion of lists of individuals maintained at Athens for various purposes (see Chapter 4, n. 24)—including a register of prostitutes (Aiskhin. 1.119)—no master list of individual *politai* or of metics was ever kept (see Chapter 4, n. 26).

[143] Even modern legal systems characterized by systematically inclusive definitions are often unable to categorize phenomena within verbal formulae. Cf. Justice Stewart's classic description of "pornography": "Under the First and Fourteenth Amendments [to the U.S. Constitution] criminal laws are constitutionally limited to hard-core pornography. I shall not attempt further to define the kinds of material I understand to be embraced within that shorthand description; and perhaps I could never succeed in intelligibly doing so. But I know it when I see it." Concurring Opinion (p. 6) in *Jacobellis v. Ohio,* 378 U.S. 184, 84 S. Ct. 1676 (1964). Aristotle similarly recognizes the practical impossibility of inclusively systematic definition of *politai*. Quoting Gorgias of Leontini (καθάπερ ὅλμους εἶναι τοὺς ὑπὸ τῶν ὁλμοποιῶν πεποιημένους, οὕτω καὶ Λαρισαίους τοὺς ὑπὸ τῶν δημιουργῶν πεποιημένους), he draws a conclusion similar to that of Justice Stewart (εἰ γὰρ μετεῖχον κατὰ τὸν ῥηθέντα διορισμὸν τῆς πολιτείας, ἦσαν πολῖται). *Pol.* 1275b28–32.

[144] Although Todd defines *proxenos* as an individual who "continues to reside in his native polis, and to further the interests there of expatriates or visitors from the community which he represents" (1993: 394), by the fourth century many *proxenoi* appear to have come from other jurisdictions to represent foreign interests in Attika (cf. Bekker 1.298.27; Whitehead 1977: 13–14; Baslez 1984: 120–22). Even if these individuals were domiciled in Attika and involved themselves in Attic life, their continued ties with their land of origin might have marked them as *xenoi* in Athenian eyes.

[145] Λυδοὶ καὶ Φρύγες καὶ Σύροι καὶ ἄλλοι παντοδαποὶ βάρβαροι· πολλοὶ γὰρ τοιοῦτοι τῶν μετοίκων. *Por.* 2.3.

[146] For *politai* having no territorial relationship with Attika, see pp. 53–54 and n. 36.

[147] For the significant number of *nothoi* at Athens (*pace* Ogden 1996: 157–63), see Patterson 1990: 60, n. 80; Sealey 1984: 113–17; Bushala 1969: 71; Rudhardt 1962: 43–44; Harrison 1968–71: 1:14; Erdmann 1934: 111; Beauchet [1897] 1969; 1:100–103; Hruza 1892–94: 2:74. The assertion has already been made that "*nothoi*, who were not members of a phratry, could be Athenian citizens" (Harris 1996: 126, n. 14; cf. MacDowell 1976b).

[148] Cf. the young boy (παιδάριον) characterized as an ἀστός at Dem. 53.16.

again become, *politai*; and potentially many others—freedmen (*apeleutheroi*), the specially privileged "*isoteleis*,"[149] the shadowy *atimoi*,[150] some of the *proxenoi* (or their offspring), individuals possessing *egktēsis*,[151] possibly even slaves *khōris oikountes* and public servants (*dēmosioi*).[152] "Outsiders" or their descendants, over an extended period, might come to be recognized as *astoi* through involvement in the community and in communal activities—participation that was critical to self-identification even among the *politai*.[153] Because such participation—in economic, military, religious, and social functions—was generally open to all the inhabitants of Attika without regard to political categorization, personal involvement (and hence absorption into the community) was largely a matter of the realization of individual inclination over an extended period.

The situation of metics is illustrative. Not every *xenos* present in Attika was a metic, nor was every metic a *xenos*. At any given time, many foreigners would be briefly and temporarily in Athens for business or tourism or for other purposes, but only those persons who stayed for an extended period were required to enroll as metics and to pay the *metoikion* tax.[154] Among those metics permanently ensconced at Athens, however, many individuals (or their offspring) ultimately became fully involved in Athenian life, and physically and culturally indistinguishable

[149] Harp., s.v. *isotelēs; I.G.* II^2 360.19–21; Xen. *Por.* 4.12.

[150] *Politai* who had suffered *atimia*, "conventionally glossed by means of the English terms 'disfranchisement' or 'loss of citizen rights'" (Todd 1993: 142). Cf. Andok. 1.77–79; Hansen 1973; Davidson 1997: 251–52. But "the rules governing (*atimia*) have not yet been clearly explained; *atimia* remains one of the most difficult topics in the study of Athenian law" (MacDowell 1978: 74–75).

[151] On non-*politai* holding the right to own land in Attika, see Pečirka 1966: 68–70, 80–82. Cf. *I.G.* II^2 351, 505.7–41, and 624.11–20.

[152] Hence, the separate requirement of "freedom" for youths being evaluated for a share in the *politeia*. See n. 82. Slaves appear generally to have been excluded from the *astoi-xenoi* complementary polarity. Cf. Thouk. 6.27.2: εἴ τις ἄλλο τι οἶδεν ἀσέβημα γεγενημένον, μηνύειν ἀδεῶς τὸν βουλόμενον καὶ ἀστῶν καὶ ξένων καὶ δούλων.

[153] Thus Scafuro notes "an essential feature of the system of identification in Athens: that witnessed participation in communal events as a function of being born Athenian was perceived by Athenians as tantamount to 'being Athenian'" (1994: 158).

[154] The prevailing view (see Whitehead 1977: 9–10) holds that foreigners had entirely open access to Athens but were required to register as metics after a relatively short sojourn—without regard to the foreigner's subjective domiciliary intent. Although direct evidence is late and somewhat contradictory (Pollux, Aristophanēs of Byzantium [fr. 38]), Gauthier has revived the view that enrollment was requisite after a presence of only one month (1972: 122; 1988: 28–29). Lévy, however, argues that metics included only immigrants permanently settled in Attika who had the intention to establish domicile and had received explicit permission to do so (1988: 53–61).

from the mass of *politai*.[155] They participated in the numerous social groups whose broad memberships were not limited to *politai*.[156] They received local honors, paid local taxes, and performed deme liturgies—all of which appear to have been imposed or awarded without regard to political status.[157] Present throughout Attica,[158] metics actually lived in the demes where they were enrolled,[159] in contrast to the *politai* who frequently had almost no continuing contact with the deme territory to which they were hereditarily attached.[160] This physical presence facilitated metics' participation in the social and religious activities of the individual demes. Paralleling their access to the central Panathenaic ritual, the procession at the City Dionysia and other *polis*-wide religious ceremonies,[161] metics frequented deme religious shrines and participated in the propitiation of local deities.[162] They served in the armed forces,[163] sometimes in positions of high rank.[164] Because the Athenian military

[155] On the homogeneous appearance of much of the Athenian population, see Chapter 4, pp. 106–9.

[156] For the wide variety of such groupings, sometimes open to women and even to slaves, see Osborne 1990: esp. 275–76. Cf. Ober 1993: 129–39, esp. 136; Murray 1993: 199; Elverson 1988.

[157] Ikarian *chorēgoi*, for example, are memorialized entirely without demotic identification (*I.G.* II² 1178. 8–9, 3094, 3095, 3098, 3099). Similarly, in the deme of Eleusis in the mid-fourth century, a non-*politēs* (the Theban Damasias) is attested as providing both the boys' and men's dithyramb (*I.G.* II² 1186. 11–13). Other Thebans resident in Eleusis (*I.G.* II² 1185–86) and some *politai* (see *I.G.* II² 1187. 16–17, 1188. 29–30) received exemption from taxes, again without differentiation of personal position. The *egktētikon* levy (a tax on landed property within a deme) was imposed without differentiation between demesmen and other residents or property owners (see *I.G.* II² 1214. 26–28). Several fourth-century inscriptions attest to deme honors granted to nondemesmen: *I.G.* II² 1204 (Akharnian honored by Lower Lamptrai, lines 4–17); *I.G.* II² 1176+ (two Lamptrian demesmen and one from Pelekēs honored by Peiraios, lines 30–33 Kirchner); *I.G.* II² 1181 (Erkhian honored by Sounion).

[158] See Chapter 4, pp. 122–23.

[159] See Chapter 4, n. 90. Cf. Gauthier 1972: 117–18, 1988: 28–29; Whitehead 1977: 72–75.

[160] See Chapter 4, pp. 113–20.

[161] See Wohl 1996: 30, n. 13; Maurizio 1998; Hansen 1989a: 17–21; 1991: 63. Participation by male and female metics in the Dionysia: Dēm. Phal. *FRGrH* 228 F 5 (see Sourvinou-Inwood 1994: 271, n. 9). Certain high religious offices, however, were reserved for *politidēs*: see Chapter 1, pp. 46–48.

[162] Deme calendars ("*fasti*") specifically provide for the admission of local non-*politai* to many, although perhaps not all, of the cults functioning within their territories. See Pollitt 1961; Daux 1963, 1983; Saunders 1972: 144–45. The only surviving document explicitly dealing with access by non-*politai* to deme rites specifically authorizes the metics of the Skambōnid deme to participate in religious sacrifices. *I.G.* I³ 244, C, lines 4–10, esp. 7–9: καὶ] τὸς μετοίκ̣[ος λαχ]ε̄ν. Cf. Clerc 1893: 249.

[163] See Xen. *Por.* 2.2–3; Thouk. 2.13.7, 31.1–2; 3.16.1, 4.90; Lykourg. 1.16. Cf. Gerhardt [1933] 1935: 42–44; Diller 1937: 134.

[164] Metics serving as trierarchs: Kallaiskhros Siphnios (*I.G.* II² 1609.27) and his son Stēsileidēs (1623.204–5, 251–52, 268–75; 1631.435); Pasiōn, responsible for five triremes before obtaining Athenian *politeia* (Dem. 45.85; Davies 1971: 11672 IV; Trevett 1992: 5–6, 21–22); the Egyptian Pamphilos who commanded the trireme financed by Meidias (MacDowell 1990: 382–83); Hēr-

was mobilized on a deme basis,[165] metics (who actually lived in the deme territory (n. 159) would likely have contributed more to unit cohesiveness than the many *politai* who had exclusively hereditary relationships to the deme and tenuous, if any, civilian contact with the territory's actual inhabitants.[166]

The extensiveness of metics' involvement in deme functions had long ago led some modern scholars, including Wilamowitz, to conclude that metics, as such, must have been full members of their demes.[167] Yet—although many metics were clearly cognizable as *astoi*, and their male offspring were thus eligible to "share in the polis" as *politai*—actual acceptance of an individual into a deme, and hence into the *polis,*[168] required an affirmative vote of the demesmen. As we have seen (pp. 68–69), deme balloting might well be capricious. Indeed, the absence of a technical definition of *astoi* would have facilitated subjective or politicized evaluation of individual applicants, complementing demesmen's capacity—as a unit of the absolutely sovereign Athenian people[169]—to make arbitrary decisions that ignored legalistic guidelines and traditions.[170] Some demesmen might have been reluctant to allocate to

---

akleidēs Erythraios (*I.G.* II^2 1491.26, 1492.106); Antimachos of Khios (*I.G.* II^2 40.10, 1604.79; Jordan 1975: 90; Osborne 1981: 155. Some scholars reject this evidence on the a priori denial "that in the fourth century the state would have permitted non-citizens even to volunteer for the liturgy" (Clark 1990: 66). Cf. Gabrielsen 1994: 61.

[165] See Lys. 16.14 (συλλεγέντων τῶν δημοτῶν πρὸ τῆς ἐξόδου). Cf. Whitehead 1977: 83. Raising of naval crews by deme: Whitehead 1986a: 258.

[166] In most Greek armies, men from the same localities served together (Hanson 1991: 89). At Athens, as Lysias implies (16.14), men from a single deme territory fought together. Cf. *I.G.* II^2 218, 287, 351, 360, 505, 545; *Hesperia* 2 (1933): 396–97 (no. 16). See Mossé [1962] 1979: 168; Wilamowitz 1887: 215 and n. 2, 216–17. *Contra:* Maffi 1973: 950–51.

[167] Wilamowitz 1887: 213–15. In accord: Hommel 1932: 1433. Francotte ([1910] 1964) argued that a hierarchical arrangement of statuses permitted metics' progressive and eventually total integration into Athenian life.

[168] "An Athenian citizen was an Athenian citizen because, both logically and chronologically prior to that, he was a demesman of Alopeke or Themakos or wherever it might be." Whitehead 1986a: 258. There is no evidence to establish linkage between membership in a phratry and participation in the *politeia*: see n. 62.

[169] For this *kyrieia*, see Antiph. 3.1.1; Andok. 2.19; Aristoph. *Hipp.* 42; Dem. 20.107; 59.4, 88; Xen. *Hell.* 1.7.12. For the Athenian demes as microcosms of the overall state, "miniature *poleis*" whose functioning mirrored the parent unit's relationship to Attika as a whole, see Chapter 4, n. 107. Yet the rule of law ("the laws," οἱ νόμοι) is also a paramount Athenian principle (Aiskhin. 3.6; Dem. 25.20; Hyper. *Euxen.* 5): litigants on occasion even alleged the primacy of the *politai* acting through the courts over the *politai* acting in assembly (Dem. 57.56; cf. Dem. 19.297; Aiskhin. 3.3–5).

[170] Even arbitrary determinations were generally not subject to appeal: unsuccessful candidates had no right of reference to any other body unless rejected as unfree (see n. 82)—although they might ultimately seek a share in the *politeia* through naturalization decrees by the Assembly (but see my subsequent discussion and n. 173). Candidates accepted in blatant disregard of the law's

the sons of non-*politai* a participation in the "windfall profits [that] could legitimately be shared out among the citizen body" (Todd 1993: 183). Yet in considering youths for membership, the demesmen also would have been influenced by certain pragmatic realities of Attic life that would have encouraged a liberal effectuation of the guidelines: the difficulty of determining individual status without archival records and often without personal knowledge of applicants' backgrounds;[171] the obfuscation resulting from the recurrent politicized changes in the composition of the *politai* (see the previous section); the effects of legislation intended to discourage strife among the residents of Attika, including the restriction on inquiries into personal statuses prior to Eukleidēs; and the impact of factors not articulated in formal legal texts, including bribery (apparently pervasive in certain demes)[172] and the influence of personal enmities, friendships, dependencies, and other localized social and economic considerations. The official requirement of *astoi* parentage was, of course, not meaningless: for Xenophon's "Lydians and Phrygians and Syrians," *politeia* was unattainable, except through acts of naturalization requiring approval of the Assembly. Significantly, such special legislation was in fact obtained almost exclusively by foreign potentates, wealthy former slaves, bankers with businesses built on overseas relations, and other persons manifestly outside the local culture, and hence unable to claim *astoi* progenitors or, in many cases, even to present themselves to the demes in their youth[173]—a phenomenon suggesting that persons acculturated in Attika had no need to pursue this extraordinary avenue to a share in the *politeia*.

---

guidelines and procedures would, at least theoretically, be vulnerable to the legal challenge of the *graphē xenias*. But the courts too functioned on a highly politicized and often arbitrary basis (see Todd 1993: 151, n. 8).

[171] Many—perhaps most—of the Athenian *politai* living in a particular area were actually affiliated with demes that were located elsewhere and often had only the most attenuated continuing contact with their own deme. See Chapter 4. On the lack of archival records, see Preface, n. 19 and Chapter 4, n. 26.

[172] Some demes were infamous for repetitive liberality in their acceptance of new *politai*, even of former slaves. Hence, for example, the saying, "today a slave, tomorrow a demesman of Sounion!" (see Chapter 4, n. 148) or the frequent pejorative references to the "easy" acceptances by the demesmen of Potamos (Harp., s.v. Ποταμός—ἐκωμῳδοῦντο δὲ ὡς ῥαδίως δεχόμενοι τοὺς παρεγγράπτους, ὡς ἄλλοι τε δηλοῦσι καὶ Μένανδρος ἐν Διδύμαις). On the extensive evidence for the prevalence of bribery throughout the Athenian political and legal systems, see Harvey 1985.

[173] The "largest group" of recipients were "persons who normally reside abroad and who are likely to continue to do so" (Osborne 1981–83: 4:187). Of the relatively few residents of Attika who obtained grants of *politeia*, ex-slaves, especially bankers, were disproportionately represented (Davies 1981: 65–66).

The difficulty of confirming the family history of even the most prominent leaders of the *polis* suggests the impossibility of demesmen's factually evaluating the genealogical qualifications of individual applicants.[174] Demosthenes, for example, frequently attributes foreign and even slave origin to political opponents,[175] and in turn his adversaries challenge his own civic status.[176] Although modern scholars peremptorily insist on the genealogical purity of this quintessentially Athenian patriot,[177] Demosthenes' mother was not a *politis*. In fact, his checkered family history illustrates the usefulness to even well-established families of requiring only *astoi* (not *politai*) as progenitors. Although his father appears successfully and systematically to have evaded the sizable taxes that would have been due on his considerable assets,[178] Demosthenes' paternal origins and background otherwise appear unexceptional.[179] But his mother, Kleoboulē, was the daughter of a Scythian woman[180] and of an Athenian father, Gylōn, who had been condemned to death for betraying Nymphaion in the Crimea.[181] Although these "allegations are circumstantial, it is a measure of their substantial truth that Aphobos could claim, and Demosthenes admitted, that Gylōn had been a public debtor" (Davies 1971: 121). As a defaultor on financial obligations to the Athenian state, impeached and convicted,[182] Gylōn would have been deprived of his political rights—that is, those of a *politēs*—but not thereby of popular

[174] For imputation of alien or slave origin to Athenian political leaders, and the implications of such charges, see Chapter 4, pp. 111–12.

[175] See, *inter alios*, Demosthenes' remarks about Aiskhinēs (18.129–30) and Meidias (Dem. 21.149ff.). Cf. Dem. 22.61, 68; *Letters* 3.29.

[176] See Chapter 4, p. 112.

[177] "Aiskhines labels Demosthenes a Skythian, and because we know that Demosthenes is a practicing politician we readily dismiss that charge" (Todd 1994: 126).

[178] Demosthenes *père* systematically kept his extensive property "invisible" (ἀφανής) and avoided the performance of even the smallest liturgy. See Korver 1942: 21–22; Ste. Croix 1953: 55; E. Cohen 1992: 200–201.

[179] His paternal grandfather can be identified as the Δημομέλ[ης] who in 421 was the architect of a bridge at Eleusis (*I.G.* I³ 79. 16–17). Plutarch, quoting Theopompos, terms his father τῶν καλῶν καὶ ἀγαθῶν ἀνδρῶν (*Dem.* 4.1).

[180] Aiskhin. 2.78, 3.172; Dein. 1.15. See Hunter 1989. Cf. the Selymbrian mother of the speaker/putative *politēs* in P. Oxy. 31.2538; the Thracian mother of Menestheus, the Athenian general whose father was the famous Iphikratēs (Dem. 23. 129; Anaxandridēs fr. 42 [K-A]).

[181] See Dem. 27; Hyper. 1.28.1–3; Aiskhin. 3.171–72; Plut. *Mor.* 844a; *Dem.* 4.2. Cf. Gernet 1918. Gylōn had served as phrouarch at Nymphaion, then under Athenian control, some time between 410 and 405 (Meritt, Wade-Gery, and McGregor 1939–53: 1:527–28).

[182] Aiskhinēs terms him a φύγας ἀπ' εἰσαγγελίας (3.171). For the process of *eisangelia* and its implications, see Hansen 1975, 1980; Rhodes 1979. Davies finds it "a reasonable enough assumption that an original death sentence was later commuted to a fine after 403" (1971: 121). For *atimia* resulting from failure to pay an obligation to the state, cf. Dem. 59.6, and n. 150.

recognition as an *astos*. And it is this standing as a "local" person that his daughter, Kleoboulē, Demosthenes' mother, confirmed by leaving the Black Sea area, coming to Athens as a young girl, marrying (as did her sister) into an established Athenian family, and undertaking—for many years prior to Demosthenes' presentation to the Paianian demesmen—the substantial roles in family and community activities detailed in Demosthenes 27 through 32.[183] Although Kleoboulē could not claim to be the offspring of two *astoi*,[184] Demosthenes was. With a panoply of established *politai* as guardians and with the financial capacity to facilitate his acceptance, he would likely have roused no special attention (decades after his grandfather's disgrace) in qualifying as a demesman, and therefore as a *politēs*. Years later, now controversial, he is attacked by his political opponents for his impure origins. But partisan contumely in the Athenian courts, and not a successful prosecution for *xenias*, was the limit of his exposure under the prevailing Athenian law requiring of a *politēs* only parentage from two *astoi*.[185]

In no society, however, are such litigational conflicts reflective of the mundane reality of the norm. Routinely, male offspring of *astoi* would have been presented to demesmen, and routinely accepted. Those blatantly unqualified—the progeny of irregular marital arrangements, the offspring of the manifestly alien—would seldom apply: their parents would be deterred by the normative and punitive power of the laws, by

[183] For Kleoboulē's deep (and independent) immersion in local arrangements, see Hunter 1989. For her sister Philia's marriage to Dēmokharēs, son of Lakhēs, see Dem. 28.3; *I.G.* II^2 6737a, p. 891.

[184] The renowned Aspasia similarly was of foreign birth, and it is often assumed that this would have prevented her—after the enactment of the Periklean "citizenship law"—from entry into "a fully valid Athenian marriage" with Periklēs (see Henry 1995: 13) and would have kept Periklēs' son from acceptance as a *politēs* (therefore necessitating the special legislation described at Plut. *Perikl.* 37). In fact, Aspasia's life appears to have been similar to Kleoboulē's—uninterrupted residence in Attika from girlhood, with a sister who (like Philia) resided in Athens as the wife of an Athenian (see Bicknell 1982: 240–50). She may well have qualified as an *astē* under Periklēs' decree, and her offspring might have been eligible for enrollment as *politai*, provided that they met the remaining guidelines and were approved by their demesmen (although all such conjectures are hazardous because our knowledge of procedures in the Athenian demes and courts is derived almost entirely from fourth-century material). In any event, there is no clear evidence that Aspasia actually was the mother of Periklēs' son or that she was married to Periklēs κατὰ τοὺς νόμους (Henry 1995: 13–15; Schaps 1998b: 174, n. 66).

[185] Demosthenes himself is said to have married a Samian woman (Plut. *Dem.* 15.4), a report fortified by Demosthenes' lifelong relationship with his "companion" and representative, the Samian Aristiōn (Harp., s.v. Ἀριστίων). For efforts to identify this Σαμία as the daughter of an Athenian *klērouch* on Samos (and to deny the existence of two sons attributed to this Samian woman), see Blass [1887–98] 1962: 3.1:129; Davies 1971: 138–39. Cf. Aiskhin. 3.162; Golden 1990: 145.

the deterrent strength of community standards, by the organizational aura of the individual demes, and by public ethos personally internalized. For most residents of Attika, most of the time, societal processes appear to have run smoothly: despite the redistribution of political and economic benefits pursuant to the various *metabolai* of the fourth century, historians have frequently noted the striking social stability of classical Athens, the almost complete absence of the "civil strife that tore apart many Greek states in the late fifth and fourth centuries,"[186] an equanimity wholly incompatible with the standard modern conceptualization of Athens as a closed society that denied any possibility of political integration to the tens of thousands of free persons in Attika who were not of autochthonous stock but had been permanently resident, often for generations. Politicized competition among the inhabitants of Attika for participation in the perquisites of power made revolution and cataclysmic upheaval alien to fourth-century Athens.

[186] Ober 1989: 308. Cf. Lintott (1982: 179), who notes how "the rest of Greece was plagued by revolution and counter-revolution" in the fourth century prior to the Makedonian conquest.

✦ 3 ✦

An Ancient Construct: The Athenian Nation

> And I will plant them upon their land, and they shall no more be plucked up out of their land which I have given them, saith the Lord thy God.[1]
>
> Amos 9.15

> A national identity connects a group of people to a particular geographical place.
>
> D. Miller, *On Nationality*, p. 25

THE EXISTENCE of ethnic groups in antiquity has long been acknowledged.[2] Yet until the relatively recent abandonment by anthropologists of the assumption that "nations" are "cultural products of relatively recent historical processes,"[3] scholars seldom recognized ancient ethnic groups as "nations." But as academic definition of a "nation" has moved from racially based "essentialism" through economically oriented "instrumentalism" to the currently prevailing "subjectivism,"[4] many past "ethnic groups" have been recognized as manifesting the characteristics now accepted as definitive of modern "nations."[5] For both ancient and modern

ונטעתים על אדמתם
ולא ינתשו עוד
מעל אדמתם אשר נתתי להם
אמר יהוה אלהיך

[2] See Weber [1922] 1968: 389. J. M. Hall surveys early studies of ethnic identity in antiquity (1997: 4–16). Cf. Goudrian 1988: 8–13, 1992; Barth 1969: 11 and 13ff.

[3] Danforth 1995: 15. Cf. Gellner 1964: 169; 1983: 8–14; Smith 1986: 69; Shennan 1989: 14.

[4] "Ethnicity [is] a subjective sense of loyalty based on imagined origins and parentage rather than something to be measured by objectively visible present cultural criteria or historical facts" (Romanucci-Ross and de Vos 1995: 13). Cf. Introduction, pp. 3–5, esp. n. 5.

[5] See Kemper 1991: 7. Cf. Armstrong 1982; Mukhopadhyay [1876] 1969. However, nations, in the sense of self-recognized ethnic groups, should not be confused with "nation-states" (sovereign units whose political and cultural boundaries coincide): see Smith 1981; Connor 1978.

peoples, the creation and perpetuation of a sense of national identity have been generally accompanied by the creation and perpetuation of origin tales set in historical fabrications that establish or reinforce a group's claim to its land[6]: in creating a sense of ethnic identification, emergent nations characteristically claim "to be 'born of' and indissolubly linked to a bounded territory and a particular history."[7] Ethnic theorists thus would anticipate—if an Athenian nation had actually developed in Attika in classical times—the parallel development of origin myths strengthening this nation's claim to have been "'born of' and indissolubly linked" to the land of Attika.[8] And so it happened. As Attika moved from its earlier division among separate villages ("demes"), each in size and function comparable with typical classical *poleis*,[9] toward the far more complex "imagined society" described in this book, nation-building tales emerged. Legends of individual "earthborn" chieftains ("kings") and traditions of a relatively recent mixture of non-Hellenic newcomers with the original non-Athenian Pelasgian inhabitants of Attika were transmuted into stories claiming that the Athenians, as a whole, were "autochthonous"—descendants individually and literally of progenitor(s) "born from the earth" (*gēgenēs*) of Athens. Paradoxically, these tales of autochthony—of Erikhthonios, the first Athenian, born from the Attic soil on which Hēphaistos (pursuing the Virgin Goddess Athēna) had spilled his sperm,[10] of Erekhtheus, Thēseus, and Iōn—the "historical" bases for Athenian claims of common origin and homogeneity of population, appear only after the relatively late changes (*metabolai*) described in Chapter 2 that transformed the Athenians into a diversified society of variant origins. While the Athenian-based originators of literary and scientific history were first providing the world with

[6] See Connor 1993: 194–95; Gellner 1983: 48; Geertz 1983: 259. Cf. Eriksen 1993: 12; Tambiah 1989: 335; Fishman 1977: 17; Keyes 1976: 205–6.

[7] Handler 1988: 154. For Hellenic antiquity, cf. Gehrke 1995: 184, n. 49; Nielsen forthcoming; Malkin forthcoming. The Romany (the "Gipsies" of Europe) appear to be the prime exception to this territorial focus: see de Vos 1995: 20.

[8] I use myth in its basic notation of a "story" (*mythos*) that has political, moral, and social significance to a particular group. For the relationships and distinctions among myth, ritual, and folktale, see, for example, Tyrrell and Brown: 1991: 3–13; Kirk 1970: ch. 1. Cf. Nilsson 1951: 12–15, 49–64; Saxonhouse 1986: 253, n. 2. For the relation between myth and history, see Hall 1989: 62–69. Cf. Hdt. 7.204 (linkage between Leōnidas and his mythical ancestor Hēraklēs); Ducat 1975 (reworking of mythic themes relating to Rhegion).

[9] On villages in Attika, see Chapter 1, n. 72; Chapter 4, nn. 93ff.

[10] See Eratosthenēs, *Catasterisms* 13; Hyginos, *Astronomika* 2, 13, p. 446 (Eur. fr. 925 Nauck^2), *Fabulae* 166. See Robertson 1985: 272; Cook 1940, 3: 218–23; Parker 1987: 193–95.

serious historiography, and natural historians were first offering rational explanations for the material universe, the Athenians were now promulgating for themselves a supernatural, and inherently incredible, ethnic origin.

Foundation tales of alleged historicity are commonplace among ancient and modern ethnic groups. The Japanese origin myth applies to an entire archipelago sharing a single nationality.[11] Swiss foundation myths center on William Tell and Gessler.[12] In New Zealand, an emergent Maori nationalism, on the basis of traditional art forms, now proclaims a unitary and indigenous ancestry.[13] For millennia, Israel's claim to the Holy Land has been buttressed by biblical passages narrating the sale of Beersheva to Abraham, and the conquest of Jerusalem by King David.[14] The Akhaian League of the Hellenistic period, a collective of *poleis* located in the Peloponnesos, "was founded on the putative notion of ethnic homogeneity, which inevitably requires the invention—or, at least, reordering—of a historical pedigree that might serve to justify the present."[15] Earlier groups in Hellenic antiquity credited the land itself with the literal creation of their founders.[16] Thus the first Boiotians were said to have arisen from the very earth, created by Cadmus's sowing of dragon's teeth into the "motherland" of Boiōtia.[17] An Arkadian tradition regarded its first settler, Pelasgos, as having been born directly from the soil.[18] Argos claimed that Panoptēs was earthborn.[19] In Plato's *Republic*, the ideal community's cohesion and homogeneity are explicitly dependent on its inhabitants' false belief, purposefully inculcated by the law-

[11] De Vos and Wagatsuma 1995: 265, 289.

[12] See Steinberg 1976. Cf. Smith 1991: 19–42.

[13] Schwimmer 1992: 70–71. Cf. Schwimmer 1990.

[14] In 1948, Israel's founding Declaration proclaimed not the establishment of a new nation, but the "re-establishment of the Jewish state," "in other words the re-establishment of a nation-state ceded to the Israelites by divine covenant, a state that reached its apogee under David and Solomon" (*Chronicle of Higher Education*; Nov. 21, 1997, p. A12).

[15] Morgan and Hall 1996: 165.

[16] Cf. the primordial, creative function of Gaia in Hesiod's *Theogony,* 117ff. Aristophanes, in Plato's *Symposion,* finds the Earth to be the source of the human female: τὸ μὲν ἄρρεν ἦν τοῦ ἡλίου τὴν ἀρχὴν ἔκγονον, τὸ δὲ θῆλυ τῆς γῆς (190b1–2).

[17] Pl., *Laws* 663. Cf. Edwards 1979; Vian 1963: chs. 2, 3, 11.

[18] As Rosivach has shown (1987: 305–6), the concept of an earthborn Pelasgos is attested no earlier than Ephoros, a fourth-century historian who expanded on texts of Hesiod and Asios. See Hesiod, fr. 160 (Merkelbach/West) (incorporating Apollod. *Bibl.* 2.1.1, 3.8.1; Serv. *Aen.* 2.84). Cf. Paus. 2.1.4–6 (= Asios, fr. 8K). In other material, Pelasgos is variously identified as the son of Niobē, Triopas, Phorōneus, Argos, or Inakhos.

[19] Aiskhyl. *Prom.* 567, 677; *Iket.* 305; Akousilaos *FGrHist* 2.27. Panoptēs is elsewhere variously identified as the son of Inakhos, Agēnōr, or Arestōr.

giver, that their precursors were not born of human parents but fashioned in the earth itself.[20] In the sixteenth century, the newly independent Dutch Republic went further: to confirm their autochthonous origins, the Dutch attributed to a distant folk hero and his followers, ancestors of the sixteenth-century inhabitants, not only original residence in the land but (through their legendary building of dikes against the North Sea) the actual "creation" of "Batavia," the territory of the northern Netherlands.[21]

Although such narratives are generally rejected by outside commentators as transparent fabrications, nationalistic proponents often insist on the absolute historical truthfulness of even the most farfetched fictions connecting their people and their land.[22] These constructions often lie at the heart of ethnic traditions, institutions, and prejudices—and their close study can sometimes provide explanations and clarifications for otherwise inexplicable elements and aspects of national life. A "mythological notion of pure origins" is often connected with "social and cultural form; innovations are co-opted by being treated as the realization of an eternal essence" (Herzfeld 1997:21). Ancient Attika is a prime exemplar of such cooptive interconnection.

Motherland and Myth

Modern studies of Athenian history and society often leave the impression that the literature and art of the Athenians are pervasively filled with *topoi* of autochthony—fulsome and repetitive expressions of Athenian pride in their origin, individually and as a people, from the Attic earth itself.[23] This seminal cultural belief supposedly underlay the Athenians' commitment to democracy (shared origin made all

[20] *Rep*. 3.414d2–e3: ἐπιχειρήσω πρῶτον μὲν αὐτοὺς τοὺς ἄρχοντας πείθειν καὶ τοὺς στρατιώτας, ἔπειτα δὲ καὶ τὴν ἄλλην πόλιν, ὡς ἄρ' ἃ ἡμεῖς αὐτοὺς ἐτρέφομεν . . . ἦσαν δὲ τότε τῇ ἀληθείᾳ ὑπὸ γῆς ἐντὸς πλαττόμενοι καὶ τρεφόμενοι . . . καὶ ἡ γῆ αὐτοὺς μήτηρ οὖσα ἀνῆκεν.

[21] See Gouthoeven 1636; Schama 1987: 67–93; de Vos 1995: 24.

[22] For the "fury" that meets any challenge to the alleged archaeological or ethnographic "evidence" for such claims, see Herzfeld 1997: 65. Cf. the heated dispute currently raging over the historicity of the foundation tales narrated in the Bible (1 and 2 Samuel, Kings, and Chronicles), now acknowledged by scholarly *opinio communis* to have been recorded long after the relevant periods. Contrast arguments supportive of the biblical narrative (*Biblical Archaeology Review* 1997) with denial of even the existence in the Iron Age of the biblical kings of a united Israel (Whitelam 1996; Davies 1992; Thompson 1992: esp. 353–423).

[23] Since the pioneering work of Ermatinger in 1897, scholars have struggled, without consensus, to explain the Athenian claim of autochthony. See recently, inter alia, Bérard 1974; Stupperich

citizens equal)[24] and purportedly explains the periodic witch-hunts for possible penetration into the *polis* by persons not born from citizen parents themselves both descended from the Attic soil (shared origin precluded the admission of outsiders into the *polis*).[25] Yet no fifth-century author deals explicitly with Athenian self-perception, except for Thucydides, who rejects the mythological tradition of autochthony.[26] In fourth-century literature, boasts of autochthony are found unequivocally only among the platitudinous banalities of encomia delivered at public funerals for soldiers who had lost their lives in battle, ceremonies of nation building where personal and communal grief for the dead, intensified by religious and patriotic emotions, produced a genre that strung together formulaic tales to reify state ideology and mythological tradition[27]—from which the Athenians' everyday values and beliefs were systematically elided.[28] But even in these speeches, autochthony typically means only the Athenians' residence in Attika for many generations without widespread changes in population as a result of war, rather than a claim of literal birth of the Athenian nation from Attic earth.

In fact, only in the late nineteenth century C.E. did there arise the hypothesis, now dominant among modern writers, that "at some uncertain, but nonetheless very early date the Athenians came to believe that, as a nation, they had always lived in Attica; and that these early Athenians expressed this belief in mythological terms, as relatively primitive people would do, by saying that their nation was, literally, sprung from the soil of its native land."[29] In reality, however, prior to the Persian Wars no

---

1977: 40–53; Loraux 1979, [1984] 1993, 1996; Montanari 1981; Miller 1983; Saxonhouse 1986; Rosivach 1987.

[24] Loraux [1984] 1993: 41: the "funeral eulogy . . . establishes the roots of democracy in autochthonous origins, and thus makes Athens into a progressive city from its birth." Cf. van Groningen 1953: ch. 5; Montanari 1981: 59 (for whom belief in autochthony is connected with the democratic reforms of Kleisthenēs and hence are symbolic of "una tendenzialità politico-democratica"). But such a relationship would be inherently contradictory: "an autochthonous society must also be xenophobic and aristocratic" (Saxonhouse 1986: 256). "For an Athenian, to be earthborn (γηγενής) and indigenous (αὐτόχθων) was also to be well-born (εὐγενής)." Walsh 1978: 301. Cf. Ober 1989: 261–63; Walsh 1978: 309–10.

[25] On these *diapsēphismoi*, see Chapter 2, pp. 63–64, with notes 92–93.

[26] Cf. Mills 1997: 45; and my discussion on pp. 91–92.

[27] See pp. 94–102.

[28] The funeral oration (*epitaphios logos*) was an "expression of the official ideology" (Loraux [1981] 1986: 263). On the "words absent" from funeral speeches, see ibid., 221, 428, n. 3. Cf. Mills 1997: 48–49, n. 13; Duby 1974: 1: 156–57.

[29] Rosivach 1987: 294 (who questions this prevailing view). For its original promulgation and elaboration, see Ermatinger 1897. In agreement: Loraux 1979: 10; Bérard 1974: 31–38; Sommer

surviving citation or even oblique allusion relates the origins of the population of Attika with ancestral tales of the magical generation from the earth of serpentine quasi deities such as Erekhtheus who only much later, probably not until the fifth century, came to be identified in local myth as ancestral chieftains ("kings").[30] The Peisistratids in the late sixth century, to be sure, did evoke "Thēseus" as a national unifier, but he was a newcomer to Attika on both his paternal and maternal sides.[31] Arriving in Athens polluted by his encounters en route, he is the ultimate outsider, the antithesis of autochthonic claims and, thereby, a potent symbol of Athens's "receptivity, or rather its need to incorporate, outsiders."[32] The other Athenian "kings," however, are not encountered as monarchical personages before the fifth century[33] and then, only in a contradictory "profusion of rival identitities" (Loraux [1984] 1993: 57), offered in "an unusually complex form" (Zeitlin 1993: xiv). Erekhtheus is originally a cult figure, a serpentine or quasi-serpentine deity identified with Poseidōn.[34] Although he is alluded to as "earthborn" in the *Iliad* (albeit in a passage often construed as a late Athenian interpolation), his daemonic characteristics still predominate: raised by Athēna and installed in her sanctuary on the Akropolis, he is worshiped with offerings of bulls and rams.[35] By the fifth century, "Erekhtheus," son of the Earth (Gē),[36] is hopelessly conflated with "Erikhthonios," who in one version, for example, is born of Gē alone; in another, of Gē and Hēphaistos; and

---

1948: 84. Connor (1994: 43, n. 16) follows Rosivach in favoring a late origin for tales of Athenian autochthony.

[30] For various interpretations of the murky political arrangements of archaic Attika, and the disputed roles of "chieftains," "big men," and/or "kings," see Stahl 1987: 150–55; Welwei 1992a: 80, n. 9; van Wees 1992: 281–94.

[31] Peisistratid promotion of Thēseus: Tyrrell and Brown 1991: 161–65; Connor 1987: 42–47. Theseus's father was Poseidōn, Aigeus (or both); his mother, Troizenian. See Mills 1997: 5; Walker 1995: 83–111, 172; Simon 1996: 12.

[32] Connor 1996a: 120. Cf. Connor 1970; Shapiro 1992; Lardinois 1992. Note the similar Athenian receptivity to Oidipous, another monarchical outsider.

[33] See Brommer 1957: 163–64, who concludes that the *basileis*, in their royal forms, were politically motivated, anachronistic inventions of the classical period.

[34] "Poseidōn Erekhtheus" (perhaps an allusion to Poseidōn the Earthshaker [ἐρέχθω= smash, break]). See Kron 1976: 32–83, 149–59; 1981–: 4:923–51; Loraux [1984] 1993: 37–57; Parker 1987: 193–202; Kearns 1989: 113–15, 160, 210–11.

[35] 2.547–51: δῆμον Ἐρεχθῆος μεγαλήτορος ὅν ποτ' Ἀθήνη | θρέψε Διὸς θυγάτηρ, τέκε δὲ ζείδωρος ἄρουρα· | κὰδ δ' ἐν Ἀθήνης εἷσεν, ἑῷ ἐν πίονι νηῷ· | ἔνθα δέ μιν ταύροισι καὶ ἀρνειοῖς ἱλάονται | κοῦροι Ἀθηναίων περιτελλομένων ἐνιαυτῶν. Cf. Hom. *Od.* 7.80–81. For possible late Athenian influence on the Homeric text, see Seaford 1994: 144–54, 183; West 1988: 38, n. 15; Kron 1976: 33–37.

[36] Hdt. 8.55. Cf. Hom. *Il.* 2.548.

in a third of Hēphaistos and Athena.[37] Their congruence, including the similarity in name, is so extreme that some scholars have characterized the duo as merely variant manifestations of a common conceptualization, a "doublet."[38] In any event, by the fifth century reference in the *Iliad* to the Athenians as "Erekhtheus's people,"[39] has been superseded by the appellation "Erekhtheidai," figuratively "the people of Erekhtheus" but literally the "sons of Erekhtheus." After the early-fifth-century poet Pindar refers to the Athenians as Erekhtheidai,[40] the appellation is thereafter found with some frequency in authors of the classical period. But it is only in Sophoklēs' *Ajax* that the adjective "earthborn" (*khthonios*) was first appended directly to "Erekhtheidai,"[41] completing the transformation of the Athenians from "the people of earthborn Erekhtheus" to "the sons of earthborn Erekhtheus" and finally to "the earthborn sons of Erekhtheus." The early serpentine deities have now become human beings, while the human Athenians, individually and as a group, now trace their origin to a supernatural union with the Motherland.

The Athenians' belief in their divine origin is set forth most strikingly, and mocked most damningly, in Euripides' *Iōn*, a dazzling work of the late fifth century that offers its audience at Athens juxtaposed paradoxical, contradictory, antithetical, and inconsistent views of Athenian origins and Athenian identity—a dramatic presentation of the discontinuities that the "real" Athenians daily amalgamated. Although the inhabitants of Attika are recurrently denominated in *Iōn* as autochthonous—Hermēs goes "to the indigenous people of renowned Athens"; "the indigenous, renowned Athenians are not an imported species"; "the earth brought forth Erikhthonios, the Athenians' earliest ancestor"[42]—Euripides has

[37] Son of Gē: Eur. *Iōn* 267. Son of Gē and Hēphaistos: Isok. *Panath.* 126; Pl. *Tim.* 23e102 (cf. Plut. *Bioi Rhēt.* 843e; Paus. 1.2.6). Son of Hēphaistos and Athēna: Cook 1940: 3.1:218–33.

[38] See Ermatinger 1897, who emphasizes the presence of χθών in both names. Cf. Rosivach 1987: 294–95, n. 4. Although Athenian claims of autochthony are, in the classical period, based on their being "the sons of earthborn Erekhtheus," it is actually Erikhthonios whom Euripides characterizes as the earliest ancestor of the Athenians, and the one who was brought forth from the motherland itself (*Iōn* 999–1000: ΚΡ.· Ἐριχθόνιον . . . | ΠΡ. ὃν πρῶτον ὑμῶν πρόγονον ἐξανῆκε γῆ;).

[39] Cf. *Il.* 2.547: δῆμος Ἐρεχθῆος.

[40] Pind. *Isthm.* 2.19: Ἐρεχθειδᾶν.

[41] Tekmēssa refers to the Salaminians as Erekhtheidai "sprung from Athenian earth" (Moore's translation of lines 201–2: ναὸς ἀρωγοὶ τῆς Αἴαντος, | γενεᾶς χθονίων ἀπ' Ἐρεχθειδᾶν . . .). Jebb offers "of the race that springs from the Erekhtheidai, sons of the soil." For the literal meanings of *khthonios*, *autokhthōn*, *gēgenēs*, and *eugenēs*, see pp. 92–93.

[42] ἐλθὼν λαὸν εἰς αὐτόχθονα | κλεινῶν Ἀθηνῶν (29–30); ΙΩΝ. εἶναί φασι τὰς αὐτόχθονας | κλεινὰς Ἀθήνας οὐκ ἐπείσακτον γένος (589–90); ΚΡ. Ἐριχθόνιον . . . | ΠΡ. ὃν πρῶτον ὑμῶν πρό-

Xouthos, the leader of Athens, insist that birth from the earth is a factual impossibility.[43] By setting the drama formally in Delphi (but suffusing it with an Athenian orientation),[44] Euripidēs is simultaneously able to present the Athenian protagonists as foreigners (at Delphi) objecting to possible foreign influence or power (at Athens).[45] Further disorienting is Euripides' depiction of Erikhthonios rather than Erekhtheus as the source of Athenian autochthony.[46] While other authors refer to the Athenians as the "earthborn descendants of Erekhtheus," Athens of the Erekhtheid period, for Euripides, is already peopled by a considerable population,[47] few of whom could literally be offspring of Erekhtheus. Although the chorus does assert that Athenian rulers should always be descendants of Erekhtheus,[48] in the *Iōn* only foreigners appear as actual rulers of Athens, present and future.[49] Xouthos is an Aiolian, whose power in Attika derives solely from the military prowess that has gained him the bed of the native princess, Kreousa.[50] Iōn, despite his illustrious parentage, despite his future glory, will remain a foreigner at Athens.[51] And

---

γονον ἐξανῆκε γῆ. . . (999–1000). Cf. τῶν εὐγενετᾶν Ἐρεχθειδᾶν (1060). For *eugeneia* as a synonym for autochthony, see Dougherty 1996: 267, n. 31; Walsh 1978.

[43] ΙΩΝ. γῆς ἄρ' ἐκπέφυκα μητρός; ΞΟ. οὐ πέδον τίκτει τέκνα (542).

[44] "The scene is Delphi but in a sense it is Athens," because Delphi provides only "a one-dimensional image, while the reality of civic space is at Athens" (Owen 1939: xxii). Cf. Immerwahr 1972: 281; Zeitlin 1996: 198.

[45] The "local" authorities at Delphi seek to punish the "foreigner" Kreousa (ἀρχαὶ δ' ἁπιχώριοι χθονὸς ζητοῦσιν αὐτὴν ὡς θάνηι πετρουμένη [lines 1111–12], Ὦ γαῖα σεμνή, τῆς Ἐρεχθέως ὕπο, ξένης γυναικός, φαρμάκοισι θνήισκομεν [1220–21]). Cf. 1292: ΙΩΝ. οὔτοι σὺν ὅπλοις ἦλθον ἐς τὴν σὴν χθόνα. Playing with the χθών- and other elements of mother earth, Euripides attaches it throughout the play to areas and peoples other than Attika, for example, Asian soil (Ἴωνα δ' αὐτόν, κτίστορ' Ἀσιάδος χθονός, 74), majestic Delphic earth (Ὦ γαῖα σεμνή, 1220).

[46] See lines 20–21 (προγόνων νόμον σώιζουσα τοῦ τε γηγενοῦς Ἐριχθονίου). But lines 1464–66 are more equivocal: δῶμ' ἑστιοῦται, γᾶ δ' ἔχει τυράννους, | ἀνηβᾶι δ' Ἐρεχθεύς· | ὅ τε γηγενέτας δόμος οὐκέτι νύκτα δέρκεται.

[47] This is shown most vividly in Praxithea's musing in Euripides' *Erekhtheus* (which survives only in fragments): πόλεως δ' ἁπάσης τοὔνομ' ἕν, πολλοὶ δέ νιν | ναίουσι· τούτους πῶς διαφθεῖραί με χρή, | ἐξὸν προπάντων μίαν ὕπερ δοῦναι θανεῖν; fr. 360 (*TrGF*), lines 16–18.

[48] μηδέ ποτ' ἄλλος ἥ- | κων πόλεως ἀνάσσοι | πλὴν τῶν εὐγενετᾶν Ἐρεχθειδᾶν (1058–60). For the substitution of ἥκων for manuscript οἴκων, see Diggle 1994: 20.

[49] Iōn is seen as destined (but foreign) ruler of Attika: ἄπαιδες οὐκέτ' ἐσμὲν οὐδ' ἄτεκνοι· | δῶμ' ἑστιοῦται, γᾶ δ' ἔχει τυράννους (Kreousa, lines 1463–64); κἀς θρόνους τυραννικοὺς | ἵδρυσον· ἐκ γὰρ τῶν Ἐρεχθέως γεγὼς | δίκαιος ἄρχειν τῆς ἐμῆς ὅδε χθονός (Athena about Iōn, lines 1572–74).

[50] Lines 1295–99: ΚΡ. ἔμελλες οἰκεῖν τἄμ', ἐμοῦ βίαι λαβών. | ΙΩΝ. πατρός γε γῆν διδόντος ἣν ἐκτήσατο. | ΚΡ. τοῖς Αἰόλου δὲ πῶς μετῆν τῆς Παλλάδος; | ΙΩΝ. ὅπλοισιν αὐτὴν οὐ λόγοις ἐρρύσατο. | ΚΡ. ἐπίκουρος οἰκήτωρ γ' ἂν οὐκ εἴη χθονός. (Nauck places lines 1300–1303 between 1295 and 1296, a transposition followed by Diggle in his 1981 Oxford Classical Text.) Throughout the play, the chorus characterizes Xouthos as an intrusive foreigner (290, 592, 702, 813).

[51] ἐλθὼν δ' ἐς οἶκον ἀλλότριον ἔπηλυς ὢν (line 607); δύο νόσω κεκτημένος, | πατρός τ' ἐπακτοῦ καὐτὸς ὢν νοθαγενής (591–92). The chorus hopes οὐ γὰρ δόμων γ' ἑτέρους | ἄρχοντας ἀλλοδαποὺς | ζῶσά ποτ' <ἐν> φαεν- | ναῖς ἀνέχοιτ' ἂν αὐγαῖς | ἁ τῶν εὐπατριδᾶν γεγῶσ' οἴκων (1069–73). In fact, Athenian mythology (and "history") generally present Iōn as the son of Xouthos: see Hdt. 7.94, 8.44. Cf. Dougherty 1996: 257.

while Apollo, through the Pythia,[52] and later through the goddess Athēna, seems to convince Kreousa that Iōn is the mixed offspring of divinity and Athenian royalty, Apollo continues to assure Xouthos that Xouthos had fathered Iōn,[53] and even Iōn (anticipating some modern editors) continues to doubt that Apollo is his father.[54]

Euripides traumatizes Athenian norms by deriving the "autochthonous" line through maternal, not paternal, filiation (while the putative father is forced into the usually feminine role of trying to gain entry into the family for a supposititious child). Euripides further unsettles received mythology by replicating through Iōn various traits of his putative male autochthonous predecessors, Erekhtheus and Erkikhthonios.[55] Euripides also tantalizes the audience with protagonists' suggestions concerning Iōn's maternal origins. Iōn sees the prophetess at Delphi as his true mother, and his factual parentage as autochthonous birth from the earth; Xouthos is convinced that Iōn's mother is a Delphian wench with whom he had a premarital coupling.[56] In effect, Euripides brilliantly reifies the Homeric plaint of Tēlemakhos that "nobody really knows his own begetting."[57] Add Euripides' mystic and misty references to Hēraklēs and Bellerophōn, to Titans, Centaurs, and Amazons, and the drama presents "a bewildering array of possibilities and strategies for engendering children, with or without partners, of which the 'true' versions here belong to the world of the myth and the 'false' to the world of reality" (Zeitlin 1996: 290).

And yet the *Iōn*'s complex, challenging, and ambivalent treatment of autochthonous origin is actually consonant with other Athenian views expressed in literature and art throughout the classical period. In contrast to modern scholars' assumption that autochthony was a fundamental

[52] The priestess of Apollo speaks for herself in the play, and occupies a pivotal role (lines 1320ff.). Her male "handlers," projected as dominant by much modern scholarship, go unnoted. See Chapter 1, nn. 216, 217.

[53] See lines 775, 781, 788, 1532, 1561. He greets Xouthos as his father: χαῖρέ μοι, πάτερ (561). Kreousa on her part insists to Iōn that no one must ever know of his claim to divine paternity: τοῦ θεοῦ δὲ λεγόμενος | οὐκ ἔσχες ἄν ποτ' οὔτε παγκλήρους δόμους | οὔτ' ὄνομα πατρός (1541–43).

[54] ὅρα σύ, μῆτερ, μὴ σφαλεῖς' ἃ παρθένοις | ἐγγίγνεται νοσήματ' ἐς κρυπτοὺς γάμους | ἔπειτα τῶι θεῶι προστίθης τὴν αἰτίαν | καὶ τοὐμὸν αἰσχρὸν ἀποφυγεῖν πειρωμένη | Φοίβωι τεκεῖν με φήις, τεκοῦσ' οὐκ ἐκ θεοῦ (1523–27). On modern editors' inclination toward a more "rational" interpretation of Iōn's plot, see Barlow 1971: 49; Verrall 1895.

[55] On this parallel, see Burnett 1970: 2–3.

[56] Iōn muses: γῆς ἄρ' ἐκπέφυκα μητρός; (542). Iōn and Xouthos reason: ΙΩΝ. Πυθίαν δ' ἦλθες πέτραν πρίν; (550) ΞΟ. Δελφίσιν κόραις . . . Βακχίου πρὸς ἡδοναῖς. ΙΩΝ. τοῦτ' ἐκεῖν'· ἵν' ἐσπάρημεν ΞΟ. ὁ πότμος ἐξηῦρεν, τέκνον (551–54).

[57] Literally, "his own begetting": μήτηρ μέν τ' ἐμέ φησι τοῦ ἔμμεναι, αὐτὰρ ἐγώ γε | οὐκ οἶδ'· οὐ γάρ πώ τις ἑὸν γόνον αὐτὸς ἀνέγνω (*Od.* 1.215–16).

"belief" of the Athenians, but one incompatible with the secular workings of life,[58] the Athenians seem easily to have rationalized their nationalistic myths with the historical fact of widespread immigration and assimilation of aliens over a long period,[59] and with constitutional arrangements that did not wholly preclude participation in the *politeia* by the offspring of newcomers (see Chapter 2). We know from non-Hellenic sources that a "belief" in the supernatural origins of the individual members of a group is not absolutely irreconcilable with the presence within that group of newcomers. The Jewish people, for example, throughout the ages has asserted that each individual Jew, as a descendant of a closed system based on rigid conditions of birth, himself personally experienced the relevant deeds of God and was personally a descendant of the Patriarchs Abraham, Isaac, and Jacob. Yet many Jews in many periods were actually converts to Judaism. Spiritual kinship, however, superseded genetic alterity. The rabbis soberly asserted that all future converts had been present within Israel from the beginning and had actually entered the covenant from the first.[60] Similarly, the Athenian orators garlanded their own contemporaries with the performance of deeds actually committed by Athenians of much earlier periods—without the slightest suggestion that all of the present-day Athenians were literally individual descendants of an ancestor "born from the Attic earth." Thus Lykourgos (1.127) asserts to an Athenian jury in 330 that "you Athenians" had sworn an oath at Plataea (150 years earlier!). Ancestral heroes are routinely assumed to be the progenitors of each and everyone of the present-day auditors,[61] despite the multitudinous historical evidence to the contrary (see Chapter 2, pp. 63ff.).

This accommodation of such apparently irreconcilable elements was facilitated at Athens by the cultural phenomenon that "truth," for the Greeks, was multifaceted: *mythos* (myth) and *logos* (reason) might be antithetical, but they were also complementary; it was "possible to half-believe, or believe in contradictory things."[62] Because of the Athenian

[58] "Professing to believe in autochthony" necesssarily conflicts with "the knowledge that human beings are actually born from the union of man and woman" (Lévi-Strauss 1968: 212).

[59] Cf. Rosivach 1987: 290, n. 10: "the Athenians did not seem bothered by the contradiction between traditions which spoke of immigrants incorporated into the citizen body on the one hand, and the claim of autochthony, on the other."

[60] Shebuot 39a, reflecting Deutonomy 29. See Isaiah 44:5; Rambam: Letter to Obadiah. Cf. Greenberg 1995: 380–82; Twersky 1972: 474–76.

[61] See, for example, Lys. 18.12; Aiskhin. 3.259.

[62] Veyne 1988: xi (*pace* Nestle 1940). Cf. Forsdyke 1957; Veyne 1995: 160–68.

penchant for shaping perception and organizing cognition through bipolarities,[63] *logos* and *mythos* did not fall into unconnected spheres but rather interacted symbiotically: it was often necessary to "purify myth (*mythos*) by reason (*logos*)."[64] Public speakers at Athens frequently offered "mythological" (*mythōdes*) argument as evidentiary justification for a thesis—and often prevailed because of the audience's favorable inclination toward marvel-filled and tradition-laden *testimonia*, even those transparently replete with apparent falsehood (*pseudologia)*.[65] By defending the use of such evidence not as literally true but as proper where appropriate to the situation, orators implicitly argued for the reliability of myth—that is, for the relevance of tales that could not satisfy epistemological analysis. Even the *logoi* (speeches) recorded in the history of Thucydides, who averred disdain for the mythological,[66] were a compromise between the "appropriate" (*ta deonta*) and the factual.[67] Because it is "appropriate" for the education of the young, Lykurgos defends his use, as evidence, of a *logos* that he acknowledges to be *mythōdes* (mythological).[68] In his Panegyric Speech, Isokratēs admits that a *logos* about Dēmētēr is *mythōdes*, but insists that its capacity for generating patriotic fervor, not its ontological "truth," justifies its introduction.[69] In Isokratēs' Panathenaic Speech, an interlocutor is portrayed as "not wishing to disbelieve but not being able entirely to believe" in the ancient tales, *mythos* not "purified" by *logos*, from which Isokratēs has been arguing—namely, the invasion of Athens by the god Poseidōn's son seeking to vindicate Poseidōn's claim to priority over the goddesss Athena in the land of Attika; the Amazons' incursion to seize Hippolytē,

[63] See Chapter 1, pp. 22–23.

[64] Plut. *Thēs*. 1.3: ἐκκαθαιρόμενον λόγῳ τὸ μυθῶδες. Cf. Hyper. *Lyk*. 11.

[65] Isok. 12.1: προῃρούμην γράφειν τῶν λόγων οὐ τοὺς μυθώδεις οὐδὲ τοὺς τερατείας καὶ ψευδολογίας μεστούς, οἷς οἱ πολλοὶ μᾶλλον χαίρουσιν ἢ τοῖς περὶ τῆς αὐτῶν σωτηρίας λεγομένοις. Cf. Isok. 2.48. Nouhaud enumerates the presence of mythological references in the Attic orators (1982: 19). Cf. Rydberg-Cox 1998: 2, n. 3.

[66] See n. 76.

[67] ὅσα μὲν λόγῳ εἶπον ἕκαστοι . . . ὡς δ᾽ ἂν ἐδόκουν ἐμοὶ ἕκαστοι περὶ τῶν αἰεὶ παρόντων τὰ δέοντα μάλιστ᾽ εἰπεῖν, ἐχομένῳ ὅτι ἐγγύτατα τῆς ξυμπάσης γνώμης τῶν ἀληθῶς λεχθέντων, οὕτως εἴρηται (1.22.1). The difficulty of reconciling a claim to accuracy (ἐχομένῳ ὅτι ἐγγύτατα . . . τῶν ἀληθῶς λεχθέντων) with the presentation of material as "appropriate" (τὰ δέοντα) has generated a mountainous volume of disputation among modern scholars for whom the two categories are usually treated as inherently contradictory. See Walbank [1967] 1985: 245; Macleod 1983: 52–53, 88. Cf. Schmid 1955; Wilson 1982; Garrity 1998.

[68] Lykourg. 1.95: λέγεται γοῦν ἐν Σικελίᾳ (εἰ γὰρ καὶ μυθωδέστερόν ἐστιν, ἀλλ᾽ ἁρμόσει καὶ νῦν ἅπασι τοῖς νεωτέροις ἀκοῦσαι) ἐκ τῆς Αἴτνης ῥύακα πυρὸς γενέσθαι κ.τ.λ.

[69] 4.28: οὗ πρῶτον ἡ φύσις ἡμῶν ἐδεήθη, διὰ τῆς πόλεως τῆς ἡμετέρας ἐπορίσθη· καὶ γὰρ εἰ μυθώδης ὁ λόγος γέγονεν, ὅμως αὐτῷ καὶ νῦν ῥηθῆναι προσήκει. Δήμητρος γὰρ ἀφικομένης εἰς τὴν χώραν κ.τ.λ.

who was cohabiting with Thēseus in violation of sororal principles; the unsuccessful effort by the Peloponnesians to capture Hēraklēs's children who had found refuge in Athens.[70] Demosthenes contrasts "mythical" tales about the Areopagos Council with facts known personally and directly by contemporary Athenians—but claims that both are worthy of consideration.[71]

Where *logos* prevailed, *mythos* might be relatively inappropriate; where *mythos* held sway, *logos* might be infelicitous. But both elements resided in Athenian culture and potentially affected each resident of Attika at every moment. The Athenians could "believe" both in the literal generation from the earth of their collective and individual ancestors and also in the interpretation of that claim as merely a mythically expressed formulation of the tradition that the Athenians had inhabited Attika for a very long time, and that Attika—unlike other regions of Hellas—had never, through invasion and conquest, experienced a cataclysmic demographic alteration once its Athenian identity had crystallized. Hellenic usage tolerated, and indeed facilitated, alternative, and often contradictory, versions of the same "events," as well as alternative levels of acceptance and understanding of the same narrative. A single story might be interpreted by one person as *logos* (a "reasonable belief"), and by another as *mythos* (a "traditional tale"): in Sōkratēs' words, "what you consider *mythos*, I judge *logos*."[72] Unexamined, the *mythos* of autochthony might promote xenophobic exclusivity; purified by reason, the *logos* of autochthony offered no insurmountable barrier to assimilation of relative newcomers.

[70] 12.234: ἀπορεῖν ἔφασκεν ... οὔτε γὰρ ἀπιστεῖν βούλεσθαι τοῖς ὑπ' ἐμοῦ λεγομένοις οὔτε πιστεύειν δύνασθαι παντάπασιν αὐτοῖς. Isokratēs had earlier argued from *mythos*: περὶ δὲ τοῦ τρίτου ποιήσομαι τοὺς λόγους, ὃς ἐγένετο τῶν μὲν Ἑλληνίδων πόλεων ἄρτι κατῳκισμένων, τῆς δ' ἡμετέρας ἔτι βασιλευομένης (191). He then discourses about Poseidōn's son, ὃς ἠμφισβήτησεν Ἐρεχθεῖ τῆς πόλεως, φάσκων Ποσειδῶ πρότερον Ἀθηνᾶς καταλαβεῖν αὐτήν; about the Amazons, αἳ τὴν στρατείαν ἐφ' Ἱππολύτην ἐποιήσαντο; and about Eurystheus, ὃς Ἡρακλεῖ μὲν οὐκ ἔδωκε δίκην ὧν ἡμάρτανεν εἰς αὐτὸν, στρατεύσας δ' ἐπὶ τοὺς ἡμετέρους προγόνους ὡς ἐκληψόμενος βίᾳ τοὺς ἐκείνου παῖδας (193–94).

[71] Dem. 23.65: τὸ ἐν Ἀρείῳ πάγῳ δικαστήριον, ὑπὲρ οὗ τοσαῦτ' ἔστιν εἰπεῖν καλὰ παραδεδομένα καὶ μυθώδη καὶ ὧν αὐτοὶ μάρτυρές ἐσμεν, ὅσα περὶ οὐδενὸς ἄλλου δικαστηρίου· ὧν ὡσπερεὶ δείγματος εἵνεκ' ἄξιόν ἐστιν ἓν ἢ δύ' ἀκοῦσαι.

[72] Ἄκουε δή, φασί, μάλα καλοῦ λόγου, ὃν σὺ μὲν ἡγήσῃ μῦθον, ὡς ἐγὼ οἶμαι, ἐγὼ δὲ λόγον. Sōkratēs proceeds to narrate ("as though it were true:" "ὡς ἀληθῆ γὰρ ὄντα σοι λέξω ἃ μέλλω λέγειν") the divine law that at death the person living justly goes to the Islands of the Blessed while the unjust man goes to eternal punishment. But while Sōkratēs believes the *mythos* to be true (ταῦτ' ἔστιν ἃ ἐγὼ ἀκηκοὼς πιστεύω ἀληθῆ εἶναι), through *logos* (καὶ ἐκ τούτων τῶν λόγων τοιόνδε τι λογίζομαι συμβαίνειν) he interprets it as signifying "nothing other" than death's marking

Fatherland and Nationalism

> No more arresting emblems of the modern culture of nationalism exist than cenotaphs and tombs of Unknown Soldiers.
>
> Anderson, *Imagined Communities*, p. 7.

For the Athenians, autochthony was a theme to boast of where appropriate (especially in works consciously trumpeting patriotic themes), to be avoided or rationalized where irrelevant or unhelpful (as in the historical writings of Thucydides, Herodotos, and others), and even to be exploited in condemnation of Athens (as in Plato's *Menexenos*). But wherever encountered—and especially in funeral orations for fallen soldiers, paeans to Athenian nationalism, and militaristic devotion to the fatherland (*patris*)—the motif of autochthony offers insight into the cultural construction of Athenian ethnicity. Unfortunately, in modern scholarship's explication of autochthony it is the banter of Plato, explicit advocate of the "noble lie" of myths of origin,[73] that has been appropriated as a leit motif: "autochthony is the basis for the unity of the city," and autochthony means "having been born from the soil."[74]

1. Leading historians at Athens treat the autochthonous origin of the Athenians from Attic soil as a poetic formulation of the underlying truth of Athenian occupation of Attika from time immemorial, a continuity that supposedly differentiated the Athenians from other Hellenic groups.[75] Thus Thucydides, faulting earlier historians for embracing "the mythological" instead of the factual,[76] proffers a reductionist interpretation of the Athenian people's tie to its land: Attika, "enjoying from a very remote

the separation of body and soul (ὁ θάνατος τυγχάνει ὤν, ὡς ἐμοὶ δοκεῖ, οὐδὲν ἄλλο ἢ δυοῖν πραγμάτοιν διάλυσις, τῆς ψυχῆς καὶ τοῦ σώματος, ἀπ' ἀλλήλοιν·). Pl., *Gorg.* 523a1–524b4.

[73] See pp. 100–3.

[74] Loraux [1981] 1986: 278, n. 87; [1984] 1993: 66. Cf. Ober 1989: 263: "Because their ancestors were born of the soil of Attica, all Athenians were, in effect, a single kinship group."

[75] Thouk. 1.2.1: φαίνεται γὰρ ἡ νῦν Ἑλλὰς καλουμένη οὐ πάλαι βεβαίως οἰκουμένη, ἀλλὰ μεταναστάσεις τε οὖσαι τὰ πρότερα καὶ ῥᾳδίως ἕκαστοι τὴν ἑατῶν ἀπολείποντες βιαζόμενοι ὑπό τινων αἰεὶ πλειόνων. Herodotos characterizes the other Greeks as "highly migratory" (πολυπλάνητον) (1.56.2). In contrast with the Libyans and Ethiopians who are αὐτόχθονες, the Greeks as a group are ἐπήλυδες (4.197.2). The majority of individual Hellenic *ethnē* were likewise ἐπήλυδα (8.73).

[76] 1.22.4: καὶ ἐς μὲν ἀκρόασιν ἴσως τὸ μὴ μυθῶδες αὐτῶν ἀτερπέστερον φαινεῖται. Thucydides explains his methodology in dealing with *logos* (here the actual language used before or during the war): ὅσα μὲν λόγῳ εἶπον ἕκαστοι . . . ἐχομένῳ ὅτι ἐγγύτατα τῆς ξυμπάσης γνώμης τῶν ἀληθῶς λεχθέντων, οὕτως εἴρηται (1.22.1).

period freedom from faction, never changed its inhabitants."[77] Similarly the fourth-century author Kleidēmos, adopting a view similar to that of Thucydides,[78] "in an allusion to the Athenian claim to autochthony, avoid(s) the term *autochthones*."[79] Another historian of Athens, Hellanikos, seems also to have interpreted the claim of autochthony as meaning only that "Attika was not involved in the migrations."[80] Even Herodotos, supposedly addicted to "patriotic stories in particular and sentimental chauvinism in general,"[81] avoids the presentation of supernatural origin tales. He soberly characterizes the Athenians as an "extraordinarily old nation, the only Greeks never to change their homeland,"[82] and explicitly chronicles the time when the original inhabitants of Attika, the "Athenian nation," were joined by other "Pelasgians": at this early period, the residents of Attika were transforming themselves into persons recognizably Greek, adopting the Greek language, and coming to be identified as Hellenes.[83] Herodotos thus implicitly, and explicitly, portrays an Athens of diverse origins—a mixture of sources, primordially not even Greek.[84] Like Thucydides, Herodotos treats Athenian authochthony as merely a statement of the Athenian population's long and continuous residence in its own country.[85] For Attic historians of the fifth and fourth centuries, "the Athenians are children of the earth since they have lived there forever, rather than because of any miraculous birth" (Saxonhouse 1986: 257).

2. Etymology confirms the appropriateness of the historians' rendering of the Greek word *autokhthōn* by the prosaic "living in the same land for a long time." "Born from the earth" is the literal meaning of another ancient Greek word, *gēgenēs*, which is used to describe any object or

[77] Crawley translation of 1.2.5: τὴν γοῦν Ἀττικὴν ἐκ τοῦ ἐπὶ πλεῖστον διὰ τὸ λεπτόγεων ἀστασίαστον οὖσαν ἄνθρωποι ᾤκουν οἱ αὐτοὶ αἰεί.

[78] Jacoby [1954] 1968: 64. Cf. Jacoby 1949: 83.

[79] Loraux [1981] 1986: 419, n. 149, with reference to fr. 3 (Jacoby).

[80] Jacoby [1954] 1968: 55, with reference to fr. 27.

[81] Flory 1990: 194. Thucydides's oblique criticism of his predecesssors is believed to have been directed primarily at Herodotos: see the scholia (at 1.22.4; see n. 76) on τὸ μὴ μυθῶδες and ἀγώνισμα (Hude 1927).

[82] The assertion of the Athenian ambassador to Syrakuse: ἀρχαιότατον μὲν ἔθνος . . . μοῦνοι δὲ ἐόντες οὐ μετανάσται Ἑλλήνων (7.161.3).

[83] τὸ Ἀττικὸν ἔθνος ἐὸν Πελασγικὸν ἅμα τῇ μεταβολῇ τῇ ἐς Ἕλληνας καὶ τὴν γλῶσσαν μετέμαθε (1.57.3); Ἀθηναίοισι γὰρ ἤδη τηνικαῦτα ἐς Ἕλληνας τελέουσι Πελασγοὶ σύνοικοι ἐγένοντο ἐν τῇ χώρῃ, ὅθεν περ καὶ Ἕλληνες ἤρξαντο νομισθῆναι (2.51.2). Cf. Connor 1994: 43, n. 16.

[84] The Pelasgians were "barbaroi" (τὸ Πελασγικὸν ἔθνος, ἐὸν βάρβαρον: 1.58).

[85] Cf. Hdt. 1.56.2: εὕρισκε Λακεδαιμονίους τε καὶ Ἀθηναίους προέχοντας . . . ἐόντα τὸ ἀρχαῖον τὸ μὲν Πελασγικόν, τὸ δὲ Ἑλληνικὸν ἔθνος. καὶ τὸ μὲν οὐδαμῇ κω ἐξεχώρησε, τὸ δὲ πολυπλάνητον κάρτα.

person of chthonic origin.[86] *Autokhthōn*, in contrast, "is always used to describe a people which has lived in its homeland since time immemorial."[87] As with many other ancient Greek terms,[88] the clearest definition of *autokhthōn* arises from its interplay with its antithesis, *epēlys* or "incomer," "immigrant."[89] One who is not an *epēlys* is perforce *not* an "incomer" to a new land, but an *autokhthōn* ("one always having the same land").[90] Thus Herodotos employs *autokhthōn* to describe indigenous peoples outside Attika, without any suggestion of earthly or other supernatural origin.[91] To this "original meaning of *autokhthōn* ("always having the same land")," there did develop at Athens a secondary notation of "a people who had literally been born from the earth," a "relatively late appearance" of a usage contrary to the natural sense of "*autos* + *khthōn*" (Rosivach 1987: 301).[92] But while the secondary notation is occasionally encountered in mythically based poetic compositions, as in Euripides, "living in the same land for a long time" dominates elsewhere, even amid the exuberant prose and mythical tales of the encomia honoring fallen Athenian soldiers.

3. While Athenian artistic presentations are often proffered by modern scholars as confirmatory of the Athenians' pervasive attachment to a literal interpretation of their earthborn origins, many of these illustrations entirely lack ideological or historical context, and virtually all are subject to multitudinously varied interpretations. Events in Erekhtheus's life, for example, including his sacrifice of his daughters, are supposedly depicted in the sculptural decorations of various classical temples in Attika, but the specificity and even the general accuracy of these attributions are often quite doubtful.[93] Similarly, notwithstanding frequent efforts to explain individual scenes on Athenian pottery by reference to

[86] Γηγενής explicitly describes supernatural objects. Cf. Eur. *Ph.* 931 (δράκων ὁ γηγενής); Hdt. 8. 55 (Ἐρεχθέος τοῦ γηγενέος λεγόμενου).

[87] Rosivach 1987: 297. Rosivach studies in detail the usage of αὐτόχθων, and even surveys the full range of cases in which αὐτο- is compounded with verbal or nominal roots (1987: 299–301).

[88] See, for example, the preceding discussion of *logos/mythos* and the discussion of ἀστός/πολίτης in Chapter 2, pp. 50–63. Cf. Cohen 1992: 44–60 (τόκος ναυτικός and ἔγγειος).

[89] LSJ, s.v. ἔπηλυς, II.

[90] For use of the two terms in vivid opposition, see (for example) Hdt. 4.197.2; Isok. 4.63, 12.124; Pl. *Men.* 237b; Dem. 60.4. Cf. Hdt. 1.78; Eur. *Iōn* 589–90, fr. 362.7.

[91] See Hdt. 1.171–72, 4.197.2, 8.73.

[92] Although some historians have sought to connect this usage with the growth of egalitarian democracy (cf. Miller 1983: 11–34; Rosivach 1987: 302–5), Montanari (1981: 59) has noted the possible connection between this linguistic phenomenon and a preclassical Athenian "tribal" or "ethnic" orientation ("una tendenzialità etnico-genetica").

[93] See Kron 1981– : s.v. Erechtheus; Collard, Cropp, and Lee [1995] 1997: 153–54.

autochthonous legend, in fact only in the fifth century does Athenian pottery even begin to present figural representations of legendary heroes and early chieftains, and then often only in a generalized, nonspecific manner, whose implications for the Athenians were necessarily far different from those posited by scholars influenced by modern preconceptions. Consider, for example, Loraux's explanation of a red-figure lekythos in the Louvre (CA 681), from the period about 450: "Athena and Erichthonios: the goddess 'raises up' a child, and we have no trouble recognizing it as the autochthonous hero, *despite the absence of Ge (and also of Hephaistos and Kekrops)*."[94] Similar ambiguous representations, presenting a timeless contemporaneity that does not require, or confirm, a narrative interpretation, are often identified as the "birth of Erikhthonios."[95]

4. "Funeral speeches" (*epitaphioi logoi*, sing. *epitaphios*) celebrating the soldiers who had died in recent warfare were delivered periodically through most of the fifth and fourth centuries.[96] Yet only a half-dozen examples survive, chronologically scattered over the entire classical period, several only in fragmentary form, and all but one of disputed context. A brief quotation from an *epitaphios* attributed to the sophist Gorgias offers a stunning example of rhetorical flourishes and figures, but the preserved single paragraph of platitudes makes no mention of Athenian autochthony or even of Attika: the only mother or father mentioned are the human parents of the decedents.[97] The remaining testimonia include only a single example of an actual oration clearly attributable to a known historical figure (Hypereidēs), and even that sole exemplar is very late and quite fragmentary.[98] We also have single speeches of unclear context attributed (falsely, by general belief) to Lysias and

[94] [1984] 1993: vii, plate 1. Emphasis added.

[95] See, for further example, Beasley 1963: 1268, 2 (Kodros Painter). Cf. Brommer 1957; Kron 1976: 246–47; Metzger 1976: 298.

[96] See Humphreys [1983] 1993: 89–90; Pritchett 1971–91: 4:106–24. Jacoby (1944a, 1944b) has argued that there was no separate funeral ceremony for recently deceased soldiers: their eulogy occurred during the annual Genēsia festival celebrating all the dead.

[97] D.K. 872.B: 5a–b, 6. ὅσιοι δὲ πρὸς τοὺς τοκέας τῆι θεραπείαι (6, line 30). The most detailed study of this speech (Vollgraff 1952) interprets it as essentially a manifesto for Sophistic education. Cf. Méridier 1964: 5:69–70.

[98] See Hess 1938. There is also a "funeral address" of Arkhinos that is known only from a reference by the ninth-century C.E. Byzantine scholar Phōtios (*Bibliothēkē* 487b34), but that *may* be reflected in the *Strōmateis* of Clement of Alexandria, a Christian writer of the second century C.E (627 and 749). See Huby 1957: 109; Treves 1937: 135. Plutarch makes mention of an *epitaphios* delivered by Periklēs for those who had died at Samos in 440 (*Perikl.* 28.5). Cf. Schneider 1912.

Demosthenes,[99] Thucydides's version of the famous speech of Periklēs, and Plato's mischievous composition of a funeral speech that he attributes to Aspasia. Although the Athenians attributed the institution of the public funeral to "ancestral custom" (*patrios nomos*),[100] the first funeral address was actually given only after the end of the Persian Wars:[101] the institution of these speeches seems thus to have paralleled the fifth-century advent of Athenian imperial hegemony and the nation-building adaptation of early tales of serpentine deities into claims for the supernatural origin of human Athenians (see pp. 83–85).

Although the ancillary themes of the encomia are inherently incredible (victory over the mythical Amazons, exploits relating to the legendary offspring of the shadowy Hēraklēs, accomplishments involving the "Seven against Thebes," and so forth), these speeches have been uniformly accepted as important evidence for Athenian beliefs and values, supposedly supporting the modern portrayal of Athens as an exploitative "club" inherently limited to men of select genealogy and birth. For prevailing scholarship, a belief in a mutually shared supernatural origin precludes the admission of outsiders into the blood-determined *polis* of "citizens" (see pp. 82–83) and justified for the Athenians the tripartite caste system that supposedly dominated all aspects of their lives (see Chapters 4 and 6). These interpretations, however, are based not on the actual texts of the surviving *epitaphioi logoi*, but almost entirely on a single jocular and ironic presentation, the funeral address attributed to Periklēs' companion, Aspasia, in Plato's *Menexenos* (a literary tour de force of purposeful falsity, a mockery of the idealization of Athens, its beliefs and values as expressed in the famous funeral address of Periklēs).[102] But in funeral orations purporting to be actual encomia over the dead[103]—the surviving speeches attributed to Periklēs, Hypereidēs,

[99] Demosthenes 60 and Lysias 2 are usually, but perhaps erroneously (Loraux [1981] 1986: 10), deemed spurious: see Jacoby 1944a. On Lysias 2, cf. Girard 1872; Walz 1936; Henderson 1975: 30, n. 20; on Demosthenes 60, Sykutris 1928; Colin 1938; and Pohlenz 1948 (cf. Habicht 1997: 7, n. 1).

[100] Thouk. 2.34.1: Ἀθηναῖοι τῷ πατρίῳ νόμῳ χρώμενοι δημοσίᾳ ταφὰς ἐποιήσαντο τῶν ἐν τῷδε τῷ πολέμῳ πρώτων ἀποθανόντων.

[101] Introduction of the *epitaphios* soon after the Persian Wars: Kierdorf 1966: 93ff.; Thomas 1989: 207–8; Clairmont 1983; Hauvette 1898. But others opt for an even later date, for example, Jacoby 1944a: 50–54 (465); Schneider 1912: (439). The first public burial ceremonies may not have included an *epitaphios logos*: see Ziolkowski 1981: 13ff.; Bradeen 1969.

[102] See pp. 100–2.

[103] Even these four must be interpreted with care: "perhaps only one or two of them were actually delivered in anything like their present form at one of the memorial services for those who perished in war" (Kennedy 1963: 154).

Demosthenes and Lysias—the orators treat Attika largely as a figurative motherland and present the Athenians as autochthonous only in the sense of being a people resident for many generations in a land that, unlike other territorial entities, had not in recent memory experienced widespread change in population as a result of war or other cataclysm. The funeral speeches actually are striking illustrations of nation building—literally "the invention of Athens," as Nicole Loraux titled her exhaustive scholarly treatment of these eulogies—Athenian examples of the common use of historical fabrication and mythical tales to confirm a nation's connection to a particular territory and a specific history (see pp. 79–82).

The earliest encomium, Periklēs' funeral oration,[104] does take Athenian ancestry as its starting point and does focus explicitly on communal memory of ancient accomplishments,[105] but makes no mention of the birth of primeval Athenians from Attic soil and offers no suggestion of any genealogical basis for limiting participation in *politeia*.[106] To the contrary, in a speech often judged the quintessential declaration of Athenian beliefs and values,[107] Periklēs merely notes that "our ancestors dwelt in the country without break in the succession from generation to generation, and handed it down free to the present time by their valor."[108] Speaking in the fifth century, at the beginning of the Peloponnesian War, Periklēs rouses patriotic zeal by emphasizing recent history, the personally known and still-verifiable accomplishments of "our own fathers, who are even more worthy of praise [than earlier ancestors], because having acquired the empire which we now hold, in addition to what they received, not without effort they bequeathed it to those now living."[109] Periklēs appeals repeatedly to the collective imagination of his audience—vividly creating with consummate artistry that connection between people, land, and

[104] Thouk. 2.35–46. For the historicity of Thucydides's rendering, see Connor 1983: 63–75; Landmann 1974; Flashar 1968. On the general historical value of the speeches contained in Thucydides's history, see n. 67.

[105] 2.36.1: Ἄρξομαι δὲ ἀπὸ τῶν προγόνων πρῶτον· δίκαιον γὰρ αὐτοῖς καὶ πρέπον δὲ ἅμα ἐν τῷ τοιῷδε τὴν τιμὴν ταύτην τῆς μνήμης δίδοσθαι.

[106] This is consistent with Thucydides's own treatment of Athenian autochthony. See Chapter 3, pp. 91–92.

[107] See, for example, Oppenheimer 1933: 12; Popper 1950: esp. 182; Goldhill 1986: 63; Farrar 1988: 163; Saxonhouse 1996: 60–62.

[108] Crawley translation of 2.36.1: τὴν γὰρ χώραν οἱ αὐτοὶ αἰεὶ οἰκοῦντες διαδοχῇ τῶν ἐπιγιγνομένων μέχρι τοῦδε ἐλευθέραν δι' ἀρετὴν παρέδοσαν.

[109] 2.36.2: ἄξιοι ἐπαίνου καὶ ἔτι μᾶλλον οἱ πατέρες ἡμῶν· κτησάμενοι γὰρ πρὸς οἷς ἐδέξαντο ὅσην ἔχομεν ἀρχὴν οὐκ ἀπόνως ἡμῖν τοῖς νῦν προσκατέλιπον.

history that modern ethnologists have identified as integral to nation building. "Our fathers, and we ourselves, have eagerly repulsed any enemy, Greek or barbarian, invading our territory"[110]—"a land that we have made totally self-sufficient in war and in peace"[111]; "you must yourselves realise the power of Athens, and feed your eyes upon her from day to day, till love of her fills your hearts; and then when all her greatness shall break upon you, you must reflect that it was by courage, sense of duty, and a keen feeling of honor in action that men were enabled to win all this, and that no personal failure in an enterprise could make them consent to deprive their country of their valor, but they laid it at her feet as the most glorious contribution that they could offer."[112]

In this sublime rousing of national consciousness, Periklēs tellingly addresses his audience not as *politai* but as *astoi* (and *xenoi*)[113]—appropriately, because at Athenian funeral ceremonies the orators (themselves perhaps not always Athenian *politai*)[114] speak directly to an audience that encompasses a spectrum of persons present in Attika: local men and women of varied status, visiting foreigners, perhaps family members of foreigners who had fought for Athens. The author of the *epitaphios* attributed to Demosthenes even appeals directly for the favorable attention of those members of the audience who are not of Athenian blood.[115] Thucydides explicitly identifies the crowd at the funeral activities as including anyone who wished to participate, "of both the *astoi* and the *xenoi*, and women."[116] Periklēs, Lysias, Hypereidēs all speak explicitly

[110] 2.36.4: αὐτοὶ ἢ οἱ πατέρες ἡμῶν βάρβαρον ἢ Ἕλληνα πολέμιον ἐπιόντα προθύμως ἠμυνάμεθα.

[111] 2.36.3: τὴν πόλιν τοῖς πᾶσι παρεσκευάσαμεν καὶ ἐς πόλεμον καὶ ἐς εἰρήνην αὐταρκεστάτην.

[112] Crawley translation of 2.43.1: μᾶλλον τὴν τῆς πόλεως δύναμιν καθ' ἡμέραν ἔργῳ θεωμένους καὶ ἐραστὰς γιγνομένους αὐτῆς, καὶ ὅταν ὑμῖν μεγάλη δόξῃ εἶναι, ἐνθυμουμένους ὅτι τολμῶντες καὶ γιγνώσκοντες τὰ δέοντα καὶ ἐν τοῖς ἔργοις αἰσχυνόμενοι ἄνδρες αὐτὰ ἐκτήσαντο, καὶ ὁπότε καὶ πείρᾳ του σφαλεῖεν, οὐκ οὖν καὶ τὴν πόλιν γε τῆς σφετέρας ἀρετῆς ἀξιοῦντες στερίσκειν, κάλλιστον δὲ ἔρανον αὐτῇ προϊέμενοι.

[113] 2.36.4: τὸν πάντα ὅμιλον καὶ ἀστῶν καὶ ξένων. Gorgias also explicitly refers to the *astoi* (πρὸς τοὺς ἀστοὺς) in his laudation of τοὺς ἐν πολέμοις ἀριστεύσαντας Ἀθηναίων. D.K. 872.B6.8, 31. (The *xenoi* would be foreigners who were present in Athens as visitors. For the distinction between *astoi* and *politai*, and between *astoi* and *xenoi*, see Chapter 2, pp. 50–63, 71–74). The orators do, on occasion, allude also to *politai*: see, for example, Hyper. *Epitaph*. 27.

[114] Of the six surviving exemplars, only two, those of Periklēs and Leōsthenēs, are known to have been delivered by Athenian *politai*. Demosthenes was chosen to speak on behalf of the dead after Khairōneia (Dem. 18. 285), but the *epitaphios* contained in his forensic corpus is of doubtful attribution (see n. 99).

[115] 60.13: Ἀνάγκη . . . τοὺς ἔξω τοῦ γένους πρὸς τὸν τάφον ἠκολουθηκότας πρὸς εὔνοιαν παρακαλέσαι.

[116] 2.34.4: ξυνεκφέρει δὲ ὁ βουλόμενος καὶ ἀστῶν καὶ ξένων, καὶ γυναῖκες πάρεισιν. . . . Cf. Pl. *Men*. 235b3–4: ἀεὶ μετ' ἐμοῦ ξένοι τινὲς ἕπονται καὶ συνακροῶνται. This inclusiveness may mirror the fact that the funeral address was merely part of a complex of burial rites, such as the funeral

to the wives, mothers, and/or sisters of the fallen.[117] This diversified audience Periklēs addresses continually in the first-person plural ("we"), in stark contrast to his use of the second-personal plural ("you") when he addresses an audience of *politai*, as in his final speech to the Assembly in 429.[118] His auditors are thus drawn into the combination of persons, physical environment, and shared experience that constituted the imagined community of Athens, a spiritual *imaginaire* that, for Periklēs in this context (as for modern nationalists generally),[119] is ultimately defined by its members' commitment to self-sacrifice. An individual's dying for the fatherland (*patris*), Periklēs insists, may expiate any prior personal inadequacies.[120] To die for the community is a sacrifice that Periklēs's idealized Athens demands, and deserves: "such is the Athens for which these men, in the assertion of their resolve not to lose her, nobly fought and died; and well may every one of their survivors be ready to suffer in her cause."[121]

But in the classical period many who died for Athens were not *politai*. The Athenian armed forces encompassed even in the fifth century residents of Attika who were metics. By the fourth century, at the latest, organization of the army on a deme basis had resulted in the integration into the military of large numbers of metics and perhaps even of slaves.[122] Hired fighters, not *politai* or even *astoi*, appear to have constituted the bulk of the Athenian forces honored by Hypereidēs in 323/22 in the latest surviving *epitaphios*, an encomium honoring the Athenian general Leōsthenēs and those who died with him in the first part of the Lamian War.[123] In this speech, allusions to the fatherland (*patris)* are ever pres-

banquet, that were organized not by the *polis* but through the *oikoi* (see Wolters 1913: 7; Jacoby 1944a: 60, 62; Lacey 1968: 78; cf. above Chapter 1, pp. 45ff.

[117] Thouk. 2.45.2; Lys. 2.75; Hyper. *Epitaph.* 27. See Kallet-Marx 1993: 139–40.

[118] 2.60–64. Connor (1983: 65–66) explores the relationship between the funeral oration, the final address, and the text of the other speech attributed to Periklēs by Thucydides (1.140–44). Cf. Flashar 1968: 38.

[119] "[T]he nation is always conceived as a deep horizontal comradeship. Ultimately it is this fraternity that makes it possible, over the past two centuries, for so many millions of people, not so much to kill, as willingly to die" (Anderson 1991: 7).

[120] καὶ γὰρ τοῖς τἆλλα χείροσι δίκαιον τὴν ἐς τοὺς πολέμους ὑπὲρ τῆς πατρίδος ἀνδραγαθίαν προτίθεσθαι· (2.42.3).

[121] Crawley translation of 2.41.5: περὶ τοιαύτης οὖν πόλεως οἵδε τε γενναίως δικαιοῦντες μὴ ἀφαιρεθῆναι αὐτὴν μαχόμενοι ἐτελεύτησαν, καὶ τῶν λειπομένων πάντα τινὰ εἰκὸς ἐθέλειν ὑπὲρ αὐτῆς κάμνειν.

[122] For metics and slaves in the military, see Chapter 2, pp. 56–57, 73–74, and nn. 51, 163–66.

[123] For the date and context of the speech, see Colin 1946: 276. Cf. Jaschinski 1981: 52–54.

ent,[124] but Hypereidēs does not discuss the actual origins and pedigree of the dead, martyred members of an Athenian force in which residents of Attika (both *politai* and non-*politai*) had been a minority.[125] Instead, eliding all reference to supernatural origins and miraculous original birth from Attic soil, Hypereidēs briefly contrasts the Athenians' long sojourn in Attika and their "common origin" with the situation of others who, having come together from a variety of places into a single *polis,* could not claim even a figurative form of shared pedigree.[126]

The two other speeches in this "scanty corpus" (Loraux [1981] 1986: 11) offer similar passing allusions. A presentation attributed to Lysias insists that the Athenians, in contrast to other groups, had not come together from many places to inhabit a foreign land after having cast out earlier inhabitants "but, being autochthonous [*autokhthones*], had acquired the same mother and fatherland [*patris*]."[127] Although some scholars tautologically translate the single word *autokhthones* here as "having been born from the soil" (Loraux [1984] 1993: 66), the seminal meaning of *autokhthones* ("living in the same land for a long time": see pp. 92–93) eliminates the otherwise patent contradiction of the Athenians' "acquiring" (without ousting anyone else) the soil from which they were born. The speech proceeds to refer to the "genuine and *autokhthonous* courage" that the Athenians showed at the Battle of Salamis.[128] Courage in defense of your own homeland and that of your ancestors—an *aretē* arising from "living in the same land for a long time"—makes sense. An *aretē* arising from literally "having been born from the soil" does not. In the *epitaphios* attributed to Demosthenes, the common origin of the Athenians is attributed not to the Attic soil but to the fatherland

[124] *Epitaph.* 9, 10, 19, 35, 37, 39, 41.

[125] At the commencement of hostilities, Leōsthenēs headed an army of 8,000 experienced mercenaries gathered from Asia Minor, many of whom had formerly been employed by Persian satraps (Diod. Sik. 17.111.3, 18.8.7–9.4). Athens sent Leōsthenēs some 5,500 troops from its own population—and an additional 2,000 mercenaries (Diod. Sik. 18.11.3). The force that fought in the north with Leōsthenēs also included many allies (Diod. Sik. 18.10.5–11; Schmitt 1969: no. 413; Broneer 1933: 397, no. 17). Cf. Habicht 1997: 35–37; Lehmann 1988.

[126] *Epitaph.* 7: τὸ<ν> μὲν <γὰρ> ἄλλους τιν(ὰ)ς ἀνθρώπους ἐγκωμιάζοντα, | οἵ, πολλαχόθεν εἰς μίαν πόλιν συνεληλυθότες, οἰκοῦσι, γένος ἴδιον ἕκαστος συνεισενεγκάμενος, τοῦτον μὲν δεῖ κατ᾽ ἄνδρα γενεαλογεῖν ἕκαστον· περὶ δὲ Ἀθηναίων ἀνδρῶν τοὺ <ς> λόγου <ς> ποιούμενον, οἷς ἡ κοινὴ γένεσις α<ὐτόχ>θοσιν οὖσιν ἀνυπέρβλητον τὴν εὐγένειαν ἔχει, περίεργον ἡγοῦμαι εἶναι ἰδίᾳ τὰ γένη ἐγκωμιάζειν.

[127] Lys. 2.17: οὐ γάρ, ὥσπερ οἱ πολλοί, πανταχόθεν συνειλεγμένοι καὶ ἑτέρους ἐκβαλόντες τὴν ἀλλοτρίαν ᾤκησαν, ἀλλ᾽ αὐτόχθονες ὄντες τὴν αὐτὴν ἐκέκτηντο καὶ μητέρα καὶ πατρίδα. For the alternative formulation μητρίδα καὶ πατρίδα, see Pl. *Rep.* 9.575d7.

[128] 2.43: γνησίαν δὲ καὶ αὐτόχθονα τοῖς ἐκ τῆς Ἀσίας βαρβάροις τὴν αὐτῶν ἀρετὴν ἐπεδείξαντο.

(*patris*).[129] The claim here—"for they alone of all men have inhabited and have passed on to their descendants the fatherland from which they sprang"[130]—is essentially an iteration of Periklēs's concept of Athenian autochthony based on long habitation and continuity of generations. In the Demosthenic oration, mystical union with the Attic motherland has been entirely superseded by militaristic and nationalistic attachment to the fatherland, and "the land of the fathers takes the place of the mother, to the extent of supplanting her as the signifier."[131] The speech presents, albeit in patriarchal garb, the characteristic claim of emergent nations (in Handler's words) "to be 'born of' and indissolubly linked to a bounded territory and a particular history" (1988: 154).

A very different formulation is found in Plato's *Menexenos*. This dialogue (now generally accepted as authentically Platonic precisely because of its ironic satirization of Athenian beliefs)[132] ridicules the claims of the traditional *epitaphioi logoi*[133] and mocks Periklēs's famed presentation in particular.[134] In the *Menexenos*, a teasing Sōkratēs[135] proffers the text of a funeral oration composed by Periklēs's *amour*, Aspasia, and memorized by Sōkratēs under her direction.[136] But this encomium (replete with "fragments" of Periklēs's own address, which according to Sōkratēs was itself composed by Aspasia)[137] is actually a lampooning distortion of Periklēs's idealized Athens. The constitutional system extolled in the Periklean oration is also lauded in the *Menexenos*, but as

[129] Dem. 60.4: οὐ γὰρ μόνον εἰς πατέρ' αὐτοῖς καὶ τῶν ἄνω προγόνων κατ' ἄνδρ' ἀνενεγκεῖν ἑκάστῳ τὴν φύσιν ἔστιν, ἀλλ' εἰς ὅλην κοινῇ τὴν ὑπάχρουσαν πατρίδα, ἧς αὐτόχθονες ὁμολογοῦνται εἶναι.

[130] 60.4: μόνοι γὰρ πάντων ἀνθρώπων, ἐξ ἧσπερ ἔφυσαν, ταύτην ᾤκησαν καὶ τοῖς ἐξ αὑτῶν παρέδωκαν.

[131] Loraux [1984] 1993: 66, commenting on Dem. 60.4. She continues: "Instead of the binominal *mētēr kai patris*, the couple *patēr/patris* will take on the function of a parental couple from this point onward, but it is a parental couple that is wholly masculine." In fact, the orator has not entirely abandoned maternal analogy: Attika's bountiful sustenance supposedly proves that "the land is the mother of our ancestors" (§5: τὸ τοὺς καρπούς . . . φανῆναι . . . ὁμολογούμενον σημεῖον ὑπάρχειν τοῦ μητέρα τὴν χώραν εἶναι τῶν ἡμετέρων προγόνων).

[132] See Tsitsidiris 1998: 21–41; Henry 1995: 33; Dean-Jones 1995: 52; Bloedow 1975. The dialogue was often read without humor in the nineteenth century, and its inclusion in the Platonic corpus was accordingly often questioned. (Isolated twentieth-century denials of Platonic authorship persist: see, for example, the youthful article of Momigliano [1930]; Spelman 1994: 107, n. 20.)

[133] See, for example, 234c, 235a, 235d, 236a, 246a. Cf. Henderson 1975: 29–33; Thomas 1989: 210–11.

[134] See Kahn 1963; Loraux 1974; Berndt 1881.

[135] Menexenos claims: Ἀεὶ σὺ προσπαίζεις, ὦ Σώκρατες (235c6); Sōkratēs admits: ἴσως μου καταγελάσῃ, ἄν σοι δόξω πρεσβύτης ὢν ἔτι παίζειν (236c8–9).

[136] 236b7–c1: MEN. Ἦ καὶ μνημονεύσαις ἂν ἃ ἔλεγεν ἡ Ἀσπασία; ΣΩ. Εἰ μὴ ἀδικῶ γε· ἐμάνθανόν γέ τοι παρ' αὐτῆς, καὶ ὀλίγου πληγὰς ἔλαβον ὅτ' ἐπενλανθανόμην.

[137] 236b5: συνετίθει τὸν ἐπιτάφιον λόγον ὃν Περικλῆς εἶπεν.

an example not of democracy but of aristocracy![138] And Periklēs's pride in the Athenians' long residence in Attika ("our ancestors dwelt in the country without break in the succession from generation to generation") is echoed and parodied. "The forefathers of these men were not of foreign origin—a pedigree that would brand them, the offspring, as sojourners in a country to which their ancestors had come from elsewhere. Rather they are native to the country [*autokhthons*], truly living and residing in their fatherland [*patris*]."[139] The *Menexenos* sardonically offers actual birth from the soil as the basis for Athenian democracy/aristocracy ("or whatever")[140] but with a twist that directly mocks Periklēs. Attic soil *was* the literal motherland of the war dead and of the audience ("this earth begat the ancestors of these men and of us"), an assertion that can easily be proved: "for every parent provides appropriate nourishment for its offspring, by which true motherhood may be determined . . . [sustenance] which our earth and mother provides sufficiently."[141] Of course, Attika was actually massively dependent on imported food to nourish its population,[142] a shortfall that Thucydides' Periklēs had finessed by boasting of Athens's unparalleled capacity to command the importation of food and other products from the entire world ("the magnitude of our city draws the produce of the world into our harbour, so that to the Athenian the fruits of other countries are as familiar a luxury as those of his own").[143]

The *Menexenos* presents this mutually shared autochthonous origin as the foundation underlying Athens's egalitarian arrangements (which Plato, of course, abhors): "Equality of birth is the basis of our constitution [*politeia*]. Other *poleis* have been fashioned from unequal men of varied origin; the result is that their constitutions are unequal . . . but in our

[138] 238c2–6: ὡς οὖν ἐν καλῇ πολιτείᾳ ἐτράφησαν οἱ πρόσθεν ἡμῶν, ἀναγκαῖον δηλῶσαι. . . . ἡ γὰρ αὐτὴ πολιτεία καὶ τότε ἦν καὶ νῦν, ἀριστοκρατία, ἐν ᾗ νῦν τὲ πολιτευόμεθα.

[139] 237b3–6: ὑπῆρξε τοῖσδε ἡ τῶν προγόνων γένεσις οὐκ ἔπηλυς οὖσα, οὐδὲ τοὺς ἐκγόνους τούτους ἀποφηναμένη μετοικοῦντας ἐν τῇ χώρᾳ ἄλλοθεν σφῶν ἡκόντων, ἀλλ᾽ αὐτόχθονας καὶ τῷ ὄντι ἐν πατρίδι οἰκοῦντας καὶ ζῶντας.

[140] 238c7–d2: καλεῖ δὲ ὁ μὲν αὐτὴν δημοκρατίαν, ὁ δὲ ἄλλο, ᾧ ἂν χαίρῃ, ἔστι δὲ τῇ ἀληθείᾳ μετ᾽ εὐδοξίας πλήθους ἀριστοκρατία.

[141] 237e1–7: ἥδε ἔτεκεν ἡ γῆ τοὺς τῶνδέ τε καὶ ἡμετέρους προγόνους. πᾶν γὰρ τὸ τεκὸν τροφὴν ἔχει ἐπιτηδείαν ᾧ ἂν τέκῃ, ᾧ καὶ γυνὴ δήλη τεκοῦσά τε ἀληθῶς καὶ μή . . . ὃ δὴ καὶ ἡ ἡμετέρα γῆ τε καὶ μήτηρ ἱκανὸν τεκμήριον παρέχεται ὡς ἀνθρώπους γεννησαμένη·.

[142] See Chapter 1, p. 16 and n. 31.

[143] Crawley translation of 2.38.2: ἐπεσέρχεται δὲ διὰ μέγεθος τῆς πόλεως ἐκ πάσης γῆς τὰ πάντα, καὶ ξυμβαίνει ἡμῖν μηδὲν οἰκειοτέρᾳ τῇ ἀπολαύσει τὰ αὐτοῦ ἀγαθὰ γιγνόμενα καρποῦσθαι ἢ καὶ τὰ τῶν ἄλλων ἀνθρώπων.

case we—all of us natural brothers from a single mother—do not deem it appropriate to be slaves or masters of one another: equality of birth naturally compels us to seek equal legal rights."[144] Plato's Sōkratēs has offered his audience a rare mixture of falsifications and absurdities, a farrago of the spellbinding absurdities and inconsistencies that he attributes to funeral addresses generally.[145] Plato's mockery of Periklēs is so skillful that Aspasia's presentation has often been taken at face value as a serious encomium of Athens.[146] In the postclassical period, Aspasia's encomium was recited annually at Athens as a statement of classical values (Cicero, *Orator* 151). Even more strikingly—although Sōkratēs claims that the funeral orators with their hypnotic praise of Athens can transport their listeners to the Islands of the Blessed, producing an illusion that takes days to wear off (235b1–2)—almost twenty-four hundred years after the dramatic date of the *Menexenos*, scholars continue to rely on Plato's fable of autochthonous birth as an important element in modern savants' portrayal of Athens as an inherently closed society.

But the persuasive sway, and patriotic importance, of myths of origin were candidly explained by Plato himself. In the *Republic,* promulgating a foundation "myth" for Kallipolis (the ideal community of that dialogue), Sōkratēs contends that such stories—immune from disproof because of people's lack of direct knowledge of distant prior events[147]—are critical to group cohesion. Even if communal leaders know these origin tales to be false, says Sōkratēs, such a creation tale is a "noble lie" (*pseudos gennaion*): communal interest justifies the myth's promulgation or perpetuation.[148] Its patent falsity should not inhibit its dissemination: at least part of the population will accept the local soil as its "mother," and therefore worthy of sacred defense.[149]

[144] αἰτία δὲ ἡμῖν τῆς πολιτείας ταύτης ἡ ἐξ ἴσου γένεσις. αἱ μὲν γὰρ ἄλλαι πόλεις ἐκ παντοδαπῶν κατεσκευασμέναι ἀνθρώπων εἰσὶ καὶ ἀνωμάλων, ὥστε αὐτῶν ἀνώμαλοι καὶ αἱ πολιτεῖαι . . . ἡμεῖς δὲ καὶ οἱ ἡμέτεροι, μιᾶς μητρὸς πάντες ἀδελφοὶ φύντες, οὐκ ἀξιοῦμεν δοῦλοι οὐδὲ δεσπόται ἀλλήλων εἶναι, ἀλλ' ἡ ἰσογονία ἡμᾶς ἡ κατὰ φύσιν ἰσονομίαν ἀναγκάζει ζητεῖν κατὰ νόμον (238e1–239a3).

[145] 235a2: γοητεύουσιν ἡμῶν τὰς ψυχάς. Cf. Clavaud 1980, esp. 117–18; Loraux 1974.

[146] See, for example, Scholl 1957; von Loewenclau 1961. Cf. Lattanzi 1935; 1953.

[147] *Rep.* 2.382c10–d3: καὶ ἐν αἷς νυνδὴ ἐλέγομεν ταῖς μυθολογίαις, διὰ τὸ μὴ εἰδέναι ὅπῃ τἀληθὲς ἔχει περὶ τῶν παλαιῶν, ἀφομοιοῦντες τῷ ἀληθεῖ τὸ ψεῦδος ὅτι μάλιστα, οὕτω χρήσιμον ποιοῦμεν;

[148] *Rep.* 3.414b8–c2: Τίς ἂν οὖν ἡμῖν μηχανὴ γένοιτο . . . γενναῖόν τι ἓν ψευδομένους πεῖσαι μάλιστα μὲν καὶ αὐτοὺς τοὺς ἄρχοντας, εἰ δὲ μή, τὴν ἄλλην πόλιν; *Rep.* 3.415c6–d4: τοῦτον οὖν τὸν μῦθον ὅπως ἂν πεισθεῖεν, ἔχεις τινὰ μηχανήν; Οὐδαμῶς, ἔφη. . . . Ἀλλὰ καὶ τοῦτο, ἦν δ' ἐγώ, εὖ ἂν ἔχοι πρὸς τὸ μᾶλλον αὐτοὺς τῆς πόλεώς τε καὶ ἀλλήλων κήδεσθαι. Sōkratēs has devoted most of book 3 to demonstrating the moral wrong of even poetic license (οἷα νῦν καταψεύδονται: 391d3).

[149] *Rep.* 3.414d2–e4: ἐπιχειρήσω πρῶτον μὲν αὐτοὺς τοὺς ἄρχοντας πείθειν καὶ τοὺς στρατιώτας, ἔπειτα δὲ καὶ τὴν ἄλλην πόλιν, ὡς ἄρ' ἃ ἡμεῖς αὐτοὺς ἐτρέφομέν τε καὶ ἐπαιδεύομεν . . . ἦσαν δὲ τότε

Athenian nationalism likewise was served by stories claiming for the Athenian people, and for each individual Athenian, an eternal tie to Attika. But metaphorical interpretations of otherwise incredible myths, and the simultaneous flourishing of disparate historical traditions and multiple contemporary dialogues, allowed the inhabitants of fourth-century Attika to enjoy this "noble lie" helpful to national definition, while largely avoiding the social agonies that would have been generated by a society in which full participation was truly limited to persons whose progenitors had lived in Attika from time immemorial, descendants of ancestors born from Attic soil. As I have described at length in Chapter 2, classical Athenian reality—in its openness to newcomers and in its willingness to accept offspring of acculturated *astoi* as *politai*—contradicted traditional Athenian claims to homogeneity through autochthony, even in their figurative, not literal, formulations. This conflict between tradition and reality did not, however, generate intolerable tension for the residents of Attika: social contradictions and conflicting discourses are everywhere prevalent in complex civilizations.[150]

τῇ ἀληθείᾳ ὑπὸ γῆς ἐντὸς πλαττόμενοι καὶ τρεφόμενοι . . . καὶ ἡ γῆ αὐτοὺς μήτηρ οὖσα ἀνῆκεν, καὶ νῦν δεῖ ὡς περὶ μητρὸς καὶ τροφοῦ τῆς χώρας . . . ἀμύνειν αὐτούς.

[150] Cf. Chapter 6, nn. 190–94 and accompanying text.

✦ 4 ✦

A Modern Myth: The Athenian Village

For present-day historians of ancient Greece, classical Athens is largely the incarnation of "the Athenian citizen body, a closed group inaccessible from outside" (Davies 1978: 73), sharing a culture of indigenous and coherent mutuality, a "consensus based on the common outlook of citizens" (Millett 1991: 39). This false premise has infected a multitude of significant contemporary Western scholars and thinkers—from so-called communitarians through Kuhnians—who often cite Athens as historical exemplar of a hermeneutically sealed society functioning as a face-to-face community.[1] In fact, ancient historians have not derived from Athenian sources this characterization of classical Athens as the face-to-face model that contemporary commentators and critics—Charles Taylor, Michael Sandel, Michael Walzer, Alasdair MacIntyre, William Galston, Philip Selnick, and Mary Ann Glendon among others—are perceived to offer as "a retreat from the larger institutions of the state and economy."[2] Instead scholars have merely appropriated Laslett's conceptualization of English village life to identify Athens as the "model of a face-to-face society" where the entire population knew one other intimately and interacted closely on a societywide basis.[3] According to this conceptualization, which has achieved wide currency and accep-

[1] MacIntyre (1981: esp. 49–59; 1989: 196), for example, contrasts modern society—purportedly overdetermined by an excess of narratives and a plurality of incompatible backgrounds—with a conceptualization of "premodern culture" characterized by hermeneutically coherent concepts and beliefs. "Beauty and wisdom such as the Athenians loved them and lived them could exist only in Athens." Castoriadis 1991: 123 (cf. 1987: esp. 146–64).

[2] Himmelfarb 1996. Cf. Kymlicka 1990: 199–237; Sandel 1982; 1996; Barber 1984.

[3] See Laslett 1956; 1972; Finley [1973] 1985: 17 and 1983: 28–29, 82. Laslett cited the Greek *polis* as the prime example of his face-to-face society, ignorantly arguing that the number of citizens was "never more than 10,000" and that "every citizen would know every other citizen" (1956: 158, 163).

tance, especially in comparative studies,[4] Athens is "a university community," "living the typically Mediterranean out-of-doors life" (Finley [1973] 1985: 17). But this idyllic, sunlit life of personal interaction "now unknown" (ibid.), is enjoyed in the chill of a totalitarian exploitation not at all "now unknown." In an oppressive tripartite society—supposedly consisting of free "citizens," free resident aliens, and slaves—a small minority of adult male *politai* supposedly held all the power.[5] Within a "face-to-face society," in a community without anonymity, such a regime would have been especially onerous: caste would have permeated daily living and turned even casual contacts into manifestations of hierarchical dominance.

But against this canonical formulation, historical reality obtrudes. Living in the largest of all Hellenic groupings, with a population and area greater than that of many modern nations (see Chapter 1, pp. 12–15), the inhabitants of Attika enjoyed, in the fourth century, a relative anonymity. In stark contrast to other societies in which status has corresponded to markers immediately discernible (of attire, skin color, size, economic function, or language, for example), the residents of Attika were remarkably homogeneous in appearance and worked in commerce, agriculture, and craft without differentiation of status or compensation.[6] In daily life, individuals would have had little or no knowledge of the "status" of the persons with whom they had contact, and virtually no way of determining to which of the three groups a person belonged. Even control over participation in the Assembly and Council, the bastions of male "citizen" power, was haphazard: differentiation of *politēs* from foreigner was so uncertain that the origins and status of even the most prominent leaders of the *polis* might be unclear. A society characterized by murky and complex multidimensional social affiliations and arrangements that were continually being modified by internal demo-

[4] Following its promulgation, this "notion of a face-to-face society" was "eagerly taken up by ancient historians . . . widely adopted" (Osborne 1985a: 64–65) and underlies much recent research: see, for example, Hunter 1994: esp. 96–119; D. Cohen 1991b: 155–56; Holmes 1979; Thomas 1989: 82. In recent years, a few specialists have challenged the characterization of Athens itself as a face-to-face society, and instead have proffered the Athenian "demes" as models of communal and personal intimacy (see the second section in this chapter).

[5] See Preface, pp. 10–12. The composition of Athens's population is discussed in Chapter 1, pp. 17ff.

[6] On the lack of visible "markers" of personal status at Athens, see Winkler 1990a: 180; Raaflaub 1994: 143; Lauffer 1958.

graphic mobility and by extensive immigration and emigration, Athens was not a "face-to-face" community—not on a *polis*-wide scale and not within its demes (the hereditary subdivisions, which, in their attenuated and bifurcated fourth-century form, cannot be equated to "villages"—see the second section in this chapter).

"Not Knowing One Another" in Attika

During the first half of the fourth century, the Athenians occupied in Attika the largest politically unified territory in the Hellenic world. Massively larger than other Greek entities, in both territory and population, Athens was comparable with a number of modern nation-states.[7] Ancient Attika's scale, however, was magnified in its inhabitants' perception by prevailing primitive modes of communication and by its difficult terrain. Thus Thucydides emphasizes how the oligarchic counterrevolution of 411 engendered fear and a sense of helplessness among the population precisely because Attika's perceived vastness ("the great size of the *polis*") and the resultant absence of community-wide person-to-person relationships ("because they did not know one another") prevented people from realizing how few the conspirators actually were.[8] Isokratēs insists that because of Athens's "great size and the large number of its inhabitants," the population was not "cognizable at a glance" (*eusynoptos*), giving rise to impossibly false conjectures about individual residents, sometimes the exact opposite of reality.[9] (This ability to identify one another at a glance is, for Aristotle, the essence of the paradigmatic *polis:* in a society that is not easily "cognizable" [*eusynoptos*], the *politai* cannot "know one another," and there is no possibility of personalized participation in decision making and office holding, the critical element of a "true" *polis.*)[10]

Within this Greek colossus, the difficulty of identifying an individual's legalistic position—both on casual contact and even after extensive

[7] See Chapter 1, pp. 12–13.

[8] Thouk. 8.66.3: καὶ τὸ ξυνεστηκὸς πολὺ πλέον ἡγούμενοι εἶναι ἢ ὅσον ἐτύγχανεν ὂν ἡσσῶντο ταῖς γνώμαις, καὶ ἐξευρεῖν αὐτὸ ἀδύνατοι ὄντες διὰ τὸ μέγεθος τῆς πόλεως καὶ διὰ τὴν ἀλλήλων ἀγνωσίαν οὐκ εἶχον.

[9] Isok. 15.172: διὰ γὰρ τὸ μέγεθος καὶ τὸ πλῆθος τῶν ἐνοικούνων οὐκ εὐσύνοπτός ἐστιν οὐδ' ἀκριβής, . . . καὶ δόξαν ἐνίοις τὴν ἐναντίαν τῆς προσηκούσης περιέθηκεν.

[10] See Chapter 1, nn. 7, 8.

dealing—is frequently attested. Aristotle is thought to be alluding to Athens, the most populous of *poleis*, in insisting that "for foreigners and aliens it's easy to participate politically in an overpopulated *polis:* because of the excessive number of inhabitants it's not difficult to elude notice."[11] The satiric *Constitution of the Athenians* (attributed to Xenophon) emphasizes the impossibility at Athens of distinguishing, by dress or physical appearance, free men from slaves, Athenians from aliens.[12] The sober *Constitution of the Athenians* (attributed to Aristotle) even specifies a complex procedure, including rights of appeal, for determining whether youths being evaluated for *politeia* are "free"—provisions responsive to the absence at Athens of visible markers readily differentiating free persons from slaves.[13] Court presentations routinely posit a similarity of appearance among the inhabitants of Attika. During a raid on a "citizen" 's farm, for example, by persons seeking to enforce a judgment, the debtor's son was carried off—he was assumed to be a slave (Dem. 47.61). The maltreatment of a free woman, described at Demosthenes 47.58–59, demonstrates the difficulty of differentiating female slaves from free women. We even hear of a young man who was sent into a neighbor's garden to pluck flowers in the hope that, mistaking the intruder for a slave, the neighbor might strike or bind him and thus become subject to damages for *hybris* (Dem. 53.16).[14]

Owing deference only to the free adults in their own *oikoi* ("households"), slaves not only were similar to free persons in appearance but frequently dealt as equals, sometimes even contemptuously, with unenslaved adversaries.[15] Plato in the *Republic* claims that "men and women purchased as slaves" find themselves at Athens "no less free than

[11] *Pol.* 1326b19–22. Scholars generally assume an Athenian focus for much of the argumentation and many of the allusions in the *Politics.* See Mossé 1967, 1979.

[12] Xen. *Ath. Pol.* 1.10: εἰ νόμος ἦν τὸν δοῦλον ὑπὸ τοῦ ἐλευθέρου τύπτεσθαι . . . πολλάκις ἂν οἰηθεὶς εἶναι τὸν Ἀθηναῖον δοῦλον ἐπάταξεν ἄν· ἐσθῆτά τε γὰρ οὐδὲν βελτίων ὁ δῆμος αὐτόθι ἢ οἱ δοῦλοι καὶ οἱ μέτοικοι, καὶ τὰ εἴδη οὐδὲν βελτίους εἰσίν. Cf. Pl., *Rep.* 563b. Although the *Ath. Pol.* attributed to Xenophon is generally dated to late in the fifth century (420s [Fisher 1993: 53], 420–415 [Gomme (1940) 1962: 68], and sometimes even earlier ["some date between the late 440's and late 420's": Stockton 1990: 168]), a fourth-century origin cannot be ruled out: cf. the anachronistic funeral speech of Aspasia, who lived in the fifth century, set in Plato's *Menexenos,* which had a dramatic date of 386.

[13] Aristot. *Ath. Pol.* 42.1. I follow here the prevailing interpretation of this passage: ἐλεύθερος should be understood in its usual meaning, "free" as opposed to "slave" (cf. Rhodes 1981; Scafuro 1994: 187, n. 43; see Chapter 2, n. 82).

[14] On *hybris*, see Chapter 6, pp. 160–66.

[15] See Chapter 5, pp. 146–48.

their purchasers."[16] Unfree persons occupied positions of significance in many aspects of Athenian business.[17] Some slaves were even themselves slave owners,[18] and many slaves—albeit formally still in bondage—actually maintained their own households, operated their own businesses, and had contact with their owners only periodically, sometimes merely to confirm commercial arrangements.[19]

Slaves and metics—and Athenian *politai*—dealt indiscriminately with one another as principals in overseas commercial transactions.[20] Slaves owned by the state (*dēmosioi*) often exercised discretionary authority in regulating matters of commercial significance and enjoyed the benefits, material and social, arising from the ability to enrich, or to penalize, traders, merchants, and contractors.[21] Women also often participated actively and significantly in commerce: in fact, it is a woman, Antigona, who plays a leading part in the only domestic Athenian business deal known in detail, a complex financial transaction in which Antigona negotiates the sale of a business, directs the form of finance, and outmaneuvers (defrauds, he claims) the male purchaser (Hyper. *Athēn.* 4–5).[22]

This frequent interchangeability of roles, especially business functions, among persons free and slave, Athenian and foreigner, was facilitated by "the functional incapacity of the Attic bureaucracy to identify its polis inhabitants" (Scafuro 1994: 182). Appearances of freedom (or of slavery) were not subject to confirmation or refutation through official records: at Athens manumission was entirely private; no public document or action was required for the freeing of a slave.[23] Nor could "citizenship"

[16] *Rep.* 563b5–7 (written sometime in the first half of the fourth century): οἱ ἐωνημένοι καὶ αἱ ἐωνημέναι μηδὲν ἧττον ἐλεύθεροι ὦσι τῶν πριαμένων.

[17] See Chapter 5, pp. 134–37.

[18] See Chapter 5, n. 32.

[19] See Chapter 5, third section, p. 148.

[20] See Chapter 5, pp. 134–35. Cf. Hansen 1984; Erxleben 1974: 462–77; Millett 1983: 36–39.

[21] See Chapter 5, pp. 136–37.

[22] For some of the many examples of female commercial activity at Athens, see Herfst [1922] 1980; D. Cohen 1990: 156–57; Brock 1994. On the economic primacy of the household, and the business importance of both its female and male members, see Chapter 1, pp. 40–45.

[23] In contrast, a valid manumission in republican Rome required the presence of a public official (cf. Chapter 5, n. 18). At Athens, even voluntary efforts to publicize manumission were difficult: proclamation of a slave's new freedom was sometimes made in the theater during dramatic festivals, but by 330 such public announcements had been prohibited as disturbing to spectators and performers (Aiskhin. 3.41–44). On the *phialai exeleutherikai*, as possible late manifestations of official recognition of individual liberation, see Todd 1997: 120.

be determined through state records. Although for varied purposes the Athenians maintained many lists of individuals[24]—including a register of prostitutes[25]—no master list of individual *politai*, or of metics, was ever kept.[26] As a result, it was quite difficult to identify an individual or to determine his status, even in the case of a person of high profile and even after extensive investigation.

This difficulty is shown clearly by Lysias 23 and Demosthenes 57, the only surviving Athenian legal cases focused on personal status,[27] two court presentations that are often adduced as prime evidence for the functioning of Athens as a "face-to-face" society of hierarchical ordering.[28] But consider the actual content of these speeches.

After extensive prior contacts,[29] the plaintiff in Lysias 23 believed Pankleōn to be a metic and sued him as such.[30] But Pankleōn asserted that he was a *politēs*, whereupon the plaintiff sued him as a *politēs* (23.2)! Following an extended investigation, the complainant finally concluded that Pankleōn, a person of high profile illuminated by prior extensive litigation,[31] was neither a *politēs* nor a metic, but a slave—albeit one with a mass of supporters who supply physical and financial assistance to keep him from being seized, and who insist that he has a brother who is a *politēs* (9–11). Although Pankleōn continues to claim

[24] Thomas (1989: 66) finds it "striking" that lists constituted so much of the public material preserved on stone inscriptions at state direction. Examples include the names of public debtors (Dem. 58.16, 25.99; cf. Boegehold 1972: 26ff.); lists of public benefactors (Lys. 13.70–72; Dem. 20.64); the names and holdings of persons whose property had been publicly sold (*I.G.* I³ 421–30); the names of persons who failed to pay promised military contributions (Isai. 5.38); the list of Plataians granted *politeia* (Dem. 59.105; cf. *I.G.* II/III² 237); names of traitors (Lykourg. *Leōk.* 117–19); lists of deserters (Andok. 1.78).

[25] Aiskhin. 1.119. Cf. Dover [1978] 1989: 40.

[26] Biscardi 1970: 301 and 1991: 140; Hansen 1985: 14; Rhodes 1981: 497; Paoli [1930] 1974: 258–61. The absence of such a master list explains why "litigants in cases that require status identification never bring [archival] documents into court" (Scafuro 1994: 164). Central registers of *politai*, in fact, were not unknown in the Hellenic world: Syrakuse, like Athens a Greek *polis* of unusual complexity, did maintain a unified listing; see Plut. *Nikias* 14.6. On the absence of marriage registries at Athens: Ledl 1907: 215–23.

[27] Except for Lysias 23, all extant "pleas against jurisdiction" (Dem. 32–38; Isok. 18) deal with issues other than personal status. In the few cases in which a party's persona is relevant (e.g., that of Neaira, the female defendant in Dem. 59), issues of personal status are ancillary to the gravamen of the dispute.

[28] See, for example, Whitehead 1986a: 69: "The speakers in Lysias 23 and Demosthenes 57 are clear on the point: a body of demesmen could be expected to vouch for one of their number as a *face*, not merely a name on a list—someone whom they knew personally as neighbor, colleague, and fellow *dēmotēs*."

[29] Lys. 23.2: Ὡς γὰρ ἀδικῶν με πολὺν χρόνον οὐκ ἐπαύετο.

[30] Ibid.: προσεκαλεσάμην αὐτὸν πρὸς τὸν πολέμαρχον, νομίζων μέτοικον εἶναι.

[31] 23.3 : ἑτέρας δίκας τὰς μὲν φεύγοι τὰς δ' ὠφλήκοι παρὰ τῷ πολεμάρχῳ.

politeia, a woman (clearly not one of the secluded, diffident Athenian females enshrined in much modern scholarship)[32] publicly asserts her ownership of Pankleōn and personally prevents his seizure (10–11). And after further inquiry, the plaintiff ultimately insists on Pankleōn's status as a metic—but in Thebes (15)!

The only other surviving court presentation focused on personal status—Demosthenes 57, involving the Halimous deme's ouster of a *politēs*—replicates the pattern of conflicting claims, ignorance, and uncertainty found in Lysias 23. Here too, contradictory statuses are attributed to the defendant, ranging from slavery through aristocratic "citizenship." Although Euxitheos admits to being the son of a father who was a former slave (57.18) and of a mother who was alleged to have been a slave (34), four separate prior evaluations had confirmed—without challenge—his right to *politeia*.[33] Yet he admits that after his father's return from slavery in Leukas, his mother sold ribbons in the central market (29) and worked as a wet nurse (35)—servile pursuits inappropriate for an Athenian *politēs* (although many *politai* were so engaged).[34] Nevertheless, this background of servitude, demeaning commerce, and sale of bodily function did not deny the family a glorious *cursus honorum*: Euxitheos's father had served as a deme officer (25–26); he himself had been a specially honored deme president (*dēmarkhos*, 63, 64), head of his phratry (*phratriarkhos*, 23), and aristocratically involved in local shrines and cults (46–48, 62).[35]

Indeed, Euxitheos attributes his loss of *politeia* to his failure to conform to prevailing—and, for us, revealing—deme practices:[36] unlike many other members (he implies), he had never even tried to falsify his true parentage and family origins;[37] despite his alleged wealth, he had not,

[32] "It is a cornerstone of the prevailing school(s) of thought that the low status of Athenian women was particularly marked by their confinement to their homes, their exclusion from social, public and economic life." D. Cohen 1989: 3. Cf. Padel 1983; Keuls 1985; Cantarella 1987: 46.

[33] See Dem. 57.27, 46, 62. For the unanimity of acceptance of Euxitheos and Thoukritos as members of the deme and hence as *politai*, see 57.61–62. Euxitheos claims that his father had been captured in war and sold into servitude.

[34] So many *politai* worked in the marketplace that a statute had been enacted punishing reproaches to *politai* or *politides* for working in the *agora*. Dem. 57.30: cf. Wallace 1994: 116, 122–23. Cf. 57.45: πολλαὶ καὶ τιτθαὶ καὶ ἔριθοι καὶ τρυγήτριαι γεγόνασιν ὑπὸ τῶν τῆς πόλεως κατ' ἐκείνους τοὺς χρόνους συμφορῶν ἀσταὶ γυναῖκες, πολλαὶ δ' ἐκ πενήτων πλούσιαι νῦν.

[35] For the family stemma, see Lacey 1980; Andrewes 1961: 6–8.

[36] For the evidentiary value of assertions ancillary to or presupposed by litigational claims, even where we cannot evaluate the truth of such claims, see Preface, pp. xiii–xiv.

[37] 57.51: καίτοι εἰ τοῖς ἐξελεγχομένοις ὧν μέν εἰσιν ἀποκρυπτομένοις, ὧν δ' οὐκ εἰσὶν προσποιουμένοις, δίκαιον ὑπάρχειν παρ' ὑμῖν τοῦτο σημεῖον ὡς εἰσὶ ξένοι, ἐμοὶ δήπου τοὐναντίον

like many others, obtained *politeia* through bribes;[38] to the contrary, as deme leader, he had pursued many demesmen who had evaded their financial obligations to the deme.[39] Halimous was a deme where a large percentage of the membership had previously been expelled as imposters (but then readmitted),[40] where *politeia* allegedly was a commodity frequently bought and sold,[41] and where behavior and demeanor, not legal documentation, were said to be consulted to determine whether an individual was slave or free.[42] Euxitheos insists that the truth of individual origin was actually irrelevant: his family had lived in the country "before Eukleidēs" and hence was protected by enactments effectively safeguarding early if illegal appropriation of deme membership.[43] Again, however, as in Lysias 23, definitive evidence concerning Euxitheos's actual status is never provided.[44] Significantly, this tale of deceit, ignorance, and confusion concerns not one of the "great demes" (*megaloi dēmoi* [Dem. 57.57]) but one of the smallest, one where a majority of hereditary members still lived, a deme territory close to Athens proper and therefore likely to have been relatively immune from the alleged massive migration in the classical period toward urban attractions (see p. 116)—in short, precisely that kind of "village" where, if anywhere in Attika, knowledge of family origin and situation would have been high.

Identification of individuals in Attika was so uncertain that both the ownership of "slaves" functioning in state capacities[45] and the origins and status of even the most prominent leaders of the *polis* were often

---

ὡς εἰμὶ πολίτης. οὐ γὰρ ἂν ξένην καὶ ξένον τοὺς ἐμαυτοῦ γονέας ἐπιγραψάμενος μετέχειν ἠξίουν τῆς πόλεως·

[38] 57.59: οὗτοι βουλομένους τινὰς ἀνθρώπους ξένους πολίτας γενέσθαι, Ἀναξιμένην καὶ Νικόστρατον, κοινῇ διανειμάμενοι πέντε δραχμὰς ἕκαστος προσεδέξαντο. Cf. 52–53 (δι' εὐπορίαν φασὶ πάντα μ' ὠνεῖσθαι. . . . οὐκ ἔστι ταῦτα). For Whitehead's attempts to avoid giving "excessive credence" to this evidence, see 1985a: 293–95. Cf. 57.60 (see n. 41).

[39] 57.63: Εἰ δὲ δεῖ τὴν δημαρχίαν λέγειν . . . ἐν ᾗ διάφορος ἐγενόμην εἰσπράττων ὀφείλοντας πολλοὺς αὐτῶν μισθώσεις τεμενῶν καὶ ἕτερ' ἃ τῶν κοινῶν διηρπάκεσαν.

[40] 57.60: κατηγορῶν δέκα τῶν δημοτῶν ἐξέβαλεν, οὓς ἅπαντας πλὴν ἑνὸς κατεδέξατο τὸ δικαστήριον. Cf. 57.26, 58, 61. Total deme membership may not have exceeded eighty members. See n. 78.

[41] 57.60: πολλούς οἱ μετ' Εὐβουλίδου συνεστῶτες καὶ ἀπολωλέκασιν καὶ σεσῴκασιν ἕνεκ' ἀργυρίου.

[42] Cf. 57.69: ἐμαυτὸν ἐπέδειξα πάντων μετειληφόθ' ὅσων προσήκει τοὺς ἐλευθέρους.

[43] 57.30: τοῖς χρόνοις τοίνυν οὕτω φαίνεται γεγονὼς ὥστε, εἰ καὶ κατὰ θάτερ' ἀστὸς ἦν, εἶναι πολίτην προσήκειν αὐτόν· γέγονε γὰρ πρὸ Εὐκλείδου.

[44] 57.12–13: ἀξιοῦντος δέ μου ἀναβαλέσθαι . . . ἵνα τούτῳ τ' ἐξουσία γένοιθ' . . . μάρτυρας εἴ τινας ἔχοι παρασχέσθαι. . . . οὗτος ὧν μὲν ἐγὼ προὐκαλούμην οὐδὲν ἐφρόντισεν . . . οὔτ' ἔλεγχον οὐδέν' ἀκριβῆ ποιήσας.

[45] Aiskhinēs insists that the prominent Pittalakos is a slave belonging to the *polis*; Hēgēsandros asserts that he is privately owned; others insist that he is free (1.62). On Pittalakos, see Chapter 5, p. 136, Chapter 6, p. 163.

unclear. Although it is difficult to evaluate the reality underlying the frequent jibes by comic writers imputing alien or slave origins to Athenian political leaders,[46] such charges recur in sober court settings and in legislative debate. Demosthenes often attributes foreign, and even slave origin to political opponents.[47] In turn Aiskhinēs characterizes Demosthenes as "servile,"[48] claiming that the Athenian leader had only narrowly avoided being branded as a runaway slave (Aiskhin. 2.79). Deinarchos, himself a metic born at Korinth, attributes Skythian birth to Demosthenes (on his mother's side) and denies his legitimacy as an Athenian *politēs* by birth (*genēi*).[49] Andokidēs charged the prominent politician Hyperbolos with being a foreigner and a non-Greek whose father was a "branded slave" working in the state mint.[50] The politically involved defendants Agoratos and Nikomakhos are identified as slaves and as of slave origin.[51] Such charges, regardless of the facts underlying each specific case (which are generally beyond our critical evaluation),[52] further illustrate the difficulty in ancient Athens of establishing or confirming the personal legal status of any individual, even a prominent person, resident in Attika.

Anonymity and Mobility: The Reality of Deme Life

Despite the widespread adoption of Finley's model of Athens as a village, especially in works by nonspecialists, a few Greek historians, recognizing the factual and conceptual impossibility of characterizing Attika itself

[46] See, for example, the sallies against Kleōn and Kleophōn in Aristophanes's plays. Even the taunts of political leaders sometimes incorporated comic elements (see Harding 1987).

[47] See, for example, his remarks about Aiskhinēs and Meidias: Chapter 2, n. 175.

[48] ἀνδραποδώδης, the opposite of ἐλευθέριος, which refers to a free person (for the antithesis, see, e.g., Aristot. *NE* 1128a21: ἡ τοῦ ἐλευθερίου παιδιὰ διαφέρει τῆς τοῦ ἀνδραποδώδους). Plato (among others) sometimes uses the word metaphorically: cf. Pl., *Laws* 880a4–5 (ἄγροικος καὶ ἀνελεύθερος ἂν λεγόμενος ἀνδραποδώδης τε); *Alk.* 1.120b2–3 (τὴν ἀνδραποδώδη τρίχα ἔχοντες ἐν τῇ ψυχῇ ὑπ' ἀμουσίας).

[49] Dein. 1.15, 95; cf. Aiskhin. 3.171–72.

[50] Andok. fr. 5 (Blass)(F III.2 [Maidment]): περὶ Ὑπερβόλου λέγειν αἰσχύνομαι, οὗ ὁ μὲν πατὴρ ἐστιγμένος ἔτι καὶ νῦν ἐν τῷ ἀργυροκοπείῳ δουλεύει τῷ δημοσίῳ, αὐτὸς δὲ ξένος ὢν καὶ βάρβαρος λυχνοποιεῖ (Schol. Aristoph. *Sphēk.* 1007).

[51] Lys. 13.18: Ἀγόρατον . . . δοῦλον καὶ ἐκ δούλων ὄντα (cf. 13.64: Ἀγόρατος . . . δοῦλος καὶ ἐκ δούλων ἐστίν). Lys. 30.2: ὁ πατὴρ ὁ Νικομάχου δημόσιος ἦν (cf. 30.6, 27, 29).

[52] Because prevailing scholarship assumes a "pure" citizen body of essentially autochthonous origin living in a society where everyone "knew" everyone else, these claims are routinely disregarded or dismissed a priori as "certainly false" (e.g., Fisher 1993: 56 with reference to Andokidēs' charge against Hyperbolos; cf. Chapter 2, n. 177).

as a closely knit hamlet,[53] have recently proffered the 139 or so ancestral "demes"[54] as the true Attic villages of face-to-face living, the embodiment of "'face to face' communities. . . . Life in these villages, towns, and neighborhoods was exceptionally stable and unchanging, with links between demesmen not only close and firm but ancestral" (Hunter 1994: 149). But such assertions conflict with the fact that an Athenian "deme" actually encompassed two distinct and disparate entities: (1) an ancestral deme composed of hereditary members, many of whom did not reside in the deme territory, and often had, at most, only infrequent and superficial contact with one another; and (2) a physical deme comprising the persons actually living in a particular geographical area (who, because of demographic mobility and residential anonymity, often possessed only unreliable and sometimes entirely false information concerning their neighbors).

The Hereditary Deme

Although the sixth-century division of Attika into demes was supposedly intended to "make fellow demesmen of those persons living in each of the demes,"[55] their descendants thereafter retained deme affiliation on a hereditary basis unaffected by changes in residence.[56] As a result, by the fourth century, literary texts and physical evidence such as the distribution of gravestones suggest that many—perhaps most—of the Athenian *politai* living in a particular area were actually affiliated with demes that were located elsewhere.[57] A study of Attic funereal markers,

[53] This "absurd model" (Osborne 1985a: 65) has "serious flaws when extrapolated to the polis level" (Ober 1989: 31). Cf. Hansen 1993: 60.

[54] "Deme" is also used, in a separate and distinct notation, to refer to the *politai* of Athens as a whole: see, for example, Dem. 18.169, 24.80; Aiskhin. 3.224; Aristot. *Pol.* 1291b17–29.

[55] Aristot. *Ath. Pol.* 21.4: διένειμε δὲ καὶ τὴν χώραν κατὰ δήμους. . . . καὶ δημότας ἐποίησεν ἀλλήλων τοὺς οἰκοῦντας ἐν ἑκάστῳ τῶν δήμων. Cf. Hdt. 5.69.2: δέκαχα δὲ καὶ τοὺς δήμους κατένειμε ἐς τὰς φυλάς. But Psellos Ὀνόματα Δικῶν (Boissonade 103, Migne p. 1015 §31) makes no mention of demes in describing Kleisthenēs' action: Κλεισθένης γὰρ τις, εἰς τριάκοντα μοίρας τὴν Ἀττικὴν ἅπασαν διανείμας.

[56] Aristot. *Ath. Pol.* 42.1: μετέχουσιν μὲν τῆς πολιτείας οἱ ἐξ ἀμφοτέρων γεγονότες ἀστῶν, ἐγγράφονται δ' εἰς τοὺς δημότας ὀκτοκαίδεκα ἔτη γεγονότες. Cf. Dem. 57.55: ἐν οἷς ὁ πάππος ὁ τοῦ πατρός, ὁ ἐμός, <ὁ> πατήρ, ἐνταῦθα καὶ αὐτὸς φαίνομαι δημοτευόμενος. *Politai* could change their hereditary deme affiliation only through the process of adoption. See Isai. 7.28; Dem. 44.35ff. Cf. Rubinstein 1993: 37–39, 114.

[57] Even prior to recent studies of the locational patterns of funerary monuments (Damsgaard-Madsen 1988; Osborne 1991; and Meyer 1993), Whitehead had concluded that "in certain demes, especially (though not exclusively) those of Athens itself, the category of non-*dēmotai* may well have come to constitute a substantial minority" (1986a: 75).

"comparing the distribution of gravestones of men of a given demotic, to the location of the deme from which they, or at least their ancestors, come," has shown that "in all demes substantial numbers of men who could contemplate a memorial, did die away from their home deme and did not have themselves carried home for burial"[58]—a phenomenon highly significant because of Athenians' tendency to bring home for burial even the remains (sometimes cremated) of relatives who had died abroad.[59] Funereal inscriptions also attest to the relatively large number of marriages involving couples from mutually distant demes, a pattern especially manifest among members of demes located relatively close to central Athens.[60] This separation of hereditary demesmen from the physical territory of their political units explains the otherwise surprising announcement at the City Dionysia (rather than in local areas) of honorific "crowns" awarded by the demes;[61] the social gathering of demesmen from Dekeleia not in deme territory but in central Athens;[62] and the convening of deme meetings outside the deme territory.

Although it has been assumed that meetings of the deme assembly normally took place within deme territory,[63] not a single local meeting is actually attested.[64] In fact, the only locus attested for deme meetings

[58] Osborne 1991: 239, 242. Even in Kerameis—site of the prominent Kerameikos cemetery, in which burial was sought even by those having no relation to the deme—fully 38 percent of members' gravestones have been found far from the deme (one even in far-distant Erkhia in the Mesogeia [modern Spata, site of the new intercontinental airport that has been criticized as excessively removed, even by modern transportation, from downtown Athens, and thus from the Kerameikos section]).

[59] Cf. Isai. 9.4; Lys. 14.27; Plut. *Bioi Rhēt.* 849c.

[60] Cox's investigation of Athenian marital domiciles, focused on inscriptional evidence from the fourth century, concludes that an "urban setting encouraged to a higher degree the association of individuals from far-flung parts of Attica" (1998: 214).

[61] Aiskhinēs (3.41–45) notes the prohibition (at some time before 330) of such announcements "at the tragedies," namely, the City Dionysia performed in the urban center. See Whitehead 1986a: 257, n. 8. The decrees of the Dēmotiōnidai similarly call for the posting of notices not in Dekeleia but in the city center (*asty*): (*I.G.* II^2 1237.B 63–64 [cf. lines 122–23]).

[62] At the barbershop in the Street of the Herms: Lys. 23.3.

[63] Cf. Haussoullier 1884: 5; Schoeffer 1903: col. 13; Busolt and Swoboda 1926: 2:969 and n. 9; Whitehead 1986a: 86–90.

[64] The sole evidentiary basis for the assumption of local meetings lies in occasional references in deme decrees to the setting up of inscriptions "in the *agora*" (see, e.g., *I.G.* II^2 1202. 1–2 [ἐν τεῖ ἀγορᾶι τεῖ κυρίαι]; cf. *I.G.* II^2 1174. 13–15, 1176+.27, 1180. 21–25), which has been interpreted as referring to a place of meeting within the deme. But the word *agora* has a wide range of meanings, often political or commercial rather than locative. When used in the context of demes (or other kinship groups), *agora* generally refers to an actual gathering, rather than to the place of meeting (Osborne 1990: 269, 271–73). Even before the 1978 publication of the deme decree from Eleusis, Ste. Croix had suggested that meetings outside the deme might not have been unusual (1972: 400–401).

is central Athens. There the members of the deme Halimous (whose ancestral territory was located some four or five miles away) assembled in 345 for the only deme assembly whose proceedings are known in any detail. Although the meeting, chronicled in Demosthenes 57, began in the late afternoon and continued into the night, causing the departure of a number of demesmen who actually lived in the deme (or at some other location away from the walled city), more than sixty ballots were finally cast in a meeting which had begun with seventy-three members in attendance.[65] The speaker, Euxitheos, even admits in passing that many (although, he claims, not most) members did live outside the deme's territory.[66] Significantly, although Euxitheos's case depends on establishing the irregularity of this assembly (in which he was deprived of *politeia*), he never even suggests, in attacking various aspects of the meeting as improper or illegal, that there was anything exceptional in its being convened outside the Halimous area.

Epigraphical evidence confirms the gathering of deme members in central Athens. The decrees of the Demotionidai, found in the ancient territory of Dekeleia, refer to "the place in the city [*asty*] where the Dekeleians meet."[67] More specifically, a deme decree from Eleusis in 332/1, preserved on stone and first published in 1978,[68] provides that future rent under a lease of stone-quarrying rights shall be paid "in the month Metageitniōn, when the demesmen hold their assembly in the Thēseion to choose magistrates."[69] Since there is no known "Thēseion"

[65] Dem. 57.9–13: [Εὐβουλίδης] κατέτριψεν τὴν ἡμέραν δημηγορῶν καὶ ψηφίσματα γράφων. . . . καὶ τῶν μὲν δημοτῶν οἱ ὀμόσαντες ἐγενόμεθα τρεῖς καὶ ἑβδομήκοντα, ἠρξάμεθα δὲ τοῦ διαψηφίζεσθαι δείλης ὀψίας, ὥστε συνέβη . . . σκότος εἶναι ἤδη· . . . ἡνίχ᾽ οἱ μὲν πρεσβύτεροι τῶν δημοτῶν ἀπεληλύθεσαν εἰς τοὺς ἀγρούς· τοῦ γὰρ δήμου ἡμῖν, ὦ ἄνδρες δικασταί, πέντε καὶ τριάκοντα στάδια τοῦ ἄστεως ἀπέχοντος καὶ τῶν πλείστων ἐκεῖ οἰκούντων, ἀπεληλύθεσαν οἱ πολλοί· . . . αἱ δὲ ψῆφοι ἠριθμήθησαν πλείους ἢ ἑξήκοντα. The speaker concedes that at least thirty members actually remained at the assembly when the balloting took place (10), but claims that some demesmen voted more than once—καὶ ἦν μὲν σκότος, οἱ δὲ λαμβάνοντες δύο καὶ τρεῖς ψήφους ἕκαστος παρὰ τούτου ἐνέβαλλον εἰς τὸν καδίσκον (13). But the Athenians maintained elaborate safeguards against such ballot stuffing: cf. Aristot. *Ath. Pol.* 68.2.

[66] Dem. 57.10: καὶ τῶν πλείστων ἐκεῖ οἰκούντων, ἀπεληλύθεσαν οἱ πολλοί.

[67] Hedrick's translation (1990: 15) of ὅπο ἂν Δεκελειῆς προσφοιτῶσιν ἐν ἄστει (*I.G.* II^2 1237.B 63–64 [cf. lines 122–23]). The primary signification of προσφοιτῶσιν, however, is "go or come to frequently" (LSJ), a meaning compatible with social gatherings rather than formal political meetings.

[68] *S.E.G.* 28.103, decree II = Coumanoudis and Gofas 1978.

[69] Lines 27–28: εἰς τὸν Μεταγειτνιῶνα μῆνα ταῖς ἀρχα|ιρεσίαις, ὅταν οἱ δημόται ἀγοράζωσιν ἐν τῶι Θησείωι. For the use of ἀγοράζω as denoting "hold an assembly," cf. *S.E.G.* 3.115.19. For the impossibility of interpreting the meeting in the Thēseion as a tribal, rather than a deme meeting, see Osborne 1985a: 77.

in Eleusis, these deme meetings, as the editors of the editio princeps noted, must have taken place in the Thēseion in central Athens, paralleling the gathering of the Halimousian demesmen in the *asty*. Such meetings in the city proper—convenient to a dispersed population of hereditary members—would have been consonant with the long-conjectured[70] widespread migration from the country into areas in and near the *asty* proper, and consistent with the evidence for demographic movement among nonurban demes, even some far distant from one another.[71]

The difficulty of gathering, even at a central site, demesmen whose residences were widely disbursed (and in many cases distant from the deme territory) would also explain, at least in part, the infrequency of deme gatherings, and their low quorum requirements. Although deme assemblies theoretically might be convened "whenever necessary,"[72] no extraordinary meetings are actually attested,[73] and the mundane, routine nature of deme proceedings suggests that there would have been little need for special or frequent gatherings. Resolutions adopted by the assemblies and preserved on stone—the sole surviving sources for the range and nature of deme discussions—testify to the inconsequential focus of demesmen's deliberations and show that "the issues which got discussed seem rarely to have risen above the routine."[74] The only functions common to all demes—selection of officers and admission of new members—recurred only annually, and are known to have been handled at single meetings.[75] Other business, as surviving decrees attest, was far from urgent: the award of honorific encomia to demesmen (and,

[70] See Schoeffer 1903: col. 7; Busolt and Swoboda 1926: 2:878–79; Gomme 1933: 37–48; Damsgaard-Madsen 1988: 55–56.

[71] For example, Philokēdēs Acharneus who lived in Coastal Lamptrai (*I.G.* II[2] 1204); Meidias Anagyrasios, resident of Eleusis (Dem. 21.158); and numerous residents of the Piraeus including Kallidamas Kholleidēs (*I.G.* II[2] 1214), the famous Timotheos Anaphlystios (Dem. 49.22), and Demosthenes Paianieus himself (Dein. 1.69; Aiskhin. 3.209). Many demesmen, of course, are known to have continued to live within deme territory (Traill 1975: 74, n. 8). For most entities, however, explicit evidence is lacking: from the vast majority of demes, for example, not a single deme inscription from any period survives (see Whitehead 1986a: 374–93). In fact, such decrees are extant from less than thirty subdivisions (for a partial list, see Traill 1975: 74–75, n. 10).

[72] Ὁπότε δεήσειεν: Harpokratiōn (cf. Suda, s.v. δήμαρχος, and Schol. Aristoph. *Clouds*, line 37).

[73] Speculation that the assemblies dealing with the *diapsēphiseis* of 346/5 were extraordinary "is admittedly no more than an assumption" (Whitehead 1986a: 92, n. 26). Cf. Chapter 2, nn. 73, 93; Lambert 1993: 390, n. 5.

[74] Osborne 1985a: 79, who specifically notes the "limited activity of the deme acting as a whole." For detailed analysis of the content of deme decrees, see Osborne 1985a: 206 (table 6).

[75] Dem. 44.39 (Otrynē) and Isai. 7.27–28 (deme unspecified). For the extent to which synoptic conclusions can be drawn, with care, from practices attested for individual demes, see Whitehead 1986a: 56–63.

significantly, to nondemesmen) for various modest services and contributions, and the consideration of motions dealing with religious matters (especially calendars), with the leasing of deme property, and with provision for the demes' limited expenses. Even at the meeting of Halimous to evaluate members' qualifications, the demesmen first transacted their ordinary business (Whitehead 1986a: 92, n. 26). At Eleusis, a meeting of the deme assembly itself was utilized for the receipt of rents from deme properties (*S.E.G.* 28.103, decree II, lines 27–28).

Quorum requirements for these meetings were minimal. At Myrrhinous, the only deme for which the fourth-century quorum requirement is explicitly preserved, only thirty members were needed in order to transact business validly:[76] these thirty demesmen would have constituted no more than one-seventh of the total membership, and probably much less.[77] A similarly low quorum can be inferred for the meeting at Halimous in 345: the speaker in Demosthenes 57, although emphasizing alleged procedural irregularities, offers no procedural objection to action taken, he alleges, by "no more than thirty" of a total membership that has been estimated at not less than eighty, and as high as two hundred or more.[78]

[76] *I.G.* II^{2} 1183.21–22 (sometime after 340): ἐξορκούτω ὁ δήμα[ρ] χος τοὺς) δημότας καὶ διδό[τω] | [τ]ὴν ψῆφον ἐὰν παρῶσιν μὴ [eta doubtful reading] ἐλάττους ἢ ΔΔΔ.

[77] Myrrhinous sent six representatives to the Athenian Council, or Boulē. Because the Boulē consisted of five hundred male *politai* over thirty who had not already served more than once, it is possible to calculate the *minimum* number of demesmen needed to meet each deme's alloted representation. Using United Nations model life tables for underdeveloped countries (see Hopkins 1966), R. Osborne has demonstrated that for each seat allocated to a deme, at least 32.5 demesmen aged thirty or over would have been required (1985a: 43–44, 196 [table 1]). Actual numbers of demesmen were probably much higher: "it must be stressed that these are minimum figures" (ibid., p. 44). Busolt and Swoboda (1926: 2:965, n. 2) even cite Myrrhinous's low quorum requirement as an indication that "many" Myrrhinousians resided outside the deme. Quorum requirements (and affiliates' actual residence within the deme territory?) may have been somewhat higher in the fifth century: Lower Paiania, with an indicated bouleutic representation of eleven, mandated a minimum presence of one hundred members at deme assemblies (*I.G.* I^{3} 250.11–14: τὰ χσυνγεγραμμ|ένα μὲ ἒναι ἀναφερίσα[ι] | ἐὰμ μὲ *h*εκατὸν παρõσιν | τõν δεμοτõν [dated to 450–430]). But Lower Paiania may have been egregiously underrepresented in the Boulē. In the reform of 307/6—which otherwise made only minor adjustments and, in most cases, no change in deme representation—Lower Paiania had its bouleutic quota doubled (see Meritt and Traill 1974: 57ff.).

[78] Dem. 57.10: οἱ δὲ κατάλοιποι ἦσαν οὐ πλείους ἢ τριάκοντα. Gomme, on population assumptions significantly different from those of R. Osborne (see note 77), observes that Halimous's allocation of three *bouleutai* would have required as many as two hundred demesmen (1933: 54–55). Lambert (1993: 389–91), reasoning solely from the information provided in the speech, identifies a total of eighty to eighty-five demesmen (on the assumption that the total number of demesmen equaled numbers mentioned in the speech—the "approximately" sixty [περὶ ἑξηκοστόν, §10] who had allegedly already been examined, and the "more than twenty remaining" [πλείους ἢ εἴκοσιν ὑπόλοιποι, §15]). But other inferences can be drawn from the text: for example, the "more than eighty" may have constituted only those scheduled to be examined that day; the seventy-three initially present may have been only part of the deme membership (with many

Such minimal attendance standards mirror the low proportions mandated for the conduct of business at *polis* assemblies (*ekklēsiai*),[79] where modest quorum requirements have been explicitly tied to the difficulty of gathering *politai* from throughout Attika.[80] Significantly, actual attendance at *polis* assemblies never substantially exceeded the minimum requirements.[81]

Also significant was the vast number of expatriate Athenians whose prolonged absences from Attika would have been a further source of obfuscation of the identity of individual inhabitants of Attika. During much of the fourth century a quarter or more of deme members actually lived abroad—as *klērouchs* in Athenian-sponsored settlements, as aliens resident in other *poleis*, or as military mercenaries.[82] Even *politai* born in Athens but taken abroad at an early age, such as Euxitheos's father, might speak with a foreign accent.[83] Such Athenians, or their descendants, on returning to Attika could easily be confused with foreigners, especially if lengthy absence had combined with the changing composition of individual deme populations to extirpate or dim communal memory of the expatriates' origins.[84] Furthermore, many non-Athenians lived in the various Athenian settlements abroad (Cargill 1995: 66–67): such people

---

members unable or unwilling to attend, but confident that friends or relatives would protect their interests, and aware that in any event an adverse outcome was subject to review in the courts). The inconsistency between the anticipated number of demesmen based on bouleutic representation and the low numbers in the text has led some scholars to suggest that the figures given may simply be an "understatement" (cf. Traill 1975: 65, n. 23), or that the text may be corrupt (see Nabers in the Oxford text who suggests ὑπερεξηκοστός, "more than sixty," as a correction for περὶ ἑξηκοστόν).

[79] At the statewide *ekklēsiai*, a minimum of six thousand *politai*—approximately a third to a seventh of the total eligible (see Chapter 1, n. 41)—was required to transact business such as the granting of *politeia* (see Hansen 1976).

[80] Hansen 1991: 60. For the willingness of some portion of the populace to traverse relatively long distances on foot or by primitive transportation, see Forrest 1966: 30–31; Harding 1981.

[81] Archaeological evidence shows that the fourth-century Pnyx, even after renovation and slight enlargement from the fifth-century gathering site, could barely contain the six thousand *politai* needed for a quorum. See Thompson 1982: 138–39. The remains now visible date from the Hadrianic period (M. H. Hansen 1989b: 141, *pace* Thompson and Scranton 1943: 278–79).

[82] Hansen 1985: 14. Cf. Sinclair 1988: 224; Beloch 1912–27: 3:402–3. Cargill (1995: 77–83 and appendix B) positively identifies no less than 626 individual Athenians as certain or likely fourth-century settlers in Athenian colonies—a figure that includes very limited representation from the Khersonēsos (which has been little excavated) and other continental areas.

[83] Dem. 57.18 (τὸ ξενίζειν αὐτοῦ); see Chapter 2, n. 74. Despite his accent, he was able to hold office in the deme of Halimous: ἀρχὰς ἔλαχεν καὶ ἦρξεν δοκιμασθείς (57.25). In contrast, Nikias's associate, Dionysios, participated in the founding of Thourioi, but left his son in Athens. In time of war, a number of Athenians are known to have sent their wives and children abroad. See Lys. 16.4; Lykourg. 1.53.

[84] On the frequency and large numbers of such returnees, see Francotte [1910] 1964: 206; Maffi 1971: 178; Whitehead 1977: 72. Cf. Chapter 2, nn. 36, 112.

coming to Athens would also have been difficult to distinguish from descendants of Athenians who had settled much earlier in these colonies.[85] In contrast, in Attika some "foreigners" were scions of families who had resided in Athens for decades. The metic Lysias, for example, had been born in Athens in 459/8 to a family already ensconced in Attika, had moved at fifteen to the Athenian colony of Thourioi, where he remained for decades until ousted in anti-Athenian disturbances, after which he returned to Attika for additional decades (punctuated by a brief intervening sojourn in Megara).[86] How could a resident of Attika easily differentiate such a native-born "alien" from a foreign-born "citizen" like Demosthenes' mother who was from Thrace?[87]

Attenuation of the hereditary deme in the fourth century accords with the infrequent use of deme attribution for personal identification. Although Kleisthenēs in the sixth century had sought to encourage self-identification by demotic rather than by patronymic (Arist. *Constitution of the Athenians* 21.4), deme affiliation is seldom noted in Athenian literature.[88] Even in court presentations, deme reference is erratic and inconsistent: *politai* are often mentioned without demotic designation, sometimes differentiated only by nickname (e.g., "the shopkeeper").[89] Fully half of the Kerameikos *ostraka*, in effect documentation in a legal process, omit demotic reference.[90] As in life, so in death: throughout classical history, most residents of Attika—*politai*, resident aliens, foreigners—were commemorated, if at all, by a funerary epitaph that contained no demotic reference or other differentiation of status (Meyer

[85] Lēmnos, for example, had originally been settled at Miltiadēs' invitation at about the beginning of the fifth century (Hdt. 6.136–40; cf. Diod. Sik. 10.19.6, *I.G.* I[3] 1466.522bis (= Touchais 1985: 768 and fig. 17).

[86] See Chapter 1, n. 62.

[87] On Kleoboulē's origins, see Chapter 2, pp. 76–77. Even the philosopher Plato himself may have been born on Aigina where his father Aristōn reportedly had settled with a group of Athenian *klēroukhoi* (see Schmitz 1988: 86–87; Figueira 1991: 57–59).

[88] Among historians, for example, Thucydides and Xenophon never designate a single Athenian by his demotic (although at *Apom.* 2.7.6 [in a list of single names] Xenophon does identify one person by demotic—the sole use of identification by deme in all of Xenophon's works). Herodotos does mention demes, but in the sense of villages—on occasion (e.g., 5.74.2) denoting as a "deme" a settlement, not constitutionally a deme. See Eliot 1962: 79.

[89] Thus Pythodōros ὁ σκηνίτης (Isok. 17.33), whose shops situated near the Leōkorion were well known to Athenians (cf. Dem. 54.7), is not to be confused with his grandson Pythodōros ὁ Ἀχαρνεύς (Dem. 50.28) or with Pythodōros ὁ Φοίνιξ (Isok. 17.4). See Mathieu and Brémond [1929–42] 1963: 1:81, n. 1; Davies 1971: 481. Cf. Τίμαρχος ὁ πόρνος (Aiskhin. 1.130), τὸν ὀρφανὸν καλούμενον Διόφαντον (Aiskhin. 1.158), Μνησίθεον τὸν τοῦ μαγείρου καλούμενον (ibid.). Until 352/1 the proposer of a decree in the Assembly was identified only by name and patronymic.

[90] Willemsen and Brenne 1991: 147–56. Cf. Hansen 1996e: 176–78.

1993: 99). In the fourth century, for example, hundreds of epitaphs contain only the decedent's name (sometimes accompanied by patronymic). Far fewer are identified by deme; a yet smaller number, as foreigners—notwithstanding the huge proportion of the resident population who were not Athenian *politai*.[91] Even in the relatively rare cases where a decedent's name is accompanied by a demotic attribution, no explicit differentiation is made thereby between hereditary deme members and nonmembers merely residing in the deme territory[92]—a homogeneity of funerary markers corresponding to the typically homologized life experiences of the residents of Attika.

The Territorial Deme

Scholars have long equated Athenian demes with villages,[93] in particular (and anachronistically) with the villages (*khōria*) of modern Greece—homogeneous groups supposedly "living in a single population center," enjoying mutual support and close social concourse, punctuated by walks to and from their nearby fields for agricultural labor.[94] In fact, however, most demes in Attika were inhabited by a heterogeneous population for whom settlement patterns precluded daily interaction on a communal basis. Local populations were highly variegated and generally included, in the fourth century, many persons who were not lineal descendants of the original Kleisthenic demesmen. Recent archaeological excavations

[91] See Meyer 1993: fig. 2; Vestergaard et al. 1992: 5–7. The disparity between the relatively large number of aliens resident in Attika (Chapter 1, pp. 17ff.) and the extremely small number of tombstones explicitly identifying a decedent as a foreigner (Meyer 1993: fig. 2) challenges the frequent assertion that "foreigners" in their grave inscriptions "usually identified their dead . . . as members of their polis of origin" (Meyer 1993: 111—cf. Whitehead 1977: 33–34; Hansen 1991: 117).

[92] Adjectival deme references on gravestones need not be limited specifically to hereditary deme relationships. To be sure, living *politai*, when using the demotic, appended to their given name and patronymic an adjectival form of their deme affiliation (Whitehead 1986a: 73–75), while metics in life appended to their names the specific phrase "living in . . ." (οἰκῶν, or for a woman, οἰκοῦσα) followed by the deme name. This "nomenclature would have been useless and nonsensical if it had not indicated the metic's actual, current deme of residence" (Whitehead 1986a: 83). But reference to a *deceased* metic as "living in" a deme would have been nugatory. Use of the short adjectival deme form on metics' gravestones would have conformed with the general brevity of funerary epitaphs.

[93] Chapter 1, n. 72. See Osborne 1985a: 37: "the settlements designated by deme names were perhaps most frequently single villages." Cf. Thompson 1971; Osborne 1985b and 1992: 21–23.

[94] For full exposition of this paradigm, see Stanton 1994: 217. Vari (ancient Anagyrous), for example, is sometimes cited as exemplifying this pattern: see Langdon 1988: 43–45; Eliot 1962: 35–46. But archaeological activity has revealed multiple settlements (Lauter 1980), and the Vari "Cave House" is a notorious example of an isolated farmstead, three kilometers up into the hills (Jones, Graham, and Sacket 1973; Jones 1976: 80).

and topographical surveys, confirming literary and epigraphical evidence,[95] show that most demes lacked a single residential center,[96] and were populated either through isolated houses spread widely over the deme territory (with neighbors sometimes no closer than several hundred meters)[97] or through multiple small settlements at some distance from each other.[98] Demes adjacent to the walled city or the harbor area seem often to have had only limited residential populations:[99] their fields were tended by persons living within Athens or Piraeus—a pattern of habitation that would have added further complexity to the already high heterogeneity of the deme populations located within these urban areas.

Residents might even have been uncertain as to the deme area in which they actually lived, and the identity of most other residents. Although the deme in its territorial expression seems generally to have had an initial geographical focus—a harbor, a valley, a shrine, a particular group of houses[100]—this focus "was a point rather than an area."[101] There were no "exact boundaries" separating the demes.[102] When Athenians

[95] See the survey by Arrigoni (1969–71).

[96] Steinhower 1994: 183, 188, n. 17, citing the results of excavations since 1960 by the Ephoreia of Antiquities of Attika, as published periodically in *Arkhaiologikon Deltion*. Recent excavations show even Thorikos (Oikonomakos 1990) and Halai Aixōnides (Andreou 1994) conforming to this pattern. Some demes appear entirely to have lacked a built-up center (Jameson 1994: 61).

[97] See, for example, the deme of Atēnē (Lohmann 1991, 1992) and the demes contiguous to modern Spata (Steinhower 1994). Although R. Osborne some years ago argued that "isolated residences" were "rare" (1985a: 37), recent surveys suggest a shift in Greek residential patterns in classical times from nucleated urban settlements to dispersed farm residences (see Alcock 1993: 33–49; Steinhower 1994: 183–87). Considerable evidence has now accumulated for isolated dwellings scattered over the countryside, in some cases clearly farmsteads. For southern Attika, see Lohmann 1992: 29–57; Young 1956: 122–46. For northern Attika, Munn and Zimmermann-Munn 1989: 100–110, 122–23, 1990. Although intensive analytical surveying of the Attic plains has not yet occurred, numerous potential fourth-century farmstead sites have been identified through excavations and through chance finds. See Petropoulakou, Tsimbidis, and Pendazos 1973: fig. 24. Cf. Eliot 1962: 75; Traill 1975: 101; Hanson 1983: 39–41; Langdon 1990–91; Jameson 1994: 55; 61, n. 33; 63.

[98] Examples of this pattern include Akharnai (Patrinakou-Eliakou 1989), Aixōnē (Yiannopoulou-Konsolakē 1990), Anagyrous (Lauter 1980), Sounion (Travlos 1988: 406), Phrearrhioi (Steinhower 1994: 188, n. 25), Anaphlystos (Travlos 1988: 15–16), Bēsa and Amphitropē (Eliot 1962: 112–14).

[99] Despite extensive excavation in recent years in the deme areas close to the ancient walled city, not one site has been definitely identified as a farmstead (Steinhower 1994: 183).

[100] Modern scholars have attempted to correlate political subdivisions and topographical features (see Traill 1986: 123–49; Thompson 1971) but not always successfully: while the highly developed central port of Piraeus always constituted a single deme (see Whitehead 1986a: 394–96), a number of demes were encompassed within the city of Athens proper (which geographically constituted a single entity focusing on the Akropolis).

[101] Hansen 1991: 47.

[102] Eratosthenēs in Strabo 1.65 (1.4.7): μὴ ὄντων γὰρ ἀκριβῶν ὅρων καθάπερ Κολυττοῦ καὶ Μελίτης, οἷον στηλῶν ἢ περιβόλων, τοῦτο μὲν ἔχειν φάναι ἡμᾶς, ὅτι τουτὶ μέν ἐστι Κολυττός, τουτὶ δὲ Μελίτη,τοὺς ὅρους δὲ μὴ ἔχειν εἰπεῖν. Although some *horoi* with deme attributions have been

spoke of property in Sphēttos or Kikynna (as at Lys. 17.5), they conveyed only an inexact indication, not a precise demarcation—much as modern urban "neighborhoods," although they lack exact boundaries, are frequently used as directional or locational references. No precise physical borders had been required for groupings originally perpetuated not on a geographical but on a hereditary basis.

By the fourth century, however, hereditary demesmen represented only a fraction of the complex populations resident in the various deme territories. In addition to the many *politai* who were unaffiliated with the political organization (the hereditary deme) of the territory in which they lived, non-*politai* were present in significant numbers in virtually every deme throughout Attika. While scholars have long emphasized the relatively large number of free non-*politai* (metics) known to have been domiciled within close proximity to central Athens,[103] aliens, many of whom engaged in farming,[104] actually resided in virtually every political subdivision. Despite the unrepresentative nature of surviving evidence (which disproportionately records those metics—and *politai*—who lived within the urban environs of ancient Athens),[105] metics are attested in more than forty separate demes scattered around Attika, including many rural divisions, and even in a number of areas lacking political organization.[106] Confounding modern preconceptions, less than

found (such as *I.G.* II² 2623: ὅρος Π[ει]ραέων [χώ] | [ρ]ας), in most cases they clearly serve purposes other than marking boundaries (for example, *I.G.* II² 1180 delineating the dimensions of a new *agora* for Sounion). These markers appear analogous to similar *horoi* containing phratry designations (e.g., *I.G.* II² 2621, 4974): such *horoi* could not be boundary markers since phratries were not territorial units (Lambert 1993: 8–14). A few *horoi*, however, for extraordinary reasons may have delineated deme borders (Stanton 1994: 221–22): see, for example, the inscriptions from Lamptrai, dated sometime after 307/6, interpreted by Traill (1982) as marking boundaries in connection with the transfer of Upper Lamptrai to the new tribe Antigonis (although Lower Lamptrai remained in Erekhtheis). Cf. Lauter 1982; Stanton 1984: 298–301; Langdon 1985: 10; Traill 1986: 116–22.

[103] See, inter alia, Davies 1981: 51; Whitehead 1977: 75, 100, n. 31; Diller 1937: 120–22, 161–79, esp. 177; Gerhardt [1933] 1935: 15–16; Hommel 1932: col. 1433; Scherling 1898: 89–95; Clerc 1893: 384–86, 450–57.

[104] For metics active in agriculture, see, for example, *I.G.* II² 10.10, 18, 20, 22, 25. Cf. *I.G.* II² 1553. 24–25, where the metic tenant Nikias may be manumitting his *epitropos,* who is there described as a *geōrgos*. See Burford 1993: 179.

[105] Epigraphic evidence is skewed by the extensive modern excavation undertaken in the environs of the ancient urban center, and by chance factors such as the ancient location of prominent burial sites immediately outside the city walls. The building accounts, for example, disproportionately record payments to workmen who resided in demes within or close to the city. (See *I.G.* II² 1553–78, 1654, 1672–73, 1951; *I.G.* I³ 475–76.). In contrast, at least ten separate citations of metics are recorded for Eleusis, a location removed from both the port and from the inner city. Cf. Haussoullier 1884: 187–93.

[106] Whitehead 1986a: 83–84. Nondeme areas: Ōrōpos (Lewis 1968: 371), Pentelē (*I.G.* II² 1673.37), Salamis (*I.G.* II² 1570.42; 1574. 4, 10); possibly Kynosargēs (Lewis 1959: 231, note

20 percent of these aliens resided in the Piraeus (Whitehead 1986a: 82–85). Because the residential districts of only about four hundred metics are known (a fraction far below 1 percent of the metic population),[107] at the very least "an entirely metic-less deme was a rarity" (Whitehead 1986: 84). In addition, a portion—possibly a considerable portion—of Attika's total cultivable land was tended by slaves who lived apart from their masters in villages or in houses adjacent to one of their owners' scattered landholdings.[108] Of these many "slaves living independently,"[109] the vast majority appear to have resided in areas other than that of their owners' deme affiliation and to have moved there relatively recently.[110]

The devolution of political power to hereditary demesmen, mirroring Athens's own separation of political rights from other aspects of society,[111] allowed local inhabitants to ignore, in everyday life, such essentially political concerns as personal status. While the infrequent gatherings of the political deme might attract only a limited number of hereditary demesmen, local metics participated in a deme's religious rites and cults, and did military service with deme units.[112] Metics

on line 98). Since the publication of Whitehead 1986a, metics have been attested in additional demes, for example, in Halai Aixōnides, and Anagyrous (Steinhower 1994: 189, n. 51).

[107] Information for *politai* is similarly fragmentary. For example, only about 1 percent of fourth-century *politai* are memorialized on funerary inscriptions (Hansen et al. 1990: 27, who claim that "even 1% of the evidence is quite sufficient for quantification, provided that the sample is representative, and not unduly biased").

[108] For such a slave χωρὶς οἰκῶν operating in agriculture, see the farmer at Hagnous (now Markopoulo) listed on the *phialai eleutherikai* lists (Chapter 5, pp. XXX–XX) as owned by an individual of Pallēnē. The fragmentation of Attic land into separated, relatively small landholdings is well documented in both literary and epigraphic sources: see Jameson 1977–78: 130ff.; 1994: 59; Burford 1993: 66–71; Osborne 1987: 37–40; Wood 1983: 31; Hanson 1983: 38; Davies 1981: 52–55. The "largest single Athenian estate" has been estimated at not more than one hundred acres (Ste. Croix 1966: 112), less than 0.1 percent of the total arable land in Attika. For the much larger proportion of total arable acreage represented by the largest holdings in regions of the Roman Empire, see Duncan-Jones 1990: 129–40.

[109] On these slaves *khōris oikountes*, see the last section in Chapter 5.

[110] See the dedications of the fourth-century *phialai exeleutherikai* (Chapter 5, pp. 152–53). Because these manumission inscriptions record (for owners who were *politai*) hereditary demotic affiliations, and (for metic owners and slaves being manumitted) their actual place of residence, this material provides information on movement of individuals, "on the assumption that at some time the slave has been present in the master's household, so that where place of residence of slave, and demotic or place of residence of owner are different, either the slave has moved from his owner's or her owner's residence, or the owner has moved from his own deme" (Osborne 1991: 244). According to R. Osborne's calculations, of 156 cases where slaves' and owners' residences or deme affiliation is known, in 137 they differ.

[111] Athenian demes are often described as microcosms of the overall state, "miniature *poleis*" whose functioning mirrored the parent unit's relationship to Attika as a whole. Cf. Osborne 1990: 269, n. 8; Parker 1996: 128, n. 23; Hopper 1957: 13–17. For political mirroring, see Whitehead 1986a: 86–148; for religious parallelism, cf. Kearns 1985: 189–207; Jameson 1982: 73 (financing of deme cults by liturgies).

[112] See Chapter 2, nn. 161–65 and accompanying text.

received local honors, paid local taxes, and performed deme liturgies—as did *politai* hereditarily affiliated with another deme but residing in or owning land in the local area—creating a further separation of the residential from the hereditary deme.[113]

Other aspects of land ownership and property use promoted a heterogeneity of deme population. Although it is often assumed—as a corollary to the premise of Attika as a face-to-face society—that "everyone in each deme knew who owned what land,"[114] in fact widespread absentee ownership of realty, lack of registration of land ownership,[115] and frequent changes in occupancy contributed to constant uncertainty (and considerable misinformation) concerning the identity of landowners and property occupants. Even the frequent presence of "mortgage stones" (*horoi*) on encumbered properties offered no information concerning the owner: while creditors were sometimes identified, the mortgagors never were.[116]

Most land was owned by a relatively small, wealthy elite, people who usually were not hereditary demesmen of the district. These absentee landlords controlled widely scattered, fragmented holdings, which were not practicably cultivable or inhabitable by the persons living in a landholder's own main residence.[117] As a result, tenants or associates (free and slave) of these absentee owners occupied many parcels, often through a succession of short-term leasing arrangements.[118] Records relating to

[113] See Chapter 2, n. 157. On Wilamowitz's early contention that metics, because of the extensiveness of their involvement in the territorial deme, were "full members" of the demes in which they resided, see Chapter 2, n. 167.

[114] Thomas 1989: 82 (who offers no explanation or evidence for this assumption).

[115] See Gabrielsen 1986: 113, n. 40; Christ 1990: 158; Todd 1993: 247; Whitehead 1993. This absence of registration may explain the absence of "regular direct taxes on the landed property of citizens" (Pleket 1972: 251–52—cf. Whitehead 1993: 148). For disputes that might have been resolved through reference to land records, had they existed, see Dem. 40.58–59; 47.34; 50.8; 55; Lys. 7.9–11, 18.

[116] Finley [1951] 1985: 77. Even on those relatively rare occasions when public bodies put the names of lessees on stone *stēlai* and placed the inscriptions in a sanctuary or meeting place, the status of the lessees—whether demesmen, *politai* unaffiliated with the deme, guardians, slaves "living independently," metics—generally went unmentioned. See, e.g., *I.G.* II^2 2492 (Pleket 1964: no. 42). Cf. Whitehead 1986a: 154–59; Guiraud 1893: 421ff.

[117] Foxhall has estimated that less than 10 percent of households controlled almost half of the total usable agricultural land in Attika (1992: 158, figs. 1 and 2). For similar conclusions, see Osborne 1991: 128–36; 1992: 23; 1995: 32–33. Comparative data suggest the reasonableness of these projections: Morris 1994: 362, n. 53.

[118] R. Osborne has shown that in Attika "all the signs are that both properties to lease and lessees to rent properties were in plentiful supply" (1988: 311). Cf. Burford 1993: 177–81; Wood 1988: 181–84. In the city proper and in the Piraeus, however, an imbalance occasionally may have existed between supply and demand: see Xen. *Por.* 2.6 (εἶτα ἐπειδὴ καὶ πολλὰ οἰκιῶν ἔρημά ἐστιν ἐντὸς τῶν τειχῶν καὶ οἰκόπεδα, εἰ ἡ πόλις διδοίη οἰκοδομησομένοις ἐγκεκτῆσθαι οἳ ἂν αἰτούμενοι

mine leases, for example, reveal that most owners of land in mining demes were entirely unaffiliated with the subdivision—and even with the area—where the mines were located: of one hundred owners with attested demotics, sixty-five were affiliates of demes geographically outside the mining areas.[119] Records of state confiscation of property, although preserved only in a few cases in any detail, reveal a similar pattern of outside ownership and fragmented holdings. Thus the so-called Attic Stēlai, dating from the period after the mutilation of the Hermai in 415, catalog significant property holdings but reveal only one individual, Polystratos of Ankylē, who owned any land in his own deme.[120] In 367/6, records of the *pōlētai* reveal that a purchaser from Lakiadai had acquired property at Alōpekē previously owned by an individual affiliated with Xypetē: here too adjoining property is owned by an outsider, a demesman of Agrylē.[121] In a document recording the confiscation in 341 of a holding in the deme of Piraeus,[122] the buyer is a demesman of Akharnai, and only one of the five landowners mentioned is an affiliate of the Piraeus deme.[123] Property at Aphidna was confiscated in the same year: the owner is a demesman from Oinoē; the purchaser, from the deme of Rhamnous.[124] In fact, analysis of all surviving confiscation inscriptions indicates that about three-fourths of the real property sold was owned by persons unaffiliated with the deme in which

ἄξιοι δοκῶσιν εἶναι, πολὺ ἂν οἴομαι καὶ διὰ ταῦτα πλείους τε καὶ βελτίους ὀρέγεσθαι τῆς Ἀθήνησιν οἰκήσεως). Thür (1989: 120–21) suggests that Xenophon's proposal refers to restrictions on metics' residences imposed by *prostatai*. By the fourth century, however, the Athenian *prostatēs* had no continuing relationship with his metic—whether of slave or free origin. See Chapter 5, n. 104.

[119] See Osborne 1985a: 112–15 and 208 (table 10).

[120] See Pritchett, Amyx, and Pippin 1953; Lewis 1966.

[121] *S.E.G* 12.100; *Hesperia* 10 (1941): 14 (records of the *pōlētai*). Cf. Finley 1953; Kränzlein 1963: 84ff., 125.

[122] *Hesperia* 5 (1936): 393, no. 10 (an extension of *I.G.* II^2 1582). For the real-estate implications of this inscription, see Finley [1951] 1985: 92–95; Osborne 1985a: 1–5. For legal connotations, see Rhodes 1981: 559; Harrison 1968–71: 1:242, n. 1, 2:213, n. 1; MacDowell 1978: 167, 270, n. 380.

[123] Akharnai lies about fifteen kilometers to the northeast of Piraeus. The owners of the property and of the adjoining holdings are all affiliated with distant Myrrhinous, which was on the Aegean coast about thirty kilometers, on a direct line, southeast of Piraeus on the Saronic Gulf. (The Hymettos ridge lies between the two areas, and road connections even today are indirect.) Similarly, of the three beneficiaries of the guarantees that led to the confiscation, only one is connected with the Piraeus, and he is a metic. Another beneficiary was a metic residing in the deme of Bēsa (located in the mining area far to the southeast of Piraeus). The sole *politēs* beneficiary was affiliated with the deme of Aixōnē (about ten kilometers from the Piraeus).

[124] See Osborne 1985a: 5–6, 217. This appropriation was handled immediately after the court adjudication of the holding in the Piraeus purchased by a demesman of Akharnai and is preserved on the same fragmentary inscription (see n. 123).

the holding was located,[125] a pattern similar to that found in literary texts where the majority of the multiple-parcel holders identifiable by deme own no real estate in the subdivision with which they are affiliated.[126] The confiscation case described in Demosthenes 53 is typical: the dispute centers on Apollodōros who owned real estate in three separate demes.[127]

Such fragmented holdings by distant owners generated ubiquitous leasing arrangements that facilitated the dispersion into deme territories of outsiders, especially non-*politai* (who generally lacked the right to buy Athenian real estate).[128] Leasing (*misthōsis*) was so commonplace a means of acquiring the use of property that Plato equates it with gift or sale.[129] The easy availability and routine utilization of rental realty is illustrated by a humorous vignette sketched by Lysias: when Aiskhinēs the Sokratic proved intolerable to his neighbors, they all are said to have moved out and *rented* new homes.[130] Hundreds of properties were leased out by public bodies and private groups that were often unconnected to the deme in which the land was located.[131] Many families were lessors of multiple parcels: the estate holdings described at Isaios 11.37ff., for example, included rental properties at Thria, Melitē, and Eleusis (and yet other properties for personal use);[132] the estate of Euktēmōn contained two *synoikiai* under lease (in addition to a bathhouse, a house in the city, and a farm).[133] Of the many decedents' estates whose assets are

[125] Ibid., 52. Fully half of these properties are owned by persons affiliated with demes located far from the situs of the parcels listed.

[126] See ibid., 47–50. Of sixteen instances of multiple property holdings, only in seven are both the location of the holdings and the deme affiliation of the owners known: four appear not to have owned any parcels in their own deme.

[127] Dem. 50.8: δόξαν γὰρ ὑμῖν ὑπὲρ τῶν δημοτῶν τοὺς βουλευτὰς ἀπενεγκεῖν τοὺς προεισοίσοντας τῶν τε δημοτῶν καὶ τῶν ἐγκεκτημένων, προσαπηνέχθη μου τοὔνομα ἐν τριττοῖς δήμοις διὰ τὸ φανερὰν εἶναί μου τὴν οὐσίαν. For Apollodōros's real-estate holdings, see Trevett 1992: 162–64. On Apollodōros's deme affiliation, see Davies 1971: 430–31; 481, n. 1.

[128] For grants of *egktēsis*, see generally Pečirka 1966; Steltzer 1971.

[129] *Sophist* 219d5. Cf. Aristot. *E.E.* 1232a. In Lys. 17, a creditor describing his seizure and immediate "lease" of a debtor's land in Sphēttos offers the jurors no explanation of the term or any suggestion that the transaction was not routine: (5) καὶ τὰ μὲν Σφηττοῖ ἤδη τρία ἔτη μεμίσθωκα; (8) τοὺς μεμισθωμένους παρ' ἐμοῦ τὸ Σφηττοῖ χωρίον. The debtors in Lys. 17 owned another parcel in Kikynna that was also occupied by tenants (who appear to have been metics). Ancient evidence offers no support for Zimmern's early impression that leasing "in our sense of the word was practically unknown in Greece" (1911: 234: cf. Foxhall 1990).

[130] Lys. fr. 38 [Gernet and Bizos]: οἱ δὲ γείτονες οὕτως ὑπ' αὐτοῦ δεινὰ πάσχουσιν ὥστ' ἐκλιπόντες τὰς αὑτῶν οἰκίας ἑτέρας πόρρω μισθοῦνται.

[131] For the enormous amount of public and association land in Attika under lease (perhaps close to one thousand separate parcels), see Osborne 1988: 285–87. Cf. Rahe [1992] 1994: 1:75.

[132] Cf. Davies 1971: 87; Wyse [1904] 1967: 671–78.

[133] Isai. 6.19–20, 33. Cf. Davies 1971: 562; Wyse [1904] 1967: 483–88.

known in detail, only two (those of Phainippos and of Demosthenes's father) did not contain real property under lease.[134] Estates administered for the benefit of orphans—fatherless children whose numbers were legion in a land of limited adult life expectancies[135]—provided many additional parcels for rent.[136] Indeed, the law encouraged fiduciaries to use their wards' funds to purchase real estate for lease to others (which was perceived as a prudent, income-producing investment): guardians are known even to have eliminated income-producing loans in order to purchase urban rental property (*synoikiai*).[137]

Because many lessees had no hereditary affiliation with the deme territories to which they came to live, the proliferation of leasing arrangements contributed to increasing residential heterogeneity. Religious and social associations, for example, often leased local property to *politai* from other demes and to metics:[138] even parcels owned by demes not infrequently were leased to persons unaffiliated with the lessor-deme.[139] Orphans' real property was "peculiarly attractive to those not from the neighborhood" (Osborne 1988: 316); analysis of mortgage stones (*horoi*) confirms that the vast majority of orphans' estates were secured by lessees' property located outside the deme area where the fiduciary real estate was located (ibid.).

[134] Osborne 1988: 311–13. While these estates confirm the "large scale" of real-estate leasing (p. 313), inventories of testamentary assets tend to exaggerate the dominance of real property among decedents' assets. Formal estate procedures were used primarily to dispose of real estate; other assets often belonged to the "unseen" (ἀφανής) economy and did not pass through public testamentary procedures. See E. Cohen 1992: 191, n. 4; MacDowell 1978: 108. R. Osborne does note the extent to which the assets of Demosthenes senior were "tied up in invisible property."

[135] Hansen (1985: 10–11) argues plausibly that the demographic structure of fourth-century Athens resembled that of the early Roman Empire. Extrapolation from detailed Roman demographic studies (by Saller 1986, 1987; Frier 1982, 1983; Hopkins 1983; and others) suggests that approximately two-thirds of the children in such a society would have lost their fathers by age twenty-two, and that 80 percent of these decedents would leave at least one living child. For the Greek world as a whole, see Sallares 1991; Angel 1947; 1975. Cf. Chapter 1, n. 147.

[136] R. Osborne (1988: 309) calculates that "something over half Athenian estates would have been liable to be leased out as orphan estates every century." In fact, twenty-four *horoi*, over 10 percent of the total surviving from Attika, mark property pledged as security by lessees of orphan estates. Guardians had incentives to lease their wards' property: beyond the general suasion of the eponymous archon who participated directly in the effectuation of such leases (see Isai. 6.36–37; Aristot. *Ath. Pol.* 56.7), prosecution by *phasis* threatened those who failed to do so (see Harrison 1968–71: 1:115–17). Cf. Lys. 32; Dem. 27.

[137] See Dem. 38.7; Lys. fr. 91 (Thal.). Cf. E. Cohen 1992: 132; Finley [1951] 1985: 235. For the inclusion of multiple-occupancy buildings in dowries, see Isai. 5.26–27; Dem. 45.28.

[138] See Osborne 1985a: 56–59, and table 4; 1988: 290–91.

[139] Osborne 1985a: 204, table 3 (who finds that almost 25 percent of such lessees lack local ties). Of the four lessees of the Piraeus theater, for example, two are from other demes. *I.G.* II^2 1176. See Stroud 1974a: 292–93.

Because leases of both land and buildings were generally for relatively brief terms, rapid turnover of tenants was not unusual. Private land leases seldom exceeded a single year (Osborne 1988: 314). Residential rental terms were even shorter.[140] Subleases were common. The landlord Euktēmōn, for example, rented his building as a unit, but his prime tenant entered into various subleases (Isai. 6). Even the master lease must have been for a brief term: although Athenian rents were generally payable by a single tender for the entire period, Euktēmōn came so frequently to collect the rent that he was alleged to have developed a close personal relationship with his female lessee (6.19–21). In Lysias 7 (4, 9–11), a lessor of land enumerates how, within a period of less than five years, five separate tenants had farmed the property, including at least one metic.[141] Similarly, in a period of three years multiple renters, including metics, appear to have occupied the land at Sphēttos mentioned in Lysias 17.

In this society of absentee owners, mobile inhabitants, frequent turnover of short-term leases, residents of homogeneous appearance but varied origin—all exacerbated by the absence of archives or registered data for the investigation or confirmation of personal and property attributes—rampant unreliable rumors and widespread personal misinformation were dominant.[142] Many persons believed to be wealthy often at death were found to have owned virtually nothing.[143] An individual of extraordinary wealth might often conceal his property and be despised as impoverished.[144] The banker Pasiōn, who only late in life became a *politēs*, somehow accumulated huge holdings in land and housing (*epi gēi kai synoikiais*), to the bafflement of his contemporaries and of modern scholarship.[145] His successor, Phormiōn, even before he became a *politēs*,

[140] R. Osborne (1988: 315) suggests that rent may have been payable on a daily basis. This would have paralleled the practice attested for imperial Rome (see Frier 1977: 27–37; 1980).

[141] Lys. 7.10: τῷ δὲ τετάρτῳ Ἀλκίᾳ Ἀντισθένους ἀπελευθέρῳ ἐμίσθωσα. Nothing is known concerning the other tenants. Humphreys (forthcoming) suggests that these short terms may have been atypical since the land under lease "was being held in trust" for Periander (Foxhall 1992: 155). But, as discussed earlier, fiduciary properties were a major source of parcels available for lease.

[142] For the centrality of rumor and gossip as a source of information (or misinformation) in Attika, see Ober 1989: 148–51; Winkler 1990b: 58–66; Dover 1974: 30–33; 1989: 45–52; Hunter 1994: 96–119. For the limited content of the archive in the Mētrōon, see Preface, n. 19.

[143] Lys. 19.45: οὐ νῦν μόνον ἀλλὰ καὶ ἐν τῷ ἔμπροσθεν χρόνῳ πολλῶν ἐψεύσθητε τῆς οὐσίας, οἳ ζῶντες μὲν πλουτεῖν ἐδόκουν, ἀποθανόντες δὲ πολὺ παρὰ τὴν δόξαν τὴν ὑμετέραν ἐφάνησαν. Cf. Gabrielsen 1986: 110–11 and 1987: 12.

[144] Humphreys [1983] 1993: 10.

[145] Dem. 36.5: ἡ μὲν γὰρ ἔγγειος ἦν οὐσία Πασίωνι μάλιστα ταλάντων εἴκοσιν, ἀργύριον δὲ πρὸς ταύτῃ δεδανεισμένον ἴδιον πλέον ἢ πεντήκοντα τάλαντα. See Davies 1971: 431, who ultimately is

controlled vast holdings of real estate but, as a creditor, maintained his interests indirectly, and anonymously, through a third party.[146] Even the famous Isokratēs, whose life and property were far from anonymous, complains bitterly of an opponent's ability grossly to exaggerate the extent of the great man's property[147]—misrepresentations reflecting the frequent impossibility of identifying the actual owner of a specific parcel or of differentiating a freeholder from a lessee, or a farmer-*politēs* from a metic or slave independently engaged in agriculture. Although Aristotle insists that, in a society like the Athenian, "for foreigners and aliens it is not difficult to elude notice" (see n. 11), cases like Demosthenes 57 and Lysias 23 demonstrate that, even when noticed, the inhabitants of Attika were difficult to identify. The murky truth underlying the Athenian saying "today a slave, tomorrow a demesman of Sounion!"[148] merely suggests the mobility and anonymity of Athenian life chronicled in this chapter—a dynamic complexity incompatible with the prevailing conceptualization of Athens as exemplar of a primitive social simplicity within a hermeneutically closed "face-to-face society."

---

unable to explain the accumulation. Cf. Bogaert 1986: 37. In antiquity, the effort to untangle Pasiōn's estate led to prolonged litigation that was never fully resolved.

[146] Dem. 36.6: ὁρῶν ὅτι, μήπω τῆς πολιτείας αὐτῷ παρ' ἡμῖν οὔσης, οὐχ οἷός τ' ἔσοιτ' εἰσπράττειν ὅσα Πασίων ἐπὶ γῇ καὶ συνοικίαις δεδανεικὼς ἦν, εἵλετο μᾶλλον αὐτὸν τὸν Πασίωνα χρήστην ἔχειν τούτων τῶν χρημάτων ἢ τοὺς ἄλλους χρήστας, οἷς προειμένος ἦν. For the techniques and motivation underlying these arrangements, see E. Cohen 1992: 133–36.

[147] Isok. 15.4: ἔγνων καὶ τούτων τινὰς οὐχ οὕτω πρός με διακειμένους ὥσπερ ἤλπιζον, ἀλλὰ τοὺς μὲν πολὺ διεψευσμένους τῶν ἐμῶν ἐπιτηδευμάτων καὶ ῥέποντας ἐπὶ τὸ πείθεσθαι τοῖς ἀνεπιτήδειόν τι λέγουσιν.

[148] Anaxandridēs (second quarter of fourth century), fr. 4, lines 3–4: πολλοὶ δὲ νῦν μέν εἰσιν οὐκ ἐλεύθεροι, | εἰς αὔριον δὲ Σουνιεῖς.

5

Wealthy Slaves in a "Slave Society"

> At Athens some slaves live magnificently and properly so.
>
> *The Constitution of the Athenians* (attributed to Xenophon)[1]

> A slave bears only this dishonor: the name. In every other way a slave is equal to the free
>
> Euripides, *Ion*[2]

DESPITE the ubiquitous presence of unfree individuals in virtually all human communities,[3] Attika constitutes one of the few attested true "slave economies"[4]—those in which the contribution of a large number of unfree persons to the totality of wealth production is so substantial that a society's overall production, distribution, and consumption is

[1] 1.11: ἐῶσι τοὺς δούλους τρυφᾶν αὐτόθι καὶ μεγαλοπρεπῶς διαιτᾶσθαι ἐνίους, καὶ τοῦτο γνώμῃ φανεῖεν ἂν ποιοῦντες.

[2] Lines 854–56: ἓν γάρ τι τοῖς δούλοισιν αἰσχύνην φέρει, τοὔνομα· τὰ δ' ἄλλα πάντα τῶν ἐλευθέρων οὐδὲν κακίων δοῦλος, ὅστις ἐσθλὸς ᾖ.

[3] See Murdock 1967: 109–236; Goody 1980: 16–42; Phillips 1985: 3; Wiedemann 1987: 1–2, 14; Patterson 1982: vii–ix, 350–64, who finds slavery omnipresent "from before the dawn of human history right down to the twentieth century, in the most primitive of human societies and in the most civilized" (p. vii). Chattel slavery continues to be extensively practiced. As of the summer of 1994, ninety thousand blacks, for example, were reported to be living as the property of Berbers in Mauritania (where slavery was officially prohibited only in 1980); in the Sudan in 1990 a woman or child could be bought for fifteen U.S. dollars at slave markets. *New York Times,* July 13, 1994, p. A19. For the extensiveness of twentieth-century slavery, see O'Callaghan 1961; Derrick 1975.

[4] On the large number of slaves in Athens, see Chapter 1, p. 17 and n. 40. For the existence of an Athenian economy in the fourth century functioning independently of political and social relationships such as reciprocity and redistribution, see Cohen 1993 (cf. Chapter 6, n. 116). On the concept of premarket economies as embedded in society, see Polanyi, Arensberg, and Pearson 1957: 68; Polanyi 1944: 63–64; Tandy 1997: 84–87; Silver 1995: xii–xxiii, 97–177; Figueira 1984 and 1998: 1; Wohl 1998: 215, n. 18; Lowry 1987: 2. Cf. Parsons's "structural differentiation" ([1944] 1951: chs. 4, 5) and Mauss's "faits sociaux totaux" (1923–24). Godelier 1986 argues that economic functions in "pre-capitalist economies" are not "embedded" in society, but are totally absent. Cf. Godelier 1978.

highly dependent on slave labor.[5] But while the prevalence and importance of slavery in ancient Athens is well known, the phenomenon of wealthy slaves and, in particular, the institution of the *khōris oikountes* (unfree persons maintaining their own households) are generally unknown, partly as a result of scholarship which has, since Roman times, denied the existence of this group of slaves (who are in fact well attested in Athenian sources).[6] Writing in the Roman imperial period, centuries after the demise of an independent Athens, the lexicographer Harpokratiōn insists that the persons described in Athenian sources as "slaves maintaining independent households" must have been "*ex*-slaves": his tautological reasoning—the term *khōris oikountes* must refer not to slaves but to freedmen, since slaves would have resided with their masters (as they did in his time).[7]

Two millennia later, confronting the description in Aiskhinēs 1 of the destruction of the slave Pittalakos's home (the ruin of his furniture, the murder of his beloved pets, and the wreckage of other property), the British scholar Todd still seeks to reject this evidence of independent servile domicile by suggesting that Pittalakos might not really have been a slave (1993: 192–94)—despite repeated, explicit reference in Aiskhinēs's text to Pittalakos's servitude.[8] Modern historians' refusal to accept the evidence of the ancient Athenian sources derives, at least in part, from preconceptions generated by the enormously influential and relatively recent slave society of North America. Yet, analyzed both within Athenian context and within the experience of other slave societies

[5] For Athens as a slave society, see Garlan 1988: 201–3; Fisher 1993: 3. (For Marx's characterization of the entire Greek world as a "slave economy" (*Sklavenhaltergesellschaft*, *Sklavenhalterordnung*), see 1970–72: 3:332, 384–85, 594–95). Finley identifies only five "genuine slave societies" among the mass of known human groupings, including "classical Greece and classical Italy" (1980: 9; cf. Finley 1985: 79). My use of "slave economies" (close to Hopkins's combination of demographic and productive criteria [1978: 99]) incorporates Patterson's "large-scale slave societies" (which focuses on the proportion of slaves to the general population [1982: 353–64]) and Ste. Croix's emphasis on the proportion of production furnished by unfree labor (1981: 52).

[6] See, for example, Lipsius [1905–15] 1966: 622, n. 6; 798, n. 29; Westermann 1955: 17, n. 106. Garlan suggests that *khōris oikountes* might have been merely a "category" of "salaried" slaves (1988: 70). Ste. Croix assumes that the term must refer "mainly if not entirely to freedmen" (1981: 563, n. 9).

[7] S.v. τοὺς χωρὶς οἰκοῦντας: Δημοσθένης Φιλιππικοῖς "καὶ μετὰ ταῦτα ἐμβαίνειν τοὺς μετοίκους ἔδοξε καὶ τοὺς χωρὶς οἰκοῦντας τῶν δεσποτῶν." οὐ μὴν ἀλλὰ καὶ χωρὶς τοῦ προσκεῖσθαι φανερὸν ἂν εἴη τὸ δηλούμενον, ὅτι οἱ ἀπελεύθεροι καθ' αὑτοὺς ᾤκουν, χωρὶς τῶν ἀπελευθερωσάντων, ἐν δὲ τῷ τέως δουλεύοντες ἔτι συνῴκουν.

[8] Aiskhin. 1.54: ἄνθρωπος δημόσιος οἰκέτης τῆς πόλεως . . . ἄνθρωπον δημόσιον οἰκέτην τῆς πόλεως. 1.62: δημόσιον οἰκέτην τῆς πόλεως. Pittalakos's prosperity is explicitly noted by Aiskhinēs at 1.54: οὗτος εὐπορῶν ἀργυρίου.

(including the American South), attainment of high position and considerable wealth at Athens by a relatively few enslaved individuals presents no cause for desperate disbelief on a priori grounds. In Babylonia and in Rome in antiquity, and in sub-Saharan Africa and the Islamic world in the medieval period, some slaves functioned as high military officers, as powerful administrators, and as important (and sometimes wealthy) businessmen.[9] In the 1820s, in the Cape Colony of southwestern Africa, then under British control, enslaved herdsmen lived on their own for extended periods, tending livestock in remote interior regions, a reflection of economic requirements and of the paucity of white authority beyond the limited area of colonial settlement (Davis 1996: 51; 1998: ix). Likewise, the *khōris oikountes* at Athens and the related phenomenon of wealthy slaves appear to have been merely an appropriate manifestation of communal realities, which virtually mandated the commercial activities of those unfree businessmen and enslaved civil servants who amassed at Athens considerable wealth and authority—a "slave economy" of significant *douloi*[10] that is sharply in conflict with prevailing scholarly assumptions and conclusions.

Unfree Wealth and Power: Slave Entrepreneurs and Civil Servants

"Slave achievement" seems, of course, oxymoronic in the context of the racially based servitude familiar from nineteenth-century North American history. Slavery there assumed the permanent exploitation

[9] Ancient Mesopotamia: Gelb 1973: 72, 90–93. For the importance of enslaved military and civilian officials in Islamic empires, see Lewis 1990: 62–77; Crone 1980; Kunt 1983, esp. chs. 3, 4. For "rich and powerful" slaves in African traditional societies, see Miers and Kopytoff 1977: esp. 5. On slaves' independent economic activity, and occasional financial success, even in the American South, see n. 14 here. Roman slaves, as early as the second century B.C.E., act as principals in buying (through borrowed funds) other slaves for training and resale (Plut. *Cato Maior* 21.7–8). This may reflect the difficult and relatively late development in Roman law of a mechanism for conducting business through agents or dependents (Wenger 1906: 125; Nicholas 1962: 201–4). When agency was ultimately recognized, "the overwhelming majority of business managers were slaves" (Aubert 1994: 417).

[10] I use slave, *doulos* and other Greek terms interchangeably as appropriate to describe the status of unfree persons at Athens. Although by Roman law definition all persons are either free or slave—there is no other category (Just. *Inst.* 1.3.pr.)—in ancient Greece the great variety of personal statuses in the various political entities (cf. Pollux 3.73–83) has generated inconsistency in modern terminology, for example, the use of the word "serf" to describe the unfree Spartan "helot" group. Cf. Lauffer 1961; Finley 1975: 63–64. Such problems of terminology are not limited to the study of classical European servitude: for objections to characterization in Western terms of traditional forms of African slavery, see Miers and Kopytoff 1977: 5–7; for the lack of consensus on vocabulary among students of modern slavery, Meillassoux 1975. On the emerging

of the slave as a member of an inferior group;[11] the perpetual easy differentiation of slaves from free persons;[12] the denial to the unfree of professional skills (and even literacy);[13] and the prohibition of business activity.[14] Athens was much different. In Attika, servitude was not racially based or inherently perpetual,[15] could befall anyone and might well be temporary.[16] No physical or other markers differentiated enslaved from free inhabitants.[17] The state, far from buttressing the institution, largely ignored it,[18] while the legal system facilitated slaves' independent

recognition of the limited applicability of contemporary Western economics, and the deleterious effect of applying culturally bound commercial analysis to alien societies, see Gudeman 1986 and Baudrillard 1988: 65–67, 98–113.

[11] In America, in a landmark case the U.S. Supreme Court held, for example, that freed blacks could not ever be U.S. citizens and that, even after obtaining their freedom, blacks "had no rights which the white man was bound to respect." *Dred Scott v. Sanford*, 60 U.S. 393, 407 (1857).

[12] The Supreme Court of the northern U.S. state of Pennsylvania in 1837 denied free blacks the right to vote under the Pennsylvania constitution and laws, but held out the hope that this ruling might be reversed if black "blood, however, may become so diluted in successive descents as to lose its distinctive character." *Hobbs v. Fogg*, 6 Watts 553, 560 (1837). See Higginbotham 1996: 170–71. But Pennsylvania harshly punished miscegenation (Pa. *Statutes at Large*, IV: 62–63; Turner 1911: 29). Even the northern state of Massachusetts (which gave African Americans the right to vote freely: see Grofman et al. 1992: 4) prohibited interracial marriage in its statutes of 1705 and 1786, and in its revised code of 1836 actually increased the penalties for transgressions.

[13] A number of southern states provided criminal sanctions for teaching a slave to read or write. See, for example, the *Va. Code* (1848), pp. 747–48. At Athens, in contrast, special efforts were made to provide young slaves with a skill: see Forbes 1955 and Burford 1972: 87–91.

[14] In the American South, slaves were severely restricted by statutory law from engaging in the professions or in business transactions. See generally Higginbotham 1978. Yet slaves' independent practice of trades and business transactions nonetheless persisted: many slaves lived and worked in cities on their own account, paying their masters monetary compensation from fees and wages earned as craftsmen, generally receiving from employers and customers compensation equivalent to that paid to free black or white practitioners. See Goldin 1976. For slaves' market-related activities in South Carolina, Virginia, and Louisiana, see Campbell 1991; Schlotterbeck 1991; and McDonald 1991.

[15] At Athens many slaves, although apparently not the majority, were of Greek origin (see Finley, 1981: 104): no legal barrier prevented the enslavement of a free inhabitant of another Greek state (Harrison 1968–71: 1:165). Where slavery is not racially based, "to be a slave is a misfortune for the individual, assuredly a grave one, but it is not inevitable, natural or necessarily permanent" (Watson 1987: 3, with reference to Roman slavery).

[16] Fisher 1993: 36. The great philosopher Plato, an aristocratic Athenian by birth (a member of the family of Kritias, with descent from Solon), is reported to have personally experienced enslavement, being captured on board ship and offered for sale at Aigina (but purchased into freedom through his friends' efforts: Diog. Laert. 3.18–21). In a similar case, the slave owner Nikostratos, while pursuing three runaway *douloi*, was himself captured by a hostile warship and taken to the island of Aigina, and there sold into slavery but ultimately returned to Athens and freedom (Dem. 53.4–9). Cf. Dem. 58.18–19. So pervasive was the need to free Athenian *politai* fallen into the control of others that Lysias lists—among a litany of routine civic undertakings (paying regular and special taxes, not causing difficulties, obeying the law, creating no enmity)—his family's "ransoming of many Athenians from the enemy" (Lys. 12.20).

[17] The residents of Attika were remarkably homogeneous. See Chapter 4, pp. 105–7.

[18] The process of manumission is illustrative. Although in many jurisdictions liberation of slaves has been carefully controlled by official regulation and formal legal provisions (cf. the Roman process of manumission [*vindicta*] yielding citizenship but validated only by the presence of a Roman official [*Dig.* 40.2]), at Athens the state provided no direction or even official

business operations—by limiting a master's liability for a slave's business debts, by allowing liberal use of agents to effectuate transactions otherwise impossible for non-*politai*, and by accepting slaves as parties and witnesses in business litigation.[19]

In fact, slaves played a leading role in Athenian business, especially in finance and the crafts.[20] The *douloi* Xenōn, Euphrōn, Euphraios, and Kallistratos—while still enslaved[21]—as principals operated the largest bank in Athens, that of Pasiōn.[22] Pasiōn himself, while still unfree, had played a major role in his owners' bank[23] and thereafter in his own *trapeza*.[24] Phormiōn (who ultimately succeeded Pasiōn as Athens's most important financier),[25] while still a slave, had been a partner in a maritime

registration. See Todd 1994: 126–27. Indeed, private efforts to publicize manumissions in the theater were ultimately proscribed as disruptive (Aiskhin. 3.41–44). (The shadowy *phialai exeleutherikai* inscriptions, all of which seem to date from the 320s [Todd 1997:120] may represent a late effort to provide some public record of manumission, but even this is highly uncertain. See my discussion on pp. 152–54.)

[19] See Cohen 1991, 1994b.

[20] For slaves' preeminence in trapezitic operations, and the social and economic factors underlying their importance in banking, see E. Cohen 1992: ch. 4. For their significance in skilled trades, see, for example, Webster 1973; Hemelrijk 1991: 255 ("the outlandish names of many artisans [Skythes, Bryygos, etc.] reveal their slave status"); for construction, Randall 1953; Burford 1963.

[21] They functioned pursuant to a leasing arrangement (*misthōsis*) with their masters that provided for a fixed rent: see Dem. 36.43, 46, 48; E. Cohen 1992: 76. Only on expiration of the lease did their owners καὶ ἐλευθέρους ἀφεῖσαν (Dem. 36.14) ("enfranchised them," see Harrison 1968–71: 1:175, n. 2.). The phrase ἐλευθέρους ἀφεῖσαν is standard Greek for manumission of slaves: cf. Hyper. *Athēn.*: εἶθ' ὕστερον ὅτε ἄν σοι δοκῇ, ἀφῇς αὐτοὺς ἐλευθέρους. (col. 3); Dem. 47.55: ἀφειμένη ἐλευθέρα ὑπὸ τοῦ πατρὸς τοῦ ἐμοῦ. συνῴκησεν δὲ ἀνδρί, ἐπειδὴ ἀφείθη ἐλευθέρα; Dem. 57.34: ἢ ὡς ἐδούλευσεν ἢ ὡς ἀφείθη ἐλευθέρα. *Pace* Todd 1993: 193, n. 42, the manumission of these slaves was related to their masters' satisfaction with their operation of the bank under lease arrangements (καὶ ἐλευθέρους ἀφεῖσαν ὡς μεγάλ' εὖ πεπονθότες, καὶ οὐκ ἐδικάζοντ' οὔτ' ἐκείνοις τότ' οὔτε τούτῳ). Dem. 36.14.

[22] Even Thompson, who sees banks as "insignificant" in the Athenian economy, recognizes the significance of "the lendable deposits (and) private resources of a tycoon like Pasion" (1979: 240).

[23] Dem. 36.43: παρὰ τοῖς αὐτοῦ κυρίοις Ἀντισθένει καὶ Ἀρχεστράτῳ τραπεζιτεύουσι πεῖραν δοὺς ὅτι χρηστός ἐστι καὶ δίκαιος, ἐπιστεύθη. Cf. Dem. 36.46, 48.

[24] Although he was an important *trapezistēs* by the 390s (Isok. 17), Pasiōn was not then a *politēs* (see 17.33 [use of Pythodōros the *politēs* as his agent], 41 [his inclusion among the ξένοι εἰσφέροντες]). While it is generally assumed that he was manumitted prior to the events described in Isok. 17 (cf. Davies 1971: 429–30), in fact we do not know when he obtained his freedom. His inclusion among the ξένοι εἰσφέροντες offers no evidence for his possible manumission: nothing is known of Athens's taxation of prosperous unfree inhabitants of Attika. Under the provisions of the grain tax law discovered in the Athenian *agora* in 1986, bidding among potential tax farmers was not limited to Athenian *politai* (see Stroud 1998: 64–66; cf. Langdon 1994). Slave entrepreneurs may therefore have been included among the *priamenoi*.

[25] Dem. 36.4, 11, 37; 45.31–32. Phormiōn's lease of Pasiōn's bank was entered into with Phormiōn ἤδη καθ' ἑαυτὸν ὄντι (4). In thus noting explicitly that Phormiōn had already obtained his freedom when he entered into operating leases giving him complete control of the bank and of a shield workshop, the speaker necessarily implies that slave status would not have been a bar to entering into these substantial obligations: otherwise the mere fact of his being lessee of the businesses would have established his status as free.

trading business.[26] Similarly the slave Lampis was the owner-operator (*nauklēros*) of a substantial commercial vessel: he entered into contracts with free persons (Dem. 34.5–10), lent substantial sums to customers (6),[27] received repayment of large amounts on behalf of other lenders (23, 31), even received the special exemption from taxes (*ateleia*) provided by Pairisadēs of Bosporos on the export of grain to Athens,[28] and provided a deposition in the arbitration proceedings relating to an Athenian legal action (18–19). Likewise Zēnothemis, identified as a slave in Demosthenes 32, was actively engaged in maritime commerce and lending: allegedly the owner of a substantial commercial cargo, he litigated in his own name as a principal in the Athenian courts.[29] Slaves often paid their owners a fixed sum while operating businesses for their own account: the *douloi* kept the profits, if any. Accordingly, we find a group of nine or ten unfree leather workers, whose leader paid their owner three obols for himself per day, two for each of the other slaves, and kept any remaining revenues (Aiskhin. 1.97); a *doulos* who operated his master's business for a fixed payment and was free to retain any additional income after expenses (Milyas in Dem. 27); a slave who ran a substantial perfume business,[30] providing his owner with reports only monthly and again subject only to a fixed payment (Meidas in Hyper. *Athēn.* 9); and slaves operating their own businesses in the *agora* and personally liable for legal transgressions without reference to their masters (Stroud 1974b: 181–82, lines 30–32).

The phenomenon of slave wealth at Athens did not go unnoted in antiquity: the author of the satiric *Constitution of the Athenians* observed, and complained, that at Athens, where the mass of foreigners and slaves

[26] See Dem. 49.31, where Timosthenēs, active in overseas commerce ("ἀφικνεῖται κατ' ἐμπορίαν ἰδίαν ἀποδημῶν"), is characterized as Phormiōn's κοινωνός at a time when Phormiōn was still a *doulos*. (Κοινωνός is difficult to translate: see E. Cohen 1992: 76, n. 71.) Davies 1971: 432 sees "Phormiōn's later activity as a shipowner" as having its "roots" in this earlier business involvement in maritime trade.

[27] See Thompson 1980: 144–45. Although it is often categorically asserted that this Lampis cannot be the same person as his homonyme, the maritime Lampis of Dem. 23, we have no independent information concerning either person, and their congruence cannot be ruled out (Todd 1993: 193, n. 43).

[28] Cf. Hervagault and Mactoux 1974: 90–91; Perotti 1974: 52–54.

[29] Dem. 32.4: ὑπηρέτης Ἡγεστράτου. A Massilian, he borrowed money at Syrakuse (χρήματ' ἐν ταῖς Συρακούσαις ἐδανείζεθ' οὗτος), claimed to have lent the funds against the security of maritime cargo, and litigated with other claimants to the collateral upon its arrival at Athens (9: τοῦ σίτου τοῦ ἡμετέρου ἀμφισβητήσας ἡμῖν δίκην προσείληχεν).

[30] The considerable scale of the business is suggested by the colossal amount of debts incurred in its operation: five talents composed of both conventional (*khrea*) and *eranos* loans (Hyper. *Athēn.* 7, 14, 19).

could not easily be differentiated in appearance from the *politai*, there could be found "rich slaves" (*plousioi douloi*), even "some who lived magnificently."[31] (We know from inscriptional evidence that some slaves at Athens themselves owned slaves.)[32] Xenophon, in the *Oikonomikos*, even urges owners of large estates to make special efforts to enrich their slave estate-managers (*epitropoi*) lest the slaves' "love of lucre" lead them to misappropriate the owners' assets; honest housekeepers (*tamiai*) should live with greater honor, freedom, and wealth than the dishonest.[33]

Persons owned by the Athenian state, so-called public slaves (*dēmosioi*),[34] also are known to have prospered: as civil servants exercising considerable independent discretion, they were in a position to aid the persons whom they regulated and to enrich themselves. The *dokimastēs*, a state servant empowered to rule on the purity of silver coinage, had the discretionary power to confiscate coins if he determined them to be counterfeit.[35] The public slave handling the revision of Athenian laws allegedly took bribes to confirm or to eliminate provisions, and was vilified as so arrogant that he came to "consider the state's possessions to be his own."[36] One *dēmosios*, a certain Pittalakos, even battles with a powerful *politēs*, Hēgēsandros, for the sexual favors of Timarkhos, a young male *politēs* and alleged prostitute: the slave not only makes use of his wealth to maintain Timarkhos in the slave's own home for a prolonged period of sexual exploitation—he ultimately brings a legal action against his rival, seeking through the Athenian courts redress for

[31] Xen. *Ath. Pol.* 1.11: εἰ δέ τις καὶ τοῦτο θαυμάζει, ὅτι ἐῶσι τοὺς δούλους τρυφᾶν αὐτόθι καὶ μεγαλοπρεπῶς διαιτᾶσθαι ἐνίους, καὶ τοῦτο γνώμῃ φανεῖεν ἂν ποιοῦντες. ὅπου γὰρ ναυτικὴ δύναμίς ἐστιν, ἀπὸ χρημάτων ἀνάγκη τοῖς ἀνδραπόδοις δουλεύειν. Despite its political bias and ironic orientation, the *Ath. Pol.* attributed to Xenophon should not be disregarded as an evidentiary source: see my Preface, p. 14; Chapter 4, n. 12.

[32] See *I.G.* II^2 1570.78–79, with regard to [. . .]leidēs (whose name has been incompletely preserved). Ownership of slaves by persons themselves enslaved is not unique to Athens: under Roman practice, for example, slaves routinely owned other slaves, sometimes in large numbers. See Watson 1987: 95.

[33] Xen. *Oik.* 14.7: ὁρῶντες πλουσιωτέρους γιγνομένους τοὺς δικαίους τῶν ἀδίκων πολλοὶ καὶ φιλοκερδεῖς ὄντες εὖ μάλα ἐπιμένουσι τῷ μὴ ἀδικεῖν. 9.13: καὶ δικαιοσύνην δ' αὐτῇ ἐνεποιοῦμεν τιμιωτέρους τιθέντες τοὺς δικαίους τῶν ἀδίκων καὶ ἐπιδεικνύοντες πλουσιώτερον καὶ ἐλευθεριώτερον βιοτεύοντας τῶν ἀδίκων.

[34] On *dēmosioi* (enslaved individuals owned by the state), see Jacob 1926, [1928] 1979. The total number of *dēmosioi* at Athens is unknown: cf. Garlan 1988: 41, 68.

[35] Stroud 1974b: lines 10–13. For similar examples, see Aristot. *Ath. Pol.* 47.5, 48.1, 50.2, 54.1.

[36] Lys. 30.2: καθ' ἑκάστην δὲ ἡμέραν ἀργύριον λαμβάνων τοὺς μὲν ἐνέγραφε τοὺς δὲ ἐξήλειφεν. 30.5: καὶ εἰς τοῦτο ὕβρεως ἥκεις, ὥστε σαυτοῦ νομίζεις εἶναι τὰ τῆς πόλεως, αὐτὸς δημόσιος ὤν. Although Fisher (1995: 46) identifies Nikomakhos as "the state slave in charge of the revision of the laws" (cf. Fisher 1992: 117–18), others arbitrarily assume the impossibility of a slave holding a position of such importance, and accordingly identify Nikomakhos as a "legitimate citizen," "whatever [his] origins" (Todd 1994: 126).

the *politēs's* jealous assault against his house and person, an action that even awakened the slave's neighbors, offensive behavior defended by Hēgēsandros not as the exercise of a free man's right to violate a slave's person and his quiet enjoyment of home, but as culpability diminished by wine's nocturnal influence (Aiskhin. 1.54–64).

There were also, of course, innumerable exploited and impoverished *douloi.* Slave opportunity was not a right. Even after Phormiōn had gained unequaled prosperity (Dem. 45.54 and 72), an adversary insists that his success was entirely dependent on his good fortune in serving as a slave to a banker:

> You [jurors] all know that if a caterer, or an artisan of some other skilled calling [*tekhnē*], had purchased Phormiōn, then—having learned the *tekhnē* of this master—he would have been far from his present benefits.[37] But since . . . a banker acquired him and taught him lettered accounts and instructed him in this *tekhnē* and made him responsible for large sums of money, he has become prosperous, taking as the foundation of all of his present prosperity the good fortune which brought him [to a banking family].[38]

There were, of course, worse fates, at Athens, than being the *doulos* of a food provider or a craftsman. Unfree labor was important in such areas as mining, where thousands of *douloi* undoubtedly endured short lives of anguish.[39] Yet it is not the slaves of suffering, but the slaves of power and wealth who have endured scholarly oblivion.

"Corrective Interpretations": Evidence Rejected, Preconceptions Maintained

Prevailing methodology explicitly sanctions—indeed, demands—a "corrective approach" to the ancient evidence: "all our documentation

[37] An Athenian *politēs* working in a field other than banking was, as a general matter, equally unable to achieve the financial success possible as a *trapezitēs*. But, theoretically at least, he would have been able to change his profession; the slave, theoretically at least, had no such choice.

[38] Dem. 45.71–72: οἶμαι γὰρ ἅπαντας ὑμᾶς εἰδέναι, ὅτι τοῦτον, ἡνίκ᾽ ὤνιος ἦν, εἰ συνέβη μάγειρον ἤ τινος ἄλλης τέχνης δημιουργὸν πρίασθαι, τὴν τοῦ δεσπότου τέχνην ἂν μαθὼν πόρρω τῶν νῦν παρόντων ἦν ἀγαθῶν. ἐπειδὴ δ᾽ ὁ πατὴρ ὁ ἡμέτερος τραπεζίτης ὢν ἐκτήσατ᾽ αὐτὸν καὶ γράμματ᾽ ἐπαίδευσεν καὶ τὴν τέχνην ἐδίδαξεν καὶ χρημάτων ἐποίησε κύριον πολλῶν, εὐδαίμων γέγονεν, τὴν τύχην, ἣ πρὸς ἡμᾶς ἀφίκετο, ἀρχὴν λαβὼν πάσης τῆς νῦν παρούσης εὐδαιμονίας.

[39] See esp. Lauffer 1979. *Pace* Kudlien 1991, slavery in classical antiquity was overwhelmingly negative, "an abomination for which no apology is possible and in which no redeeming features can be found" (Bradley 1997: 274—cf. Garnsey 1996: 110–14; Annequin 1992: 290–97).

relating to slaves is 'overdetermined' in one way or another and, as such, demands a 'diagnostic' or 'symptomatic' reading" (Garlan 1988: 19).[40] Such pursuit of a "lecture symptomale," rather than the "plain meaning" of a text, in reality has meant either the arbitrary dismissal of the ancient testimonia as merely "the exceptions that prove the rule" of slave nullity[41]—even though there is no body of affirmative testimonia supporting conventional analyses[42]—or contorted efforts to force the ancient sources to conform to modern preconception.

A good illustration of this phenomenon is found in two recent treatments of the text of Aiskhinēs that discusses the slave Pittalakos's loves, luxuries, and lawsuits (1.54–60; see p. 131). While Todd seeks to reject this evidence by suggesting that Pittalakos might not really have been a slave at all (1993: 192–94), Fisher accepts the passage's identification of Pittalakos as a slave but attributes his control of his own property, money, and time to an alleged "special status: Pittalakos was apparently free from the laws that said slaves could not 'love' free boys and were unable to bring legal actions themselves" (1993: 57). Dealing with the claim by Andokidēs that the prominent politician Hyperbolos was a foreigner, indeed a non-Greek whose father was a "branded slave" working in the state mint, Fisher immediately and peremptorily dismisses the allegation as "certainly false,"[43] rather than seeking an explanation for the charges of slave or foreign origin frequently made against Athenian political leaders.[44]

Such "'diagnostic' or 'symptomatic' reading" has long and rarefied pedigree. A century ago, Wilamowitz (1893: 2:368ff.) rejected a plaintiff's claim that his action has been properly lodged in the polemarch's court because the defendant, Pankleōn, is a slave, although the largest part of the plaintiff's speech (Lys. 23.7–12) is devoted to elaborations

[40] In French terms, "documentation 'surdéterminée' " requires "une lecture 'symptomale' " (Garlan 1982: 31). "Diagnostic reading" is viewed as merely a defensive response to the inevitable subjectivity of those espousing objective pretensions: "very few of the apparently purely scholarly debates on [Greek slavery] avoid, in one way or another, consciously or unconsciously, adopting a particular ideological perspective" (Garlan 1988: 23).

[41] Garlan 1988: 68, warns against "regarding these examples (of banking dynasties of slave origin) as anything but exceptional success stories."

[42] Although the number of individual situations providing detailed information on slaves' involvement in commercial activity is highly limited—perhaps a dozen situations—forensic attestation does provide a sound basis for generalization (see Preface, pp. xiii–xiv).

[43] Fisher 1993: 56; Andok. fr. 5 (Blass) (F III.2 [Maidment]): Greek text at Chapter 4, n. 50.

[44] At Athens, affirmative establishment of political status was quite difficult: the antecedents of even prominent politicians were frequently uncertain. See Chapter 4, pp. 111–12.

on the defendant's slave status, with the triumphant conclusion that Pankleōn has by his own actions acknowledged his unfree status.[45] The speaker's insistence upon the defendant's servitude presupposes the admissibility in the polemarch's court of cases against slaves involved in commerce,[46] an impossibility under the modern scholarly preconception that Athenian slaves, denigrated and nullified by an exploitative society, could not conceivably have litigated as independent parties in Athenian courts.[47] In support of this shibboleth, Wilamowitz explains that the plaintiff *really* had no interest in pursuing an action against the defendant! Instead, the plaintiff, we are to believe, was arguing for his right to pursue the litigation only in order to obtain his real goal—to have his suit dismissed.[48] A century later, Wilamowitz's odd explanation is still accepted as a means of explaining away the implications of the plaintiff's assertions (Todd 1993: 168–69).

Similar logic has been employed to reject ancient evidence concerning a deposition provided by a slave in the arbitration of an Athenian business dispute. The slave Lampis was a substantial shipowner-operator (Dem. 34.18–19) but is termed at 34.5 an *oiketēs*, the "word most frequently used" in ancient Greek to denote an unfree person (Garlan 1988: 21). At 34.10, Lampis is again referred to as a slave, here as a *pais*: the repetition of the characterization and the textual distance separating the two citations would seem to preclude even paleographical objections to recognizing Lampis's servile status. But Lampis's situation

[45] Lys. 23.12: εὖ εἰδὼς ἑαυτὸν ὄντα δοῦλον ἔδεισεν ἐγγυητὰς καταστήσας περὶ τοῦ σώματος ἀγωνίσασθαι.

[46] The speech provides no information concerning the nature of the plaintiff's underlying claim other than a reference to the defendant's commercial activity in a fuller's shop.

[47] The prevailing presumption allows no exceptions: "slaves could not enter into litigation" (Finley [1951] 1985: 104–5). Carey (1992: 102) cites Finley in asserting that "a slave lacks legal personality," although Finley's conclusion was based not on evidence from classical Athens, but on much later material from Delphi (see Finley [1951] 1985: 292, n. 78). Cf. Garlan 1988: 42. But modern preconception on this issue conflicts with ancient Greek assumption. In considering the possible bases for "friendship" between slave and master, Aristotle explicitly recognized a slave's inherent capacity to participate in legal matters and specifically to enter into contracts (*synthēkai*): ᾗ μὲν οὖν δοῦλος, οὐκ ἔστι φιλία πρὸς αὐτόν, ᾗ δ' ἄνθρωπος· δοκεῖ γὰρ εἶναί τι δίκαιον παντὶ ἀνθρώπῳ πρὸς πάντα τὸν δυνάμενον κοινωνῆσαι νόμου καὶ συνθήκης· καὶ φιλία δή, καθ' ὅσον ἄνθρωπος (*NE* 1161b5–8). Contractual arrangements with slaves would have meaning (because legally enforceable) only if slaves could be parties to commercial litigation.

[48] The speaker's alleged true goal—"to give Nikomedes [an alleged master] the implicit backing of the court to recapture him" (Todd 1994: 131, n. 15)—is nowhere alluded to in the speech or elsewhere in antiquity (see Gernet and Bizos [1924, 1926] 1967: 93–94) who adopt Wilamowitz's explanation despite their recognition that "cette connivence n'apparaît pas trop dans le discours").

and actions are so variant from prevailing preconception that scholars for a century have sought other characterizations for him: the *oiketēs* of our text becomes an "independent agent," an "ex-slave," a "metic," a "freedman."[49]

Many other examples can be cited of abrogation of the "plain meaning" of evidence for independent slave activity in commerce: Demosthenes 36.14, where the text shows slaves operating a bank, but where scholars have contended that since slaves could not actually have operated a *trapeza* as principals, the Greek text cannot mean here, as elsewhere, "enfranchised them later";[50] Demosthenes 27.19, where Demosthenes's father's longtime slave, Milyas, supposedly must have been free at the time that he managed on a profit basis the father's business;[51] Hypereidēs's *Against Athēnogenēs,* where the perfume business operated by the slave Meidas must have been insignificant because operated by slaves,[52] despite clear textual evidence to the contrary; Aristotle's *Politics* 1277a7–8, where textual reference to a slave's possessions has been arbitrarily dismissed by striking the word *ktēsis* from the Greek text, without the slightest paleographical justification.[53] And despite the abundant evidence for the *khōris oikountes*—slaves maintaining independent households—the very existence of such *douloi* has often been summarily rejected (see n. 6).

Why has there been such scholarly determination to force the evidence to conform to preconception, rather than to amend preconception to conform to ancient testimonia? Although the ideological preferences mentioned by Garlan (see n. 40) may have consciously motivated some scholars, even self-styled "positivist" historians would be disturbed by the apparent inconsistency between documentation describing wealthy slaves and the contempt for slaves prominent in elite literature and legal

[49] "Independent agent" (Seager 1966: 181, n. 82); "ex-slave" (Schäfer [1885–87] 1979: 3.2:305–6; Blass [1887–98] 1962: 3.1:577; Lipsius [1905–15] 1966: 797, n. 28; Partsch 1909: 136) ; "metic" (Beauchet [1897] 1969: 2:461) ; "freedman" (Paley and Sandys [1896–98] 1979: 1:5n; Ste. Croix 1981: 563, n. 9).

[50] See Todd 1994: 137 and n. 31; MacDowell 1978: 265, n. 161. Cf. my n. 21.

[51] Dem. 27.19; Pearson 1972: 122. Demosthenes, many years later, does refers to Milyas as "our freedman" (ὁ ἀπελεύθερος ὁ ἡμέτερος) but there is no indication that Milyas was not still a slave when he was operating the workshops.

[52] Millett 1991: 310, n. 40. But see my n. 30.

[53] οἰκία ἐξ ἀνδρὸς καὶ γυναικός, καὶ κτῆσις ἐκ δεσπότου καὶ δούλου (V^{m} reads κτησεις [*sic*]). Lord 1984 translates the passage as "a household of man and woman and master and slave," following Bernays in bracketing κτῆσις, but noting that the text manuscripts actually read "and a household of man and woman, and possessions of master and slave."

texts from Athens, especially allusions to physical maltreatment and even torture of unfree persons.[54] Yet literature often reflects normative assumptions acceptable to elite auditors, and legal texts—inevitably part of an ideological "discourse" prizing consistency—often mask inconsistencies and incongruities in practice.[55] In recent years, scholars have come to recognize that, for any society, the formal rules of legal substance and procedure cannot be understood, and are not applied, in disassociation from psychological, economic, and social realities, and that these rules, "the law," perform functions beyond the narrow control of behavior, including the statement of communal values that may be quite different from social reality.[56] And it is this social reality that explains the accumulation of wealth by certain *douloi* at Athens.

An Athenian Explanation for the Athenian Slave Economy

The phenomenon of "wealthy slaves" in Attika reflects several key elements of Athenian social organization and values:

1. the unwillingness of free persons to work as continuing employees in businesses conducted by others, an ethical orientation that provided slaves with the opportunity to gain commercial skills and economic power;

[54] Allusions to torture provide a further example of the gap between text and reality. Despite much rhetorical posturing, no slave ever gave testimony under torture at Athens in private disputes. Thür (1977) has definitively established the fictitious nature of this forensic jousting. Todd (1990: 33–34) summarizes: "on forty-two occasions in the orators we find the challenge, either 'torture my slaves for evidence' or 'let me torture yours.' Forty times this challenge was flatly rejected; twice (Isok. 17.15–16; Dem. 37.42) it was accepted but not carried through." Cf Gagarin 1996; Mirhady 1996.

[55] See Humphreys 1985; E. Cohen 1991. On the discontinuities and contradictions endemic at Athens, see Chapter 6, pp. 190–91.

[56] Consider, for example, the deviation between values and reality regarding selection of spouses. Speaking on behalf of a banker of enormous wealth but of slave origin, Demosthenes explains to a jury of *politai* how persons of wealth who were not born into Athenian *politeia* necessarily place supreme value on the retention of economic power, "preferring piles of money over pedigree" in selecting spouses for themselves and others—however strange this preference might seem by elite values. (Τοῖς γένει πολίταις, οὐδὲ ἓν' πλῆθος χρημάτων ἀντὶ τοῦ γένους καλόν ἐστιν ἑλέσθαι [Dem. 36.30]). But in reality, by the fourth century, legislation was required forbidding marriage between *astoi* and *xenoi*. Even for the most aristocratic of *politai*, dynastic marriages—commonplace in the sixth century—appear to have disappeared by the fourth. For the period of more than forty years prior to the regime of Dēmētrios, "an exceptionally well-documented period," not a single marriage link can be discerned among political personages. Davies 1981: 120.

2. the severance after manumission of virtually all legal relationship between former master and freed slave, in sharp contrast to other systems, such as the Roman, that imposed on former slaves substantial obligations to their ex-owners, including financial commitments: this Athenian abrogation of ties largely precluded liberation as a device for economic enrichment of the master and as an incentive for the gifted slave—and provided impetus for the development of a similar symbiosis not involving manumission;
3. the organization of Attika through households (*oikoi*) which facilitated the flourishing of the *khōris oikountes*—slaves maintaining independent households and autonomous businesses.

Not for Hire: Free Employees

In Attika, free persons were not available for "employment." As Aristotle observed, "the nature of the free man prevents his living under the control of another."[57] Numerous Athenians, however, were self-employed in crafts or trade,[58] and many others followed entrepreneurial pursuits.[59] Employment by a master for brief periods, a day or two, might have been acceptable to a few *politai*,[60] but extended service was intolerable.[61]

[57] Aristot. *Rhetoric* 1367a32: ἐλευθέρου γὰρ τὸ μὴ πρὸς ἄλλον ζῆν. It was not manual labor itself, but dependence on a master that was despised. Cf. Isai. 5.39: τοὺς δὲ περιεώρα τοὺς μισθωτοὺς ἰόντας δι' ἔνδειαν τῶν ἐπιτηδείων. See Isok. 14.48; Dem. 57.45; Xen. *Apom.* 2.8.1–5. See also Humphreys [1983] 1993: 10. Metics of free Greek origin would likely have harbored the same attitudes as Athenian *politai* toward "servile" employment.

[58] See Hopper 1979: 140; Finley 1981: 99; Ehrenberg 1962: 162; Osborne 1995: 30.

[59] See Thompson 1983; Garnsey 1980. For the significance of such activities in the ancient world, see Goody 1986: 177–84.

[60] Although most of those standing daily for hire at Kolonōs Agoraios in Athens were slaves, some might have been free men (Pherekratēs, fr. 142 (K-A)). Cf. Fuks 1951: 171–73. Marx believed that the formation of a labor market meant the introduction of "wage slavery," a precursor to classical capitalism (1970–72: 1:170). Cf. Lane 1991: 310–11. But the Athenian labor market appears to have been, in the main, a market actually composed of juridically unfree persons.

[61] In Xen. *Apom.* 2.8, Sōkratēs suggested permanent employment as an estate supervisor to Euthēros, an aging free man who feared that he would not long be able to continue earning a living through physical labor on an ad hoc basis. Such *epitropoi*, Sōkratēs notes, were well compensated (§6) even if they merely preserved existing wealth (2.8.3: ἔργων τε ἐπιστατοῦντα καὶ συγκομίζοντα τοὺς καρποὺς καὶ συμφυλάττοντα τὴν οὐσίαν, ὠφελοῦντα ἀντωφελεῖσθαι). The impoverished Euthēros curtly rejects the suggestion of a supervisory position under a single employer: such executive positions were only for slaves (2.8.4: χαλεπῶς ἂν ἐγὼ δουλείαν ὑπομείναιμι). Cf. 2.8.5: Ὅλως τὸ ὑπαίτιον εἶναί τινι οὐ πάνυ προσίεμαι. Jameson (1997: 100) alludes to free persons "reluctant to admit to the need of working for someone else."

It was also unnecessary: even for those unable to support themselves from their own property or from independent craft or business, the availability to *politai* of public maintenance funds and public service provided a practical means to avoid employment arrangements considered demeaning.[62]

Yet many businesses required repetitive service on a regular basis over an extended period of time, employment that was inherently incompatible with the "work ethic" of free Athenians. Although in many fields at Athens the same functions might be performed by slaves or by free persons hired for a specific task or for a limited period of time,[63] service by free persons was seldom exclusive to a single employer: instead we encounter businessmen working on their own for a variety of customers, or agents undertaking a specific, limited task for a single client.[64] Conversely, only slaves were considered appropriate as managers of large estates—where it was assumed that they would become wealthy if they performed well.[65] Because of the need for confidentiality and control, slaves were preferred over free persons in financial businesses, even when free persons were available.[66] As a result, *douloi* engaged in such activities (albeit in all probability a small minority of the unfree inhabitants of Attika) were frequently able to acquire skills, to obtain business knowledge, to develop valuable contacts—and to prosper. But an owner's full exploitation of this servile resource had to conform with prevailing institutional structures. In other societies, the promise of liberation, or even its actual grant, might serve the master's interest by increasing a skilled slave's motivation without adverse effect on the owner's financial position. But at Athens manumission could not achieve this result.

[62] The Athenian state offered paid service in the armed forces, and compensation for frequent jury duty and Assembly meetings; for "incapacitated" *politai* of limited means, there were outright public grants. See E. Cohen 1992: 71, n. 50.

[63] See Ehrenberg 1962: 183, 185. For parallel functioning by slave and free labor in the construction trades, see Randall 1953; Burford 1972. Cf. Chapter 6, pp. 186–87.

[64] Cf. the maritime entrepreneur who introduces a client to the bank of Hērakleidēs in Dem. 33.7; Agyrrhios who serves Pasiōn as a representative in litigational matters (Isok. 17.31–32; cf. Stroud 1998: 22; Strauss 1987: 142); Arkhestratos who provided the bond for Pasiōn (Isok. 17.43); Stephanos's relationship with the banker Aristolokhos at Dem. 45.64.

[65] See Xen. *Oik.* 12.3: ὅταν δεηθῇς ἐπιτρόπου, καταμαθὼν ἄν που ᾖ ἐπιτροπευτικὸς ἀνήρ, τοῦτον πειρᾷ ὠνεῖσθαι. Aristot. *Oik.* specifically recognizes the supervisor (ἐπίτροπος) as a category of slave separate from that of the unfree worker (ἐργάτης).

[66] For the application of these principles to the operation of *trapezai*, for example, see E. Cohen 1992: 72–73.

Manumission: Unprofitable Severance at Athens

In classical Rome, the wealth of some former slaves was proverbial,[67] and their former masters continued to benefit from such freedmen's success: for Roman law, the manumission of profit-providing slaves did not end the masters' economic rights.[68] *Operae* (labor) and *bona* (property rights) guaranteed the ex-owner an interest in the future prosperity of his former slave.[69] Under the Praetor's Edict, for example, the former owner retained the right to succession in the event of a freedman's death, even against the decedent's will.[70] With the institutionalized rights of patronage as a determining guide, the owner's movement from *dominus* to *patronus* might be financially beneficial (as the jurist Gaius observes explicitly).[71] In turn, the promise of manumission, appropriate after six years of service (Cic. *Phil.* 8.32), provided incentive for slaves of commercial capability.[72]

[67] Martial *Epigrams* 5.13. Cf. Pliny *Natural History* 33.134–35 (many ex-slaves wealthier than the tycoon Crassus; one freedman in 8 B.C.E., even after substantial losses from civil war, owned 4,116 slaves, 3,600 pairs of oxen, 257,000 other animals, and 60 million sesterces in cash—the minimum wealth of a senator, in contrast, was only 1 million sesterces).

[68] The original owner's position as *patronus* was protected even when manumission occurred by force of law as a result of the breach of a sales covenant prohibiting the use of a female slave in the sale of sexual services—even where the violator was a later purchaser not in privity with the original owner and presumably "had not been warned of the existence of the covenant" (McGinn 1990: 325). See Mod. (lib. sing. de manumiss.) *Dig.* 37.14.7 pr.: "Divus Vespasianus decrevit ut, si qua hac lege venierit, ne prostitueretur et, si prostituta esset, ut esset libera, si postea ab emptore alii sine condicione veniit, ex lege venditionis liberam esse et libertam prioris venditoris." On the grant of freedom by force of law, see Wagner 1967: 172; Mitteis 1908: 182, n. 62 ("nach Analogie des Statusliber"). On covenants forbidding prostitution of female slaves, see generally Sicari 1991; Sokala 1993.

[69] This entitlement to days of work resembles the payment to masters—in lieu of labor—by slaves *khōris oikountes*. See pp. 148ff. Like the Athenian arrangement, the Roman contribution of *operae* was determined by agreement. But *operae* had to be reasonable: see *Dig.* 38.1.15.1 (Paul, book 40 on the *Edict*); 38.1.14.pr. (Ulpian); 38.1.46 (Valens, book 5 on *Trusts*). Cf. Lenel [1927] 1966: 338ff.; Waldstein 1986: 234–35, 273. Significantly we find virtually no evidence at Athens for *paramonē* arrangements (i.e., manumission on condition of continued service). Such agreements (appearing at Athens only in the probably apocryphal philosophers' "wills" found in Diogenēs Laertios, an author of the Roman period) are fairly common centuries later in other parts of the Greek world: of 1,237 manumissions recorded at Delphi in the second and first centuries B.C.E., 400 are conditional (Hopkins 1978: 140).

[70] See Gaius *Inst.* 3.41–54, esp. 41–44. Cf. *Epit. Ulp.* 29.3, and, generally, Fabre 1981. Even under the Twelve Tables, in the event of intestacy, the former master inherited the former slave's property. See Watson 1987: 35.

[71] Gaius *Inst.* 1.19: "Iusta autem causa manumissionis est si quis . . . servum procuratoris habendi gratia aut ancillam matrimonii causa apud consilium manumittat." Cf. D'Arms 1981: 142; Wilson 1935: 66; Meiggs 1973: 224.

[72] Although the mass of Roman slaves engaged in menial tasks probably had no realistic anticipation of freedom, in late republican and early imperial times tens of thousands of ex-slaves

A slave's liberation brought much different financial consequences at Athens. There the freedman and his ex-master had no continuing legal relationship. This may partly have reflected the limited public effect of manumission in Attika: in contrast to the Roman procedure, liberation at Athens could not confer *politeia* ("citizenship"). In turn, manumission at Athens imposed on the freedman no continuing, legally sanctioned obligation toward his former master (see pp. 150–51). An owner accordingly could not anticipate financial benefit through Roman-style manumission and the creation of a *patronus-cliens* relationship. But implicit in communal organization by "household" (*oikos*) was the possibility of a similar symbiosis—the institution of the *khōris oikountes*.

Slaves Maintaining Independent Households

While modern Westernized societies focus on the individual persona and on individual rights and obligations, at Athens "the basic unit of social and economic organisation was the household,"[73] or *oikos*,[74] which encompassed the physical house and its accoutrements, the persons presently or previously living in that house, and the property relating to those persons[75]—in Aristotle's words, a "natural association for everyday purposes."[76] This association included all the persons living in the residence: husband, wife, children, and (explicitly in the ancient testimonia) slaves.[77] Indeed, in a ceremony analogous to that which greeted the entry of a bride, a newly purchased slave was welcomed into the *oikos* with an outpouring of figs, dates, and other delicacies intended to portend a

---

are known to have lived in the city of Rome itself: App., *Emph. Pol.* 1.100, 104; Dio Cass. 55.26; Just. *Inst.* 1.42, 43. Cf. Alföldy 1972: 97ff.; Bradley 1984: 81ff.

[73] Foxhall 1989: 42. Cf. Pomeroy 1994: 41 ("the polis was a community of oikoi"). For the seminal role of the *oikos* at Athens, see Chapter 1, pp. 32ff.

[74] Although the *oikos* was an important social and economic organization throughout classical Greece (see E. Cohen 1992: 85–86), its dominance appears to have been greatest in Attika (cf. Schaps 1979, who offers numerous examples of greater individual rights of ownership in other Greek societies).

[75] For the fullest discussion of the various aspects of the word *oikos*, see MacDowell 1989; Karabēlias 1984.

[76] *Pol.* 1252b12–14: ἡ μὲν οὖν εἰς πᾶσαν ἡμέραν συνεστηκυῖα κοινωνία κατὰ φύσιν οἶκός ἐστιν.

[77] Aristot. *Pol.* 1253b4–7 (οἰκία δὲ τέλειος ἐκ δούλων καὶ ἐλευθέρων). In fact, the slave, as a member of the *oikos*, was frequently referred to as an *oiketēs*. Acceptance of slaves as inferior members of a family is also characteristic, for example, of precolonial slavery in West Africa (Miers and Kopytoff 1977: 11). Even paternalistic treatment of slaves in North America fell far short of incorporating black dependents into slave owners' families: see Kolchin 1993: 111–18; Scarborough 1976.

"sweet and pleasant" future.[78] The *doulos's* permanence as a household member, albeit inferior and exploited, is confirmed by the remarkable absence from our sources of even a single instance of a slave being abandoned because of the infirmities of old age.[79] To the contrary, Xenophon claims that a prime responsibility for the mistress of the house was to provide for the care of her own offspring and of slaves who might become ill.[80] Although numerous tangible and personal incentives for increasing a slave's loyalty and economic contribution are suggested in the *Oikonomikos*, the possibility of freedom (and the slave's resultant departure from the *oikos*) is never mentioned.[81] The promise of manumission is unknown as an incentive to motivate slaves once ensconced in an Athenian household.[82]

Yet kind treatment of slaves was merely an option that might be chosen by self-interested masters:[83] within the *oikos*, the slave was largely without rights, other than an entitlement not to be murdered or sexually abused.[84] But outside the household, relative to other inhabitants of Attika, free or slave, the Athenian *doulos* was under no legal obligation

[78] Lex. Seguer. (Bekker) 269.9: καταχύσματα ἰσχάδες καὶ φοίνικες καὶ κάρυα ἄλλα τοιαῦτα ἐδώδιμα κατέχεον αἱ κύριαι τῶν οἴκων κατά τι ἔθος ἐπὶ τὰς κεφαλὰς τῶν ἄρτι ἐωνημένων δούλων παραδηλοῦσαι, ὅτι ἐπὶ γλυκέα καὶ ἡδέα πράγματα εἰσεληλύθασιν. Cf. Aristoph. *Plout*. 768 and schol.; Dem. 45.74; Pollux 3.77; Harp. and Sud. s.v. καταχύσματα.

[79] Pomeroy 1994: 223. Cf. Ste. Croix 1988: 25–26. Dem. 47.55–56 tells of an elderly servant who after manumission had lived independently with her husband, but on his death, in need, had come back to her ex-master's family—who professed an obligation to care for her.

[80] *Oik*. 7.24, 37: τῇ γυναικὶ καὶ ἐνέφυσε καὶ προσέταξε τὴν τῶν νεογνῶν τέκνων τροφήν. . . . ὃς ἂν κάμνῃ τῶν οἰκετῶν, τούτων σοι ἐπιμελητέον πάντων ὅπως θεραπεύηται.

[81] At *Oik*. 5.16, Xenophon insists on the need for slave incentives. These include a share in the profits of the *oikos* (9.11–13; 12.9, 15), the opportunity to reproduce (9.5), good clothing (13.10), and food (13.9)—but not manumission. Cf. Pomeroy 1994: 65–66. In contrast, Aristotle, writing in a pan-Hellenic context, urges that "all slaves" should be motivated by the possibility of freedom (καὶ διότι βέλτιον πᾶσι τοῖς δούλοις ἆθλον προκεῖσθαι τὴν ἐλευθερίαν, ὕστερον ἐροῦμεν: *Pol*. 1330a32–33), but "it is not clear whether [he is] encouraging existing trends or making radical proposals" (Fisher 1993: 69). In contrast, Greeks enslaved by war, brigandage, or piracy might anticipate relatively expeditious emancipation through ransom: see Dem. 53.6–13; cf. Thompson 1979: 224.

[82] Some manumissions did occur (see Aiskhin. 3.41–44). But in support of his assumption that at Athens "the inducement of freedom was a strong weapon in the slaveowners' armoury," Fisher adduces only a single example of manumission by a private owner—and that occurred at Korinth! (See Fisher 1993: 67–70; Dem. 59.29–32.) Other possible cases of manumission at Athens are clearly exceptional: the freeing by the Athenian state of slaves who fought in the final, traumatic stages of the Peloponnesian War (cf. Aristoph. *Batr*. 33–34, 290–91, 693–94: cf. Chapter 2, pp. 67–68). For the mysterious *phialai exeleutherikai* documents, see pp. 152–54.

[83] Plato is explicit in urging that masters should treat their slaves well, but not so much for the slaves' advantage, as for the masters' (*Laws* 6.777d).

[84] Protection from murder by his master(s): Antiph. 5.48; Schol. Aiskhin. 2.87; Harrison 1968–71: 1:171–72. On legislation prohibiting sexual abuse of slaves, even by *kyrioi*, see the first section of Chapter 6.

of subservience.[85] Thus even the prominent Kallippos, *proxenos* of the Hērakleōtes, pressing a claim at a bank, was dismissed by a slave functionary with the derisive "And what business is it of yours?"[86] A slave's ability to deal on a basis of equality with free persons outside the *oikos* was frequently critical to business operation. *Douloi* employed in banking, for example, often had access to large sums of money:[87] if they felt compelled to defer to free customers, the banks would be endangered. A contemporary observer saw this clearly. Noting (and lamenting) the elevated economic and social position of Athenian slaves, including their failure to show obeisance to free persons,[88] the author of the Xenophonic *Constitution of the Athenians* (1.10–11) attributes it all to money (*apo khrēmatōn*): for persons receiving a share of the earnings of their slaves, "it is not profitable" to have their slaves "fear" the free persons whom they encounter. Indeed, "if your slave fears me, there will be a danger that he will give you the money in his possession so as not himself to be at risk."[89] This egalitarian reality underlay the state's protection of a slave's "honor" (*timē*)—against transgressions from outside his *oikos*. A slave's honor? The very term is inconceivable within the prevailing scholarly conceptualization of hierarchical relationships in Attika.[90] Yet Demosthenes explains that a prosecution for *hybris* (any action that intentionally damaged a person's *timē*)[91] lay "whenever someone

[85] Athens differed from some other Greek jurisdictions where a slave might be treated with disdain and even struck with impunity by any free person. MacDowell 1978: 81. When, for example, outsiders attempted to enforce a judgment by seizing property (Dem. 47), the establishment's slaves did not hesitate to resist (§§53, 56).

[86] Dem. 52.5–6: τύχης δὲ συμβάσης τοιαύτης τῷ Λύκωνι τούτῳ ὥστε . . . ἀποθανεῖν, ἔρχεται ἐπὶ τὴν τράπεζαν Κάλλιππος οὑτοσὶ εὐθὺς ἐρωτῶν . . . "ἆρα καὶ ἐχρῆτο ὑμῖν;" ἔφη ὁ Φορμίων· "ἀλλὰ πρὸς τί ἐρωτᾷς;" For Kallippos's official position, personal prestige, and considerable power, see 52.1, 5, 11.

[87] The slave Kittos, without the bank owner's involvement, was able to advance six talents in a single transaction (Isok. 17.4); another *doulos* on his own is known to have paid out to a third party 1,640-odd drachmas (Dem. 52.7). Pursuant to a loan request from an Athenian general (Dem. 49.6), the same slave delivered loan proceeds to one of the commander's financial assistants (49.7). Slaves are even reported to have been dispatched to deal with foreign potentates concerning significant bank deposits at Athens by their nationals (Isok. 17.51).

[88] Xen. *Ath. Pol.* 1.10: οὔτε ὑπεκστήσεταί σοι ὁ δοῦλος. Cf. Preface, pp. xiv–xv.

[89] ἐὰν δὲ δεδίῃ ὁ σὸς δοῦλος ἐμέ, κινδυνεύσει καὶ τὰ χρήματα διδόναι τὰ ἑαυτοῦ ὥστε μὴ κινδυνεύειν περὶ ἑαυτοῦ.

[90] "The idea of a law on *hubris* concerning the *timē* of an individual in any sense other than that of his citizen rights seems contrary to the conceptions prevalent in Athenian legislation of the Classical period." (Murray 1990b: 140). See Chapter 6, pp. 160ff.

[91] See Chapter 6, pp. 160–65 and especially n. 23. A slave's *timē*, however, might have been conceived as so slight that *hybris* against a slave would require "gross and brutal treatment" (Fisher 1992: 40). Cf. Schaps 1998b: 170, n. 44.

intentionally insults the honor [*hybrizei*] of another, whether a child or a woman or a man, whether free or slave, or does something improper (*paranomon*) against any such person."[92]

This dichotomy between a slave's protected status outside the *oikos* and rightless inferiority within would have evoked special tension whenever the slave was potentially or actually of extraordinary economic benefit to the household, as many *douloi* were in a society open to servile commercial opportunity and training. In Xenophon's treatise on household management, slaves are assumed to be the subject when reference is made to "certain persons" (*tinas*) who had the skills and resources, but not the motivation, to increase household wealth.[93] To provide such slaves with the opportunity to "maintain their own households," to be *khōris oikountes*,[94] was a natural symbiosis in a society organized by household—going far beyond the better living conditions routinely offered as an incentive to profitable slaves (n. 81) but falling short of the manumitted liberation that would have eliminated the masters' legal interest in slaves' earnings. In fact, many "slaves who main-

[92] 21.47: Ἐάν τις ὑβρίζῃ εἴς τινα, ἢ παῖδα ἢ γυναῖκα ἢ ἄνδρα, τῶν ἐλευθέρων ἢ τῶν δούλων, ἢ παράνομόν τι ποιήσῃ εἰς τούτων τινά. Other authors confirm the law's protection of a slave's honor. Ἐάν τις ὑβρίζῃ εἰς παῖδα (ὑβρίζει δὲ δή που ὁ μισθούμενος) ἢ ἄνδρα ἢ γυναῖκα, ἢ τῶν ἐλευθέρων τινὰ ἢ τῶν δούλων, ἢ ἐὰν παράνομόν τι ποιῇ εἰς τούτων τινά, γραφὰς ὕβρεως εἶναι πεποίηκεν (Aiskhin. 1.15). Cf. Hyper. fr. 120: ἔθεσαν οὐ μόνον ὑπὲρ τῶν ἐλευθέρων, ἀλλὰ καὶ ἐάν τις εἰς δούλου σῶμα ὑβρίσῃ, γραφὰς εἶναι κατὰ τοῦ ὑβρίσαντος. Harris (1992b: 77) treats ἢ παράνομόν τι ποιήσῃ εἰς τούτων τινά as "covering every imaginable crime" (for him παράνομόν is simply "an illegal action"), arguing that "this all-embracing clause cannot have stood in the actual law on *hybris*" and that Dem. 21.47 is therefore a "forgery." But the protection of a slave's honor is confirmed by Demosthenes' direct text (21.48: τοῦ νόμου τῆς φιλανθρωπίας, ὃς ουδὲ τοὺς δούλους ὑβρίζεσθαι ἀξιοῖ).

[93] Xen. *Oik.* 1.16–17: ὁπόταν ὁρῶμέν τινας ἐπιστήμας μὲν ἔχοντας καὶ ἀφορμὰς ἀφ' ὧν δύνανται ἐργαζόμενοι αὔξειν τοὺς οἴκους, αἰσθανώμεθα δὲ αὐτοὺς ταῦτα μὴ θέλοντας ποιεῖν, καὶ διὰ τοῦτο ὁρῶμεν ἀνωφελεῖς οὖσας αὐτοῖς τὰς ἐπιστήμας. . . . Περὶ δούλων μοι, ἔφη ὁ Σωκράτης, ἐπιχειρεῖς, ὦ Κριτόβουλε, διαλέγεσθαι; Disaffected (or dishonest) slave overseers, because of their knowledge of household finance and their access to assets, could do grave damage. The slave Moskhiōn, who had total knowledge of Komōn's household affairs, used it to enrich himself: οὗτος ὁ οἰκέτης σχεδόν τι ᾔδει τά τε ἄλλα τὰ τοῦ Κόμωνος ἅπαντα, καὶ δὴ τὸ ἀργύριον οὗ ἦν . . . καὶ πρῶτον μὲν ὑφαιρεῖται αὐτοῦ χιλίας δραχμὰς χωρίς που κειμένας τοῦ ἄλλου ἀργυρίου, ἔπειτα ἑτέρας ἑβδομήκοντα μνᾶς (Dem. 48.14–15).

[94] Although failure to focus on the evidentiary context and economic implications of the term *khōris oikountes* has often forced scholars to leave the phrase untranslated, or described by inaccurate periphrasis, literal translation of *khōris oikountes* ("slaves who maintain [i.e., direct or manage] their own households") makes both economic and philological sense. One of the basic meanings of the verb *oikeō* (whence the form *oikountes*) is to "manage or direct a household" (LSJ, s.v. II). See Xen. *Oik.* 1.2, 1.3; Isok. 2.19. Cf. Soph. *Oid. Kol.* 1535; Thouk. 3.37; Eur. *Elek.* 386. Not all uses of the verb are transitive. Paralleling the intransitive form of *khōris oikountes*, Xenophon recalls Sōkratēs as urging youth to seek that excellence "by which cities and households manage well (*oikousi*)." Xen. *Apom.*. 1.2.64: ἀρετῆς, ᾗ πόλεις τε καὶ οἶκοι εὖ οἰκοῦσι. Cf. Pl. *Khrm.* 162a; *Rep.* 462d, 472e, 473a, 543a.

tained their own households" are attested at Athens. We know, for example, of the charcoal burner in Menander's *Epitrepontes*, a slave who lives outside the city with his wife and merely pays to his owner a portion of his earnings;[95] Lampis, the ship-owning slave of Demosthenes 34, who is specifically described as one of the *khōris oikountes* residing at Athens with his wife and children;[96] the slave Aristarkhos, a leather worker who is listed on the Attic Stēlai with an assortment of chattels that, in defiance of modern conceptualization, are described as belonging to the slave rather than to his master Adeimantos;[97] the leather-working slaves whose independent arrangements are described in Aiskhinēs 1; the slave in Hypereidēs's *Against Athēnogenēs*, whose only contact with his master was to provide him with a monthly accounting; and numerous other literary references to slaves in similar autonomous arrangements.[98]

Yet the very existence of such independent slaves has been summarily denied by some modern scholars and ignored by others.[99] Here, classical Roman preconception has reinforced modern prejudgment. On the tautological argument that slaves by definition necessarily resided with their masters, and that any persons living independently would therefore ipso facto be free, references to *khōris oikountes* have been construed as referring not to present but to former slaves, that is, freedmen.[100] This circular argument, entirely in conflict with Athenian evidence, originated with Harpokratiōn, a lexicographer writing in Roman imperial times, who formulates his opinion in precisely this tautology: the term *khōris*

[95] See lines 378–80. Cf. Biezunska-Malowist 1966: 65–72.

[96] Dem. 34.37: καὶ ταῦτ' ἔπραξεν, οἰκῶν μὲν 'Αθήνησιν, οὔσης δ' αὐτῷ γυναικὸς ἐνθάδε καὶ παίδων.

[97] Stēlē 6.21, 31–46 (Pritchett, Amyx, and Pippin 1953). The sales described in the stēlai appear to have occurred over an extended period between 415 and 413.

[98] In addition to the testimonia cited in the text, see, for example, Andok. 1.38; Telēs fr. 4.b (pp. 46–47 Hense); Theophr., *Khar.* 30.15; Xen. *Ath. Pol.* 1.10–11 ("sans doute": Perotti [1974: 50, n. 15]); and the activities of slaves identified as μισθοφοροῦντα , many of whom may have maintained their own *oikoi* (Xen. *Ath. Pol.* 1.17; Xen. *Por.* 4.14–15, 19, 23; Isai. 8.35; Dem. 27.20–21, 28.12, 53.21; and Theophr. *Khar.* 30.17). Dem. 59.31, although preserved in an Athenian context, *stricto sensu* refers to a non-Athenian situation.

[99] Ste. Croix (1981: 563, n. 9) laments the absence of even a single "satisfactory treatment" of the *khōris oikountes*. Garlan (1988: 70) devotes one paragraph to them, offering one ancient and one modern reference. Of more than five thousand items listed in the *Bibliographie zur Antiken Slaverei* (1983), only two (Kasakevitch 1960, in Russian, and Perotti 1974) deal with the *khōris oikountes*. For scholars' outright denial of their existence, see my n. 6. In fact, slaves maintaining independent households are not uniquely Athenian: in precolonial West Africa, "settled slaves" closely resembled the *khōris oikountes* (see Meillasoux 1991: 117–18).

[100] For translation of χωρὶς οἰκοῦντες as "freedmen," see, for example, the Loeb and Budé translations of Dem. 4.36. Cf. Gernet 1955b: 169: "le fait d' 'habiter à part' est caractéristique de l'affranchi."

oikountes must refer not to slaves but to freedmen, since slaves would have resided with their masters.[101] But this Roman conjecture reflects not Hellenic reality but Roman practice. As we have seen, Roman society did routinely posit a continuing legal, social, and economic relationship between slave and freedman; Athenian practice did not.[102] At Athens, in contrast to some other Greek jurisdictions,[103] a freedman did not differ at all in legal status from other free non-*politai*: the freedman, enrolled by the city as a metic, had no continuing legal relationship with his former master.[104]

But allowing a slave to "maintain his own household" offered a master continued (possibly enhanced) economic benefits without diminution of his legal rights, and provided the slave many of the benefits of manumission (most importantly, perhaps, respite from the continual indignity of living virtually without rights in a household controlled by others).

[101] Harp., s.v. τοὺς χωρὶς οἰκοῦντας: οὐ μὴν ἀλλὰ καὶ χωρὶς τοῦ προσκεῖσθαι φανερὸν ἂν εἴη τὸ δηλούμενον, ὅτι οἱ ἀπελεύθεροι καθ' αὑτοὺς ᾤκουν, χωρὶς τῶν ἀπελευθερωσάντων, ἐν δὲ τῷ τέως δουλεύοντες ἔτι συνῴκουν. Harpokratiōn does refer to Dem. 4.36–37 ("καὶ μετὰ ταῦτα ἐμβαίνειν τοὺς μετοίκους ἔδοξε καὶ τοὺς χωρὶς οἰκοῦντας τῶν δεσποτῶν"), but the citation is misleading. Demosthenes mentions only the mustering into Athenian military service of those who "lived by themselves, independently of their masters" (in Harpokratiōn's transcription), without any suggestion that these persons were free. Because Greek has a specific term for freedman, *apeleutheros*, used often and in a multitude of contexts, Demosthenes would more naturally have specified "freedmen" rather than *khōris oikountes* if he were speaking of *former* slaves (as Perotti has observed: 1974: 47). Another late lexicographer, quoted in *Anekdota Graeca*, likewise assumes that the term *khōris oikountes* refers to freedmen (although he concedes that it can also refer to slaves): οἱ ἀπελεύθεροι, ἐπεὶ χωρὶς οἰκοῦσι τῶν ἀπελευθερωσάντων· ἢ δοῦλοι χωρὶς οἰκοῦντες τῶν δεσποτῶν (Lex. Seguer. [Bekker] 316, s.v. χωρὶς οἰκοῦντες). In fact, Demosthenes does speak of a freedwoman who χωρὶς ᾤκει (Dem. 47.72). For the circumstances, see n. 79.

[102] Although the Roman commentator Harpokratiōn (s.v. ἀποστασίου) claims that an action lay if manumitted slaves "failed to do what the laws prescribed" (ἃ κελεύουσιν οἱ νόμοι μὴ ποιῶσιν), by the fourth century the only obligation imposed by the state on a manumitted slave was enrollment as a metic with his ex-master as *prostatēs*, an undertaking of no continuing significance (see n. 104). Harrison (1968–71: 1:185) suggests that a δίκη ἀποστασίου might be brought if a former slave failed to do "all those things which he agreed to do at his manumission." But for the (non)binding effect on a freedman of his commitments to a former master made during his servitude, see n. 108.

[103] For example, Megara, Hellenistic Kōs, Rhodes: see Gauthier 1972: 126–36.

[104] Whitehead 1977: 16–17. Cf. Harrison 1968–71: 1:184–85; Gernet 1955b: 168–72 Although it is possible that the former master did serve as a freedman's *prostatēs* ("sponsor" or "patron") when the ex-slave became a metic, by the fourth century the Athenian *prostatēs* had no continuing relationship with his metic. Whitehead 1977: 91. Although Aristotle indicates that a metic in many places (πολλαχοῦ) needed a *prostatēs* in order to litigate (*Pol.* 1275a7–14), and scholars have sometimes assumed that Athens was one of these places, the *prostatēs* nowhere appears as a legal representative in proceedings at Athens involving metics (although a *prostatēs* is called as a witness at Dem. 25.58). Davidson offers no evidence for his assertion that at Athens "freedmen maintained very close relationships with their former masters, relationships that were reinforced by ill-defined but legally binding obligations" (1997: 100).

For example—because the permanent physical premises of an Athenian bank, like those of many Athenian businesses,[105] were generally coextensive with the personal residence of the *trapeza*'s proprietor—a slave operating a bank would have had to maintain his own household in order to separate the banking business from the master's other assets (and thus offer his owner potential insulation from personal liability for the business's obligations [E. Cohen 1992: 94–96]). Many other independent slave enterprises likewise could not easily have operated within the master's residence: consider the extensive leather-working operation of Aiskhinēs 1, the multiple perfume businesses of Hypereidēs's *Against Athēnogenēs*, the large cargo vessel of Lampis (Dem. 34), and the maritime trading business conducted by the slave Phormiōn in association with a free partner (Dem. 49).

Yet despite the separate premises, legalistically the property and earnings of *khōris oikountes* still belonged to the master. Thus, the Attic Stēlai record the simultaneous confiscation of a slave owner's property and of the property of his slave who had been operating *khōris oikōn*:[106] because the slave's possessions were *stricto sensu* owned by his master, they too went to the state.[107] In solvent circumstances, however, the master's legal rights would likely facilitate a favorable business arrangement with his slave, in contrast to the difficulties that might beset an ex-master negotiating with a former slave over whom he had no continuing power.[108] A good illustration is the quagmire of difficulties encountered

[105] See Jameson 1990: 185; Aiskhin. 1.124.

[106] Stēlē 6, 31–46 (Pritchett, Amyx, and Pippin 1953). Cf. Lewis 1966: 182, n. 32.

[107] Athenian law, however, seems to have accommodated slave enterprise by limiting a master's *liability* for the debts of a slave independently operating a business: see E. Cohen 1992: 94–96; Gernet 1955b: 161–62.

[108] Economic agreements and "contractual" arrangements between masters and their slaves are frequent in those societies where unfree labor is a significant factor in the overall economy, evoking recurrent scholarly discussion of the legal status of the slaves' commitments (which theoretically should be legal nullities because of the slave's position as his master's chattel, his incorporation into his master's legal personality, and/or similar objections). Although economic and social considerations rather than legal recourse seem alone to have sustained such commitments at Athens, Roman law ultimately devised the legal fiction of the *peculium*, "the juristic existence of fictitious assets pertaining de facto to the dependent, but belonging de iure to the principal" (Aubert 1994: 65). A special conundrum ("un cercle vicieux" [Gernet 1955b: 169]) arises when a slave's manumission is conditional on his satisfying obligations continuing after his liberation. Although Roman law devised a form of obligatory confirmation ("renovation") of the slave's commitment(s)—the initial religiously sanctioned *iusiurandum liberti*, and the subsequent civil *iurata promissio* (see *Dig.* 40.12 [Ulpian], 44 [Modestinus])—the Athenian δίκη ἀποστασίου did not lie to enforce private arrangements, but only ἃ κελεύουσιν οἱ νόμοι (Harp., s.v. ἀποστασίου).

by the banker Pasiōn and his sons. Phormiōn, one of the bank's managers while still a slave,[109] was freed and thereafter operated the bank for his own account under a lease (*misthōsis*).[110] Although Phormiōn's manumission and the resultant end of his personal legal relationship with Pasiōn were addressed in complex contractual arrangements—including a "non-competition" covenant restricting Phormiōn's activities[111] and a contorted effort to enable Phormiōn, now free but not a *politēs*, to collect loans secured by real estate[112]—the arrangement between ex-master and freedman itself became a focus of protracted litigation and bitter antagonism.[113] When Phormiōn's lease expired, the owners entered into a similar arrangement, but this time with persons who continued to be their slaves (including a certain Euphraios, who had worked at the bank with Phormiōn when the latter was still unfree).[114] For these bankers, status as *khōris oikountes* was merely a "halfway house" to freedom: only on expiration of the lease did their owners manumit them.[115] In permitting slaves to become *khōris oikountes*, masters thus retained one final incentive to prompt their *douloi*'s continued full contribution to the master's economic welfare: the promise of full liberation.

This hypothesis of slaves' possible progression, first to maintenance of an independent household and thereafter sometimes to full freedom, is confirmed by the group of inscriptions commonly referred to as the *phialai exeleutherikai* documents, dating from the 320s, published in *Inscriptiones Graecae* II[2] and republished (in part) by Lewis in 1959 and 1968 to incorporate additional finds from the Athenian Agora excavations.[116] Lewis accepts the conventional interpretation of the inscriptions

[109] See, for example, Dem. 45.72; 49.7; 52.5, 6, 29.

[110] Dem. 36.4, 11, 37; 45. 31–32. The lease was entered into with Phormiōn ἤδη καθ' ἑαυτὸν ὄντι.

[111] The lease document specifically forebade Phormiōn to pursue banking activity on his own account. Dem. 45.31: μὴ ἐξεῖναι δὲ τραπεζιτεῦσαι χωρὶς Φορμίωνι, ἐὰν μὴ πείσῃ τοὺς παῖδας τοὺς Πασίωνος. Cf. 45.34.

[112] Dem. 36.4–6. Cf. E. Cohen 1992: 129–36.

[113] In one lawsuit against Phormiōn, brought many years after Pasiōn's death, Pasiōn's son, Apollodōros, sought damages of twenty talents, alleging various wrongful acts. The clearest explanation of this much discussed claim is Thompson 1981a. Wolff clarifies the procedural aspects (1966: 52–57).

[114] Along with Phormiōn, Euphraios had disbursed loan funds to Timotheos in 373. See Dem. 49.44.; Bongenaar 1933: 207.

[115] See Dem. 36.14 (cited in n. 21).

[116] *I.G.* II[2] 1553–78; Lewis 1959, 1968. The texts consist of some fifteen to twenty stones (*I.G.* II[2] 1553, 1560–78)—seemingly separate inscriptions—and a single large inscription (Lewis 1959) assembled from *I.G.* II[2] 1554–59 and additional texts from the Agora excavations. Lewis 1968 is the publication of an important additional fragment. The single large document (Lewis 1959) includes about half of the known dedications. See Kränzlein 1975 for a survey of

as manumission texts, in the form of the dedication of a 100-drachma silver bowl (*phialē*) by each ex-slave after his or her acquittal in formalistic (i.e., fictitious) actions (*dikai apostasiou*)[117] brought by ex-owners. The inscriptions document the manumission of approximately 375 slaves at Athens but offer no direct information as to who paid for the containers dedicated. Because owners are unlikely to have made such an expenditure in order to *free* their slaves, we might expect this process of manumission to involve a disproportionate number of slaves *khōris oikountes*—the "wealthy slaves" of the *Constitution of the Athenians* attributed to Xenophon. These were the *douloi* who would have been able to accumulate the funds necessary for such dedications, or to induce lenders (who appear frequently on the inscriptions) to advance the cost of the dedication—and the presumably higher price of manumission.[118]

Confirming this theoretical expectation, a disproportionately high percentage of the persons manumitted are in fact engaged in commercial business pursuits, and numerous ex-slaves appear on the *phialai* lists not as individuals but as members of a "*de facto* family."[119] In short, "the majority of occupations listed of the ex-slaves on these lists come, as would be expected, from those 'living apart.' "[120] A good example is provided by an inscription discovered in 1939 at the north foot of the Areopagos hill in Athens,[121] setting forth the manumission by the metic Hippokratēs of three persons who operated a perfumery shop. This liberation is suggestive of the transaction described at length in the speech of Hypereidēs, *Against Athēnogenēs* (23–24), where three slaves *khōris oikountes*, likewise engaged in selling perfume some time after 330,[122] were freed through the manipulations of the metic Athēnogenēs. The slaves of Hypereidēs's presentation easily could have provided the

scholarly work on these texts; for early work on the original nineteenth-century fragments (starting with Pittakis in Ἐφ. ἀρχ. 1830), see Calderini [1908] 1965: 424–34.

[117] On the *dikē apostasiou*, see n. 108.

[118] Lenders (operating as groups of *eranistai*) appear with frequency on the *phialai exeleutherikai* texts. See *I.G.* II^2 1553.7–10, 20–23; 1556.B27–29; 1557.B105–7; 1558.A37–43; 1559.A II 26–31; 1566.A27–29; 1568.B18–23; 1569.A III 18–21; 1570.24–26, 57–62, 82–84; 1571.8–13; and 1572.8–11; Lewis 1959: face A, lines 141–42 and 566–67, face B, lines 2 and 153; Lewis 1968: 368, line 8. We have no reliable information on prices paid to owners at Athens in connection with manumissions.

[119] Todd 1997: 123. Cf. Rosivach 1989: esp. 365.

[120] Fisher 1993: 70. In contrast, the estates confiscated on the Attic Stēlai, relating almost entirely to noncommercial assets, include only a few slaves for whom occupations are noted. See Todd 1997: 118–20.

[121] Lewis 1968: 369–74 (Agora Excavations Inventory no. I 5656), lines 29–37.

[122] All of the *phialai exeleutherikai* texts date to the decade after 330 (Todd 1997: 120); the Hypereidēs speech was delivered some time following 330.

several hundred drachmas in silver needed for the dedication: their business had been able to generate borrowed funds that exceeded thirty thousand drachmas (9). In fact, the slave Neaira, working independently as a *hetaira* in Korinth, had no difficulty in raising two thousand drachmas for her freedom (Dem. 59.30–32). Once free, however, she immediately moved to Athens (59.33) where she lived a life of conspicuous consumption—showing that not all the wealthy inhabitants of Attika were slaves.

✦ 6 ✦

The Social Contract: Sexual Abuse and Sexual Profit

> The medieval *Bürger* was a *homo oeconomicus* . . . the ancient *Bürger* was a *homo politicus*.[1]
>
> M. Weber, *Die Stadt* (p. 756)

> Man is not only a Political but also an Economic Being.[2]
>
> Aristotle, *Eudemian Ethics*

MODERN scholarly focus on the political organization of the male "citizens," and hence on Athens as a *polis* (rather than an *ethnos*), has encouraged exclusively political explanations of Athenian civilization and institutions, interpretations often focusing on the juridical-political "status" of individuals, and especially on the political "order" to which they belong: "citizen" (*politēs*), "resident foreigner" (metic), or "slave."[3] Even business activity has been explained not in economic terms, but as a manifestation of political power: according to a thesis dominant for decades, "citizens" uniformly lived on incomes derived from capital investments and property; only noncitizens worked personally and actively in trade and production.[4] Sexual activity also has been

[1] Studies of medieval prostitution do tend to emphasize economic and sexual factors, and to minimize ideological and political considerations: see, for example, Rossiaud 1982, 1988; Trexler 1981; Pavan 1980. For similar focus on the economic aspects of commercial sex in the Renaissance, see Larivaille 1975.

[2] ὁ γὰρ ἄνθρωπος οὐ μόνον πολιτικὸν ἀλλὰ καὶ οἰκονομικὸν ζῷον (*EE.* 1242a23–24). Contrast the frequently quoted ὁ ἄνθρωπος φύσει πολιτικὸν ζῷον (*Pol.* 1253a2–3).

[3] On the importance of "orders' in modern discussions of Athens, see Preface, pp. x–xii.

[4] Scholars have long accepted Hasebroek's claim, largely derivative from Weber, of a fundamental economic division in the *polis* between the noncitizens (who were actively involved in trade and production) and citizen-*rentiers* living on income generated from property (especially real estate, supposedly enjoyed by *politai* with monopolistic exclusivity and assumed to be the basic source of wealth in an agrarian and "primitive" society). See Hasebroek [1933] 1978: 22, 28,

characterized as responsive not to erotic but to political considerations.[5] Metics, totally lacking political rights but often of high economic and social position, allegedly "had few sexual rights" (Posner 1992: 41). In contrast, a *politēs* "might do whatever he wished with a slave boy or foreigner" (D. Cohen 1991a: 182). While "the sexual behavior of citizen women was regulated by laws" (Pomeroy 1975: 86), for noncitizens "the conventions of sexual segregation and protection did not apply" (Just 1989: 144). Even the obtaining of sexual pleasure through active, insertive use of the penis reflects not biology or socially constructed behavior (neither "a universal category of the human psyche [nor] a universal structure of patriarchal society") but a political "image of the citizen body as masculine and assertive" (Halperin 1990: 102–3).

At the intersection of business and *erōs,* the commercial exchange of sex for compensation[6]—"prostitution"[7]—has likewise been approached

---

35; Weber, especially [1909] 1924: 32–33). But more recent studies have refuted this politically-oriented thesis. See Millett 1983: 38 ("Hasebroek's comments . . . cannot be reconciled with the actual evidence"); Hansen 1984: 88, 92, n. 74. Cf. Oertel's earlier criticism (1928: 1624–25). Despite the frequently high heuristic value of Weber's conceptualizations, they are often, as here, counterproductive in analyzing actual historical phenomena: see Aron 1950: 232–36; Veyne 1971: 173–75.

[5] Contemporary scholarship, following Dover ([1978] 1989: 60–68, 81–109) and Foucault (e.g., 1984: 47–62, 98–99), generally views the Greek conceptualization of sexuality as focused not on gender or genital differentiations but on politicized opposition between activity (inherently masculine) and passivity (demeaned as inherently feminizing). See Chirassi Colombo 1984: 110; Cantarella 1988: 35–78; Halperin 1990; Winkler 1990a, 1990b; Bremmer 1989: 8; Larmour, Miller, and Platter 1998: 23. But Loraux ([1989] 1995: 250, n. 29) is "not convinced"; for D. Cohen (1991a: 172), "major issues remain"; for Davidson, the prevailing model is an "absurd simplification" (1997: 25).

[6] Despite frequent assertion that "the meaning of 'prostitution' is self-evident" (Pateman 1988: 195), the defining line, if any, between prostitution and other forms of sexual exchange is often unclear. For the multitude of modern definitional efforts (generally focusing on considerations of payment, promiscuity, and emotional indifference), see, for example, Palmer and Humphrey 1990: 150; Bloch 1912: 7; McGinn 1998: 17–18. For the Athenians, "submission in gratitude for gifts, services or help is not so different in kind from submission in return for an agreed fee" (Dover [1973] 1984: 152; cf. Aristoph. *Plout.* 153–59). Marriage itself has often been seen as a form of prostitution: in early Greek antiquity, the poet Hesiod assumes marriage to involve—to the male's potential detriment—an exchange of women's sexual services for economic benefits (*Works and Days* 373–75); since the eighteenth century, modern marriage has often been characterized as "legal prostitution" (see, e.g., Wollstonecraft [1790] 1983: 247; Hamilton [1909] 1981: 37; Goldman 1969: 179; Beauvoir 1974: 619).

[7] Ancient Greek actually employs two principal clusters of words for persons and acts relating to prostitution, those cognate to *pernanai* ("sell") and those cognate to *hetairein* ("be a companion"). The terms are not synonymous. For Aiskhinēs, promiscuity was the prime differentiation between the two forms of sexual labor (1.51–52). Traditional scholarly analysis focuses on "emotional attitude" as determining the difference between a *hetaira* ("sometimes nearer to 'mistress' than to 'prostitute' ") and "a common prostitute" (*pornē*) (Dover [1978] 1989: 21). Discursive analysis finds the "opposition . . . constituted along the axis of gift- vs. commodity-exchange, identified with the *hetaira* and the *pornē* respectively" (Davidson 1994: 141–42). Cf.

in strictly political terms. Alleged proscriptions at Athens on male prostitution by "citizens" supposedly had "very little to do with sex and everything to do with political ambitions and alliances in the highstakes game of city leadership" (Winkler 1990b: 60). For both male and female "citizens,"[8] formal political considerations supposedly precluded their employment as prostitutes. Athenian *politai* were "perpetually on the superordinate side of a series of hierarchical and roughly congruent distinctions in status: master vs. slave, free vs. unfree, dominant vs. submissive, active vs. passive, insertive vs. receptive, customer vs. prostitute, citizen vs. non-citizen, man vs. woman."[9] Since "the body of a citizen is sacrosant" (Winkler 1990b: 48), "male prostitutes . . . were presumably for the most part foreigners" (Dover [1978] 1989: 32). Female prostitutes confirmed the male citizens' "privileges of free status, citizenship, money, class, and gender" (Keuls 1985: 174) . Here too a political criterion—the male citizen's right to the exclusive sexual use or protection of members of his own household—supposedly mandated foreign predominance in female prostitution.[10]

In reality, however, commercial sex at Athens reflected economic and sexual determinants far removed from hierarchical considerations of status. In other trades and endeavors, "citizens," free foreigners, and slaves are known to have worked at the same tasks—sometimes at identical, sometimes at varying compensation—without differentiation based on personal juridical status. Prostitution similarly encompassed all segments of the population: "citizen" courtesans served foreigners and even slaves. Fees reflected market, rather than theoretical political, considerations. Higher prices were commanded by prostitutes whose

---

Davidson 1997: 117–27; Kurke 1997: 107–12; Reinsberg 1989: 80–86. For male prostitutes, differentiation between *pornos* and *hetairos* is often "analogous to the distinction between the *pornē* and the *hetaira*" (Dover [1978] 1989: 21). Cf. Hauschild 1933: 7–9; Herter 1957: 1154, 1181–82; 1960: 83; Peschel 1987: 19–20; Calame 1989: 103–4.

[8] For women as πολίτιδες ("citizenesses"), see the last section of Chapter 1.

[9] Halperin 1990: 102–3. For Todd, the congruity of citizenship and superordinate masculinity is supposedly so complete that the differentiation "between male and female with which we are familiar is in fact specific to citizens" (Todd 1997: 114). Scholars have attributed a similar sexual construction to the Roman world: "the Roman sex/gender system . . . like that of classical Athens, corresponded to social patterns of dominance and submission" (Skinner 1997: 3); Walters (1997: 31) identifies "Roman (and classical Greek) sexual protocols, which view the sexually 'active' role as the only appropriate one for an adult male citizen. . . . a sexually passive male . . . was a slave, an ex-slave, or a non-citizen."

[10] Krenkel 1988: 1291: "Female prostitution . . . was the province of slaves, freed persons, and foreigners." In accord: Pomeroy 1997: 152; Keuls 1985: 154.

qualities were perceived as in short supply or who appealed to specialty markets willing and able to pay a premium price.

Yet while prostitution was a lawful activity for all adult inhabitants of Attika,[11] and the sale of sexual services (by both men and women) was a commonplace aspect of Athenian life,[12] Athenian laws purported to provide widespread protection from sexual abuse for the entire resident population (free or slave, male or female, and especially for children). Partly as a result, there arose the practice of "whoring under contract" (*kata synthēkas hētairēkenai*), an arrangement that emphasized the mutuality and market egalitarianism underlying the sale of sex at Athens. The only juridical disincentive to sale by *politai* of their own sexual services—a rarely enforced exclusion from leadership roles in political activities[13]—mirrors similar limitations imposed for such financial offenses as waste of one's household estate through profligate living or neglect, or for failure to provide material support for one's parents,[14] economic behavior that compromised the independence of the *oikos* and thereby undermined a key conservative value by commercializing functions that traditionally had been performed within the household without monetary exchange or other exterior payments. Female prostitution offered women economic opportunity and independence that were similarly in conflict with the traditional encapsulation of women within the *oikos*.[15] The market transactions of fourth-century Athens—the leas-

[11] Although Harrison (1968–71: 1:37) infers from the charges set forth in Aiskhin. 1 the existence of a γραφὴ ἑταιρήσεως, there is no allusion in the speech to any such statute (although Aiskhinēs does invoke a host of other proscriptions). Lipsius ([1905–15] 1966: 436) correctly dismisses the possibility of a legal ban on prostitution.

[12] Ancient sources treat both male and female prostitution as routinely present. See, for example, Dem. 22.61, *Epistle* 4.11; Aristoph. *Plout.* 155; Xen. *Apom.* 1.6.13; Antiph., fr. 210; Alexis, fr. 257 (K-A); Ephippos, fr. 20 (K-A); Eupolis *Philoi*, fr. 286 (K-A); Kratinos, fr. 4; Aiskhin. 1 and Lys. 3. Cf. Diog. Laert. 2.9.105. Cf. Keuls 1985: 153–205; Licht (Brandt) [1932] 1952: 329, 410, 436–40; Herter 1960; Krenkel 1978, 1988; McGinn 1989.

[13] Cf. Davidson 1997: 252: "The real figures of authority, the real 'leaders' of the city were the *rhētores*, those who made speeches in the Assembly . . . everyone was assumed to be eligible unless challenged. Such challenges were issued very rarely. I know of only one certain example in the whole history of the democracy."

[14] Aiskhin. 1.28–32, 154, 194–95.

[15] Some feminists see present-day prohibitions of female prostitution as yet another manifestation of patriarchal determination to deny women economic freedom otherwise obtainable through unfettered market transactions: "prostitution enables women to make more money than they can earn at most other jobs open to women in patriarchal capitalism" (Pateman 1988: 194). In classical Athens, prostitution "could be extremely lucrative, indeed more profitable than most women's work, though, of course, not open to respectable citizen women" (Pomeroy 1997: 151–52). But explicit examples of Athenian "citizen women" working as *hetairai* survive: see n. 66.

ing of land for payment in cash,[16] the production of consumer items by commercial workshops,[17] business deals involving unrelated participants seeking only monetary profit independent of social and political relationships,[18] the commodification and commercial vending of sex—all were incompatible with a nostalgic commitment to the self-sufficient *oikos*. But all reflected the reality of fourth-century Attica.

An Academic Fantasy: Sexual Exploitation as Political Entitlement

A prime tenet of contemporary scholarship is the belief that the majority of the residents of Attika were wantonly exploited sexually by the adult male citizen minority[19]—a manifestation, for prevailing dogma, of the general "oppression of noncitizen groups within the Polis."[20] Virtually without dissent, scholars insist that Athens prohibited only liaisons that violated the property rights of male "citizens" (such as their wives' adultery), couplings that might upset prevailing hierarchical arrangements (e.g., marriage between aliens and local residents), and sexual relations that implied or articulated acceptance by male "citizens" of a submissive sexual role, as in the sale of erotic favors by a *politēs*.[21] Yet the substantial protections against sexual abuse or exploitation provided

[16] D. Lewis (1973) has posited the existence by the later fourth century of a "base price" in cash (fifty drachmas per plethron per year) for the lease of agricultural land. Cf. Burford 1993: 79–80. See, for example, *I.G.* II^2 2492 (Pleket 1964: no. 42).

[17] Such commercial workshops are known only after the end of the Peloponnesian War (see Lys. 12.8, 19; Pl. *Rep.* 8; Plut. *Orators' Lives* 835 b–c). For similar fourth-century manufacturing facilities for consumer goods, see Dem. 27.9, 36.11; Aiskhin. 1.97. Compare the high proportion of slaves engaged in specialized craft activity in the mid-320s (documents recording the manumissions of about 375 slaves: Chapter 5, n. 116) with the very low percentage listed on the Attic Stēlai (recording in c. 414 the sale of some 53 slaves: *I.G.* I^3 421–30 and Pritchett, Amyx, and Pippin 1953, 1956; Kliacko 1966).

[18] These transactions were not only "disembedded" from society (see n. 116): they were seen by theoreticians in their writings and litigants in their court cases as carrying significant threat to traditional social and familial methods of handling production and consumption (see pp. XXXff.).

[19] On the composition of the population of Attika, see Chapter 1, p. 188ff.

[20] See Preface, n. 15 and related text.

[21] See Just 1989: 146–48; Posner 1992: 38–44; Halperin 1990: 92–104; Winkler 1990a, 1990b; Keuls 1985: 153–299; Dover [1973] 1984: 148–49; 1974: 205–16; [1978] 1989; Foucault 1985, 1986; and Pomeroy 1975, ch. 5. The dependency inherent in male prostitution is supposedly incompatible with the "hoplite" culture of a state conceptualized by its citizens as a military force of kinsmen (cf. Rahe [1992] 1994: 32; Sagan 1991: 353), and therefore inherently closed to nonkinsmen. But in the Athenian armed forces of the fourth century, contrary to the traditional reliance of the *polis* on its own members (cf. Aristot. *Pol.* 1327a40–b8), metics and slaves (and mercenaries, many of whom did not even reside in Attika: see McKechnie 1989: 79–100)

by both Athenian law and communal practice were actually directed toward, and applied for the benefit of, Attika's entire residential population, "citizen" or foreigner, and (to some extent) even for the protection of slaves. Correspondingly, personal inclinations, private situations, and financial considerations—not political classification—largely determined individual involvement in the sexual market.

A fundamental Athenian law purported to protect every inhabitant of Attika, "whether a child or a woman or a man, whether free or slave," from sexual exploitation or abuse. Legislation cited by Demosthenes authorized a public prosecution (*graphē*) for *hybris* "whenever someone intentionally insults the honor [*hybrizei*] of another, whether a child or a woman or a man, whether free or slave, or does something improper [*paranomon*] against any such person."[22] The law thus prohibits "the deliberate infliction of serious insult on another human being,"[23] a broad coverage confirmed explicitly by other contemporary sources, including Demosthenes' prime rival, Aiskhinēs, who in independent context cites the legislation in language virtually identical with that of Demosthenes.[24] Accordingly, there is "general agreement [that] we possess the actual text of the law as it stood in the fourth century" (Fisher 1992: 36), the "genuine law" (MacDowell 1990: 263)—albeit a text that in its wide protection of Attika's *Untermenschen* conflicts starkly with the allegedly unlimited right of male "citizens" to exploit Attika's residents. As a result of this contradiction, the law's "plain meaning"—its extension of protection far beyond adult male "citizens"—has tended to be disregarded, or even dismissed as "incoherent" or theoretically impossible.[25]

constituted a significant portion of total personnel. For military service by metics, see Chapter 2, nn. 163–66 and related text. For service by slaves, see Chapter 2, n. 51.

[22] Dem. 21.47. Greek text: Chapter 5, n. 92.

[23] Fisher 1995: 45. In accord: Todd 1993: 270, 379, following Fisher 1990: 126; 1992: 36–82; D. Cohen 1991b; Lipsius [1905–15] 1966: 420–29; Morrow 1939: 38–41; Harrison 1968–71: 1:168, 172; MacDowell 1976a; 1978: 129–32; Dover [1978] 1989: 34–39; Cantarella 1983; Cole 1984: 99. Ruschenbusch (1965) even sees *hybris* as inclusively covering all offenses against the person. Gagarin, in contrast, finds *hybris* distinguished by the use of inordinate force or violence (1979: 232). For other interpretations, see Cairns 1996.

[24] Aiskhin. 1.15; cf. Hyper. fr. 120 (Greek text of both: Chapter 5, n. 92). The "law" preserved at Aiskhin. 1.16 is patently a forgery: MacDowell 1990: 263–64.

[25] The enshrinement of slaves' rights, for example, leaves distinguished scholars grasping (unsuccessfully) for words: "such a law would have had to envisage a situation involving the treatment of free men as if they were slaves, or citizens as if they were foreigners, or slaves (who are specifically mentioned as within the scope of the law) as if they were—what?" (Murray 1990b: 140). "Incoherent": Gernet 1917: 183–97. Cf. Fisher 1992: 59ff.

Athenian legislation against *hybris*, however, was far from theoretical. Demosthenes notes that harsh punishment had actually been meted out in many cases involving victimization of slaves.[26] To mitigate the lengthy legal delays endemic within the Athenian court system,[27] actions charging *hybris* had to be heard within thirty days after the day on which the charges were first brought,[28] a virtually unique acceleration of process.[29] Should the prosecutor prevail, there was to be an immediate determination of penalties.[30] Upon conviction, an offender was held in prison until payment of any fine that had been assessed[31]—an extraordinary remedy in a system where private litigants generally had to enforce court judgments without official assistance[32] and where even debts owed to the state often were allowed to languish for months before obligors, subject to no restraint, fled.[33] To avoid the chimera of a protection not practically available to those unable personally to vindicate their rights against a more powerful abuser, prosecution could be pursued by any Athenian *politēs,*[34] in contrast to the usual requirement in a private action (*dikē*)

[26] Dem. 21.48–49: Ἀκούετ', ὦ ἄνδρες Ἀθηναῖοι, τοῦ νόμου τῆς φιλανθρωπίας, ὃς οὐδὲ τοὺς δούλους ὑβρίζεσθαι ἀξιοῖ . . . καὶ πολλοὺς ἤδη παραβάντας τὸν νόμον τοῦτον ἐζημιώκασιν θανάτῳ.

[27] For the systemic prevalence and causes of protracted and postponed litigation, see E. Cohen 1973: 10–12; Charles 1938: 9–10.

[28] Dem. 21.47: οἱ δὲ θεσμοθέται εἰσαγόντων εἰς τὴν ἡλιαίαν τριάκοντα ἡμερῶν ἀφ' ἧς ἂν γραφῇ, ἐὰν μή τι δημόσιον κωλύῃ, εἰ δὲ μή, ὅταν ᾖ πρῶτον οἷόν τε. In practice, as anticipated by the statute, state considerations could still sometimes delay prompt resolution of the charges: γραφὴν δ' ὕβρεως γράφομαι πρὸς τοὺς θεσμοθέτας αὐτόν. χρόνου δὲ γιγνομένου, καὶ τῆς μὲν γραφῆς ἐκκρουομένης, δικῶν δ' οὐκ οὐσῶν, γίγνονται παῖδες ἐκ τούτου τῇ μητρί (Dem. 45.4).

[29] MacDowell (1990: 266–67) refutes Hansen's claim (1981: 167–70) that requirement of trial within thirty days was not uncommon: no other provision for εἰσαγωγὴ τριάκοντα ἡμερῶν is known at Athens (although we do know of "thirty-day cases" [τριακοσταῖαι δίκαι] from Naupaktos [Meiggs and Lewis 1988: 35–37, no. 20] and from Hēraklea [Dareste (1892–1904) 1965: 1: 194ff., face II, lines 26–27]). Cf. Gofas 1979: 180, n. 21. For the δίκαι ἔμμηνοι at Athens, see E. Cohen 1973: 23–26; Vélissaropoulos 1980: 242–45.

[30] Dem. 21.47: ὅτου δ' ἂν καταγνῷ ἡ ἡλιαία, τιμάτω περὶ αὐτοῦ παραχρῆμα, ὅτου ἂν δοκῇ ἄξιος εἶναι παθεῖν ἢ ἀποτεῖσαι.

[31] Dem. 21.47: ἐὰν δὲ ἀργυρίου τιμηθῇ τῆς ὕβρεως, δεδέσθω ἐὰν ἐλεύθερον ὑβρίσῃ, μέχρι ἂν ἐκτείσῃ. Imprisonment thus was not automatically available in cases of transgressions against slaves.

[32] See Todd 1993: 144–45; Allen 1997: 134. In the case of *hybris*, the fine was paid to the state, not to the victim or prosecutor, thereby giving the *polis* a direct financial interest in extracting payment. See Dem. 21.45: καὶ τῆς ὕβρεως αὐτῆς τὰς μὲν γραφὰς ἔδωκεν ἅπαντι τῷ βουλομένῳ, τὸ δὲ τίμημ' ἐποίησεν ὅλον δημόσιον·

[33] For the rarity of imprisonment as a procedural or punitive process at Athens, see E. Cohen 1973: 74–83; MacDowell 1990: 268; Hunter 1997. On the state's laxity even in cases involving public debtors, note the famous case of Demosthenes's father-in-law, Gylōn (Dem. 28.1–3; Aiskhin. 3.171; Davies 1971: 121).

[34] Dem. 21: 47: γραφέσθω πρὸς τοὺς θεσμοθέτας ὁ βουλόμενος Ἀθηναίων οἷς ἔξεστιν. Some potential cases, however, may have been discouraged by the absence of monetary incentive for

of suit by the victim directly or through his or her male representative (*kyrios*).[35]

Because of "the centrality of *hybris* . . . in Athenian social relations" (D. Cohen 1991b: 171), this legislation potentially affected many aspects of Athenian behavior. Yet its prime impact was felt in sexual context, for eroticized misconduct was a fundamental and frequent manifestation of *hybris*.[36] Of approximately five hundred occurrences of *hybris* or its cognates in the principal surviving Athenian prose authors, eighty-two incidents relate to sexual misconduct—more cases by far than of any other typology.[37] Rape is repeatedly denominated as *hybris*.[38] In fact, Aristotle specifically warns rulers that of the various manifestations of *hybris*, sexual abuse of boys and girls and physical violation of individuals are most to be avoided.[39] (Aristotle significantly does not differentiate between male and female youngsters, or between freemen and slaves in cases of bodily violence.) Deinarchos even brands as *hybris* the Macedonians' assignment of Theban women and children to barbarian tents (Dem. 19.24).

Erotic insult did not require physical contact. Alkibiadēs is said to have committed *hybris* against his wife by merely bringing other women into their home (Andok. *Alk.* 14.3, 15.8, 29.2). Nor did protection require "citizenship." Although Arkhippē, widow of the Athenian banker Pasiōn,

---

a voluntary prosecutor (ὁ βουλόμενος) and by the requirement (see Lipsius [1905–15] 1966: 243–44; Harrison 1968–71: 1: 195, n. 1) that the prosecutor be an Athenian citizen. For *graphai* open also to prosecution by non-Athenians, see Dem. 59.66 (Epainetos "certainly a foreigner" [Carey 1992: 121]), 59.16, 21.175, 24.105, possibly 59.52.

[35] Just 1985: 173, n. 8: "κύριος, the head of the household to which (an Athenian woman) was attached"—an improvement over the traditional translation of *kyrios* as guardian or "master" (Wolff 1944: 46–47, n. 22). In fact, "*kyrieia* is a much fuzzier, less formalized institution than social and legal historians have generally thought" (Foxhall 1996: 150). Some women were even αὑτῆς κυρία (Dem. 59.46), and some *kyrioi* were merely public representatives of familial interests or of powerful females (cf. Hunter 1989a: 46–47; 1994: 9–13, 15–19). Cf. Chapter 1, n. 174.

[36] Despite Athenian law's harsh penalties against *hybris*, and the general recognition among specialists that the word denotes behavior seriously injurious and subject to rigorous punishment, "more 'traditional' interpretations of *hybris*, still commonly found in scholarly discourse and perhaps even more commonly among the 'chattering classes,' see it as human arrogance, overconfidence or unawareness of the reasons for one's own good fortune" (Fisher 1995: 45–46).

[37] Even physical assault against free persons is reported less frequently. See D. Cohen 1991b: 172–73; MacDowell 1976a; Fisher 1976–79.

[38] See D. Cohen 1991b: 175; Doblhofer 1994; Dover [1978] 1989: 36.

[39] *Pol.* 1315a14–23: ἔτι δὲ πάσης μὲν ὕβρεως εἴργεσθαι, παρὰ πάσας δὲ δυεῖν, τῆς τε εἰς τὰ σώματα [κολάσεως] καὶ τῆς εἰς τὴν ἡλικίαν. . . . μὴ χρῆσθαι δεῖ τοῖς τοιούτοις, ἢ . . . φαίνεσθαι ποιούμενον . . . τὰς δὲ πρὸς τὴν ἡλικίαν ὁμιλίας δι' ἐρωτικὰς αἰτίας, ἀλλὰ μὴ δι' ἐξουσίαν.

appears never to have received Athenian *politeia,* her son Apollodōros brought on her behalf an action for *hybris* against his mother's second husband, the family's former slave.[40] Even women of low status might complain of *hybris*—as did Neaira, allegedly a foreign whore born into slavery, who charged the Athenian *politēs* Phryniōn with *hybris* for various indignities, including consensual intercourse with her in public.[41] In homoerotic situations, charges of *hybris* likewise can arise from a dishonoring abuse of power. The public slave Pittalakos brands as *hybris* the actions of the well-connected Athenian *politai* Hēgēsandros and Timarchos who, as the dénouement of a sexual triangle, had sadistically tied Pittalakos to a column and whipped him during a nocturnal revel. Although he had the support of *politai* who were prepared to act for him and who might have brought a public action for this *hybris*, the slave instead brought a private suit (*dikē*) on his own behalf against the two *politai*.[42] Indeed, from the varied evidence of Aiskhinēs 1, the Italian scholar Montuori has contended that *anyone* who prostituted a male slave could be charged with *hybris* (1976: 12–14).

But even those scholars who accept the law's explicit statement of protection for slaves and other dependents often assume the provision to have been meaningless in actual practice. Harrison, for example, considers that there was not even a "slender chance" that any outsider would actually prosecute an alleged act of *hybris* by a master against his slave.[43] But Athenian values encompassed a strong ideological commitment to aid unrelated persons who might be victimized. Solon reportedly considered the ideal state to be one in which otherwise uninvolved persons came to the aid of those being wronged and punished the wrongdoers: a key element in his legislation was authorization for volunteers

[40] Dem. 45.4. For Arkhippē's continuing status as an alien, see Carey 1991. Cf. E. Cohen 1992: 102–6; Whitehead 1986b.

[41] Dem. 59.33–37: ἐκώμαζέ τ' ἀεὶ μετ' αὐτοῦ, συνῆν τ' ἐμφανῶς ὁπότε βουληθείη πανταχοῦ, φιλοτιμίαν τὴν ἐξουσίαν πρὸς τοὺς ὁρῶντας ποιούμενος. . . . διηγησαμένη πάντα τὰ πεπραγμένα καὶ τὴν ὕβριν τοῦ Φρυνίωνος . . . προΐσταται Στέφανον τουτονὶ αὑτῆς.

[42] Aiskhin. 1.62: βαρέως δὲ φέρων τὴν ὕβριν αὐτῶν ὁ ἄνθρωπος, δίκην ἑκατέρῳ αὐτῶν λαγχάνει. . . . Ἐν παντὶ δὲ κακοῦ γενόμενος ὁ Πιττάλακος προσπίπτει ἀνδρὶ καὶ μάλα χρηστῷ. Ἔστι τις Γλαύκων Χολαργεύς· οὗτος αὐτὸν ἀφαιρεῖται εἰς ἐλευθερίαν. In P. Hamb. 133, a freedwoman's suit against Zoilos for killing her child was later undertaken by her former master. Cf. P. Oxy. 13.1606 (Lys. fr. 1 [Gernet and Bizos]) where Lysias (or a colleague) defends a *therapaina* who had been sued by Hippothersēs for her role in the effort to reclaim property confiscated by the Thirty and sold to Hippothersēs.

[43] Harrison 1968–71: 1:172. Cf. Humphreys [1983] 1993: 5.

to act on behalf of outside victims.[44] In his enunciation of Athenian values in the funeral address, Periklēs alludes to the Athenians' obedience to the laws that provided aid for persons being wronged.[45] Even our sparse knowledge of actual Athenian litigation provides numerous examples of third parties instituting actions on behalf of women, children, and other dependents, and even confirms Demosthenes' statement (see n. 26) that offenders had actually been executed for acts of *hybris* against slaves. Deinarkhos reports that at the Eleusinian festival the Athenian *politēs* Themistios had been put to death for *hybris* against a Rhodian lyre girl,[46] and that a certain Euthymakhos was executed for forcing an Olynthian slave woman into a brothel.[47] Legal actions also appear to have been brought over the hybristic treatment of another enslaved Olynthian woman by Athenians at a Macedonian symposium after Philip's destruction of Olynthos,[48] although "we do not know enough about these cases to know in what circumstances they did, or might, reach the courts" (Fisher 1995: 69–70).

Even where the wrongdoing involved only allegation of financial mismanagement, third parties are known to have come forward. In Demosthenes 38, under a statute permitting "anyone" to act on behalf of the alleged victims, a certain Nikidas, not otherwise involved or even known, denounced a guardian for mismanagement of an estate intended to benefit minor children.[49] Legislation permitting "anyone" to take action on behalf of an abused individual allowed persons otherwise lacking standing the opportunity to intervene on behalf of individuals to whom they were not directly related by blood, as Arkhedamos did when he charged Eupolis with having ravaged the estate of the son of Arkheda-

[44] Aristotle cites as among the provisions most favorable to the masses τὸ ἐξεῖναι τῷ βουλομένῳ τιμωρεῖν ὑπὲρ τῶν ἀδικουμένων (*Ath. Pol.* 9.4). See Plut. *Sol.* 18.3–8: ἐρωτηθεὶς γάρ, ὡς ἔοικε, ἥτις οἰκεῖται κάλλιστα τῶν πόλεων, ἐκείνη, εἶπεν, ἐν ᾗ τῶν ἀδικουμένων οὐχ ἧττον οἱ μὴ ἀδικούμενοι προβάλλονται καὶ κολάζουσι τοὺς ἀδικοῦντας. Cf. Pl. *Rep.* 462d.

[45] οὐ παρανομοῦμεν . . . ἀκροάσει καὶ τῶν νόμων, καὶ μάλιστα αὐτῶν ὅσοι τε ἐπ' ὠφελίᾳ τῶν ἀδικουμένων κεῖνται (Thouk. 2.37.3).

[46] Dein. *Dem.* 23: ὑμεῖς Μένωνα μὲν τὸν μυλωθρὸν ἀπεκτείνατε, διότι παῖδ' ἐλεύθερον ἐκ Πελλήνης ἔσχεν ἐν τῷ μυλῶνι· Θεμίστιον δὲ τὸν Ἀφιδναῖον, διότι τὴν Ῥοδίαν κιθαρίστριαν ὕβρισεν Ἐλευσινίοις, θανάτῳ ἐζημιώσατε. Cf. Worthington 1992: 169. Demosthenes mentions by name a number of other persons executed for misdeeds at such religious gatherings (21.175–81).

[47] Dein. *Dem.* 23: Εὐθύμαχον δέ <θανάτῳ ἐζημιώσατε> διότι τὴν Ὀλυνθίαν παιδίσκην ἔστησεν ἐπ' οἰκήματος.

[48] Dem. 19.196–98; Aiskhin. 2.4, 153–55.

[49] Dem. 38.23: οὐκ ἐμίσθωσαν ἡμῶν τὸν οἶκον, ἴσως ἐροῦσιν. οὐ γὰρ ἐβούλεθ' ὁ θεῖος ὑμῶν Ξενοπείθης, ἀλλὰ φήναντος Νικίδου τοὺς δικαστὰς ἔπεισεν ἐᾶσαι αὐτὸν διοικεῖν· For *phasis* as a procedure against κάκωσις οἴκου ὀρφανικοῦ, see Harp., s.v. φάσις, Aristot. *Ath. Pol.* 56.6.

mos's wife by an earlier marriage (Isai. 7.5–7). Friends frequently take an active role as arbitrators in reconciling various members of an *oikos*, in many cases effectively protecting dependent members of a household.[50] But total outsiders are also known to have come to the aid of dependent persons. When Neaira, an ex-slave staying in Megara, had been subjected to *hybris* by the Athenian *politēs* Phryniōn (who claimed to be her master), she sought assistance from the Athenian *politēs* Stephanos, whom she had only recently met. He responded to her appeal—for Stephanos the beginning of substantial litigation on her behalf, including defense of her freedom through a claim of *aphairesis* against Phryniōn.[51] Similarly the slave Pittalakos was able to call on the influential *politēs* Glaukōn to vindicate his legal rights against harassment by the prominent Hēgēsandros, who claimed that Pittalakos was his slave.[52]

Athenian concern for the rights, especially the sexual sanctity, of dependents, contrasts with modern Western societies' long history of ignoring or trivializing sexual abuse against minor and female family members (and against slaves, even where miscegenation statutes prohibited interracial sexual relations).[53] But at Athens social structures and communal values (especially commitment to *philanthrōpia*) encouraged effective protection against the sexual abuse of children, slaves, and women.[54] Accordingly, Aiskhinēs sets forth in considerable detail the extraordinarily strong Athenian laws against child abuse, which affected a wide circle of men who might have contact with children, but targeted with special rigor *kyrioi* and other adult male family members.[55] Legal

[50] See, for example, Dem. 36.15, 41.14. Cf. Scafuro 1997: 131–35.

[51] Dem. 59.37–40: ἐπιδημήσαντα Στέφανον τουτονὶ εἰς τὰ Μέγαρα . . . διηγησαμένη πάντα τὰ πεπραγμένα καὶ τὴν ὕβριν τοῦ Φρυνίωνος . . . προΐσταται Στέφανον τουτονὶ αὑτῆς . . . ἀφαιρουμένου δὲ τοῦ Στεφάνου κατὰ τὸν νόμον εἰς ἐλευθερίαν, κατηγγύησεν αὐτὴν πρὸς τῷ πολεμάρχῳ. The effect on Neaira's persona of dependence on male juridical mediation is discussed with considerable insight at Johnstone 1998: 232–33.

[52] Aiskhin. 1.62: σκέψασθε μεγάλην ῥωμην Ἡγησάνδρου· ἄνθρωπον . . . ἦγεν εἰς δουλείαν φάσκων ἑαυτοῦ εἶναι. Ἐν παντὶ δὲ κακοῦ γενόμενος ὁ Πιττάλακος προσπίπτει ἀνδρὶ καὶ μάλα χρηστῷ. Ἔστι τις Γλαύκων Χολαργεύς· οὗτος αὐτὸν ἀφαιρεῖται εἰς ἐλευθερίαν.

[53] On sexual abuse of slaves by masters in North America, see, for example, Woodward 1981: 29; Jacobs 1987: 27; Faust 1982: 87.

[54] Dem. 21.48: τοῦ νόμου τῆς φιλανθρωπίας, ὃς οὐδὲ τοὺς δούλους ὑβρίζεσθαι ἀξιοῖ. Fisher (1995) skillfully explores the inherent tension between Athenian support for the authority of the *kyrios*, and Athenian social concepts mandating protection for dependent persons.

[55] Note in particular the provisions against child prostitution: διαρρήδην δ' οὖν λέγει [ὁ νόμος], ἐάν τινα ἐκμισθώσῃ ἑταιρεῖν πατὴρ ἢ ἀδελφὸς ἢ θεῖος ἢ ἐπίτροπος ἢ ὅλως τῶν κυρίων τις, κατ' αὐτοῦ μὲν τοῦ παιδὸς οὐκ ἐᾷ γραφὴν εἶναι, κατὰ δὲ τοῦ μισθώσαντος καὶ τοῦ μισθωσαμένου (1.13). Cf. the pedagogic regulations set forth in sections 9–11 and the penalties for procurement of free minors (προαγωγεία) (§14).

protection for slaves was consonant with the recognition of *douloi* as integral members of the household.[56] A newly bought slave was ceremonially welcomed into the *oikos*; not a single case is reported where an aged slave was abandoned.[57] Although slaves were generally within the complete power of their *kyrioi,* they were entitled even within the household to protection from *hybris*—just as Athenian parents had some discretion to deny even life to newborn children but not to abuse their dependent children sexually (D. Cohen 1991b: 183).[58] And outside the household, relative to other inhabitants of Attika—free or slave—the Athenian *doulos* was under no legal obligation of subservience. Athenian slaves who need not even yield on the street to a free person had no obligation to acquiesce in sexual *hybris* from outsiders.[59]

Within the *oikos*, the adult male *politēs* had little opportunity to function as a sexual predator. Late marriage for men encouraged prolonged male dependence; early marriage for women meant early social maturation—and (because of relatively low longevity) in many cases early widowhood.[60] The tendency of many widows to reside with their married children often resulted in control of household operations, and even of household morality, by these senior women.[61] Largely because of his mother's presence, Lysias, for example, did not dare to bring his girl friend, even chaperoned by her "mother," to his own home.[62] And even free of mother or mother-in-law, the Athenian male might be far from a domineering sexual exploiter. In Menander's *Plokion*, for example, the husband of Krōbylē is portrayed as reduced to whining ineffectively after his wife has ejected from the house a servant girl in whom he was interested.[63] Because there are no other surviving detailed chronicles of the adult male's ability to take wanton sexual advantage of servile retainers, Lysias 1 is often cited as exemplar. But in this narrative, the

[56] See Chapter 5, pp. 145–46; Chapter 1, pp. 33ff.

[57] See Chapter 5, nn. 78–81.

[58] For the extent and context of infanticide at Athens, see Chapter 1, n. 164; for slaves' protection from murder by their masters, see Chapter 5, n. 84. For the flagrantly outrageous treatment required for *hybris* against a slave, see Chapter 5, n. 91.

[59] Cf. Preface, pp. 14–15; Chapter 5, nn. 88–89, and accompanying text.

[60] On delayed marriage for men, early widowhood for women, and widows' residence patterns, see Chapter 1, pp. 35–36, 44–45. On longevity, see Chapter 1, n. 138; Chapter 4, n. 135.

[61] Cf. Chapter 1, p. 43ff.

[62] See Chapter 1, n. 197.

[63] See Chapter 1, n. 200.

"master's" spouse locks him in his bedroom lest—his wife asserts—he renew his prior drunken "attempt" at the household's servant girl. With her *kyrios* dominantly imprisoned, his wife can enjoy sex with her lover without interference![64]

Equal Employment Opportunity: Prostitution Not "the Special Preserve of Foreigners"

Contemporary scholarship uniformly follows Dover in characterizing homosexual prostitution as "the special preserve of foreigners" (Dover [1978] 1989: 34). The "untouchability" of those members of "the privileged citizen class" and their right to "throw their weight around to intimidate metics and slaves" supposedly precluded for *politai* the demeaning dependence inherent in functioning as prostitutes (Winkler 1990b: 49). In fact, Athenian *politai* working as courtesans are the focus of the only surviving evidence dealing in detail with male prostitution, Aiskhinēs 1 and Lysias 3,[65] and male (and female) "citizens" are explicitly characterized as prostitutes in many other contexts.[66] In contrast, scholars such as Dover and Winkler have been able to cite only a few items of tendentious evidence—Aiskhinēs 1.43 and 1.195, Demosthenes 25.57,

[64] Lys. 1.11–13: ὁ γὰρ ἄνθρωπος ἔνδον ἦν· . . . καὶ ἐγὼ τὴν γυναῖκα ἀπιέναι ἐκέλευον καὶ δοῦναι τῷ παιδίῳ τὸν τιτθόν. "ἵνα σύ γε" ἔφη "πειρᾷς ἐνταῦθα τὴν παιδίσκην· καὶ πρότερον δὲ μεθύων εἷλκες αὐτήν." κἀγὼ μὲν ἐγέλων, ἐκείνη δὲ ἀναστᾶσα καὶ ἀπιοῦσα προστίθησι τὴν θύραν, προσποιουμένη παίζειν, καὶ τὴν κλεῖν ἐφέλκεται. Pomeroy suggests that the wife's adultery would likely not have been possible "if the mother-in-law were still living in the house" (1997: 23–24). Cf. Schaps 1998b: 185, n. 120.

[65] For the historical value (and limitations) of Athenian forensic speeches, see Preface, pp. xiii–xiv.

[66] See, for example, Dem. 22.61, where the parents of two *politai* are alleged to have been prostitutes (τοῦ δὲ τὸν πατέρ' ἡταιρηκέναι, τοῦ δὲ τὴν μητέρα πεπορνεῦσθαι). At Aiskhin. 1.165, an unnamed ἀνὴρ εἷς τῶν πολιτῶν . . . λέγεται κατὰ συνθήκας ἡταιρηκέναι. Cf. the citation of the important political leader Hēgēsandros as a *pornos* and as Laodamas's paid "woman" (Aiskhin. 1.70, 111). Hirzel early gathered evidence for Athenian women functioning as prostitutes: [1918] 1962: 71, n. 1. See, for example, Isai. 3 where the consort of a *politēs* is accused of having been a prostitute, but "her citizen status is never brought into question in the speech" [Roy 1997: 16]. In fact, Isaios (3.17–18) suggests substantial precedent for the phenomenon of young men, influenced by passionate desire, entering into marriages with prostitutes (who were necessarily *astai*: Athenian law prohibited marriage between an *astos* and a *xenē* [Dem. 59.16]). Cf. the ἀστή characterized as a ἑταίρα (see n. 135), and the vignettes in Dem. 59 discussed later in this chapter. The prostitute Theodotē (Xen. *Apom.* 3.11) appears to have been a *politis*: note Sōkratēs's inquiry as to whether she is a landowner (ἔστι σοι ἀγρός; . . . οικία προσόδους ἔχουσα; §4) and her characterization as Athenian by Athēnaios (535c); see Cox 1998: 175, n. 37. Note the prostitute Naïs (Lys. fr. 82 [Th.]), for whom Arkhias is explicitly termed *kyrios*. (Kilmer [1993] has noted the difficulty in erotic scenes on Attic red-figure vases of distinguishing *hetairai* from other free women.)

and Lysias 3.22–24—to confirm the view that "boys and men who made a living from homosexual prostitution would be predominantly non-Athenian" (Dover [1978] 1989: 31). These four passages, however, actually tend to confirm the relative unimportance in sexual barter of political status—and the critical significance, *mirabile dictu*!, of physical attractiveness and money.

In Lysias 3, Theodotos, pursuant to a formal contractual commitment of sex for money, had received three hundred drachmas from Simōn, but preferred the foreign travel and other enticements offered by Simōn's wealthy rival.[67] Here there are no differences of status (the two patrons and the prostitute are all *politai*),[68] but in Aiskhinēs 1 a variegated clientele is serviced by a young prostitute who is a *politēs*. At adolescence, Timarkhos had gone down to the Piraeus and sold himself to a motley crowd of customers—"traders, other foreigners, *politai*."[69] Other alleged clients are identified: Misgolas (apparently a *politēs*),[70] Antiklēs (who is on Samos "with the *klērouchs*"),[71] and the "wild men" Kēdōnidēs, Autokleidēs, and Thersandros (who are connected by an ancient scholion to the Triballoi, a Thracian tribe). Ultimately, the rich *slave* Pittalakos maintains Timarkhos in the slave's own home—along with the slave's treasured fowl and other valued personal possessions—for a prolonged period of sexual exploitation. After Pittalakos refuses a request to cede Timarkhos's services to Hēgēsandros, the wealthy treasurer of the Athenian fleet, who has returned to Athens with considerable funds, Hegesandros propositions Timarkhos directly and successfully.[72] Disgusted at

[67] Lys. 3.5: ἐγὼ μὲν εὖ ποιῶν αὐτὸν ἠξίουν εἶναί μοι φίλον. 10: ἔδοξέ μοι κράτιστον εἶναι ἀποδημῆσαι ἐκ τῆς πόλεως. λαβὼν δὴ τὸ μειράκιον . . . ᾠχόμην ἐκ τῆς πόλεως. 22: ἐτόλμησε γὰρ εἰπεῖν ὡς αὐτὸς μὲν τριακοσίας δραχμὰς ἔδωκε Θεοδότῳ, συνθήκας πρὸς αὐτὸν ποιησάμενος, ἐγὼ δ᾽ ἐπιβουλεύσας ἀπέστησα αὐτοῦ τὸ μειράκιον.

[68] Lys. 3.5: Θεοδότου, Πλαταϊκοῦ μειρακίου. 45: <Σίμων> μόνος Ἀθηναίων ὑπὸ τῶν στρατγῶν ἐξεκηρύχθη. 38: ἐγὼ εἰς τοιοῦτον ἀγῶνα καθέστηκα, ἐν ᾧ καὶ περὶ τῆς πατρίδος καὶ τῆς οὐσίας τῆς ἐμαυτοῦ ἁπάσης κινδυνεύω; 47: μὴ περιίδητε ἐκ τῆς πατρίδος ἀδίκως ἐκπεσόντα . . . καὶ κακοῦ μὲν αὐτῇ οὐδενὸς αἴτιος γεγένημαι, οὐδὲ τῶν ἐμῶν προγόνων οὐδείς, ἀγαθῶν δὲ πολλῶν.

[69] Aiskhin. 1.40: ἐκάθητο ἐν Πειραιεῖ ἐπὶ τοῦ Εὐθυδίκου ἰατρείου, . . . πωλεῖν αὐτὸν προῃρημένος. . . . Ὅσοι μὲν οὖν τῶν ἐμπόρων ἢ τῶν ἄλλων ξένων ἢ τῶν πολιτῶν τῶν ἡμετέρων κατ᾽ ἐκείνους τοὺς χρόνους ἐχρήσαντο τῷ σώματι Τιμάρχου, ἑκὼν καὶ τούτους ὑπερβήσομαι.

[70] Misgolas is identified in Aiskhinēs' text (1.41) as Μισγόλας Ναυκράτους Κολλυτεύς, but in the purported text of his deposition (1.50) as Μισγόλας Νικίου Πειραιεύς.

[71] 1.53: Ἀντικλῆς Καλλίου Εὐωνυμεύς. οὗτος ἄπεστιν ἐν Σάμῳ μετὰ τῶν κληρούχων.

[72] Aiskhin. 1.56–57: (Ἡγήσανδρος) ἧκε δεῦρο . . . ἔχων οὐκ ἐλάττους ἢ ὀγδοήκοντα μνᾶς ἀργυρίου . . . καὶ εἰσφοιτῶν ὡς τὸν Πιττάλακον συγκυβευτὴν ὄντα, καὶ τοῦτον ἐκεῖ πρῶτον ἰδών, ἥσθη τε καὶ ἐπεθύμησε καὶ ἐβουλήθη ὡς αὑτὸν ἀναλαβεῖν . . . πρῶτον μὲν οὖν τῷ Πιτταλάκῳ διελέχθη

"having spent huge sums of money in vain" on Timarkhos, the slave ultimately brings a legal action against his Athenian rival.[73]

The "status" of the parties involved in these two cases—prostitutes who are *politai* but customers of varied juridical position—directly contradicts the prevailing hierarchical model of politically based commercial sex. Scholars have accordingly sought to negate the "plain meaning" of these texts. Efforts have been made to manumit the wealthy slave Pittalakos (how could an unfree person at Athens maintain an Athenian *politēs* as sex object and bring a lawsuit in the Athenian courts to vindicate his rights?) and to disenfranchise Theodotos, the prostitute who is a *politēs*. The manuscript readings, however, are paleographically strong: Aiskhinēs 1 contains multiple separate and explicit manuscript references to Pittalakos as a slave;[74] Lysias 3 explicitly identifies Theodotos as a Plataian and hence an Athenian *politēs*. Yet Todd suggests that Pittalakos, despite the text's statements, might have been merely a "former slave" (1993: 193), while Fisher attributes to Pittalakos a "special status," arguing tautologically that he could not have been an actual slave since "Pittalakos was apparently free from the laws that said slaves could not 'love' free boys and were unable to bring legal actions themselves."[75] (Timarkhos in fact was not a "boy" and therefore was not affected by the various laws prohibiting slaves [and others] from "loving 'free boys.' ")[76] Yet more remarkably, Dover attempts to disenfranchise the prostitute Theodotos, and then to use him (now shorn of *politeia*) as *confirmation* for Dover's thesis that Athenian prostitution was the "exclusive preserve of foreigners." This contention is critically

δεόμενος παραδοῦναι τοῦτον· ὡς δ' οὐκ ἔπειθεν, αὐτῷ τούτῳ προσβάλλει, καὶ οὐ πολὺν ἀνήλωσε χρόνον, ἀλλ' εὐθὺς ἐπεπείκει.

[73] Aiskhin. 1.54–64. Aiskhinēs emphasizes the monetary resources of both the slave (εὐπορῶν ἀργυρίου [54], μάτην τοσοῦτον ἀργύριον ἀνηλωκώς [58]) and the Athenian politician (ἔχων οὐκ ἐλάττους ἢ ὀγδοήκοντα μνᾶς ἀργυρίου [56], ὢν δ' ἐν τοιαύτῃ ἀφθονίᾳ [57]).

[74] See Chapter 5, n. 8. Pittalakos's true status is, in this context, unimportant: it is the plausibility of the premise underlying Aiskhinēs's argument—that a slave could maintain a *politēs* in the slave's home for sexual purposes—that is significant. For this methodology of "forensic attestation," see Preface, p. xiii. Although Wood (1988: 48–49) has suggested that οἰκέτης might refer indiscriminately to a free or to an enslaved household servant, Pl. *Laws* 763a and 853d show that *oiketai* are necessarily a subset of *douloi*. Cf. Osborne 1995: 32. On enslaved individuals owned by the state (*dēmosioi*), see Chapter 5, p. 136 and n. 34.

[75] 1993: 57. No one in Attika could lawfully "love" children: the legal protections at Athens for minors and others are discussed in the first section of this chapter. On litigational rights of slaves, see E. Cohen 1991.

[76] For Timarkhos's maturity, see, for example, Aiskhin. 1.40: ἀπηλλάγη ἐκ παίδων.

important to Dover's argument: he is able to offer as further evidence for foreigners' functioning as prostitutes at Athens only the two passages from Aiskhinēs discussed subsequently.

But Dover's position on Theodotos depends on implausible assumptions. He first asserts that Theodotos was of "marginal citizenship status" because of his Plataian origin, and then plunges further, suggesting that "it is quite possible that the young Plataean Theodotos did not possess Athenian citizen status at all," since some Plataians may have been denied *politeia* several decades earlier when the Athenians, prior to 427, bestowed their "citizenship" on the Plataians and their descendants.[77] However, the decree providing *politeia* to the Plataians (preserved at Dem. 59.104) makes no mention of any Plataians being excepted, and explicitly provides not for "marginal citizenship status" but for full equality with all other Athenians.[78] The only limitation was a proscription on the holding of certain administrative and religious offices by the original grantees, although their descendants were fully eligible for such positions.[79] Since Lysias 3 involves events that occurred more than thirty-five years after the mass grant of "citizenship,"[80] the "young Plataian Theodotos" (as Dover calls him) is necessarily such a scion and would hold an Athenian "citizenship" entirely untruncated. Unlike Dover, fourth-century Athenians did recognize that a person of Plataian origin was, ipso facto, necessarily a full Athenian "citizen": any potential challenges based on defects in individual entitlement at the time of the original decree were precluded by the rider of Nikomenēs attached in 403 to the resolution renewing the "citizenship law" of Periklēs, specifically forbidding evaluation of the qualifications of those who had been accepted as *politai* before 403/2.[81]

A surviving court presentation (Lys. 23) focuses precisely on this point, and explicitly demonstrates that after 403 a Plataian's claim to

[77] Dover [1978] 1989: 32–33. On the mass grant of citizenship to the Plataians, see Thouk. 3.55.3, 63.2, 68.5; 5.32.1; Dem. 59.104–6; Isok. 12.94.

[78] Πλαταιέας εἶναι Ἀθηναίους . . . ἐπιτίμους καθάπερ οἱ ἄλλοι Ἀθηναῖοι, καὶ μετεῖναι αὐτοῖς ὧνπερ Ἀθηναίοις μέτεστι πάντων. On the authenticity of the decree preserved at Dem. 59.104, see Carey 1992: 139; Osborne 1981–83: 2:13–16; Lambert 1993: 115–16.

[79] καὶ μετεῖναι αὐτοῖς ὧνπερ Ἀθηναίοις μέτεστι πάντων, καὶ ἱερῶν καὶ ὁσίων, πλὴν εἴ τις ἱερωσύνη ἢ τελετή ἐστιν ἐκ γένους, μηδὲ τῶν ἐννέα ἀρχόντων, τοῖς δ' ἐκ τούτων.

[80] Lys. 3 was delivered some time (perhaps a considerable time) after 394. See Carey 1989: 86.

[81] τοὺς δὲ πρὸ Εὐκλείδου ἀνεξετάστως ἀφεῖσθαι (Schol. Aiskhin. 1.39). Cf. Dem. 57.30.

Athenian "citizenship" could be rebutted not by questioning whether an individual Plataian was entitled to Athenian "citizenship," but only by a showing that the claimant was in fact not a Plataian or of Plataian descent.[82] Pankleōn had asserted that because he was a Plataian, he could not be sued in the *polemarch*'s court (which was for metics, not *politai*).[83] The plaintiff, not disputing Pankleōn's entitlement to *politeia* if he were a Plataian or of Plataian descent, seeks instead to show that Pankleōn is not a Plataian. Modern scholars should accept the premise of the litigants in Lysias 23, rather than arguing, some two millennia later, for an ex post facto disenfranchisement of Theodotos.[84]

Dover also considers in detail two passages from Aiskhinēs 1 concerning prostitution.

Aiskhinēs 1.43[85]

Timarkhos had agreed to march with Misgolas and Phaidros in the City Dionysia parade. Greatly upset at Timarkhos's failure to appear—they had spent considerable time in preparation for the procession—Misgolas

[82] It is unclear how many years separate the adoption of Nikomenēs's amendment and the delivery of Lys. 23. Lamb (1930) suggests a date shortly before 387 (since Thebes and Plataia are portrayed as still hostile [23.15]). MacDowell (1971) has argued that the speech was delivered in 400/399. On Lys. 23, cf. Chapter 4, pp. 109–10.

[83] Lys. 23.2: προσεκαλεσάμνην αὐτὸν πρὸς τὸν πολέμαρχον, νομίζων μέτοικον εἶναι. εἰπόντος δὲ τούτου ὅτι Πλαταιεὺς εἴη, ἠρόμην ὁπόθεν δημοτεύοιτο. . . . ἐπειδὴ δὲ ἀπεκρίνατο ὅτι Δεκελειόθεν, προσκαλεσάμενος αὐτὸν καὶ πρὸς τοὺς τῇ Ἱπποθωντίδι δικάζοντας. On the implications of this passage, see Todd 1993: 167–69; E. Cohen 1994a: 146–49.

[84] Some commentators (but not Dover) have puzzled over the speaker's argument that he would not have undertaken an (allegedly) premeditated assault accompanied only by the youth Theodotos, "this child, who would have been unable to support me, but was capable of giving information under torture" (Lamb's Loeb translation of Lys. 3.33: μήτε ἄλλον ἄνθρωπον παρακαλέσαι μηδένα, εἰ μὴ τοῦτό γε τὸ παιδίον, ὃ ἐπικουρῆσαι μέν μοι οὐκ ἂν εδύνατο, μηνῦσαι δὲ ἱκανὸν ἦν βασανιζόμενον). Lamb muses on the inconsistency between his own translation here and the Plataian origins of Theodotos: "If Theodotos was a *free* Plataean, he would have the same rights as an Athenian citizen, and could not be subjected to torture" (1930: 86, n. a). Cf. Carey 1988. But in alluding to this παιδίον the speaker may not have been referring to Theodotos: an alternate meaning is "a young slave." In any event, Gagarin (1996: 2) has shown that "clearly βάσανος, in some uses at least, is not the same thing as its common modern translation, 'torture,' " "in the orators it sometimes retains the simple sense of a 'test' (Andok. 1.30; Isai. 9.29) . . . an interrogation."

[85] ἦν μὲν Διονυσίων τῶν ἐν ἄστει ἡ πομπή, ἐπόμπευον δ' ἐν ταὐτῷ ὅ τε Μισγόλας ὁ τοῦτον ἀνειληφὼς καὶ Φαῖδρος Καλλίου Σφήττιος. συνθεμένου δ' αὐτοῖς συμπομπεύειν Τιμάρχου τουτουί, οἱ μὲν περὶ τὴν ἄλλην παρασκευὴν διέτριβον, οὗτος δὲ οὐκ ἐπανῆκε. παρωξυμμένος δὲ πρὸς τὸ πρᾶγμα ὁ Μισγόλας ζήτησιν αὐτοῦ ἐποιεῖτο μετὰ τοῦ Φαίδρου, ἐξαγγελθέντος δ' αὐτοῖς εὑρίσκουσι τοῦτον ἐν συνοικίᾳ μετὰ ξένων τινῶν συναριστῶντα. διαπειλησαμένου δὲ τοῦ Μισγόλα καὶ τοῦ

and Phaidros searched for him. "They found him having lunch with some visiting foreigners. They threatened the foreigners and told them to come along to the prison, because they had corrupted a youth of free status; the foreigners were frightened and disappeared, leaving the party that had been prepared" (Dover trans., [1978] 1989: 34).

The "nationality" of the prostitute, even in Dover's translation, is clearly irrelevant. The purported offense lies in corrupting a "youth of free status" ("sc. of any nationality," as Dover concedes, ibid.). Likewise, the "nationality" of the "corruptors" is of no significance: Athenian law protected children from sexual abuse by anyone. Even a child's male relatives—"father or brother or uncle or guardian or any one responsible for him" (in Timarkhos's case all presumably would have been *politai*)—were subject to prosecution if involved in his prostitution.[86] In view of the severity of the laws against sexual exploitation of the young (see pp. 165–66) and the expedited procedures available for their enforcement, even *politai* confident of their political connections might have chosen the anonymity of flight[87] if confronted by individuals passionately angry over being stood up by a youngster of exceptionally youthful appearance.[88]

Although a claim of "corruption" (Greek *diaphtheir-*) often carries an erotic connotation, the "foreigners" here had not been caught in a sexually compromising situation (in Dover's translation, "they found him having lunch with some visiting foreigners"), and their "flight" might have been nothing more than their departure for the parade of the City Dionysia, which was about to commence. Many visitors came to Athens from abroad for festivals,[89] and foreign tourists might well have feared charges of interfering with the carefully orchestrated procession (which included

Φαίδρου τοῖς ξένοις, καὶ κελευόντων ἤδη ἀκολουθεῖν εἰς τὸ δεσμωτήριον, ὅτι μειράκιον ἐλεύθερον διέφθειραν, φοβηθέντες οἱ ξένοι φεύγοντες ᾤχοντο, καταλιπόντες τὰ παρεσκευασμένα.

[86] Cf. Aiskhin. 1.13: διαρρήδην δ' οὖν λέγει [ὁ νόμος], ἐάν τινα ἐκμισθώσῃ ἑταιρεῖν πατὴρ ἢ ἀδελφὸς ἢ θεῖος ἢ ἐπίτροπος ἢ ὅλως τῶν κυρίων τις, κατ' αὐτοῦ μὲν τοῦ παιδὸς οὐκ ἐᾷ γραφὴν εἶναι, κατὰ δὲ τοῦ μισθώσαντος καὶ τοῦ μισθωσαμένου. On legal protections against sexual oppression at Athens, see the preceding section.

[87] Dover's translation ("the foreigners were frightened and disappeared") omits the element of "flight" that is at the heart of the Greek verb φεύγω. Cf. Adams's translation in the Loeb edition of Aiskhinēs: "the foreigners were so scared that they ran away as fast as they could go"; Martin and Budé in the Budé edition: "épouvantés, les dîneurs prennent la fuite."

[88] In fact, Timarkhos actually already was an adolescent (see n. 76)—Dover refers to the threat as a "bluff" ([1978] 1989: 34)—but Greek terms for children and youth are notoriously fluid (see Garland 1990: 14, 200; Strauss 1993: 94; Forbes 1933: 60–61).

[89] See, for example, Dem. 59.24 (Σῖμος ὁ Θετταλὸς . . . ἀφικνεῖται δεῦρο εἰς τὰ Παναθήναια τὰ μεγάλα).

men and women of every status, Athenian and foreign).[90] Indeed, cultural historians have noted that this passage, fraught with ambiguity and implication, has "not been adequately analyzed" (Goldhill 1994: 361), especially for the information that it provides about the egalitarian interaction of Athenian and "foreign" elements in civic activities such as the Dionysia.[91] Foreign visitors, unlike resident metics and other local non-*politai*, seem often to have been victimized by persons of varied status preying on the targets' lack of familiarity with Athens, its customs, laws, and inhabitants.[92] Athenian literature is replete with tales not only of foreigners but of *politai* in flight from confrontation, frequently to avoid physical conflict.[93] This vignette, deprecated by Aiskhinēs himself as merely one of the many "ridiculous" episodes (*katagelasta*) in which Timarkhos was involved (1.43), certainly offers no clear basis for determining the ratio of Athenian and foreign prostitutes, or for portraying non-*politai* at Athens as cavalierly cowed in daily life by swaggering "citizens."

Aiskhinēs 1.195[94]

In this passage, Aiskhinēs contends to an audience of Athenian jurors that there would be only limited impact from enforcement of the laws precluding political activity by those who had engaged in proscribed activities, "for the law is directed not to those engaging in private pursuits, but to those involved in political activities. Bid those who have consumed their paternal assets to go to work and to gain their living from other sources, and (bid) those who are hunters of such young men as are easily caught[95] to turn to foreigners and metics, so that they should not be

[90] Participation by male and female metics: Dēm. Phal. F Gr Hist 228 F5. For full participation by free women of every "status," see Sourvinou-Inwood 1994: 271, n. 9; Menander fr. 337 (K-A).

[91] Maurizio (1998) sees this passage as one in which "Aiskhinēs describes a row among processors over whom they will march with in the parade." For Goldhill, "Timarkhos' failing to arrive for the procession because he was eating with a group of foreigners is especially galling to Misgolas and leads to a public row" (1994: 361).

[92] Cf., for example, Aiskhin. 1.158; Dem. 59.41; Lys. 9.

[93] Cf. Lys. 3; Cohen 1995.

[94] ὧν πρὶν τῆς συνηγορίας ἀκοῦσαι τοὺς βίους ἀναμιμνῄσκεσθε, καὶ τοὺς μὲν εἰς τὰ σώματα ἡμαρτηκότας μὴ ὑμῖν ἐνοχλεῖν, ἀλλὰ παύσασθαι δημηγοροῦντας κελεύετε· οὐδὲ γὰρ ὁ νόμος τοὺς ἰδιωτεύοντας, ἀλλὰ τοὺς πολιτευομένους ἐξετάζει· τοὺς δὲ τὰ πατρῷα κατεδηδοκότας ἐργάζεσθαι καὶ ἑτέρωθεν κτᾶσθαι τὸν βίον κελεύετε· τοὺς δὲ τῶν νεῶν, ὅσοι ῥᾳδίως ἁλίσκονται, θηρευτὰς ὄντας εἰς τοὺς ξένους καὶ τοὺς μετοίκους τρέπεσθαι κελεύετε, ἵνα μήτ' ἐκεῖνοι τῆς προαιρέσεως ἀποστερῶνται μηθ' ὑμεῖς βλάπτησθε.

[95] For "prostitutes" as synonymous with "such young men as are easily caught," see Dover (1978) 1989: 32, 88–91.

deprived of their preference, nor should you be harmed." The duality of this appeal to the jurors reflects the dual accusations lying at the heart of the case: by consuming his father's wealth and by prostituting himself, Timarkhos has technically forfeited his right to participate in Athenian politics.[96] But just as there is no reason to believe that a disproportionate percentage of the wastrels resident in Athens were foreigners, this passage is no guide to the demography of Athenian prostitution.

Although Aiskhinēs is seeking to assure the jury of Athenian *politai* that the Athenians will not suffer by being deprived of speakers in the assembly if prostitutes and consumers of family estates were subject to exclusion from political activities—at worst, wastrels can go to work, and *politai* can purchase their sexual preferences from foreigners and metics[97]—the passage provides no evidence that conspicuous consumption was the preserve of foreigners, or that *politai* did not work as prostitutes. To the contrary, legal scholars have long insisted that the adoption of proscriptive legislation is almost always an indication of the prevalence of the banned activity: legislative attention is seldom devoted to phenomena unknown or rare within a particular community.[98] Likewise, only if prostitution by male *politai* were a frequent occurrence would it be necessary for Aiskhinēs even to raise the question and, defensively, to assure those inclined to purchase homoerotic pleasures from "such young men as are easily caught" to turn their attention and their purses instead to non-"citizens."

FINALLY, in addition to these two passages from Aiskhinēs 1, Winkler (1990a:180) cites a passage from Demosthenes as confirmation for the sexual "untouchability" of "the privileged citizen class" and as an example of "citizens bullying metics."

[96] The gravamen of Aiskhinēs's complaint is summarized succinctly at 1.154: τί λέγω κατὰ Τιμάρχου, καὶ τίνα ποτ' ἐστὶν ἃ ἀντιγέγραμμαι; δημηγορεῖν Τίμαρχον πεπορνευμένον καὶ τὴν πατρῴαν οὐσίαν κατεδηδοκότα. "All the way through the speech, [Aeschines] refers to both charges" (Davidson 1997: 253).

[97] For the distinction between "foreigners" (ξένοι) and metics (who may be part of the *astoi*, "locals" in contradistinction to "foreigners"), see the last section of Chapter 2. For *atimia* as a punishment for male prostitution, see Rainer 1986: 106–14.

[98] With specific reference to Athenian laws regulating the prostitution of minors, Aiskhinēs concurs: νομοθετεῖ περὶ ἀδικημάτων μεγάλων μέν, γιγνομένων δ' οἶμαι ἐν τῇ πόλει· ἐκ γὰρ τοῦ πράττεσθαί τιν' ὧν οὐ προσῆκεν, ἐκ τούτου τοὺς νόμους ἔθενθ' οἱ παλαιοί (1.13).

Demosthenes 25.57[99]

In prosecuting the prominent Aristogeitōn,[100] Demosthenes charges that the defendant "with his own hands grabbed" a female metic, Zenōbia, and "dragged her off to the sales office (*pōlētērion*) for metics, and if she had not had the metic tax, she would have been sold into slavery." Although this passage is routinely cited as one of the few explicit attestations of Athenian *politai* routinely bullying non-*politai*, Aristogeitōn at the time may himself not have been a *politēs*. And if he were, his behavior reflected not random mistreatment of a foreigner by a "superordinate" male *politēs*, but one episode in a close and personal relationship between an Athenian *politēs* and a foreign woman—in which the Athenian is actually dependently obligated to his female benefactor. Aristogeitōn, as portrayed by Demosthenes, is a brute who uniformly abuses virtually everyone with whom he has contact, from Athenian officials to his own family members (he allegedly beat his mother, sold his sister into slavery, and left his father to die in prison!).[101] On one occasion, when he had escaped from jail, Zenōbia had hidden him from the authorities, and had thereafter provided him with clothing and with the substantial funds needed to travel to Megara. On his return to Athens and after a favorable change in his circumstances,[102] they lived together until her complaints over his ingratitude, and his violence and threats, led to their

[99] Dem. 25 [56] ὅτε γὰρ τὸ δεσμωτήριον διορύξας ἀπέδρα [sc. ὁ Ἀριστογείτων], τότε πρὸς γυναῖκά τιν᾽ ἔρχεται Ζενωβίαν ὄνομα, ᾗ ἐτύγχανεν, ὡς ἔοικε, κεχρημένος ποτέ· καὶ κρύπτει καὶ διασῴζει [αὐτόν] ἐκείνη . . . καὶ μετὰ ταῦτα δοῦσα δραχμὰς ὀκτὼ ἐφόδιον καὶ χιτωνίσκον καὶ ἱμάτιον ἐξέπεμψεν εἰς Μέγαρα. [57] ταύτην τὴν ἄνθρωπον, τὴν τοιαῦτ᾽ εὐεργετήσασαν αὐτόν, ὡς πολὺς παρ᾽ ὑμῖν ἔπνει καὶ λαμπρός, μεμφομένην τι καὶ τούτων ὑπομιμνῄσκουσαν καὶ ἀξιοῦσαν εὖ παθεῖν τὸ μὲν πρῶτον ῥαπίσας καὶ ἀπειλήσας ἀπέπεμψεν ἀπὸ τῆς οἰκίας, ὡς δ᾽ οὐκ ἐπαύεθ᾽ ἡ ἄνθρωπος, ἀλλὰ γυναίου πρᾶγμ᾽ ἐποίει καὶ πρὸς τοὺς γνωρίμους προσιοῦσ᾽ ἐνεκάλει, λαβὼν αὐτὸς αὐτοχειρίᾳ πρὸς τὸ πωλητηρίον τοῦ μετοικίου ἀπήγαγεν· καὶ εἰ μὴ κείμενον αὐτῇ τὸ μετοίκιον ἔτυχεν, ἀπέπρατ᾽ ἂν διὰ τοῦτον, ᾧ τῆς σωτηρίας αὐτὴ αἰτία ἐγεγόνει.

[100] Sealey (1960) claims that this Aristogeitōn (son of Kydimachos) is to be identified with Aristogeitōn II of Aphidna, a descendant of the liberator of the Peisistratid period. But this attribution is unlikely since none of the surviving speeches against Aristogeitōn (Dem. 25, 26; Dein. 2), all filled with vituperation against the defendant, contains any negative comparison to the heroic homonyme (in contrast to the animadversions of Hypereidēs against Dēmokratēs [*Phil.* 2–3]). The name Aristogeitōn is known to have been used in a number of demes other than Aphidna: see Davies 1971: 476; Osborne and Byrne 1994: 54, s.v.

[101] Dem. 25.54–55: πρὸς μὲν γὰρ τῷ τὸν πατέρ᾽ ἐν τῷ δεσμωτηρίῳ προδοὺς ἀπελθεῖν ἐξ Ἐρετρίας . . . πρὸς δὲ τῷ τῆς μητρὸς μὴ ἀπεσχῆσθαι τὼ χεῖρε . . . καὶ τὴν ἀδελφὴν τὴν ἑαυτοῦ . . . ἐπ᾽ ἐξαγωγῇ ἀπέδοτο.

[102] ὡς πολὺς παρ᾽ ὑμῖν ἔπνει καὶ λαμπρός.

separation. It was only when she, "as a woman would,"[103] persisted in complaining to friends about his behavior that he turned her in to the authorities for tax evasion (to no avail, since she was capable of meeting her obligations).

Yet Zenōbia's experience might have befallen any resident of Attika. Athenians generally felt an obligation to help their friends, and an expectation of resultant gratitude (and an entitlement to future reciprocity).[104] Despite legal and social strictures, violent behavior was not unusual, and not restricted to abuse involving "master vs. slave, free vs. unfree, dominant vs. submissive, active vs. passive, insertive vs. receptive, customer vs. prostitute, citizen vs. non-citizen, man vs. woman": *politēs*-on-*politēs* assault is well attested.[105] Imprisonment and sale into slavery were common punishments for misbehavior, both for *politai* and for other residents, but only in accordance with formal legal procedures. In Zenōbia's case, her immunity from punishment reflected not her status but her compliance with her obligations.[106] Aristogeitōn's experience was quite different. Although he was a prominent political leader of the 330s and 320s,[107] he was continually in debt to the state and supposedly spent most of his life in prison.[108] Like all such debtors, he would have become *atimos*, thus forfeiting the benefits and rights of *politeia*. But not only modern scholars (who cite his actions as the archetypical behavior of a *politēs*) have had difficulty in accurately monitoring his actual "status." It fell to Lykourgos (fr. 13) to prosecute him, successfully, for exercising the rights of *politeia* when in fact he had been disenfranchised. But while succeeding in passing as a *politēs*,[109] Aristogeitōn did not lodge charges only against foreign females with whom he had cohabitated.

[103] γυναίου πρᾶγμ' ἐποίει (Dem. 25.57).

[104] See Millett 1991: 24–52.

[105] See D. Cohen 1995.

[106] Although the obligation to pay the *metoikion* was required only of certain non-*politai*, the tax was modest (*pace* Whitehead 1977) in comparison to the confiscatory taxation (liturgies, *eisphorai*, and *proeisphorai*) that fell upon the relatively small number of persons appearing to own the largest amounts of property. Because only *politai* could directly own land (which was the most "visible"—φανερόν—and hence most taxable form of property), those persons "appearing" to have the highest personal worth were likely disproprortionately to be *politai*. See E. Cohen 1992: 194–201.

[107] At least eight of his court presentations were known in late antiquity, including a speech against Phrynē. See Athēn. 591e; Sud., s.v. 'Αριστογείτων. After the Athenian defeat in 338, he prosecuted Demosthenes and Hypereidēs (Hyper. fr. 18).

[108] Dein. 2.2: καὶ ἐν τῷ δεσμωτηρίῳ πλείω χρόνον ἢ ἔξω διατέτριφε.

[109] For the Athenians' difficulty in differentiating persons on the basis of "status," and the elasticity of various juridical categorizations at Athens, see Chapter 2.

Deinarkhos notes the irony of Aristogeitōn's disregarding his own irregular status while prosecuting persons who actually did have *politeia*.[110] As a target of Aristogeitōn, Zenōbia stands in distinguished company. Demosthenes and Hypereidēs, prominent political leaders, were also targets of Aristogeitōn's contumely (Hyper. fr. 18). But in egalitarian Athens, the metics could strike back. It is the metic Deinarkhos (born in Korinth) who, joining in the prosecution of Aristogeitōn after the death of Alexander the Great, is the author of a vitriolic attack on this abusive defendant.[111] It is again ironic that while modern scholars cite the noncitizen Aristogeitōn's ill-treatment of his metic paramour as paradigmatic of "citizens" ' abuse of non-"citizens" at Athens, in antiquity Deinarchos's status as a "foreigner" did not prevent his citation as one of the canonical ten "Attic orators"—exemplars of authentic Athenian style and avatars of Athenian excellence—a decemvirate, however, that actually included three "orators" who were residents of Attika but were not *politai*.[112]

Consensual Sex: "Prostitution by Contract," Not Status

> Now let me tell you how it happens that it has become the prevailing custom to say that persons have become prostitutes "under written agreement." One of our *politai* . . . is said to have been a prostitute in accordance with a written contract deposited with Antiklēs. Now, since he was not a private person, but active in public affairs and a lightning-rod for attacks, he caused the city to become accustomed to this expression, and that's the reason why some people inquire if the [sexual] act has been "under written agreement."
>
> Aiskhinēs 1.165[113]

[110] Dein. 2.2: ὀφείλων τῇ δημοσίῳ κατὰ τῶν ἐπιτίμων γέγραφεν οὐκ ἐξὸν αὐτῷ, καὶ ἕτερα πολλὰ καὶ δεινὰ πεποίηκε.

[111] Although Deinarkhos is known to have spoken in court in Athens in other litigation (see the extract from his speech against Proxenos quoted at Dion. Hal. *Dein.* 3 [cf. Plut. *Bioi Rhēt.* 850e]), he may not personally have delivered this speech.

[112] The other two "foreigners" were Lysias and Isaios (who may actually have been born in Athens: Dion. Hal. *Isai.* 1; Edwards 1994: 31). The so-called eleventh orator (Apollodōros) was the son of a slave who had gained freedom and wealth. For the cultural contribution of foreigners at Athens, see Chapter 1, pp. 17–18. On Apollodōros, see Introduction, n. 6. On the canonical tradition, Worthington 1994; Douglas 1956.

[113] πόθεν οὖν ἴσχυκε καὶ σύνηθες γεγένηται λέγειν, ὡς κατὰ γραμματεῖον ἤδη τινὲς ἡταίρησαν, ἐρῶ. ἀνὴρ εἷς τῶν πολιτῶν . . . λέγεται κατὰ συνθήκας ἡταιρηκέναι τὰς παρ' Ἀντικλεῖ κειμένας· οὐκ

For the many scholars who passionately deny the applicability to Athenian society of conventional economic concepts—pricing mechanisms, market principles, supply-and-demand considerations[114]—no special difficulty is posed, ipso facto, by the lack of affirmative evidence for prostitution as a "special preserve of foreigners."[115] For these analysts, a sociopolitical allocation of prostitutes is an inexorable by-product of an "economy" in which vocational functions are "embedded" in political and social arrangements, employment arrangements are "conventional rather than market-determined," and compensation is "remarkably undifferentiated."[116] The result, it is claimed, was a society of "standard prices" and "standard wages." In such an "economy," in which the assignment of labor functions reflected not monetary motivations but a "wider social context,"[117] employment as a prostitute might well have been determined by caste—a service function allocated to foreigners and slaves whose abject political position rendered such work appropriate.

But this model of "undifferentiated" and "standard" wages is internally inconsistent and factually erroneous. Ampolo and Migeotte have demonstrated the absence of a "fixed" or "normal" price for grain.[118] Loomis has shown from detailed analysis of ancient evidence that "there was

---

ὢν <δ'> ἰδιώτης, ἀλλὰ πρὸς τὰ κοινὰ προσιὼν καὶ λοιδορίαις περιπίπτων, εἰς συνήθειαν ἐποίησε τοῦ λόγου τούτου τὴν πόλιν καταστῆναι, καὶ διὰ τοῦτο ἐρωτῶσί τινες, εἰ κατὰ γραμματεῖον ἡ πρᾶξις γεγένηται.

[114] See Schaps 1998a: 1. Cf., for example, Meikle 1995a: 148; 1995b; Finley 1985: 21.

[115] In fact, a commitment to ignoring, or "shaping," evidence is espoused by many contemporary ancient historians. The author of a major work on Athenian lending boasts of "the deliberate suppression of detail which appears to be less significant in favor of material that is judged to be critical" (Millett 1991: 4). Todd, in proclaiming himself a " 'models' rather than an 'evidence' historian," decries those historians who "take as a starting-point the statements of ancient writers" (1993: 22, with n. 4).

[116] Finley 1985: 212 (n. 19), 80. Anthropologists have developed models of primitive groups where production, distribution, and consumption are accomplished solely through familial or political relationships. In such societies, economic activity supposedly cannot occur without direct social significance; the economy thus is said to be "embedded" in the society itself (cf. Chapter 5, n. 4). Finley, an associate of Polanyi from 1958 to 1963, denominated Athens such a society and claimed that in entities of this type "political rights" preempted "economic interests" (1985: 80–81). Here Finley followed Weber's sweeping conceptualization ([1909] 1924, 1921) of the subordination of economic considerations to politics in antiquity (see n. 4 for the often deleterious effect of such Weberian grandiosity on the analysis of specific historical issues). Finley's diktat has been widely accepted, even influencing analyses of Roman wages (where even less evidence is available). See, for example, Crawford 1974: 2: ch. 6.

[117] Stewart 1990: 65. A sampling of proponents of a standard wage at Athens (set by modern academic edict at one drachma per day): Burford 1972: 138; Himmelman 1979: 127–40; Gallo 1987: 19–63, esp. 47, 58. For a listing of proponents of standard pricing (especially for grain), see Migeotte forthcoming.

[118] Ampolo 1986: 146–47; Migeotte forthcoming. Cf. Reger 1993: 312–14.

no standard wage at Athens" and that wage rates were more reflective "of a market economy than the modern orthodoxy has held."[119] In any event, a theoretically consistent, politically derived allocation of resources would have mandated higher wages for *politai* than for other workers, but an egalitarian treatment among *politai* themselves—"a citizen in democratic Athens," according to a leading advocate of the primacy of status over market, "was in a position somewhat akin to that of a shareholder in a modern company: a joint owner . . . expecting in good times to receive a dividend from the profits of the enterprise."[120] Yet the *polis*, in its own wage practices, actually pursued a policy totally inconsistent with any such expectation. It indiscriminately employed *politai*, other free persons, and slaves to perform similar services for similar compensation, but paid to its "citizen" functionaries quite varying compensation for differing tasks, "akin" to a "corporation" which would pay dividends to shareholders and nonowners alike, but at varying rates unrelated to the status of the recipients.

Thus, in the period before 322, *politai* serving on juries received 3 obols per day; councillors (*bouleutai)*, 5 to 6 obols; "magistrates" (*archons*), 4 obols; assembly members (*ekklēsiastai*), 6 to 9 obols.[121] At about the same time, or slightly earlier, the compensation paid to a diverse group of "skilled" and "unskilled" workers—*politai,* metics, slaves—at Eleusis in 329/8 and 327/6 likewise varied considerably, but according to trade and task, not pursuant to the political "order" to which the worker belonged.[122] (In fact—again confuting the theory of an allocation of tasks by political status—the shoes for the public slaves working at Eleusis were made by a cobbler who was a *politēs*![123]) Without regard to "status," *politai,* slaves, and metics working on construction of the Erekhtheion between 409 and 407 were all paid precisely the

[119] Loomis 1997: 1 (emphasis in original). Cf. Loomis 1998: 232–39, 254.

[120] Todd 1993: 183. Cf. Osborne 1995: 39: "the undertaking of economic activities on any large scale within a city with a citizen body with established privileges demanded an underclass."

[121] Aristot. *Ath. Pol.* 62.2. Cf. Loomis 1998: 23–25.

[122] *I.G.* II^{2}1672–73. A sampling of wages: workers carrying construction materials (such as bricks or wood), sifting plaster, mixing mortar, breaking clods, 2 drachmas 3 obols per day (*I.G.* II^2 1672–73.28–30, 32–34, 44–46, 60–62); two sawyers, 3 drachmas (perhaps aggregate pay for both: *I.G.* II^2 1672.159–60); workers laying bricks and working on wood, 2 and 1/2 drachmas (*I.G.* II^2 1672.26–28); workers laying roof tiles, 2 drachmas (*I.G.* II^2 1672.110–11); architect, 2 drachmas (*I.G.* II^2 1672.12); mason finishing stone and plasterer, 1 drachma, 1 and 1/2 obols each (*I.G.* II^2 1672.31–32).

[123] *I.G.* II^2 1672.190.

same wage, a single drachma per day.[124] Political rights likewise appear to have played no role in the type of labor performed: we find, for example, nine *politai*, twelve metics, and sixteen slaves working as masons.[125] In the Athenian navy, *politai*, metics, and slaves served as crew members without differentiation of status or work assignment: a master and his slave even appear often to have been rowers on the same trireme.[126] But even *politai* serving as rowers received from the state only half the compensation paid to slaves working on the Erekhtheion.[127] The state's disregard of status corresponded to the pattern prevailing in private businesses, where many free residents of Attika—*politai* and metics—and many slaves worked in crafts or trades,[128] while unfree persons often conducted their own businesses, sometimes owning their own slaves.[129] Even within Athenian households, free women appear to have worked alongside domestic slaves at many tasks.[130]

Despite occasional assertions to the contrary,[131] there is no substantial evidence for governmental controls on pricing or other aspects of the sexual economy.[132] Prices for sexual services largely reflected market

[124] *I.G.* I^3 474–76. See Randall 1953; Paton 1927: 338–39, 380, 382, 398, 416.

[125] No slave sculptors or woodcarvers are attested, but *politai* are not lacking: three *politai* and five metics appear as sculptors, but five metic woodcarvers outnumber a single *politēs*. See Osborne 1995: 30.

[126] See *I.G.* I^3 1032; Thouk. 7.13.2, which together confirm that "slaves regularly formed a substantial proportion of the rowers on Athenian triremes, and their masters included fellow oarsmen" (Graham 1998: 110). Cf. Graham 1992; Welwei 1974. See the discussion of Isok. 8.48 at Burke 1992: 218.

[127] Loomis 1998: 236–38. Cf. Gabrielsen 1994: 110–14.

[128] See Hopper 1979: 140; Finley 1981: 99; Ehrenberg 1962: 162; Osborne 1995: 30. Cf. Chapter 5, pp. 134–35.

[129] For these slaves "living independently," see Chapter 5, pp. 145–54.

[130] See, for example, Iskhomakhos's wife at Xen. *Oik.* 7.6. The wife's role, however, was often essentially managerial: see Chapter 1, pp. 37–38.

[131] For example, Krenkel (1978; 1988: 1294, 1296) asserts that *polis* officials imposed a "standard fee" of four drachmas on male prostitutes, unjustifiably generalizing from an isolated prostitute's claim for four drachmas in Aiskhin. 1.158 (see n. 161).

[132] From the limitation on flute girls' compensation (that he attributes to the *agoranomoi*), Krenkel derives a general limitation on female prostitutes' "charge for a single visit" (1988: 1294). Aristot. *Ath. Pol.* 50.2 does report that the *astynomoi* set a maximum fee of two drachmas for females who played reed pipes, harps, and/or lyres: καὶ τάς τε αὐλητρίδας καὶ τὰς ψαλτρίας καὶ τὰς κιθαριστρίας οὗτοι σκοποῦσιν ὅπως μὴ πλείονος ἢ δυεῖν δραχμαῖς μισθωθήσονται. Even if we assume that these musicians "might also be called on to provide sexual entertainment" (Rhodes 1981: 574), this is not proof of a *general* limitation on the fees of female sexual workers. (On the "fluidity" of female "discursive categories," see Henry 1986: 147; Kurke 1997: 109; on the diversity and complexity of the sexual market for women in Athens, Davidson 1997: 74–76). The control of compensation for flute girls might have been intended to avoid brawls on the street from competing revelers: "on the street the flute-girls really came into their element, in

factors, especially consumer preference. Consider Demosthenes 59, a presentation focused on Neaira, a woman (according to the plaintiff) long notorious as a whore but for decades passing as an Athenian *politis* ("citizeness")—an improbable (and therefore unpersuasive) accusatory coupling if prostitution were truly incompatible with "citizenship."[133] Female "citizens" were perceived as responsive to economic factors: Apollodōros hyperbolically warns that *politides* lacking wealthy relatives to provide appropriate dowries will become prostitutes if the prohibition against marriage with foreigners (encouraging men to marry even poor *politides* of middling appearance) is not enforced.[134] (In the early third century an Athenian *astē*, who was a prostitute, is in fact parodied by Antiphanēs as having neither guardian nor kinsmen, and thus presumably lacking a dowry.)[135] Unenslaved women drew premium prices. The procuress Nikaretē, herself free, supposedly presented as her own offspring the child prostitutes whom she owned, including Neaira who allegedly came whoring to Attika before reaching puberty. Nikaretē's motivation: the "highest prices" might be obtained from customers desiring to have sex with young girls whom they believed to be the free offspring of the woman providing the children's services.[136] But customers would also pay higher fees for sexual relations with women of seemingly bourgeois

---

the *kōmos*, a conga of revellers" (Davidson 1997: 81), where "Woman is present as musician, dancer, flutist, or parasol-bearer, not as hetaira" (Frontisi-Ducroux and Lissarrague 1990: 228).

[133] Whether Neaira herself actually was a former prostitute is beyond our knowledge, but the speaker's presupposition (that such a woman could pass for decades as an Athenian "citizen") is significant; see p. xiii. For the equation of πολίτιδες and Athenian "citizens," see n. 8; for other evidence of *politides* as prostitutes, see n. 66.

[134] Dem. 59.112–13: ὥστε καὶ ὑπὲρ τῶν πολιτίδων σκοπεῖτε, τοῦ μὴ ἀνεκδότους γενέσθαι τὰς τῶν πενήτων θυγατέρας. νῦν μὲν γάρ, κἂν ἀπορηθῇ τις, ἱκανὴν προῖκ' αὐτῇ ὁ νόμος συμβάλλεται, ἂν καὶ ὁπωστιοῦν μετρίαν ἡ φύσις ὄψιν ἀποδῷ· προπηλακισθέντος δὲ τοῦ νόμου . . . καὶ ἀκύρου γενομένου, παντελῶς ἤδη ἡ μὲν τῶν πορνῶν ἐργασία ἥξει εἰς τὰς τῶν πολιτῶν θυγατέρας.

[135] Fr. 210 (K-A) (= Athēn. 13.29 [572a]): κατοικούσης τινὸς | ἰδὼν ἑταίρας εἰς ἔρωτ' ἀφίκετο, | ἀστῆς, ἐρήμου δ' ἐπιτρόπου καὶ συγγενῶν. (I am grateful to W. T. Loomis for calling this citation to my attention.) On *astai*, see Chapter 2, pp. 60ff.

[136] Dem. 59.18–22: Ἑπτὰ γὰρ ταύτας παιδίσκας ἐκ μικρῶν παιδίων ἐκτήσατο Νικαρέτη, Χαρισίου μὲν οὖσα τοῦ Ἠλείου ἀπελευθέρα . . . προσειποῦσα δ' αὐτὰς ὀνόματι θυγατέρας, ἵν' ὡς μεγίστους μισθοὺς πράττοιτο τοὺς βουλομένους πλησιάζειν αὐταῖς ὡς ἐλευθέραις οὔσαις. . . . Νέαιρα αὑτηί, ἐργαζομένη μὲν ἤδη τῷ σώματι, νεωτέρα δὲ οὖσα διὰ τὸ μήπω τὴν ἡλικίαν αὐτῇ παρεῖναι. The deposition that follows (believed to be authentic: Carey 1992: 97; Kirschner 1885: 77ff.) suggests that the deponent believed Neaira actually to have been the daughter of Nikaretē: Φιλόστρατος Διονυσίου Κολωνῆθεν μαρτυρεῖ εἰδέναι Νέαιραν Νικαρέτης οὖσαν, ἧσπερ καὶ Μετάνειρα ἐγένετο. Because the deposition is offered in support of the assertion that Nikaretē presented the girls as θυγατέρας, and because the primary and original meaning of γίγνομαι (immediately following) is "be born," it seems reasonable to treat the genitive form of Nikaretē here as denoting family relationship.

pretension (*epi proskhēmatos tinos*) living in a stable marital relationship[137]—a market phenomenon (also encountered in modern sexual commerce) of enhanced payment for denigration.[138]

Indeed, the cultural significance at Athens of "zero-sum competition" would have further enhanced the market attractiveness of free prostitutes, and especially of youths from established families: in the agonistic environment of Athens, only to the extent that sexual submission is felt to dishonor and humiliate a person or his or her "household" (*oikos*) is the purchaser's self-esteem and perceived self-worth enhanced.[139] The resultant willingness of customers to lavish huge sums on "citizen" prostitutes is exemplified by Simōn, who supposedly contracted to pay the *politēs* Theodotos 300 drachmas—when his own possessions amounted to only 250 drachmas.[140] But this desire to prevail—to enhance oneself by debasing another—could easily lead to the would-be predators' victimization. Neaira supposedly would entice a "wealthy but unknowledgeable foreigner" into a sexual relationship—after which her "husband" Stephanos, as an outraged cuckold, would extract a considerable cash settlement from the victim.[141] Similarly in Hypereidēs 5, Antigona (a former prostitute, now a brothel operator) in a complex contractual arrangement allegedly defrauds a young *politēs*, Epikratēs. She and her metic confederate, Athēnogenēs, sell an entire perfumery operation to Epikratēs, who had no interest in the business but lusted after the son of the slave, a *doulos khōris oikōn* who operated the enterprise. By

[137] Dem. 59.41: διεγγυηθεῖσα δ' ὑπὸ Στεφάνου καὶ οὖσα παρὰ τούτῳ τὴν μὲν αὐτὴν ἐργασίαν οὐδὲν ἧττον ἢ πρότερον ἠργάζετο, τοὺς δὲ μισθοὺς μείζους ἐπράττετο τοὺς βουλομένους αὐτῇ πλησιάζειν, ὡς ἐπὶ προσχήματος ἤδη τινὸς οὖσα καὶ ἀνδρὶ συνοικοῦσα.

[138] Psychological elements, especially of debasement and abuse, not directly related to genital sexuality are an important determinant of modern prostitutional compensation (Rosen 1982: 97; Pateman 1988: 259, n. 33). According to some observers, denigration is the essence of purchased eroticism: "prostitution and pornography are acts of dominance expressed through sexuality" (Kitzinger 1994: 197). But purchased debasement does not lack ideological defense: sadomasochistic lesbian groups valorize what others consider to be the "dehumanization of sexual relations" involved in customers' frequent choice of "abusive" satisfactions. See Barry 1995: 69–73, 79–90; Leidholdt 1990: ix; Goode 1978: 72. The continued erotic centrality of power within ostensibly egalitarian female relationships has evoked considerable analytical concern (see Kitzinger 1991, 1994; Hoagland 1988; Lobel 1986).

[139] On the centrality of "zero-sum" competition in Athenian culture, see Gouldner 1965: 49; Dover 1964: 31; Winkler 1990a: 178; D. Cohen 1995: 63. But cf. Davidson 1997: 169.

[140] Lys. 3.22–24: αὐτὸς μὲν τριακοσίας δραχμὰς ἔδωκε Θεοδότῳ, συνθήκας πρὸς αὐτὸν ποιησάμενος . . . σκέψασθε δὲ ὡς ἄπιστα εἴρηκε. τὴν γὰρ οὐσίαν τὴν ἑαυτοῦ ἅπασαν πεντήκοντα καὶ διακοσίων δραχμῶν ἐτιμήσατο. καίτοι θαυμαστὸν εἰ τὸν ἑταιρήσοντα πλειόνων ἐμισθώσατο ὧν αὐτὸς τυγχάνει κεκτημένος.

[141] Dem. 59.41: συνεσυκοφάντει δὲ καὶ οὗτος, εἴ τινα ξένον ἀγνῶτα πλούσιον λάβοι ἐραστὴν αὐτῆς, ὡς μοιχὸν ἐπ' αὐτῇ ἔνδον ἀποκλείων καὶ ἀργύριον πραττόμενος πολύ.

purchasing the business and freeing the slaves, Epikratēs hoped to gain the slave boy's gratitude and goodwill (*kharis*: 5.6).

For the *hetairoi* of Athens, contractual arrangements for sexual services—whether directly explicit, as in Lysias 3, or constructed with greater complexity, as in Hypereidēs 5—were the norm. Aiskhinēs, contrary to his own litigational interest (he was unable to provide written confirmation of his charges of prostitution against Timarkhos), acknowledges that male prostitutes were often said to work "under written contract."[142] References to such contractual arrangements were so commonplace that the phrase "whoring under contract" (*syngraphē*), a usage popularized by a prominent *politēs* who had worked as a prostitute, had become idiomatic in local discourse (Aiskh. 1.165). Requests were routinely anticipated in court proceedings for written confirmation of commercial sexual acts.[143] As with written agreements for other commercial undertakings, contracts for sexual services appear on occasion even to have been deposited for safeguarding with third persons,[144] and prostitutional obligations, as was the case with other contractual arrangements, were undertaken with a panoply of witnesses to confirm the agreements.[145]

Even female courtesans are known to have entered into elaborate contractual commitments. In Plautus's *Asinaria,* an adaptation of a Hellenic original,[146] there is presented, in comic version but at considerable length, a contract in writing (termed *syngraphus*, the Latin rendering of the Greek *syngraphē*), providing for Philaenium, daughter of Cleareta, to spend her time exclusively with the Athenian Diabolus for a period of one year at a price of two thousand drachmas, a "gift" paid in advance.[147] The contract contains extended provisions of humorous

[142] Loeb translation of κατὰ γραμματεῖον (Adams 1919): for *grammateion* as written contract, see Lys. 32.7 ("τὰ γραμματα would include the contracts relating to the loans": Carey 1989: 214). Cf. P. Oxy. 1012, fr. 9 ii.15. For the relevant text of Aiskhin. 1.165, see n. 113. For the distinction between *hetairoi* and *pornoi*, see n. 7.

[143] Aiskhin. 1.160: Ἐὰν δ' ἐπιχειρῶσι λέγειν ὡς οὐχ ἡταίρηκεν ὅστις μὴ κατὰ συγγραφὰς ἐμισθώθη, καὶ γραμματεῖον καὶ μάρτυρας ἀξιῶσί με τούτων παρασχέσθαι. Cf. 165: ἐρωτῶσί τινες εἰ κατὰ γραμματεῖον ἡ πρᾶξις γεγένηται.

[144] Aiskhin. 1.165: λέγεται κατὰ συνθήκας ἡταιρηκέναι τὰς παρ' Ἀντικλεῖ κειμένας· For safekeeping of maritime loan agreements, for example, see Dem. 34.6, 56.15.

[145] Aiskhin. 1.125: ἀγοραῖα τεκμήρια. Without witnesses, even written agreements were unrecognized and unenforceable until very late in the fourth century. See Thomas 1989: 41–45; Pringsheim 1955.

[146] For the validity of the use of Roman comic material as evidence for Athenian legal and social practices, see Scafuro 1997: 16–19; Paoli 1976: 76–77.

[147] Lines 751–54: Diabolus Glauci filius Clearetae | lenae dedit dono argenti viginti minas, | Philaenium ut secum esset noctes et dies | hunc annum totum.

paranoia—for example, Philaenium is not even to gaze upon another man and must swear only by female deities. Similar Greek contractual arrangements with courtesans are alluded to in a number of other Plautine comedies and in a work of Turpilius (who seems often to have adapted plays from Menander).[148] From Athenian sources, we know directly of the complex financial arrangements made by a *hetaira* in Korinth with the Athenian Phryniōn—and with Timanoridas the Korinthian, Eukratēs of Leukas, and other of her "lovers."[149] The same woman later, acting on her own behalf in a private arbitration proceeding at Athens,[150] reached agreement with two Athenian patrons requiring mutual consent for any alteration in the terms governing allocations of property and obligations of maintenance undertaken in exchange for her provision of sexual services to both men.[151] Although these arrangements are presented by the courtesan's opponent without comment and without invective (in a speech otherwise replete with personalized contumely directed at the *hetaira*), modern scholarship has been horrified: for the editor of the only commentary on the speech available in English, the contractual provisions are "a further indication of her degraded life that she can be shared in this way . . . passed back and forth daily like an object" (Carey 1992: 110–11).

Such reactions reflect, at least in part, the chasm between Athenian and modern Western conceptualizations of prostitution.[152] Contemporary Western thought and governmental regulation largely continue to "em-

[148] See Plaut. *Merc.* 536ff., *Bacch.* fr. 10 and 896ff.; Turpilius Com. fr. 112 Ribbeck *Leuc.* Cf. Schonbeck 1981: 150–51 and 203, n. 73; Herter 1960: 81, nn. 193 and 194.

[149] Dem. 59.29–32.

[150] Dem. 59.45–46: συνῆγον αὐτοὺς οἱ ἐπιτήδειοι καὶ ἔπεισαν δίαιταν ἐπιτρέψαι αὐτοῖς. . . . ἀκούσαντες ἀμφοτέρων καὶ αὐτῆς τῆς ἀνθρώπου τὰ πεπραγμένα, γνώμην ἀπεφήναντο . . . τὴν μὲν ἄνθρωπον ἐλευθέραν εἶναι καὶ αὐτὴν αὑτῆς κυρίαν.

[151] Dem. 59.46: ἃ δ' ἐξῆλθεν ἔχουσα Νέαιρα παρὰ Φρυνίωνος χωρὶς ἱματίων καὶ χρυσίων καὶ θεραπαινῶν, ἃ αὐτῇ τῇ ἀνθρώπῳ ἠγοράσθη, ἀποδοῦναι Φρυνίωνι πάντα· συνεῖναι δ' ἑκατέρῳ ἡμέραν παρ' ἡμέραν· ἐὰν δὲ καὶ ἄλλως πως ἀλλήλους πείθωσι, ταῦτα κύρια εἶναι· τὰ δ' ἐπιτήδεια τῇ ἀνθρώπῳ τὸν ἔχοντα ἀεὶ παρέχειν.

[152] In Asia, twentieth-century views are much closer to the Athenian. In the 1920s, the Japanese minister for home affairs insisted that "it is not easy for Western savants of individualism to comprehend our distinctive system" (quoted in Buruma 1998: 10). Prostitution was a licensed profession in Japan from at least the fourteenth century until immediately after the American occupation. See Garon 1997: 89–90; cf. Fowler 1998. Traditionalists still defend Japanese prostitution as compatible with Eastern, rather than Christian, social and sexual morals. Throughout Asia, in 1998, the sale of sexual services was a major and flourishing industry: Thailand's overall income from this sector was estimated at over $22 billion, Indonesia's at some $2.5 billion (Report of the United Nations International Labor Organization 1998). Japanese women in prosperous districts of Tokyo in large numbers were reported to be pursuing "economic freedom" through freelance prostitution (Buruma 1998: 12).

bed" prostitution within prevailing social, political, and religious values that see prostitution as morally degenerate and humanly exploitative, a selling of one's self rather than a contracting out of a particular type of labor for a set period in exchange for money and/or other consideration.[153] In contrast with the Athenian use of written contract to provide for the individualized sale of sexual services (in a society where written contracts are believed to have been relatively unimportant),[154] prevailing modern juridical theory rejects prostitution as falling within the ken of employment contracts, denying that "the prostitution contract is exactly like—or is one example of—the employment contract. . . . A prostitute does not . . . contract out use of *sexual services*."[155] In contrast, consensual arrangements for sexual services did not evoke moral outrage at Athens. Prostitution enjoyed the goodwill of the goddess Aphroditē, divinity of sex: "in ancient Greece prostitutes clearly functioned as mediators of Aphroditē's power, their sexual skills a sort of 'technology' that canalized her potent force."[156] Attic law, furthermore, mandated the recognition of "whatever arrangements either party willingly agreed upon with the other,"[157] and some written contracts explicitly provided for the priority of such private agreements even over laws and decrees.[158] The Athenian

[153] See, for example, Barry 1995: 220–42; Giobbe 1991: 144. Although neither of the two principal Athenian clusters of words for persons and acts relating to prostitution—those cognate to *pernanai* (sell) and those cognate to *hetairein* (be a companion) (see n. 7)—inherently denominate prostitution as a sale of sexual services alone or as a sale of the body itself, scholars have interpreted and translated both terms as though they both carried the solitary meaning, in Dover's words, of "sale of one's own body." Dover [1978] 1989: 20. But cf. Henry (1996) who explicitly deems prostitution an exchange of "sexual service" for "other resource." Greek usage is equivocal: cf. Aiskhin. 1.29: "ἡταιρηκώς"· τὸν γὰρ τὸ σῶμα τὸ ἑαυτοῦ εφ' ὕβρει πεπρακότα; 31: καταγελάστως μὲν κεχρημένου τῷ ἑαυτοῦ σώματι; 40: πωλεῖν αὑτὸν προῃρημένος . . . ἐχρήσαντο τῷ σώματι <τῷ> Τιμάρχου; 51: ἡταιρηκέναι . . . ἐπὶ μισθῷ δὲ τὴν πρᾶξιν ποιούμενος.

[154] See, for example, Thomas 1992: 89, 149; Harris 1989: 68–70. But, as Stroud argues persuasively (1998: 45–48), new evidence and fresh consideration suggest that *syngraphai* may have been used more frequently and earlier than has been acknowledged by scholars, including me (see, e.g., 1992: 124–25).

[155] Pateman 1988: 191 (emphasis in original). Cf. Richards 1982: 115, 121; Ericcson 1980: 335–66; McIntosh 1978: 54.

[156] Thornton 1997: 152. For prostitutes as devotees and beneficiaries of Aphroditē, see, for example, Paus. 8.6.5, 10.15.1; Athēn. 588c, 590e.

[157] Dem. 56.2: τοῖς νόμοις τοῖς ὑμετέροις [sc. 'Αθηναίοις] οἳ κελεύουσι, ὅσα ἄν τις ἑκὼν ἕτερος ἑτέρῳ ὁμολογήσῃ κύρια εἶναι. Similarly: Dem. 42.12, 47.77; Hyper. 5.13; Dein. 3.4; Pl. *Symp.* 196c.

[158] The maritime loan document preserved at Dem. 35.10–13, the sole surviving text of an actual Athenian sea finance agreement, provides explicitly that as to the matters encompassed therein, "nothing else has greater validity than (this) contract" (κυριώτερον δὲ περὶ τούτων ἄλλο μηδὲν εἶναι τῆς συγγραφῆς). This clause is characterized in the text of Dem. 35 as giving the contract priority over laws and decrees (35.39: ἡ μὲν γὰρ συγγραφὴ οὐδὲν κυριώτερον ἐᾷ εἶναι τῶν ἐγγεγραμμένων, οὐδὲ προσφέρειν οὔτε νόμον οὔτε ψήφισμα οὔτ' ἄλλ' οὐδ' ὁτιοῦν πρὸς τὴν

government not only tolerated prostitution by *politai*—it sought to share in the revenues! Each year the *boulē* delivered to private tax collectors a list of prostitutes subject to the occupational levy on courtesans.[159] The names of "citizens" must have been found routinely among those listed, for Timarkhos's defenders, seeking to show that he had not prostituted himself, argued that his name was absent from these lists—a nugatory contention if the names of *politai* had not regularly appeared on the annual registers.[160] Indeed, one *politēs* engaged in prostitution, the orphan Diophantos, in seeking to collect four drachmas owed as payment for a sex act, even sought the active aid of the *archon*—who was charged with protecting minors who had lost their fathers![161]

Athenian moral outrage, in its turn, was reserved for forms of labor—in particular, "gainful employment," "useful labor," "the work ethic"—that are extolled under modern Western socialism and capitalism.[162] The Athenians instead valued economic arrangements that permitted leisurely dedication to cultural and social activities.[163] Although many free residents of Attika were self-employed, the Athenians abhorred extended labor for a single employer—a "job."[164] Since prostitution was often promiscuous, involving numerous customers for short periods of time, its practice by free persons was not inherently incompatible with Athenian occupational values (although, of course, potentially violative of other

συγγραφήν·). (On the authenticity of this document, see Purpura 1987: 203–35.) A similar provision was found in the written agreement that is the subject of litigation in Dem. 56.26. Cf. *I.G.* XII 7.67, 27, and 76.

[159] Aiskhin. 1.119: καθ' ἕκαστον ἐνιαυτὸν ἡ βουλὴ πωλεῖ τὸ πορνικὸν τέλος· καὶ τοὺς πριαμένους τὸ τέλος οὐκ εἰκάζειν, ἀλλ' ἀκριβῶς εἰδέναι τοὺς ταύτῃ χρωμένους τῇ ἐργασίᾳ. From the time of Caligula (first century C.E.) to the late fifth century, the Romans likewise imposed a tax on prostitutes (and on pimps). See McGinn 1989.

[160] Aiskhin. 1.119: Ὁπότε δὴ οὖν τετόλμηκα ἀντιγράψασθαι πεπορνευμένῳ Τιμάρχῳ μὴ ἐξεῖναι δημηγορεῖν, ἀπαιτεῖν φησὶ τὴν πρᾶξιν αὐτὴν οὐκ αἰτίαν κατηγόρου, ἀλλὰ μαρτυρίαν τελώνου τοῦ παρὰ Τιμάρχου τοῦτο ἐκλέξαντος τὸ τέλος.

[161] Aiskhin. 1.158: τίς γὰρ ὑμῶν τὸν ὀρφανὸν καλούμενον Διόφαντον οὐκ οἶδεν, ὃς τὸν ξένον πρὸς τὸν ἄρχοντα ἀπήγαγεν, . . . ἐπαιτιασάμενος τέτταρας δραχμὰς αὐτὸν ὑπὲρ τῆς πράξεως ταύτης ἀπεστερηκέναι;

[162] The academic inclination to view ancient societies through modernizing lenses has a long and deleterious pedigree, and a continuing vitality. Von Reden (1992), for example—while criticizing the modern tendency to view "ancient" labor as a form of production—imports to antiquity a value-laden conceptualization of work as "kulturellen Selbstdefinition." Instead, "we are badly in need of comparative studies which overcome the tendency to base judgment on the standards of the nineteenth and twentieth centuries, which in fact constitute the exception in terms of universal history" (Nippel 1985: 419).

[163] Aiskhinēs emphasizes that Timarkhos was under no financial pressure to work as a prostitute: ὑπέστη Τίμαρχος οὑτοσί, οὐδενὸς ὢν τῶν μετρίων ἐνδεής· πολλὴν γὰρ πάνυ κατέλιπεν ὁ πατὴρ αὐτῷ οὐσίαν (§42).

[164] See Chapter 5, pp. 142–43, esp. nn. 57, 61.

putative Athenian values). Negotiated terms memorialized in writing covering the personal provision of sexual services would have further differentiated prostitution from unequal forms of employment by a controlling "boss" or business, arrangements central to modern economies but unseemly for free persons under Athenian values. The contractual arrangements of Theodotos and Neaira reflected this Athenian orientation, as did the avoidance by free persons of sexual labor in a brothel[165] or financial work in a bank.[166]

Antagonism to work under a master should not be confused with antipathy to labor itself.[167] But in the fourth century a sector of Athenian opinion did object to any form of endeavor that—violating Athenian traditions of self-sufficiency and nonmonetary reciprocity—sought financial aggrandizement through the exchange of services or goods, or that promoted nontraditional, especially flagrant expenditures. Aiskhinēs's speech against Timarkhos invokes an Athenian law that prohibited participation as a speaker in the Assembly by those who had, inter alia, accepted compensation for sex, wasted family assets or inheritances, or had failed to provide for a parent.[168] Aiskhinēs emphasizes Timarkhos's dual economic crimes:[169] although financially able to pursue the Athenian ideal of self-sufficiency, in order to satisfy his dependence on excessive consumption (expensive meals, luxurious women, and gambling), Timarkhos has enslaved himself by accepting compensation for sexual services, and has wasted his paternal estate.[170]

[165] Prevailing scholarship assumes that "houses" were staffed by servile labor. Krenkel 1988: 1295: "slave boys were forced into prostitution; they would ply their trade in brothels and in private lodgings." Cf. Davidson 1997: 83–91.

[166] For the operation of *trapezai*—even at the highest levels of financial responsibility and remuneration—exclusively by slaves and family members, see Cohen 1992: 70–82.

[167] For the distinction, and an analysis of its historical basis, see Wood 1988: 126–45, esp. 139.

[168] Aiskhin. 1.28–32: "δοκιμασία ῥητόρων· ἐάν τις λέγῃ ἐν τῷ δήμῳ τὸν πατέρα τύπτων ἢ τὴν μητέρα, ἢ μὴ τρέφων, ἢ μὴ παρέχων οἴκησιν," τοῦτον οὐκ ἐᾷ λέγειν. . . . "ἢ τὰς στρατείας μὴ ἐστρατευμένος . . . ἢ τὴν ἀσπίδα ἀποβεβληκώς" . . . "ἢ πεπορνευμένος ἢ ἡταιρηκώς" . . . "ἢ τὰ πατρῷα κατεδηδοκώς, ἢ ὧν ἂν κληρονόμος γένηται" . . . "δοκιμασίαν μέν ἐπαγγειλάτω Ἀθηναίων ὁ βουλόμενος, οἷς ἔξεστιν." Beyond participation in the Assembly, a number of other positions of honor or opportunity were also foreclosed to prostitutes (Aiskhin. 1.19–20).

[169] He summarizes the gravamen of his complaint against Timarkhos: τί λέγω κατὰ Τιμάρχου, καὶ τίνα ποτ᾽ ἐστὶν ἃ ἀντιγέγραμμαι; δημηγορεῖν Τίμαρχον πεπορνευμένον καὶ τὴν πατρῴαν οὐσίαν κατεδηδοκότα (1.154). For the equation of "patrimonies squandered and lost, young men turned to prostitution," see Davidson 1993: 62–66.

[170] ὑπέστη Τίμαρχος οὑτοσί, οὐδενὸς ὢν τῶν μετρίων ἐνδεής· πολλὴν γὰρ πάνυ κατέλιπεν ὁ πατὴρ αὐτῷ οὐσίαν, ἣν οὗτος κατεδήδοκεν. . . . ἀλλ᾽ ἔπραξε ταῦτα δουλεύων ταῖς αἰσχίσταις ἡδοναῖς, ὀψοφαγίᾳ καὶ πολυτελείᾳ δείπνων καὶ αὐλητρίσι καὶ ἑταίραις καὶ κύβοις καὶ τοῖς ἄλλοις, ὑφ᾽ ὧν οὐδενὸς χρὴ κρατεῖσθαι τὸν γενναῖον καὶ ἐλεύθερον (1.42). Cf. 1.75–76: τί χρὴ λέγειν, ὅταν μειράκιον

In the monetized economy of fourth-century Athens, conservative opinion yearned for an earlier period when services were provided not as a commodity to be paid for but more "naturally" through the self-sufficiency of households.[171] In the *Politics*, Aristotle notes the relatively recent development of a new type of economic activity, which has adversely affected traditional values and methods.[172] The "monied mode of acquisition" (*khrēmatistikē ktētikē* [*tekhnē*]),[173] has arisen from the new dominance of economic activity by persons motivated by profit considerations ("making money from one another").[174] This individualistic pursuit of profit reflected society's new functioning through the exchange of goods and services for money, a process superseding the prior system of household production-consumption supplemented by barter based on social and political relations. Although Aristotle longs for the former arrangement, its replacement by impersonal coined money is what he actually portrays—and rues.[175] Modern scholars likewise sharply differentiate the nature of economic activity at Athens in the fourth century from that prevailing earlier.[176] While coinage of high value (useful only for settling large transactions) was introduced into mainland Greece

. . . πολυτελῆ δεῖπνα δειπνῇ ἀσύμβολον, καὶ αὐλητρίδας ἔχῃ καὶ ἑταίρας τὰς πολυτελεστάτας, καὶ κυβεύῃ, καὶ μηδὲν ἐκτίνῃ αὐτός, ἀλλ' ἕτερος ὑπὲρ ἐκείνου . . . ἀντὶ τούτων ἡδονάς τινας παρασκευάζειν τοῖς τὸ ἀργύριον προαναλίσκουσιν;

[171] "Naturally": κατὰ φύσιν (Aristot. *Pol.* 1258b1).

[172] Aristotle recognizes the introduction of coinage as the precondition to the development of retail trade (τὸ καπηλικόν), but explicitly separates an earlier, "simple" state of this trade from the profit-seeking, complex market activity existing in his own time: πορισθέντος οὖν ἤδη νομίσματος ἐκ τῆς ἀναγκαίας ἀλλαγῆς θάτερον εἶδος τῆς χρηματιστικῆς ἐγένετο, τὸ καπηλικόν, τὸ μὲν πρῶτον ἁπλῶς ἴσως γινόμενον, εἶτα δι' ἐμπειρίας ἤδη τεχνικώτερον, πόθεν καὶ πῶς μεταβαλλόμενον πλεῖστον ποιήσει κέρδος (*Pol.* 1257b1–5).

[173] Χρηματιστική, an adjective, is derived from the noun χρῆμα, which carried a dual meaning of "money" or of "property" (goods, chattel, etc.) When applied to the fourth-century market, as in the Aristotelian phrase ἡ κτητικὴ χρηματιστικὴ (τέχνη) (*Pol.* 1256b 40–41), the monetary notation is clearly present. Cf. Humphreys [1983] 1993: 12: "*chrēmatistikē*, the art of money-making."

[174] Aristot. *Pol.* 1258b1–4: τῆς δὲ μεταβλητικῆς ψεγομένης δικαίως (οὐ γὰρ κατὰ φύσιν ἀλλ' ἀπ' ἀλλήλων ἐστίν), εὐλογώτατα μισεῖται ἡ ὀβολοστατικὴ διὰ τὸ ἀπ' αὐτοῦ τοῦ νομίσματος εἶναι τὴν κτῆσιν καὶ οὐκ ἐφ' ὅπερ ἐπορίσθη. For Aristotle's view on the appropriate role of money, see *EN* 1133a19–29, 1133b10–28.

[175] Aristotle explicitly recognizes the dichotomy between focus on the ideal (περὶ τῆς μελλούσης κατ' εὐχὴν συνεστάναι πόλεως: *Pol.* 1325b36–38), and perception of actual phenomena (τῶν γιγνομένων διὰ τῆς αἰσθήσεως: 1328a20–21).

[176] Polanyi, Arensberg, and Pearson 1957: 67 ("in Aristotle's writings we possess an eyewitness account . . . of incipient market trading at its very first appearance in the history of civilization"). Cf. Meikle 1995a: 153–56 (critical of Finley 1970); von Reden 1995: 105–6; Davies 1971: 38–87. Mossé connects fourth-century developments in commercial banking with "l'apparition d'une mentalité nouvelle en contradiction avec l'ethique de la cité" (1972: 143).

by the late sixth century,[177] and became widespread in the fifth,[178] only in the fourth century were there substantial issuances of fractional coinage appropriate for retail trade,[179] and only after 350 did Athens produce a regular bronze coinage.[180] A torrent of recent studies has explored the revolutionary impact of this dissemination of coined money, which was a catalyst for the resultant commoditization of wealth and economic activity, a process that culminated ultimately in the detached monetary transactions of fourth-century Athens.[181]

A law purportedly limiting the political activity of men selling sexual services (or violating other traditional standards of economic conduct) must, therefore, be seen in the context of conservative objection to all profit-making endeavour.[182] For theorists unhappy with the commoditization of society, business people were objects of contempt whose activities should be discouraged or, if possible, eliminated. Aristotle expressed "the aristocratic attitude toward wealth, with its preference for landed property and its prejudice against trade and commerce."[183] Xenophon groups the "commercial crowd" (*agoraios okhlos*) with slaves and servants.[184] Theophrastos sees "endurance of shameful deeds and words"

[177] Von Reden (1995: 171–94) dates "the establishment of state coinage in the proper sense" to the introduction of the Athena-owl pieces late in the sixth century. Vickers (1985), opposing the general preference for a sixth-century attribution, dates the earliest Athenian "owls" to sometime between 479 and 462. For the opinio communis, see Karweise 1991; Howgego 1995: 2–6; Kroll 1997: 175 (who considers von Reden's chronology improperly late).

[178] Rutter 1981. Cf. Howgego 1995: 6ff.; Kraay 1976: 317.

[179] Kraay 1964. In Asia Minor, and in a few cities in southern Italy and Sicily, there may have been significant earlier issuances of fractional coins (Kim 1994, 1997; Price 1968, 1979).

[180] Kroll 1979. In the areas to the north and west of the Black Sea, Stancomb 1993 traces a similar monetary development betwen the mid-sixth and mid-fourth centuries.

[181] For the "fundamental difference between the social consequences of exchange based on coinage on the one hand and on gift exchange on the other" (von Reden 1997: 154) and similar paradigmatic economic alterations, see Kurke 1994: 42; Seaford 1994: 199. Cf. Seaford 1998; von Reden 1998; Steiner 1994; Kurke 1989. The cultural independence of money is analyzed critically, from an anthropological perspective, in Bloch and Parry, 1989.

[182] "The advance of commercial exchange, along with *polis* institutions, at the expense of reciprocity would, with its possibilities of mere egoism, bring into the moral world of every Athenian a new kind of anxiety" (Seaford 1998: 11). "[T]he trade of Athens, its monetary commercialism, its naval policy, and its democratic tendencies . . . were hated by the oligarchic parties of Athens" (Popper 1950: 173, with regard to the fifth century).

[183] Ross 1949: 243. "The class who got their living through marketing in the agora form a distinct 'illiberal' group in Aristotle's sociology of the polis" (Millett 1998: 219). Cf. Mulgan 1977: 49. For the differentiation of the "commercial crowd" (τὸν ἀγοραῖον ὄχλον) from other groups in society, see Aristot. *Pol.* 1291b14–30. Cf. Aristot. *Pol.* 1258b1–2, 1289b27–34 (discussed in Preface, n. 10). Meikle (1996) defends Aristotle's views as reasonable in the context of his metaphysics.

[184] *Hell.* 6.2.23 (τὸν ἀγοραῖόν τε ὄχλον καὶ τὸν τῶν θεραπόντων καὶ τὸν τῶν ἀνδραπόδων).

as characteristic of the businessman (*Khar.* 6.2). For Plato, "market people" (*agoraioi anthrōpoi*) pursued monetary profit because they were incapable of anything more acceptable.[185] Decent societies would marginalize such people and minimize their activities. According to Aristotle, many oligarchic states wisely and absolutely prohibited *politai* from engaging actively in business.[186] Aristocratic thought also condemned as inherently incompatible with "citizenship" all "banausic" pursuits—production or trading of goods, labor for monetary compensation, even professional acting or musical performances.[187] Theophrastos is dismissive not only of operating brothels, but even of innkeeping (and tax collection!).[188] Plato joins as disreputable prostitution, shoemaking, and fish marketing.[189] Xenophōn finds the commercialization of sex no less disgusting than charging for education.[190] And prostitution was the paradigmatic commercial exchange of sex for compensation. Although the Athenian state did not ban this business, the existence of a law forbidding such economic activity by its political leaders, albeit often dismissed as a "dead letter,"[191] gave Aiskhinēs the opportunity to strike at Demosthenes through the indictment of Timarkhos.

But Athens was not monolithic, and such views—even where legitimatized by the force of traditional law (*patrios nomos*)—could coexist with the reality of a "city [that] lived entirely by cash transactions," an Athens whose *politai* were "farmers, fishermen, shopkeepers, market

[185] Pl. *Rep.* 371c: οἱ ἀσθενέστατοι τὰ σώματα καὶ ἀχρεῖοί τι ἄλλο ἔργον πράττειν. Cf. Pl. *Protag.* 347c (τῶν φαύλων καὶ ἀγοραίων ἀνθρώπων); *Polit.* 289e (οἱ μὲν κατ᾽ ἀγοράς, οἱ δὲ . . . νόμισμά τε πρὸς τὰ ἄλλα καὶ αὐτὸ πρὸς αὐτὸ διαμείβοντες . . . μῶν τῆς πολιτικῆς ἀμφισβητήσουσί τι;). Cf. *Laws* 705a.

[186] χρηματίζεσθαι (*Pol.* 1316b3–5). Cf. Ober 1991: 125.

[187] On the virulent opposition to *banausia*, see, for example, *Pol.* 1337b18–22; 1258b25–27, 33–39; 1260a41–b2; 1277b33–1278a13; 1277a32–b7; 1341b8–18. Cf. Humphreys 1978, esp. 148–49.

[188] *Khar.* 6.5: δεινὸς δὲ καὶ πανδοκεῦσαι καὶ πορνοβοσκῆσαι καὶ τελωνῆσαι καὶ μηδεμίαν αἰσχρὰν ἐργασίαν ἀποδοκιμάσαι. Aiskhinēs is likewise critical of the business of brothel keeping (1.188).

[189] *Khrm.* 163b: οἴει οὖν αὐτόν . . . οὐδενὶ ἂν ὄνειδος φάναι εἶναι σκυτοτομοῦντι ἢ ταριχοπωλοῦντι ἢ ἐπ᾽ οἰκήματος καθημένῳ;

[190] *Apom.* 1.6.13: παρ᾽ ἡμῖν νομίζεται τὴν ὥραν καὶ τὴν σοφίαν ὁμοίως μὲν καλόν, ὁμοίως δὲ αἰσχρὸν διατίθεσθαι εἶναι. τήν τε γὰρ ὥραν ἐὰν μέν τις ἀργυρίου πωλῇ τῷ βουλομένῳ, πόρνον αὐτὸν ἀποκαλοῦσιν, ἐὰν δέ τις, ὃν ἂν γνῷ καλόν τε κἀγαθὸν ἐραστὴν ὄντα, τοῦτον φίλον ἑαυτῷ ποιῆται, σώφρονα νομίζομεν. καὶ τὴν σοφίαν ὡσαύτως. . . .

[191] Cf. Davidson 1997: 252: "The real figures of authority, the real 'leaders' of the city were the *rhētores*, those who made speeches in the Assembly . . . everyone was assumed to be eligible unless challenged. Such challenges were issued very rarely. I know of only one certain example in the whole history of the democracy . . . Timarchus." But even Timarkhos (prior to his politically motivated indictment) for years was openly active in the Assembly (even holding public office). See Dover [1978] 1989: 19.

gardeners and small craftsmen" (Humphreys 1978: 148), and prostitutes. We need not be discomfited by the dissonance reflected in the persistence of legislative disincentives to "citizen" prostitution alongside the widespread, lawful purchase of sex from "citizen" prostitutes. Athenian culture was "fraught with ambivalence, ambiguity and conflict."[192] Although classicists and ancient historians have long been in thrall—albeit often without conscious recognition—to "functionalist" doctrines that stress the "social solidarity," "structural equilibrium," or "cultural uniformity" of societies,[193] a striving for theoretical consistency necessarily obliterates the discontinuities, contradictions, and unintegrated deviations that are inherent in complex and dynamic civilizations.[194] The Athenians were well aware of the complexity, and inconsistency, of their civilization, especially in sexual mores: "in other *poleis* erotic conventions are easy to understand and well-defined, but at Athens they are *poikilos*"—complex, intricate, many-hued.[195] Conservative thinking at Athens may have nostalgically preferred an Attika where *politai* did not sell their sexual services (or other commodities and skills). But this preference did not reflect the Athens of reality.

[192] D. Cohen 1991b: 21. Cf. Larmour, Miller, and Platter 1998: 27.

[193] See Leach's early criticism (1965:7) of British anthropologists' adherence to functional ideology. Cf. Cohen 1995: 9–13.

[194] Cf. Keiser 1986; Rueschemeyer 1984: 134; Bourdieu 1977: 98. Dougherty properly urges us "to read the multiplicity of narratives that represent Athenians as Athenians in such a way that we preserve their contradictions" (1996: 251).

[195] Pl. *Symp.* 182a7–9: ὁ περὶ τὸν ἔρωτα νόμος ἐν μὲν ταῖς ἄλλαις πόλεσι νοῆσαι ῥᾴδιος, ἁπλῶς γὰρ ὥρισται· ὁ δ' ἐνθάδε καὶ ἐν Λακεδαίμονι ποικίλος.

✦ WORKS CITED ✦

Adam, S. 1989. "Aspects de la sécurité de la navigation dans l'Antiquité grecque." In *Symposion 1985*, edited by A. Biscardi, J. Mélèze-Modrzejewski, and G. Thür, pp. 283–91. Cologne.

Adams, C. D. 1919. *The Speeches of Aeschines*. Cambridge, Mass.

Alcock, S. E. 1993. *Graecia Capta: The Landscapes of Roman Greece*. Cambridge.

Alcoff, L. 1990. "Feminist Politics and Foucault: The Limits to a Collaboration." In *Crises in Continental Philosophy*, edited by A. B. Dallery, C. E. Scott, and P. H. Roberts, pp. 69–86. Albany, N.Y.

Aleshire, S. B. 1994. "The Demos and the Priests: The Selection of Sacred Officials at Athens from Cleisthenes to Augustus." In *Ritual, Finance, Politics: Athenian Democratic Accounts Presented to David Lewis*, edited by R. Osborne and S. Hornblower, pp. 325–37. Oxford.

Alföldy, G. 1972. "Die Freilassung von Sklaven und die Struktur der Sklaverei in der römischen Kaiserzeit." *Rivista Storica dell'Antichità* 2: 97ff.

Allen, D. 1997. "Imprisonment in Classical Athens." *Classical Quarterly* 47: 121–35.

Alty, J.H.M. 1982. "Dorians and Ionians." *Journal of Hellenic Studies* 102: 1–14.

Amit, M. 1973. *Great and Small Poleis*. Brussels.

Ampolo, C. 1986. "Il pane quotidiano delle città antiche fra economia e anthropologia." *Opus* 5: 143–51.

Anderson, B. 1991. *Imagined Communities: Reflections on the Origins and Spread of Nationalism*. 2nd ed. London.

Andreades, A. [1933] 1979. *A History of Greek Public Finance*. Vol. 1. Translated by C. N. Brown. New York.

Andreou, J. 1994. "Ο δήμος των Αιξωνίδων Αλών." In *The Archaeology of Athens and Attica under the Democracy*, edited by W.D.E. Coulson, O. Palagia, T. L. Shear Jr., H. A. Shapiro, and F. J. Frost, pp. 191–209. Oxford.

Andrewes, A. 1961. "Philochoros on Phratries." *Journal of Hellenic Studies* 81: 1–15.

———. 1982. "The Tyranny of Peisistratus." In *Cambridge Ancient History*, edited by J. Boardman and N.G.L. Hammond, vol. 3, pt. 3. 2nd ed. Cambridge.

Angel, J. L. 1947. "The Length of Life in Ancient Greece." *Journal of Gerontology* 2: 18–24.

———. 1975. "Paleoecology, Paleodemography and Health." In *Population, Ecology and Social Evolution*, edited by S. Polgar, pp. 167–90. The Hague.

Annequin, J. 1992. "Recherches sur l'esclavage et la dépendance." *Dialogues d'histoire ancienne* 18, no. 2: 271–300.

Anonymous. 1828. *A Rejected Essay on the National Character of the Athenians*. Edinburgh.

Appadurai, A. 1990. "Disjuncture and Difference in the Global Cultural Economy." *Public Culture* 2, no. 2: 1–24.

Arafat, K., and C. Morgan. 1994. "Athens, Etruria and the Heuneburg: Mutual Misconceptions in the Study of Greek-Barbarian Relations." In *Classical Greece: Ancient Histories and Modern Archaeologies*, edited by I. Morris, pp. 108–34. Cambridge.

Armstrong, J. 1981. *Nations before Nationalism*. Chapel Hill.

Aron, R. 1950. *La Philosophie critique de l'histoire, essai sur une théorie allemande de l'histoire*. Paris.

Arrigoni, E. 1969–71. "Στοιχεῖα πρός ἀναπαράστασιν τοῦ τοπίου τῆς Ἀττικῆς κατά την κλασσικήν ἐποχήν." Ἀθηνᾶ 71: 332–86; 74: 25–86.

Asheri, D. 1960. "L'οἶκος ἔρημος nel diritto successorio attico." *Archivio Giuridico* 28: 7–24.

Asheri, D. 1963. "Laws of Inheritance, Distribution of Land and Political Constitutions in Ancient Greece." *Historia* 12: 1–21.

Aubert, J.-J. 1994. *Business Managers in Ancient Rome: A Social and Economic Study of* Institores, *200 B.C.–A.D. 250*. Leiden.

Auffret, S. 1987. *Mélanippe la philosophe*. Paris.

Aurenche, O. 1974. *Les groupes d'Alcibiade, de Léogoras et de Teucros*. Paris.

Bakhuizen, S. C. 1989. "The Ethnos of the Boiotians." In *Boiotika. Vorträge vom 5. Internationalen Böotien-Kolloquium*, edited by H. Beister and J. Buckler, pp. 65–72. Munich.

Baltrusch, E. 1994. *Symmachie und Spondai. Untersuchungen zum griechischen Volkerrecht der archaischen und klassischen Zeit*. Berlin.

Barber, B. 1984. *Strong Democracy: Participatory Politics for a New Age*. Berkeley.

Barlow, S. 1971. *The Imagery of Euripides*. London.

Barry, K. 1995. *The Prostitution of Sexuality*. New York.

Barth, F. 1969. *Ethnic Groups and Boundaries: The Social Organization of Cultural Difference*. Bergen.

Baslez, M. F. 1984. *L'étranger dans la Grèce antique*. Paris.

Baudrillard, J. 1988. *Jean Baudrillard: Selected Writings*. Edited by M. Poster. Cambridge.

Beasley, J. D. 1963. *Attic Red-Figure Vase-Painters*. 2nd ed. Oxford.

Beauchet, L. [1897] 1969. *Histoire du droit privé de la république athénienne*. 4 vols. Amsterdam.

Beauvoir, S. de. 1974. *The Second Sex*. Translated by H. M. Parshley. New York.

Beck, H. 1997. *Polis und Koinon*. Stuttgart.

Beloch, K. J. 1886. *Die Bevölkerung der Griechisch-Römischen Welt*. Leipzig.

———. 1912–27. *Griechische Geschichte*. 4 vols. 2d ed. Strassburg, Berlin, and Leipzig.

Bérard, C. 1974. *Anodoi: Essai sur l'imagerie des passages chthoniens*. Neuchâtel.

Bergese, L. B. 1995. *Tra* ethne *e* poleis. Pagine di storia Arcade. Pisa.

Berktold, P., et al. 1996. *Arkananien*. Würzburg.

Berlin, I. and P.D. Morgan, eds. 1991. *The Slaves' Economy*. London.

Berndt, T. 1881. *De ironia Menexeni*. Monasterii Guestfalorum.

Bertrand, J. M. 1992. *Cités et royaumes du monde grec: Espace et politique*. Paris.

Biblical Archaeology Review. 1997. "Face to Face: Biblical Minimalists Meet Their Challenges." *Biblical Archaeology Review* 23–24: 26–42, 66.

Bibliographie zur Antiken Sklaverie. 1983. Edited by E. Hermann. Bochum.

Bicknell, P. J. 1982. "Axiochus, Alkibiadou, Aspasia and Aspasios." *Acta Classica* 51: 240–50.

Bien, G. 1973. *Die Grundlegung der politischen Philosophie bei Aristoteles*. Freiburg.

Biezunska-Malowist, I. 1966. "Les esclaves payant l'apophora dans l'Egypt gréco-romaine." *Journal of Juristic Papyrology* 15: 65–72.

Bilde, P., T. Engberg-Pedersen, L. Hanestad, and J. Zahle, eds. 1992. Ethnicity in Hellenistic Egypt. Aarhus.

Biscardi, A. 1970. "Stato civile (presso i Greci)." *Novissimo Dig. Italiano* 18: 301ff.

———. 1991. Αρχαίο ελληνικό δίκαιο. Translated by P. Dimakis. Athens. Originally published as *Diritto greco antico*. Milan, 1982.

Bix, B. 1993. *Law, Language, and Legal Determinacy*. Oxford.

Blass, F. [1887–98] 1962. *Die attische Beredsamkeit*. 2d ed. 3 vols. in 4. Hildesheim.

Bleicken, J. 1985. *Die athenische Demokratie*. Paderborn.

Bloch, I. 1912. *Die Prostitution*. Berlin.

Bloch, M., and J. Parry, eds. 1989. *Money and the Morality of Exchange*. Cambridge.

Bloedow, E. 1975. "Aspasia and the 'Mystery' of the *Menexenos*." *Wiener Studien*, n.s., 9: 32–48.

Boegehold, A. L. 1972. "The Establishment of a Central Archive at Athens." *American Journal of Archaeology* 76: 23–30.

———. 1994. "Perikles' Citizenship Law of 451/0 B.C." In Boegehold and Scafuro 1994, pp. 57–66. Baltimore.

Boegehold, A. L., and A. C. Scafuro, eds. 1994. *Athenian Identity and Civic Ideology*. Baltimore.

Bogaert, R. 1986. *Grundzüge des Bankwesens im alten Griechenland*. Konstanzer Althistorische Vorträge und Forschungen, vol. 18. Konstanz.

Bongenaar, J.C.A.M. 1933. *Isocrates' trapeziticus vertaald en toegelicht*. Utrecht.

Bonner, R. J. 1910. "The Boeotian Federal Constitution." *Classical Philology* 5: 405–417.

———. [1933] 1976. *Aspects of Antiquity*. Berkeley.

Bordes, J. 1982. *Politeia dans la pensée grecque jusqu'à Aristote*. Paris.

Bourdieu, P. 1977. *Outline of a Theory of Practice*. Translated by Richard Nice. Cambridge.

Bourriot, F. 1976. *Recherches sur la nature du genos. Etude d'histoire sociale athénienne—périodes archaique et classique*. Lille.

Bowersock, G. W., ed. 1968. *Xenophon VII. Scripta Minora*. Cambridge, Mass.

Bradeen, D. W. 1969. "The Athenian Casualty Lists." *Classical Quarterly* 19: 145–59.

Bradley, K. R. 1984. *Slaves and Masters in the Roman Empire*. Brussels.

———. 1997. "The Problem of Slavery in Classical Culture." *Classical Philology* 92: 273–82.

Bremmer, J. 1989. "Greek Pederasty and Modern Homosexuality." In *From Sappho to De Sade: Moments in the History of Sexuality*, edited by J. Bremmer, pp. 1–14. London.

Brock, R. 1994. "The Labour of Women in Classical Athens." *Classical Quarterly*, n.s., 44: 336–46.

Brommer, F. 1957. "Attische Könige." In *Mélanges E. Langlotz*, pp. 152–64. Bonn.

Broneer, O. 1933. "Excavations on the North Slope of the Acropolis." *Hesperia* 2, no. 3: 329–417.

Bruce, I.A.F. 1967. *An Historical Commentary on the Hellenica Oxyrhynchia*. Cambridge.

Bruhns, H. 1987–89. "La cité antique de Max Weber." *Opus* 6–8.

Brun, P. 1983. *Eisphora, syntaxis, stratiotika*. Paris.

Bulmer, M., and A. M. Ress, eds. 1996. *Citizenship Today: The Contemporary Relevance of T. H. Marshall*. London.

Burford, A. 1963. "The Builders of the Parthenon." *Parthenos and Parthenon. Greece & Rome*, suppl. 10: 23–35.

———. 1972. *Craftsmen in Greek and Roman Society*. London.

———. 1993. *Land and Labor in the Greek World*. Baltimore.

Burke, E. M. 1990. "Athens after the Peloponnesian War: Restoration Efforts and the Role of Maritime Commerce." *Classical Antiquity* 9: 1–13.

———. 1992. "The Economy of Athens in the Classical Era." *Transactions of the American Philological Association* 122: 199–226.

Burkert, W. 1985. *Greek Religion, Archaic and Classical*. Oxford. Translation of *Griechische Religion der archäische und klassische Epoche*. Stuttgart, 1977.

Burnett, A. P. 1970. *Ion by Euripides*. Englewood Cliffs, N.J.

Buruma, I. 1998. "Down and Out in East Tokyo." *New York Review of Books* 45 (June 25): 9–12.

Bushala, E. W. 1969. "The Pallake of Philoneus." *American Journal of Philology* 90: 65–72.

Busolt, G., and H. Swoboda. 1920, 1926. *Griechische Staatskunde*. 2 vols. Munich.

Butler, J. 1990. *Gender Trouble: Feminism and the Subversion of Identity*. New York.

Cairns, D. L. 1996. "*Hybris*, Dishonour, and Thinking Big." *Journal of Hellenic Studies* 116: 1–32.

Calame, C. 1989. "Entre rapports de parenté et relations civiques: Aphrodite l'hétaïre au banquet politique des hétairoi." In *Aux sources de la puissance: Sociabilité et parenté*. Rouen.

———. 1996. *L'éros dans la Grèce antique*. Paris. Originally published as *I Greci e l'eros: Simboli, practice, luoghi*. Bari, 1992.

Calderini, A. [1908] 1965. *La manomissione e la condizione dei liberti in Grecia*. Rome.

Campbell, J. 1991. "As 'a Kind of Freeman'? Slaves' Market-Related Activities in the South Carolina Upcountry, 1800–1860." In Berlin and Morgan 1991, pp. 131–69.

Canfora, L. 1995. "The Citizen." In *The Greeks*, edited by J.-P. Vernant, pp. 120–52. Translation of *L'uomo greco*. 1991.

Cantarella, E. 1983. "Spunti di riflessione critica su *hybris* e *timē* in Omero." In *Symposion 1979*, edited by P. Dimakis, pp. 85–96. Cologne.

Cantarella, E. 1987. *Pandora's Daughters: The Role and Status of Women in Greek and Roman Antiquity.* Translated with revisions by M. B. Fant. Baltimore. Originally published as *L'ambiguo malanno.* 1981.

———. 1988. *Secondo natura.* Rome.

———. 1991. "Moicheia. Reconsidering a Problem." In *Symposion 1990,* edited by M. Gagarin, pp. 289–96. Cologne.

Carey, C. 1988. "A Note on Torture in Athenian Homicide Cases." *Historia* 37: 241–45.

———, ed. 1989. *Lysias: Selected Speeches.* Cambridge.

———. 1991. "Apollodoros' Mother: The Wives of Enfranchised Aliens in Athens." *Classical Quarterly* 41: 84–89.

———, ed. 1992. *Apollodoros against Neaira [Demosthenes] 59.* Warminster.

Cargill, J. 1981. *The Second Athenian League: Empire or Free Alliance?* Berkeley.

———. 1995. *Athenian Settlements of the Fourth Century* B.C. Leiden.

Cartledge, P. 1993. *The Greeks: A Portrait of Self and Others.* Oxford.

———. 1996. "Comparatively Equal." In Ober and Hedrick, 1996, pp. 175–85.

Cartledge, P., P. Millett, and S. von Reden. 1998. *Kosmos: Essays in Order, Conflict and Community in Classical Athens.* Cambridge.

Casson, L. 1971. *Ships and Seamanship in the Ancient World.* Princeton.

Castoriadis, C. 1987. *The Imaginary Institution of Society,* translated by K. Blamey. Cambridge, Mass. Originally published as *L'Institution imaginaire de la société.* 1975.

———. 1991. *Philosophy, Politics, Autonomy: Essays in Political Philosophy.* Edited by D. A. Curtis. New York.

Chaniotis, A. 1997. Review of Hansen 1996f and 1996g. In *Bryn Mawr Classical Review,* 16 July. An e-journal at owner_bmcr_l@brynmawr.edu.

Chantraine, P. 1956. "Le suffixe -ikos." In *Etudes sur le vocabulaire grec,* pp. 97–171. Paris.

———. 1968, 1970. *Dictionnaire étymologique de la Langue grecque.* 2 vols. Paris.

Chapot, V. 1929. "ASTOS." *Revue des études anciennes* 31: 7–12.

Charles, J. F. 1938. *Statutes of Limitations at Athens.* Chicago.

Chatterjee, P. 1986. *Nationalist Thought and the Colonial World.* Tokyo.

———. 1993. *The Nation and Its Fragments.* Princeton.

Chirassi Colombo, I. 1984. "L'inganno di Afrodite." In *I labirinti dell'Eros: materiali per una ricerca sull' identità femminile,* pp. 109–21. Florence.

Christ, M. R. 1990. "Liturgical Avoidance and *Antidosis* in Classical Athens." *Transactions of the American Philological Association* 120: 147–69.

Clairmont, C. W. 1983. *Patrios Nomos: Public Burial in Athens during the Fifth and Fourth Centuries B.C.* Oxford.

Clark, M. 1990. "The Date of I.G. II[2] 1604." *Annual of the British School at Athens* 85: 47–67.

Clark, S.R.L. 1982. "Aristotle's Woman." *History of Political Thought* 3, no. 2: 177–91.

Clavaud, R. 1980. *Le Ménexène de Platon et la rhétorique de son temps.* Paris.

Clerc, M. 1893. *Les métèques athéniens.* Paris.

Cochrane, C. N. 1944. *Christianity and Classical Culture: A Study of Thought and Action from Augustus to Augustine.* Rev. ed. London.

Cohen, D. 1989. "Seclusion, Separation, and the Status of Women." *Greece & Rome,* 2nd ser., 36: 1–15.

———. 1990. "The Social Context of Adultery at Athens." In *Nomos: Essays in Athenian Law, Politics and Society,* edited by P. Cartledge, P. Millett, and S. Todd, pp. 147–65. Cambridge.

———. 1991a. "Sexuality, Violence, and the Athenian Law of *Hubris.*" *Greece & Rome* 38: 171–88.

———. 1991b. *Law, Sexuality and Society: The Enforcement of Morals in Classical Athens.* Cambridge.

———. 1995. *Law, Violence and Community in Classical Athens*. Cambridge.

Cohen, E. 1973. *Ancient Athenian Maritime Courts*. Princeton.

———. 1990. "Commercial Lending by Athenian Banks: Cliometric Fallacies and Forensic Methodology." *Classical Philology* 85: 177–90.

Cohen, E. 1991. "Banking as a 'Family Business': Legal Adaptations Affecting Wives and Slaves." In *Symposion 1990*, edited by M. Gagarin, pp. 239–63. Cologne.

———. 1992. *Athenian Economy and Society: A Banking Perspective*. Princeton.

———. 1994a. "Status and Contract at Athens." In *Symposion 1993*, edited by G. Thür, pp. 141–52. Cologne.

———. 1994b. "Τράπεζες και τραπεζικές εργασίες στην κλασική Αθήνα—Η νομική θέση των γυναικών και των δούλων." *Συμβολές στην έρευνα του αρχαίου ελληνικού και ελληνιστικού δικαίου* 2: 149–75.

Cole, D. R. 1976. " 'Asty' and 'Polis': 'City' in Early Greek." Ph.D. dissertation, Stanford University.

Cole, S. 1984. "Greek Sanctions against Sexual Assault." *Classical Philology* 79: 97–113.

Colin, G. 1938. "L'oraison funèbre d'Hypéride, ses rapports avec les autres oraisons funèbres athéniennes." *Revue des études grecques* 51: 209–66, 305–94.

———, ed. 1946. *Hypéride*. Paris.

Collard, C., M. J. Cropp, and K. H. Lee, eds. [1995] 1997. *Euripides: Selected Fragmentary Plays*. Vol. 1. Reprinted with corrections. Warminster.

Connor, W. 1978. "A Nation Is a Nation, Is a State, Is an Ethnic Group, Is a . . ." *Ethnic and Racial Studies* 1: 377–400.

Connor, W. R. 1970. "Theseus in Classical Athens." In *Quest for Theseus*, edited by A. G. Ward, pp. 143–74. London.

———. 1983. *Thucydides*. Princeton.

———. 1987. "Tribes, Festivals and Processions: Civic Ceremonial and Political Manipulation in Archaic Greece." *Journal of Hellenic Studies* 107: 40–50.

———. 1988. " 'Sacred' and 'Secular.' Ἱερὰ καὶ Ὅσια and the Classical Athenian Concept of the State." *Ancient Society* 19: 161–88.

———. 1990. "City Dionysia and Athenian Democracy." In *Aspects of Athenian Democracy*, edited by W. R. Connor, M. H. Hansen, K. A. Raaflaub, and B. S. Strauss, pp. 7–32. Copenhagen.

———. 1993. "The Ionian Era of Athenian Civic Identity." *Proceedings of the American Philosophical Society* 137, no. 2: 194–206.

———. 1994. "The Problem of Athenian Civic Identity." In Boegehold and Scafuro 1994, pp. 34–44. Baltimore.

———. 1996a. "Religion and Power in the Ancient Greek World." *Acta Universitatis Upsaliensis: Boreas* 24: 115–20.

———. 1996b. "Civil Society, Dionysiac Festival, and the Athenian Democracy." In Ober and Hedrick 1996, pp. 217–26. Princeton.

Cook, A. B. 1940. *Zeus: A Study in Ancient Religion*. 3 vols. Cambridge.

Coumanoudis, S. N., and D. C. Gofas. 1978. "Deux décrets inédits d'Éleusis." *Revue des études grecques* 91: 289–306. Reprinted in Gofas 1993, pp. 111–22.

Cousin, G., and F. Dürrbach. 1885. "Inscriptions de Lemnos." *Bulletin de correspondance hellénique* 45–64.

Cox, C. A. 1988. "Sibling Relationships in Classical Athens: Brother-Sister Ties." *Journal of Family History* 13: 377–95.

———. 1998. *Household Interests: Property, Marriage Strategies and Family Dynamics in Ancient Athens*. Princeton.

Crawford, M. H. 1974. *Roman Republican Coinage*. 2 vols. Cambridge.

Crawford, M. H., and D. Whitehead. 1983. *Archaic and Classical Greece*. Cambridge.

Crone, P. 1980. *Slaves on Horses: The Evolution of the Islamic Polity.* Cambridge.

Curty, O. 1995. *Les parentés légendaires entre cites grecques. Catalogue raisonné des inscriptions contenant le terme συγγένεια et analyse critique*. Geneva.

Damsgaard-Madsen, A. 1988. "Attic Funeral Inscriptions: Their Use as Historical Sources and Some Preliminary Results." In *Studies in Ancient History and Numismatics Presented to Rudi Thomsen,* edited by A. Damsgaard-Madsen, E. Christiansen, and E. Hallager, pp. 55–68. Aarhus.

Danforth, L. M. 1995. *The Macedonian Conflict: Ethnic Nationalism in a Transnational World.* Princeton.

Dareste, R., B. Haussoullier, and T. Reinach, eds. [1892–1904] 1965. *Recueil des inscriptions juridiques grecques.* 1st ser., 1892–95; 2d ser., 1898–1904. Paris.

D'Arms, J. H. 1981. *Commerce and Social Standing in Ancient Rome.* Cambridge, Mass.

Darnton, R. 1984. *The Great Cat Massacre and Other Episodes in French Cultural History.* New York.

Daux, G. 1963. "La Grande Démarchie: Un nouveau calendrier sacrificiel d'Attique." *Bulletin de correspondance hellénique* 87: 603–34.

———. 1983. "Le calendrier de Thorikos au Musée J. Paul Getty." *L'Antiquité classique* 52: 150–74.

David, E. 1986. "A Preliminary Stage of Cleisthenes' Reforms." *Classical Antiquity* 5: 1–13.

Davidson, J. N. 1993. "Fish, Sex and Revolution in Athens." *Classical Quarterly* 43: 53–66.

———. 1994. "Consuming Passions: Appetite, Addiction and Spending in Classical Athens." Ph.D. dissertation, Trinity College, Oxford University.

———. 1997. *Courtesans and Fishcakes: The Consuming Passions of Classical Athens.* London.

Davies, J. K. 1971. *Athenian Propertied Families, 600–300 B.C.* Oxford.

———. 1977–78. "Athenian Citizenship: The Descent Group and the Alternatives." *Classical Journal* 73: 105–21.

———. 1978. *Democracy and Classical Greece.* Stanford.

———. 1981. *Wealth and the Power of Wealth in Classical Athens.* Salem, N.H.

Davies, P. R. 1992. *In Search of "Ancient Israel."* Sheffield.

Davis, D. B. 1996. "At the Heart of Slavery." *New York Review of Books* 43(16): 51–54.

———. 1998. "The Problem of Slavery." In *A Historical Guide to Slavery,* edited by S. Drescher and S. Engerman, pp. ix–xviii. Oxford.

Dayal, S. 1996. "Postcolonialism's Possibilities: Subcontinental Diasporic Intervention." *Cultural Critique* 33: 113–49.

Dean-Jones, L. 1995. "Menexenus—son of Socrates." *Classical Quarterly* 45: 51–57.

Derrick, J. 1975. *Africa's Slaves Today.* London.

Detienne, M. 1977. *The Gardens of Adonis: Spices in Greek Mythology.* Sussex. Originally published as *Les jardins d'Adonis*. Paris, 1971.

Deubner, L. 1908–26. "Birth." In *Encyclopaedia of Religion and Ethics,* edited by J. Hastings, 2: 648–49.

———. [1932] 1966. *Attische Feste.* Hildesheim.

Deutsch, K. W. 1966. *Nationalism and Social Communication.* 2d ed. New York.

de Vos, G. A. 1995. "Ethnic Pluralism: Conflict and Accommodation." In *Ethnic Identity: Creation, Conflict, and Accommodation,*" edited by L. Romanucci-Ross and G. de Vos, pp. 15–47. Walnut Creek, Cal.

de Vos, G. A., and L. Romanucci-Ross. 1995. "Ethnic Identity: A Psychocultural Perspective." In *Ethnic Identity: Creation, Conflict, and Accommodation,*" edited by L. Romanucci-Ross and G. de Vos, pp. 349–79. Walnut Creek, Cal.

de Vos, G. A., and H. Wagatsuma. 1995. "Cultural Identity in Japan." In *Ethnic Identity: Creation, Conflict, and Accommodation,*" edited by L. Romanucci-Ross and G. de Vos, pp. 264–97. Walnut Creek, Cal.

Dewald, C. 1981. "Women and Culture in Herodotus' Histories." *Women's Studies* 8: 93–127.
Diamond, I., and Lee Quinby, eds. 1988. *Feminism and Foucault: Reflections on Resistance*. Boston.
Diggle, J. 1994. *Euripidea: Collected Essays*. Oxford.
Diller, A. 1932. "The Decree of Demophilus, 346–345 B.C." *Transactions of the American Philological Association* 63: 193–205.
———. 1937. *Race Mixture among the Greeks before Alexander.* Urbana, Ill.
Dimakis, P. D. N.d. Ὁ θεσμὸς τῆς προικὸς κατὰ τὸ ἀρχαῖον ἑλληνικὸν δίκαιον. Athens.
Dimopoulou-Piliouni, A. Forthcoming. "La Constitution des Athéniens du Pseudo-Xénophon, une approche comparative." In *Symposion 1997*. Cologne.
Dittenberger, W. 1906, 1907. "Ethnika und Verwandtes." *Hermes* 41: 78–102, 161–219; 42: 1–34.
Doblhofer, G. 1994. *Vergewaltigung in der Antike*. Beiträge zur Altertumskunde 46. Stuttgart.
Donlan, W. 1985. "The Social Groups of Dark Age Greece." *Classical Philology* 80: 293–308.
Dougherty, C. 1996. "Democratic Contradictions and the Synoptic Illusion of Euripides' *Ion*." In Ober and Hedrick 1996, pp. 249–70.
Douglas, A. E. 1956. "Cicero, Quintilian, and the Canon of Ten Attic Orators." *Mnemosyne* 9: 30–40.
Dover, K. J. 1964. "Eros and Nomos." *Bulletin of the Institute of Classical Studies* 9: 31–42.
———. 1968. *Lysias and the Corpus Lysiacum*. Berkeley.
———. [1973] 1984. "Classical Greek Attitudes to Sexual Behaviour." In *Women in the Ancient World: The* Arethusa *Papers*, edited by J. Peradotto and J. P. Sullivan, pp. 143–57. Originally published in *Arethusa* 6: 59–73.
———. 1974. *Greek Popular Morality in the Time of Plato and Aristotle*. Berkeley.
———. [1978] 1989. *Greek Homosexuality*. London.
———. 1989. "Anecdotes, Gossip and Scandal." In *The Greeks and Their Legacy: Collected Papers*, vol. 2, *Prose Literature, History, Society, Transmission, Influence*, pp. 45–52. Oxford.
Dreher, M. 1995. "Poleis und Nicht-Poleis im Zweiten Athenischen Seebund." In Hansen 1995d, pp. 171–200.
Dreyfus, H., and P. Rabinow. 1983. *Michel Foucault: Beyond Structuralism and Hermeneutics*. Chicago.
Du Boulay, J. 1974. *Portrait of a Greek Mountain Village*. Oxford.
Duby, G. 1974. "Histoire sociale et idéologies des sociétés." In *Faire de l'histoire*, edited by J. le Goff and P. Nora, pp. 147–68. Paris.
Ducat, J. 1975. "Les thèmes des récits de la fondation de Rhégion." In *Mélanges G. Daux*, pp. 93–114. Paris.
Dull, C. J. 1985. "A Reassessment of the Boiotian Districts." In *Proceedings of the Third International Conference on Boiotian Antiquities, 1979*. McGill University Monographs in Classical Archaeology and History 2, pp. 33–39. Amsterdam.
Duncan-Jones, R. P. 1980. "Metic Numbers in Periclean Athens." *Chiron* 10: 101–9.
———. 1990. *Scale and Structure in the Roman Economy*. Cambridge.
Dworkin, R. 1986. *Law's Empire*. Cambridge, Mass.
Edwards, M. 1994. *The Attic Orators*. Bristol.
———, ed. 1995. *Andocides*. Warminster, England.
Edwards, R. B. 1979. *Kadmos the Phoenician*. Amsterdam.
Ehrenberg, V. 1946. *Aspects of the Ancient World*. Oxford.
———. 1962. *The People of Aristophanes: A Sociology of Old Attic Comedy*. New York.
———. 1969. *The Greek State*. 2d ed. London.
Eliot, C.W.J. 1962. *Coastal Demes of Attica: A Study of the Policy of Cleisthenes*. Toronto.
Elverson, S. 1988. "Aristotle on the Foundation of the State." *Political Studies* 36: 89–101.
Erdmann, W. 1934. *Die Ehe im alten Griechenland*. Münchener Beiträge zur Papyrusforschung und antiken Rechtsgeschichte 20. Munich.

Ericcson, L. 1980. "Charges against Prostitution: An Attempt at a Philosophical Assessment." *Ethics* 90: 335–66.

Eriksen, T. H. 1993. *Ethnicity and Nationalism: Anthropological Perspectives.* London.

Ermatinger, E. 1897. *Die attische Autochthonensage bis auf Euripides.* Ph.D. dissertation. Berlin.

Erxleben, E. 1974. "Die Rolle der Bevölkerungsklassen im Aussenhandel Athens im 4. Jahrhundert v.u.Z." In *Hellenische Poleis*, edited by E. C. Welskopf, 1: 460–520. Berlin.

Evans, D. T. 1993. *Sexual Citizenship.* London.

Fabre, G. 1981. *Recherches sur les rapports patron-affranchi à la fin de la République romaine*. Rome.

Fantham, E., H. Foley, N. Kampen, S. Pomeroy, and H. Shapiro. 1994. *Women in the Classical World.* Oxford.

Farrar, C. 1988. *The Origins of Democratic Thinking: The Invention of Politics in Classical Athens*. Cambridge.

Faubion, J. D. 1993. *Modern Greek Lessons: A Primer in Historical Constructivism.* Princeton.

Faust, D. G. 1982. *James Henry Hammond and the Old South: A Design for Mastery.* Baton Rouge, La.

Figueira, T. J. 1984. "Karl Polanyi and Ancient Greek Trade: The Port of Trade." *Ancient World* 10: 15–30.

———. 1991. *Athens and Aigina in the Age of Imperial Colonization*. Baltimore.

———. 1998. *The Power of Money: Coinage and Politics in the Athenian Empire.* Philadelphia.

Fine, J.V.A. 1951. *Horoi: Studies in Mortgage, Real Security, and Land Tenure in Ancient Athens. Hesperia,* suppl. 9.

Finley, M. I. [1951] 1985. *Studies in Land and Credit in Ancient Athens*. With new introduction by P. Millett. New Brunswick, N.J.

———. [1953] 1984. "Land, Debt and the Man of Property in Classical Athens." *Political Science Quarterly* 68: 249–68. Reprinted as and quoted here from chapter 4 in Finley 1981, pp. 62–76.

———. 1953. "Multiple Charges on Real Property in Athenian Law." *Studi in onore di Vincenzo Arangio-Ruiz* 3: 473–91. Naples.

———. 1963. *The Ancient Greeks*. London.

———. 1970. "Aristotle and Economic Analysis." *Past & Present* 47: 3–25. Reprinted in Finley 1974, pp. 26–52.

———. [1973] 1985. *Democracy Ancient and Modern*. London.

———, ed. 1974. *Studies in Ancient Society.* London.

———. 1975. *The Use and Abuse of History.* London.

———. 1980. *Ancient Slavery and Modern Ideology.* London.

———. 1981. *Economy and Society in Ancient Greece*. Edited by B. D. Shaw and R. P. Saller. London.

———. 1982. "Le Document et l'histoire économique de l'antiquité." *Annales (economies, sociétés, civilisations)* 37: 697–713. Reprinted in English as Chapter 3 in Finley 1986, pp. 27–46.

———. 1983. *Politics in the Ancient World.* Cambridge.

———, ed. 1984. *The Legacy of Greece: A New Appraisal.* Oxford.

———. 1985. *The Ancient Economy.* 2d ed. London and Berkeley.

———. 1986. *Ancient History: Evidence and Models*. New York.

Fisher, N.R.E. 1976. *Social Values in Classical Athens.* London.

———. 1976–79. "*Hubris* and Dishononour." *Greece & Rome* 23: 177–93; 26: 32–47.

———. 1981. Review of Schaps 1979. In *Classical Review* 31: 72–74.

———. 1990. "The Law of *hubris* in Athens." In *Nomos: Essays in Athenian Law, Politics and Society,* edited by P. Cartledge, P. Millett, and S. Todd, pp. 123–45. Cambridge.

———. 1992. *Hybris*. Westminster.

———. 1993. *Slavery in Classical Greece*. London.
———. 1995. "*Hybris*, Status and Slavery." In *The Greek World*, edited by A. Powell, pp. 44–84. London.
Fishman, J. 1977. " 'Language and Ethnicity." In *Language, Ethnicity and Intergroup Relations*, edited by H. Giles, pp. 15–57. London.
Flashar, H. 1968. *Der Epitaphios des Perikles*. Heidelberg.
Flory, S. 1990. "The Meaning of τὸ μὴ μυθῶδες (1.22.4) and the Usefulness of Thucydides' *History*." *Classical Journal* 85: 193–208.
Forbes, C. A. 1933. *"Neoi": A Contribution to the Study of Greek Associations*. Philological Monograph 2. American Philological Association.
———. 1955. "The Education and Training of Slaves in Antiquity." *Transactions of the American Philological Association* 86: 321–60.
Forrest, W. G. 1966. *The Emergence of Greek Democracy*. London.
Forsdyke, J. 1957. *Greece before Homer: Ancient Chronology and Mythology*. New York.
Fossey, J. M. 1988. *Topography and Population of Ancient Boiotia*. Chicago.
Foucault, M. 1984. *The Foucault Reader*. Edited by P. Rabinow. New York.
———. 1985. *The History of Sexuality*. Vol. 2. New York. Originally published as *L'usage des plaisirs*. Paris, 1984.
———. 1986. *The History of Sexuality*. Vol. 3. New York. Originally published as *Le souci de soi*. Paris, 1984.
Fougères, G. 1900. "Komé." In *Dictionnaire des antiquités grecques et romaines*, edited by C. Daremberg and E. Saglio, 3: 852–595. Paris.
Fowler, E. 1998. *San'ya Blues: Laboring Life in Contemporary Tokyo*. Ithaca, N.Y.
Foxhall, L. 1989. "Household, Gender and Property in Classical Athens." *Classical Quarterly* 39: 22–44.
———. 1990. "The Dependent Tenant: Land Leasing and Labour in Italy and Greece." *Journal of Roman Studies* 80: 97–114.
———. 1992. "The Control of the Attic Landscape." In *Agriculture in Ancient Greece*, edited by B. Wells, pp. 155–59. Stockholm.
———. 1994. "Pandora Unbound: A Feminist Critique of Foucault's *History of Sexuality*." In *Dislocating Masculinity: Comparative Ethnographies*, edited by A. Cornwall and N. Lindisturre, pp. 133–46. London.
———. 1996. "The Law and the Lady." In *Greek Law in Its Political Setting*, edited by L. Foxhall and A.D.E. Lewis, pp. 133–52. Oxford.
———. Forthcoming. "Household Structures and the Economy in Ancient Athens." Oral Presentation at conference on Ancient Greek Economy. Delphi, Greece, September 1994.
Fraisse, G. 1989. *Muse de la raison. La démocratie exclusive et la différence des sexes*. Aix-en-Provence.
Francotte, H. [1910] 1964. "De la condition des étrangers dans les cités grecques." *Mélanges de droit public grec* 5: 167–220.
Frier, B. 1977. "The Rental Market in Early Imperial Rome." *Journal of Roman Studies* 67: 27–37.
———. 1980. *Landlords and Tenants in Imperial Rome*. Princeton.
———. 1982. "Roman Life Expectancy: Ulpian's Evidence." *Harvard Studies in Classical Philology* 86: 213–51.
———. 1983. "Roman Life Expectancy: The Pannonian Evidence." *Phoenix* 37: 328–44.
Fritz, K. von, and E. Kapp, eds. 1961. *Aristotle's Constitution of Athens and Related Texts*. 2d ed. New York.
Frontisi-Ducrous, F., and F. Lissarrague. 1990. "From Ambiguity to Ambivalence: A Dionysiac Excursion through the 'Anakreontic' Vases." In Halperin, Winkler, and Zeitlin 1990, pp. 211–56.
Fuks, A. 1951. "*Kolonos misthios*: Labour Exchange in Classical Athens." *Eranos* 49: 171–73.

Gabrielsen, V. 1986. "φανερά and ἀφανὴς οὐσία in Classical Athens." *Classica et Mediaevalia* 37: 99–114.

———. 1987. "The *Antidosis* Procedure in Classical Athens." *Classica et Mediaevalia* 38: 7–38.

Gabrielsen, V. 1994. *Financing the Athenian Fleet: Public Taxation and Social Relations.* Baltimore.

Gagarin, M. 1979. "The Athenian Law against *Hybris.*" In *Arktouros: Hellenic Studies presented to Bernard Knox,* edited by G. W. Bowersock, W. Burkert, and M.C.J. Putnam, pp. 229–36. Berlin and New York.

———. 1996. "The Torture of Slaves in Athenian Law." *Classical Philology* 91: 1–18.

Gallant, T. W. 1991. *Risk and Survival in Ancient Greece: Reconstructing the Rural Domestic Economy.* Stanford.

Gallo, L. 1984a. *Alimentazione e demografia della Grecia antica: ricerche.* Salerno.

———. 1984b. "La donna greca e la marginalità." *Quaderni urbanati di cultura classica* 18: 7–51.

———. 1987. "Salari e inflazione: Atene tra V e IV sec. A. C." *Annali della Scuola normale superiore di Pisa,* 3d ser., 17, no. 1: 19–63.

Garlan, Y. 1974. "Quelques travaux récents sur les esclaves grecs en temps de guerre." In *Actes de Colloque d'histoire sociale 1972 sur l'esclavage,* pp. 15–28. Paris.

———. 1988. *Slavery in Ancient Greece.* Ithaca, N.Y. Originally published as *Les esclaves en grèce ancienne.* Paris, 1982.

Garland, R. 1982. "A First Catalogue of Attic Peribolos Tombs." *Annual of the British School at Athens* 77: 125–76.

———. 1987. *The Piraeus.* Ithaca, N.Y.

———. 1990. *The Greek Way of Life.* Ithaca, N.Y.

Garner, R. 1987. *Law and Society in Classical Athens.* London.

Garnsey, P., ed. 1980. *Non-Slave Labour in the Greco-Roman World.* Cambridge.

———. 1985. "Grain for Athens." In *Crux: Essays in Greek History presented to G.E.M. de Ste. Croix,* edited by P. A. Cartledge and F. D. Harvey, pp. 62–75. London.

———. 1988. *Famine and Food Supply in the Graeco-Roman World: Responses to Risk and Crisis.* Cambridge.

———. 1996. *Ideas of Slavery from Aristotle to Augustine.* Cambridge.

———. 1998. *Cities, Peasants and Food in Classical Antiquity.* Cambridge.

Garon, S. 1997. *Molding Japanese Minds: The State in Everyday Life.* Princeton.

Garrity, T. F. 1998. "Thucydides 1.22.1: Content and Form in the Speeches." *American Journal of Philology* 119: 361–84.

Gaudemet, J. 1967. *Institutions de l'antiquité.* Paris.

Gauthier, Ph. 1972. *Symbola. Les étrangers et la justice dans les cités grecques.* Nancy.

———. 1988. "Métèques, périèques et *paroikoi*: Bilan et points d'interrogation." In *L'étranger dans le monde grec,* edited by R. Lonis, pp. 24–46. Etudes anciennes 4. Nancy.

Gawantka, W. 1975. *Isopolitie.* Munich.

———. 1985. *Die sogenannte Polis. Enstehung, Geschichte und Kritik der modernen althistorischen Grundbegriffe der griechische Staat, die griechische Staatsidee, die Polis.* Stuttgart.

Geary, P. 1983. "Ethnic Identity as a Situational Construct in the Early Middle Ages." *Mitteilungen der anthropologischen Gesellschaft in Wien,* 113: 15–26.

Geertz, C. 1983. "The Integrative Revolution: Primordial Sentiments and Civil Politics in the New States." In *The Interpretation of Cultures,* pp. 255–310. New York.

Gehrke H.-J. 1985. *Stasis.* Munich.

———. 1995. "Zwischen Altertumswissenschaft und Geschichte. Zur Standorbestimmung der Alten Geschichte." In *Die Wissenschaften vom Altertum am Ende des 2. Jahrtausends n. Chr.* Stuttgart.

Gelb, I. J. 1973. "Prisoners of War in Early Mesopotamia." *Journal of Near Eastern Studies* 32: 70–98.

Gellner, E. 1964. *Thought and Change.* London.
———. 1983. *Nations and Nationalism.* Oxford.
Gera, G. 1975. *L'imposizione progressiva nell'antica Atene.* Rome.
Gerhardt, P. [1933] 1935. *Die attische Metoikie im vierten Jahrhundert.* Dissertation, Königsberg.
Gernet, L. 1909. "L'approvisionement d'Athènes en blé au Ve et au IVe siècle." *Mélanges d'histoire ancienne* 25, no. 3 (Paris): 171–385. Reprint 1979.
———. 1917. *Recherches sur le développement de la pensée juridique et morale en Grèce. Étude sémantique.* Paris.
———. 1918. "Notes sur les parents de Démosthène." *Revue des études grecques* 31:185–96.
———. [1920] 1955. "La loi de Solon sur le 'testament.'" In Gernet 1955b, pp. 121–49. Originally published in *Revue des études grecques* 33: 123–68.
———, ed. 1954–60. *Démosthène, Plaidoyers Civils.* 4 vols. Collection des Universitès de France. Paris.
———. 1955a. "Aspects du droit athénien de l'esclavage." In Gernet 1955b: 151–72. Originally published in *Archives d'histoire du droit oriental* (1950): 159–87.
———. 1955b. *Droit et société dans la Grèce ancienne.* Paris. Reprint 1964 with augmented bibliography.
Gernet, L., and M. Bizos, eds. [1924, 1926] 1967. *Lysias: Discours.* 2 vols. Collection des Universitès de France. Paris.
Gill, C., N. Postlethwaite, and R. Seaford, eds. 1998. *Reciprocity in Ancient Greece.* Oxford.
Giobbe, E. 1991. "Prostitution: Buying the Right to Rape." In *Rape and Sexual Assault III: A Research Handbook,* edited by A. W. Burgess, pp. 143–60. New York.
Giovannini, A. 1971. *Untersuchungen über die Natur und die Anfänge der bundesstaatlichen Sympolitie.* Göttingen.
Girard, J. 1872. "Sur l'authenticité de l'oraison funèbre attribuée à Lysias." *Revue archéologique* pp. 373–89.
Glazer, N., and S. Moynihan. 1975. Introduction to *Ethnicity: Theory and Experience,* edited by N. Glazer and S. Moynihan, pp. 1–26. Cambridge, Mass.
Glotz, G. 1926. *Ancient Greece at Work.* London.
Godelier, M. 1978. "Politics as Infrastructure: An Anthropologist's Thoughts on the Example of Classical Greece and the Notions of Relations of Production and Economic Determinism." In *The Evolution of Social Systems,* edited by J. Friedman and M. J. Rowlands, pp. 13–28. London.
———. 1986. *The Mental and the Material.* London. Originally published as *L'idéel et le matériel.* Paris, 1984.
Gofas, D. 1979. "Les 'emmenoi dikai' à Thasos." In *Symposion 1974,* edited by A. Biscardi, pp. 175–88. Cologne. Reprinted in Gofas 1993, pp. 71–77.
———. 1993. Μελέτες ἱστορίας τοῦ ἑλληνικοῦ δικαίου τῶν συναλλαγῶν. Athens.
Golden, M. 1981. "Demosthenes and the Age of Majority at Athens." *Phoenix* 33: 25–38.
———. 1988. "Did the Ancients Care When Their Children Died?" *Greece & Rome* 35: 152–63.
———. 1990. *Children and Childhood in Classical Athens.* Baltimore.
———. 1992. "Continuity, Change and the Study of Ancient Childhood." *Echos du monde classique/Classical Views* 11: 7–18.
Goldhill, S. 1986. *Reading Greek Tragedy.* Cambridge.
———. 1994. "Representing Democracy: Women at the Great Dionysia." In *Ritual, Finance, Politics: Athenian Democratic Accounts Presented to David Lewis,* edited by R. Osborne and S. Hornblower, pp. 347–70. Oxford.
Goldin, C. D. 1976. *Urban Slavery in the American South, 1820–1860.* Chicago.
Goldman, E. 1969. "The Traffic in Women." In *Anarchism and Other Essays,* pp. 183–200. New York.
Gomme, A. W. 1933. *The Population of Athens in the Fifth and Fourth Centuries* B.C. Oxford.

Gomme, A. W. [1940] 1962. "The Old Oligarch." In *Athenian Studies Presented to W. S. Ferguson. Harvard Studies in Classical Philology*, suppl. 1: 211–45. Reprinted in *More Essays in Greek History and Literature*, pp. 38–69. Oxford, 1962. Reprint New York 1987.

Gomme, A. W., A. Andrewes, and K. J. Dover. 1945–81. *A Historical Commentary on Thucydides*. 5 vols. Oxford.

Goode, E. 1978. *Deviant Behavior: An Interactionist Approach*. New York.

Goody, J. 1980. "Slavery in Time and Space." In *Asian and African Systems of Slavery*, edited by J. L. Watson. Berkeley.

———. 1986. *The Logic of Writing and the Organization of Society*. Cambridge.

Goudriaan, K. 1988. *Ethnicity in Ptolemaic Egypt*. Amsterdam.

———. 1992. "Ethnical Strategies in Graeco-Roman Egypt." In Bilde et al., 1992, pp. 74–99.

Gould, J. 1980. "Law, Custom and Myth: Aspects of the Social Position of Women in Classical Athens." *Journal of Hellenic Studies* 100: 38–59.

Gouldner, A. 1965. *Enter Plato: Classical Greece and the Origins of Social Theory*. New York.

Gouthoeven, W. van. 1636. *D'oude Chronijcke ende Historien van Holland*. 's Gravenhage.

Graham, A. J. 1964. *Colony and Mother City in Ancient Greece*. Manchester.

———. 1992. "Thucydides 7.13.2 and the Crews of Athenian Triremes." *Transactions of the American Philological Association* 122: 257–70.

———. 1998. "Thucydides 7.13.2 and the Crews of Athenian Triremes: An Addendum." *Transactions of the American Philological Association* 128: 89–114.

Greenberg, M. 1995. *Studies in the Bible and Jewish Thought*. Philadelphia.

Greenfield, L. 1992. *Nationalism: Five Roads to Modernity*. Cambridge, Mass.

Grofman, B., et al. 1992. *Minority Representation and the Quest for Voting Equality*. New York.

Grote, G. [1859–65] 1907. *Histories of Greece*. 10 vols. London.

Grube, G.M.A. 1974. *Plato's Republic*. Indianapolis.

Gschnitzer, F. 1955. "Stammes- und Ortsgemeinden im alten Griechenland." *Wiener Studien* 68: 120–44.

———. 1971. "Stadt und Stamm bei Homer." *Chiron* 1: 1–17.

Gudeman, S. 1986. *Economics as Culture*. London.

Guiraud, P. 1893. *La propriété foncière en Grèce jusqu'à la conquête romaine*. Paris.

Habicht, C. 1997. *Athens from Alexander to Antony*. Cambridge, Mass. Translation of *Athen. Die Geschichte der Stadt in hellenistischer Zeit*. Munich 1995.

Hall, E. 1989. *Inventing the Barbarian: Greek Self-Definition through Tragedy*. Cambridge.

Hall, J. M. 1997. *Ethnic Identity in Greek Antiquity*. Cambridge.

Hallett, J. 1984. *Fathers and Daughters in Roman Society: Women and the Elite Family*. Princeton.

Halperin, D. M. 1990. *One Hundred Years of Homosexuality and Other Essays on Greek Love*. New York.

Halperin, D. M., J. J. Winkler, and F. I. Zeitlin, eds. 1990. *Before Sexuality: The Construction of Erotic Experience in the Ancient Greek World*. Princeton.

Hamilton, C. [1909] 1981. *Marriage as a Trade*. London.

Hampl, F. 1939. "Poleis ohne Territorium." *Klio* 32: 1–60. Reprinted in *Zur griechischen Staatskunde*, edited by F. Gschnitzer, pp. 403–473. Darmstadt, 1969.

Handler, R. 1988. *Nationalism and the Politics of Culture in Quebec*. Madison, Wis.

Hansen, M. H. 1973. *Atimistraffen i Athen i Klassisk Tid*. Odense.

———. 1975. *Eisangelia: The Sovereignty of the People's Court in Athens in the Fourth Century BC and the Impeachment of Generals and Politicians*. Odense.

———. 1976. "How Many Athenians Attended the *Ecclesia*?" *Greek Roman and Byzantine Studies* 17: 115–34.

———. 1978. *Det Athenske Demokrati i 4 århundrede f.Kr I: staten, folket, forfatningen*. Copenhagen.

———. 1980a. "*Eisangelia* in Athens: A Reply." *Journal of Hellenic Studies* 80: 89–95.

———. 1981. "Two Notes on the Athenian *dikai emporikai*." In *Symposion 1979*, edited by P. Dimakis, pp. 167–75. Cologne.

———. 1982. "Demographic Reflections on the Number of Athenian Citizens." *American Journal of Ancient History* 7: 172–89.

Hansen, M. H. 1985. *Demography and Democracy*. Copenhagen.

———. 1988. *Three Studies in Athenian Demography*. Copenhagen.

———. 1989a. *Was Athens a Democracy? Popular Rule, Liberty and Equality in Ancient and Modern Political Thought*. Historisk-filosofiske Meddelelser 59. Copenhagen.

———. 1989b. "Two Notes on the Pnyx." In *The Athenian Ecclesia II. A Collection of Articles, 1983–89*, pp. 129–41. Copenhagen.

———. 1991. *The Athenian Democracy in the Age of Demosthenes*. Oxford.

———, ed. 1993. *The Ancient Greek City-State*. Copenhagen.

———. 1994a. "*Poleis* and City-States, 600–323 B.C.: A Comprehensive Research Programme." In Whitehead 1994, pp. 9–17.

———. 1994b. "*Polis, Civitas,* Stadtstaat and City State." In Whitehead 1994, pp. 19–22.

———. 1995a. "Boiotian Poleis. A Test Case." In Hansen 1995, pp. 13–63.

———. 1995b. "The 'Autonomous City-State.' Ancient Fact or Modern Fiction?" In Hansen and Raaflaub 1995, pp. 21–43.

———. 1995c. "*Kome*: A Study in How the Greeks Designated and Classified Settlements Which Were Not *Poleis*." In Hansen and Raaflaub 1995, pp. 45–81.

———, ed. 1995d. *Sources for the Ancient Greek City-State*. Symposium, August 24–27 1994. Acts of the Copenhagen Polis Centre. Vol. 2. Historisk-filosofiske Meddelelser 72. Copenhagen.

———. 1996a. "Aristotle's Two Complementary Views of the Polis." In *Transitions to Empire: Essays in Greco-Roman History, 360–146 B.C., in Honor of E. Badian,* edited by R. W. Wallace and E. M. Harris, pp. 195–210.

———. 1996b. "ΠΟΛΛΑΧΩΣ ΠΟΛΙΣ ΛΕΓΕΤΑΙ (Arist. *Pol.* 1276a23). The Copenhagen Inventory of Poleis and the *Lex Hafniensis de Civitate.*" In Hansen 1996f, pp. 7–72. Copenhagen.

———. 1996c. "An Inventory of Boiotian *Poleis* in the Archaic and Classical Periods." In Hansen 1996f, pp. 73–116. Copenhagen.

———. 1996d. "Were the Boioian *Poleis* Deprived of Their *Autonomia* during the First and Second Boiotian Federations? A Reply." In Hansen and Raaflaub 1996, pp. 127–36.

———. 1996e. "City-Ethnics as Evidence for *Polis*-Identity." In Hansen and Raaflaub 1996, pp. 169–96.

———, ed. 1996f. *Introduction to an Inventory of Poleis*. Symposium, August 23–26 1995. Acts of the Copenhagen Polis Centre. Vol. 3. Historisk-filosofiske Meddelelser 74. Copenhagen.

———, ed. 1996g. *More Studies in the Ancient Greek Polis*. Papers from the Copenhagen Polis Centre 3. *Historia*, Einzelschriften, 108. Stuttgart.

Hansen, M. H., L. Bjertrup, T. H. Nielsen, L. Rubinstein, and T. Vestergaard. 1990. "The Demography of the Attic Demes: The Evidence of the Sepulchral Inscriptions." *Analecta romana Instituti danici* 19: 25–44.

Hansen, M. H., and K. Raaflaub, eds. 1995. *Studies in the Ancient Greek Polis*. Papers from the Copenhagen Polis Centre 2. *Historia*, Einzelschriften, 95. Stuttgart.

———, eds. 1996. *More Studies in the Ancient Greek* Polis. Papers from the Copenhagen Polis Centre 3. *Historia,* Einzelschriften, 108. Stuttgart.

Hansen, M. V. 1984. "Athenian Maritime Trade in the 4th Century B.C.: Operation and Finance." *Classica et Mediaevalia* 35: 71–92.

Hansen, P. A. 1983. *Carmina epigraphica graeca saeculorum VIII–V A. Chr. N.* Berlin.

———. 1989. *Carmina epigraphica graeca saeculorum IV A. Chr. N.* Berlin.

Hanson, V. D. 1983. *Agriculture and Warfare in Classical Greece*. Pisa.

———, ed. 1991. *Hoplites: The Classical Greek Battle Experience*. London.

Harding, P. 1981. "In Search of a Polypragmatist." In *Classical Contributions: Studies in Honour of M. F. McGregor,* pp. 41–50. New York.

Harding, P. 1987. "Rhetoric and Politics in Fourth-Century Athens." *Phoenix* 41: 25–39.

Harris, E. 1992a. "Women and Lending in Athenian Society: A *Horos* Re-Examined." *Phoenix* 46: 309–21.

———. 1992b. Review of MacDowell 1990. *Classical Philology* 87: 71–80.

———. 1995. *Aeschines and Athenian Politics.* Oxford.

———. 1996. "A Note on Adoption and Deme Registration." *Tyche: Beiträge zur Alten Geschichte, Papyrologie und Epigraphik* 11: 123–27.

Harris, W. 1989. *Ancient Literacy.* Cambridge.

Harrison, A.R.W. 1968–71. *The Law of Athens.* 2 vols. Oxford.

Hart, H.L.A. 1994. *The Concept of Law.* 2d ed. Oxford.

Harvey, F. D. 1985. "Some Aspects of Bribery in Greek Politics." In *Crux: Essays in Greek History presented to G.E.M. de Ste. Croix,* edited by P. A. Cartledge and F. D. Harvey, pp. 76–113. London.

Hasebroek, J. [1933] 1978. *Trade and Politics in Ancient Greece.* Translated by L. M. Fraser and D. C. MacGregor. London. Originally published as *Staat und Handel im alten Griechenland.* Tübingen, 1928.

Hauschild, H. 1933. *Die Gestalt der Hetäre in der griechischen Komödie.* Leipzig.

Haussoullier, B. 1884. *La vie municipale en Attique: Essai sur l'organisation des dèmes au quatrième siècle.* Paris.

Hauvette, A. 1898. "Les 'Éleusiniens' d'Éschyle et l'institution du discours funèbre à Athènes." In *Mélanges Henri Weil,* pp. 159–78. Paris.

Hedrick, C. W. 1989. "The Phratry from Paiania." *Classical Quarterly* 39: 114–25.

———. 1990. *The Decrees of the Demotionidai.* Atlanta.

Hemelrijk, J. M. 1991. "A Closer Look at the Potter." In *Looking at Greek Vases,* edited by T. Rasmussen and N. Spivey. Cambridge.

Henderson, J., ed. 1987. *Aristophanes: Lysistrata.* Oxford.

Henderson, M. M. 1975. "Plato's Menexenus and the Distortion of History." *Acta Classica* 18: 25–46.

Henry, M. M. 1986. "*Ethos, Mythos, Praxis:* Women in Menander's Comedy." *Helios,* n.s., 13, no. 2: 141–50.

———. 1995. *Prisoner of History: Aspasia of Miletus and Her Biographical Tradition.* Oxford.

———. 1996. "Secular Prostitution." In *Oxford Classical Dictionary,* 3d ed., edited by S. Hornblower and A. H. Spawforth, p. 1264. Oxford.

Herfst, P. [1922] 1980. *Le travail de la femme dans la Grèce ancienne.* Utrecht.

Herter, H. 1957. "Dirne." *Reallexikon für Antike und Christentum* 3: 1149–1213.

———. 1960. "Die Soziologie der antiken Prostitution im Lichte des heidnischen und christlichen Schriftums." *Jahrbuch für Antike und Christentum* 3: 70–111.

Hervagault, M.-P., and M.-M. Mactoux. 1974. "Esclaves et société d'après Démosthène." In *Actes du Colloque d'histoire sociale 1972 sur l'esclavage,* pp. 57–102. Paris.

Herzfeld, M. 1997. *Cultural Intimacy: Social Poetics in the Nation-State.* London.

Hess, H. 1938. *Textkritische und erklärende Beiträge zum Epitaphios des Hypereides.* Leipzig.

Higginbotham, A. L., Jr. 1978. *In the Matter of Color: Race and the American Legal Process.* New York.

———. 1996. *Shades of Freedom: Racial Politics and Presumptions of the American Legal Process.* New York.

Hignett, C. 1952. *A History of the Athenian Constitution.* Oxford.

Himmelfarb, G. 1996. "The Unravelled Fabric—and How to Knit It Up: Mixed Motives among the New Communitarians." *Times Literary Supplement,* May 17, pp. 12–13.

Himmelmann, N. 1979. "Zur Entlohnung künstlerischer Tätigkeit in klassischen Bauinschriften." *Jahrbuch des deutschen Archäologischen Instituts* 94: 127–42.

Hirzel, R. [1918] 1962. *Der Name. Ein Beitrag zu seiner Geschichte im Altertum und Besonders bei den Griechen*. Abhandlungen der Philologische-Historischen Klasse der Sächsischen Akademie der Wissenschaften 36.2. Amsterdam.

Hoagland, S. L. 1988. *Lesbian Ethics: Toward New Value*. Palo Alto.

Höffe, O. 1971. *Praktische Philosophie: Das Modell des Aristoteles*. Munich.

Holmes, S. T. 1979. "Aristippus In and Out of Athens." *American Political Science Review* 73: 113–28.

Hommel, H. 1932. "Metoikoi." In Pauly-Wissowa 1894–1972, 15: 1413–58.

Hopkins, M. K. 1966. "The Probable Age Structure of the Roman Population." *Population Studies* 20: 245–64.

———. 1978. *Conquerors and Slaves*. Cambridge.

———. 1983. *Death and Renewal*. Cambridge.

Hopper, R. J. 1957. *The Basis of the Athenian Democracy*. Sheffield.

———. 1979. *Trade and Industry in Classical Greece*. London.

Hornblower, S. 1987. *Thucydides*. London.

———. 1991. *A Commentary on Thucydides*. Vol. 1: *Books I–III*. Oxford.

Howgego, C. 1995. *Ancient History from Coins*. London.

Hruza, E. 1892–94. *Beiträge zur Geschichte des griechisch und römisch Familienrechts: I. Ehebegrundung nach attischen Rechte, II. Polygamie und Pellikat nach griechischem Rechte*. Erlangen.

Huby, P. H. 1957. "The *Menexenus* Reconsidered." *Phronesis* 2, no. 2: 104–14.

Hude, C., ed. 1927. *Scholia in Thucydidem*. Leipzig.

Humphreys S. C. 1978. *Anthropology and the Greeks*. London.

———. [1983] 1993. *The Family, Women and Death*. 2d ed. Ann Arbor.

———. 1985. "Law as Discourse." *History and Anthropology* 1: 241–64.

———. Forthcoming. *Kinship in Ancient Greece*. Oxford.

Hunt, P. 1998. *Slaves and Soldiers in Classical Ideologies*. Cambridge.

Hunter, V. J. 1981. "Classics and Anthropology." *Phoenix* 35: 144–55.

———. 1989a. "Women's Authority in Classical Athens." *Echos du monde classique/classical views* 33, n.s., 8: 39–48.

———. 1989b. "The Athenian Widow and Her Kin." *Journal of Family History* 14: 291–311.

———. 1993. "Agnatic Kinship in Athenian Law and Athenian Family Practice: Its Implications for Women." In *Law, Politics and Society in the Ancient Mediterranean World*, edited by B. Halpern and D. W. Hobson, pp. 100–121. Sheffield.

———. 1994. *Policing Athens: Social Control in the Attic Lawsuits, 420–320 B.C.* Princeton.

———. 1997. "The Prison of Athens: A Comparative Perspective." *Phoenix* 51, nos. 3–4: 296–326.

Immerwahr, H. 1972. "Αθηναϊκές Εικόνες στον 'Ιονα' του Ευριπιδη." *Hellenika* 25: 277–97.

Irwin, T. H. 1996. Review of F. Miller 1995. *Times Literary Supplement*, August 16, p. 26.

Isager, S., and M. H. Hansen. 1975. *Aspects of Athenian Society in the Fourth Century B.C.* Odense.

Isager, S., and J. E. Skydsgaard. 1992. *Ancient Greek Agriculture*. London.

Ito, S. 1988. "An Interpretation of the So-called Demotionid Inscription." *Journal of History* 71: 677–713. (Japanese; English summary).

Jacob, O. 1926. "Les esclaves publics à Athènes." *Musée Belge* 30: 57–106.

———. [1928] 1979. *Les esclaves publics à Athènes*. New York. Originally published as Bibliothèque de la Faculté du philosophie et lettres de l'Université de Liège, fasc. 35. Paris.

Jacobs, H. A. 1987. *Incidents in the Life of a Slave Girl, Written by Herself*. Edited by J. F. Yellin. Cambridge, Mass.

Jacoby, F. 1944a. "*Patrios Nomos*: State Burial in Athens and the Public Cemetery in the Kerameikos." *Journal of Hellenic Studies* 64: 37–66.

Jacoby, F. 1944b. "Genesia: A Forgotten Festival of the Dead." *Classical Quarterly* 38: 67–75.

———. 1949. *Atthis, the Local Chronicles of Ancient Athens.* Oxford.

———. [1954] 1968. *Die Fragmente der griechischen Historiker.* 3b (supp.). Vols. 1–2. Leiden.

Jameson, M. H. 1977–78. "Agriculture and Slavery in Classical Athens." *Classical Journal* 73: 122–45.

———. 1982. "The Leasing of Land in Rhamnous." In *Studies in Attic Epigraphy, History and Topography Presented to Eugene Vanderpool,* pp. 66–74. *Hesperia*, suppl. 19. Princeton.

———. 1983. "Famine in the Greek World." In *Trade and Famine in Classical Antiquity,* edited by P. Garnsey and C. R. Whittaker, pp. 6–16. Cambridge.

———. 1990. "Private Space and the Greek City." In *The Greek City from Homer to Alexander,* edited by O. Murray and S. Price, pp. 171–95. Oxford.

———. 1994. "Class in the Ancient Greek Countryside." In *Structures rurales et sociétés antiques,* edited by P. N. Doukellis and L. G. Mendoni, pp. 55–63. Paris.

———. 1997. "Women and Democracy in Fourth-Century Athens." In *Esclavage, guerre, économie en Grèce ancienne: Hommages à Yvon Garlan*, edited by P. Brulé and J. Oulhen, pp. 95–107. Rennes.

Jameson, M. H., C. N. Runnels, and T. H. van Andel. 1994. *A Greek Countryside*. Stanford.

Jaschinski, S. 1981. *Alexander und Griechenland unter dem Eindruck der Flucht des Harpalos.* Bonn.

Jebb, R. C. 1893. *The Attic Orators.* Vol. 1. 2d ed. London.

Jeffery, L. H. 1962. "The Inscribed Gravestones of Archaic Attica." *Annual of the British School at Athens* 57: 115–53.

Johnstone, S. 1998. "Cracking the Code of Silence: Athenian Legal Oratory and the Histories of Slaves and Women." In *Women and Slaves in Greco-Roman Culture*, edited by S. Murnaghan and S. R. Joshel, pp. 221–35. London.

Jones, C. P. 1996. "ἔθνος and γένος in Herodotus." *Classical Quarterly* 46: 315–20.

Jones, H., ed. 1998. *Le monde antique et les droits de l'homme. Actes de la 50ᵉ session de la société Fernand de Visscher pour l'histoire des droits de l'antiquité.* Brussels, 16–19 September, 1996. Brussels.

Jones, J. E. 1975. "Town and Country Houses of Attica in Classical Times." In *Miscellanea Graeca*, fasc. 1, edited by H. Mussche and P. Spitaels, pp. 63–136. Gent.

———. 1976. "Hives and Honey of Hymettus: Beekeeping in Ancient Greece." *Archaeology* 29: 80–91.

Jones, J. E., A. J. Graham, and L. H. Sackett. 1973. "An Attic Country House below the Cave of Pan at Vari." *Annual of the British School at Athens* 68: 355–452.

Jones, N. F. 1987. *Public Organizations in Ancient Greece: A Documentary Study.* Memoirs of the American Philosophical Society, vol. 176. Philadelphia.

Jordan, B. 1975. *The Athenian Navy in the Classical Period.* Berkeley.

Just, R. 1985. "Freedom, Slavery and the Female Psyche." In *Crux: Essays in Greek History presented to G.E.M. de Ste. Croix,* edited by P. A. Cartledge and F. D. Harvey, pp. 169–88. London.

———. 1989. *Women in Athenian Law and Life*. London.

Kagan, D. 1963. "The Enfranchisement of Aliens by Cleisthenes." *Historia* 12: 41–46.

Kahn, C. 1963. "Plato's Funeral Oration: the Motive of the *Menexenos." Classical Philology* 58: 220–34.

Kalinka, E. 1913. *Die pseudoxenophontische Athenaion Politeia*. Leipzig.

Kallet-Marx, L. 1993. "Thucydides 2.45.2 and the Status of War Widows in Periclean Athens." In *Nomodeiktes: Greek Studies in Honor of Martin Ostwald*, edited by R. M. Rosen and J. Farrell, pp. 133–43. Ann Arbor.

Karabēlias, E. 1984. "Le contenu de l'oikos en droit grec ancien." In *Μνήμη Γεωργίου Α. Πετροπούλου*, edited by P. Dimakis, 1: 441–54. Athens.

Karweise, S. 1991. "The Artemisium Coin Hoard and the First Coins of Ephesus." *Revue belge de numismatique et de sigillographie* 137: 1–28.

Kasakevitch (Grace), E. L. 1960. "*Byli-li rabami* χωρὶς οἰκοῦντες?" (in Russian). *Vestnik Drevnej Istorii* 3: 23–42.

Kearns, E. 1985. "Change and Continuity in Religious Structures after Cleisthenes." In *Crux: Essays in Greek History Presented to G.E.M. de Ste. Croix*, edited by P. A. Cartledge and F. D. Harvey, pp. 189–207. London.

———. 1989. *The Heroes of Attica.* Bulletin of the Institute of Classical Studies, supp. 57. London.

Keen, A. G. 1996. "Were the Boiotian *Poleis Autonomoi*?" In Hansen and Raaflaub, 1996, pp. 113–26.

Keiser, R. 1986. "Death Enmity in Thull: Organized Vengeance and Social Change in a Kohistani Community." *American Ethnologist* 13: 489–505.

Kemper, S. 1991. *The Presence of the Past: Chronicles, Politics, and Culture in Sinhala Life.* Ithaca, N.Y.

Kennedy, G. 1963. *The Art of Persuasion in Greece*. Princeton.

Keuls, E. C. 1985. *The Reign of the Phallus: Sexual Politics in Ancient Athens*. New York.

Keyes, C. F. 1976. "Towards a New Formulation of the Concept of the Ethnic Group." *Ethnicity* 3: 202–13.

———. 1992. *Who Are the Lue Revisited? Ethnic Identity in Laos, Thailand, and China*. Cambridge.

———. 1995. "Who Are the Tai? Reflections on the Invention of Identities." In *Ethnic Identity: Creation, Conflict, and Accommodation*," edited by L. Romanucci-Ross and G. de Vos, pp. 136–60. Walnut Creek, Calif.

Kierdorf, W. 1966. *Erlebnis und Dorstellung der Perserkriege.* Göttingen.

Kilmer, M. F. 1993. *Greek Erotica on Red-figure Vases.* London.

Kim, H. S. 1994. "Greek Fractional Silver Coinage: A Reassessment of the Inception, Development, Prevalence, and Functions of Small Change during the Late Archaic and Early Classical Periods." M. Phil. thesis, Oxford.

———. 1997. Oral Communication at conference on Kerdos: The Economics of Gain in the Ancient Greek World. Cambridge, 28–30 May.

Kirchner, J. 1885. "Zur Glaubwürdigkeit der in die [Demosthenische] Rede wider Neaira eingelegten Zeug enaussagen." *Rheinisches Museum* 40: 377–86.

———. 1901–3. *Prosopographia Attica.* Vols. 1–2. Berlin.

Kirk, G. S. 1970. *Myth: Its Meaning and Functions in Ancient and Other Cultures.* Cambridge.

Kitzinger, C. 1991. "Feminism, Psychology and the Paradox of Power." *Feminism and Psychology: An International Journal.* 1, no. 1: 111–29.

———. 1994. "Problematizing Pleasure: Radical Feminist Deconstructions of Sexuality and Power." In *Power/Gender: Social Relations in Theory and Practice*, edited by H. L. Radtke and H. J. Stam, pp. 194–209. London.

Kliacko, N. B. 1966. "The *Hermokopidai stelai* as a Source for Slavery in the Fifth Century B.C." (in Russian). *Vestnik Drevnej Istorii* 97, no. 3: 114–27. Summarized in *Biblioteca Classica Orientalis* 13 (1968): 281–82.

Kocevalov, A. 1932. "Die Einfuhr von Getreide nach Athen." *Rheinisches Museum* 81: 320–23.

Kolchin, P. 1993. *American Slavery: 1619–1877*. New York.

Korver, J. 1942. "Demosthenes gegen Aphobos." *Mnemosyne*, 3d ser., 10: 8–22.

Kraay, C. M. 1964. "Hoards, Small Change and the Origin of Coinage." *Journal of Hellenic Studies* 84: 76–91.

———. 1976. *Archaic and Classical Greek Coins*. London.

Kränzlein, A. 1963. *Eigentum und Besitz im griechischen Recht des fünften und vierten Jahrhunderts v. Chr.* Berlin.

Kränzlein, A. 1975. "Die attischen Aufzeichnungen über die Einleiferung von phialai exeleutherikai." In *Symposion 1971*, edited by H. J. Wolff, pp. 255–64. Cologne.

Krenkel, W. A. 1978. "Männliche Prostitution in der Antike." *Das Altertum* 24: 49–55.

———. 1988. "Prostitution." In *Civilization of the Ancient Mediterranean: Greece and Rome*, edited by M. Grant and R. Kitzinger, pp. 1291–97. New York.

Kroll, J. H. 1979. "A Chronology of Early Athenian Bronze Coinage, ca. 350–250 B.C." In *Greek Numismatics and Archaeology: Essays in Honor of Margaret Thompson*, edited by O. Mørkholm and N. M. Waggoner, pp. 139–54. Wetteren.

———. 1997. Review of von Reden 1995. *American Journal of Archaeology* 101: 175–76.

Kron, U. 1976. *Die Zehn attischen Phylenheroen: Geschichte, Kult und Darstellungen.* Berlin.

———. 1981– . *Lexicon Iconographicum Mythologiae Classicae.* Zurich.

Kudlien, F. 1991. *Sklaven-Mentalität im Spiegel antiker Wahrsagerei.* Stuttgart.

Kuhn, E. 1878. *Ueber die Enstehung der Staedte der Alten. Komenverfassung und Synoikismos.* Leipzig.

Kullman, W. 1983. "Aristoteles' Staatslehre aus heutiger Sicht." *Gymnasium* 90: 456–77.

Kunt, I. M. 1983. *The Sultan's Servants: The Transformation of Ottoman Provincial Government, 1550–1650.* New York.

Kurke, L. 1989. "*Kapēlia* and Deceit." *American Journal of Philology* 110: 535–44.

———. 1994. "Herodotus and the Language of Metals." *Helios* 22: 36–64.

———. 1997. "Inventing the *Hetaira*: Sex, Politics, and Discursive Conflict in Archaic Greece." *Classical Antiquity* 16: 106–50.

Kurtz, D. C., and J. Boardman. 1971. *Greek Burial Customs.* London.

Kymlicka, W. 1990. *Contemporary Political Philosophy: An Introduction.* Oxford.

Lacey, W. C. 1968. *The Family in Classical Greece.* London.

———. 1980. "The Family of Euxitheos." *Classical Quarterly* 30: 57–61.

Lamb, W. R. M. 1930. *Lysias.* Cambridge, Mass.

Lambert, S. D. 1993. *The Phratries of Attica.* Ann Arbor.

Landmann, G. P. 1974. "Das Lob Athens in der Grabrede des Perikles, Thukydides II, 34–41." *Museum Helveticum* 31: 65–95.

Lane, R. E. 1991. *The Market Experience.* Cambridge.

Lane-Fox, R. 1985. "Aspects of Inheritance in the Greek World." In *Crux: Essays in Greek History presented to G.E.M. de Ste. Croix*, edited by P. A. Cartledge and F. D. Harvey, pp. 208–32. London.

Langdon, M. K. 1985. "The Territorial Basis of the Attic Demes." *Symbolae Osloenses* 60: 5–15.

———. 1988. "The Topography of Coastal Erechtheis." *Chiron* 18: 43–54.

———. 1990–91. "On the Farm in Classical Attica." *Classical Journal* 86: 209–13.

———. 1994. "Public Auctions in Ancient Athens." In *Ritual, Finance, Politics: Athenian Democratic Accounts Presented to David Lewis*, edited by R. Osborne and S. Hornblower, pp. 253–65. Oxford.

Lanza, D., and M. Vegetti. 1975. "L'ideologia della città." *Quaderni di storia* no. 1, 2: 1–37. Reprinted with changes in D. Lanza, M. Vegetti, et al., eds., *L'ideologia della città*, pp. 13–28. Naples.

Lardinois, A. 1992. "Greek Myths for Athenian Rituals." *Greek Roman and Byzantine Studies* 33: 313–27

Larivaille, P. 1975. *La vie quotidienne des courtisanes en Italie au temps de la Renaissance.* Paris.

Larmour, D., P. Miller, and C. Platter. 1998. "Situating *The History of Sexuality.*" In *Rethinking Sexuality: Foucault and Classical Antiquity*, edited by D. Larmour, P. Miller, and C. Platter, pp. 3–41. Princeton.

Larsen, J.A.O. 1945. "Representation and Democracy in Hellenistic Federalism." *Classical Philology* 40: 65–97.

Larsen, J.A.O. 1955. *Representative Government in Greek and Roman History*. Berkeley.

———. 1968. *Greek Federal States: Their Institutions and History*. Oxford.

Laslett, P. 1956. "The Face to Face Society." In *Philosophy, Politics and Society: First Series*, edited by P. Laslett, pp. 157–84. Oxford.

———, ed. 1972. *Household and Family in Past Time*. Cambridge.

Lattanzi, G. M. 1935. "Il *Menesseno* e l'epitafio attribuito a Lisia." *Il mondo classico* 5: 355–60.

———. 1953. "Il significato e l'autenticità del *Menesseno*." *La parola del passato* 8, no. 31: 303–6.

Lauffer, S. 1958. "Die Bedeutung des Standesunterschieds im klassischen Athen." *Historische Zeitschrift* 185: 497–514.

———. 1961. "Die Sklaverei in der griechisch-römischen Welt." *Gymnasium* 68: 370–95. Originally published in *Rapports*, 11th International Congress of Historical Sciences, 2: 71–97. Uppsala, 1960.

———. 1979. *Die Bergwerkssklaven von Laureion*. 2d ed. Forschungen ant. Skl. 2. Expanded edition of *Abhandlungen der Akademie der Wissenschaften und der Literatur*, Mainz, 1955, no. 12, and 1956, no. 11.

Lauter, H. 1980. "Zu Heimstätten und Gusthaüsern im klassischen Attika." In *Forschungen und Funde: Festschrift Bernhard Neutsch*, edited by F. Krinzinger, B. Otto, and E. Wade-Psenner, pp. 279–86. Innsbruck.

———. 1982. "Zwei Horos-Inschriften bei Vari." *Archäologischer Anzeiger*, 2: 299–315.

Leach, E. 1965. *Political Systems of Highland Burma*. 2d ed. Boston.

Ledl, A. 1907. "Das attische Bürgerrecht und die Frauen. I." *Wiener Studien* 29:173–227.

Lehmann, G. A. 1988. "Der 'Lamische Krieg' und die 'Freiheit der Hellenen': Überlegungen zur hieronymianischen Tradition." *Zeitschrift für Papyrologie und Epigraphik* 73: 121–49.

Leidholdt, D. 1990. Introduction to *Sexual Liberals and the Attack on Feminism*, edited by D. Leidholdt and J. G. Raymond. New York.

Lenel, O. [1927] 1966. *Das Edictum Perpetuum*. 3d ed. Leipzig.

Lévi-Strauss, C. 1968. "The Structural Study of Myth." In *Structural Anthropology*, trans. C. Jacobson and B. G. Schoepf, pp. 202–28. New York.

Lévi-Strauss, C., and D. Eribon. 1991. *Conversations with Claude Lévi-Strauss*. Translation of "De près et de loin." Chicago.

Lévy, E. [1985] 1988. "Astos et politès d'Homère à Hérodote." *Ktéma* 10: 53–66.

———. 1986. "Apparition en Grèce de l'idée de village." *Ktéma* 11: 117–27.

———. 1988. "Métèques et droit de résidence." In *L'étranger dans le monde grec*, edited by R. Lonis, pp. 47–67. Etudes anciennes 4. Nancy.

———. 1990. "La cité grecque: Invention moderne ou réalité antique?" *Du pouvoir dans l'antiquité: Mots et réalités. Cahiers du Centre Glotz* 1: 53–67.

Lewis, B. 1990. *Race and Slavery in the Middle East*. Oxford.

Lewis, D. 1955. "Notes on Attic Inscriptions (II)." *Annual of the British School at Athens* 50: 1–36.

———. 1959. "Attic Manumissions." *Hesperia* 28: 208–38.

———. 1962. "The Federal Constitution of Keos." *Annual of the British School at Athens* 57: 1–4.

———. 1966. "After the Profanation of the Mysteries." In *Ancient Society and Institutions: Studies Presented to Victor Ehrenberg*, edited by E. Badian, pp. 177–91. Oxford.

———. 1968. "Dedications of phialai at Athens." *Hesperia* 37: 368–80.

———. 1973. "The Athenian Rationes Centesimarum." In *Problèmes de la terre en Grèce ancienne*, edited by M. I. Finley, pp. 188–91. Paris.

Licht, H. (P. Brandt). [1932] 1952. *Sexual Life in Ancient Greece*. Edited by L. H. Dawson, translated by J. Freese. New York. Originally published as *Sittengeschichte Griechenlands*. Dresden, 1925–28.

Link, S. 1994. *Das griechische Kreta . . . vom 6. bis zum 4. Jh. v. Chr.* Stuttgart.

Lintott, A. 1982. *Violence, Civil Strife, and Revolution in the Classical City, 750–330 B.C.* London.

Lipset, S. M. 1959. "Political Sociology." In *Sociology Today*, edited by R. K. Merton et al. New York.

Lipsius, J. H. [1905–15] 1966. *Das attische Recht und Rechtsverfahren.* 3 vols. Hildesheim.

Lloyd, G.E.R. [1966] 1987. *Polarity and Analogy: Two Types of Argumentation in Early Greek Thought.* Bristol.

Lobel, K. 1986. *Naming the Violence: Speaking Out about Lesbian Violence.* Washington, D.C.

Lohmann, H. 1991. "Zur Prosopographie und Demographie der attischen Landgemeinde Atene (Ἀτήνη)." *Stuttgarter Kolloquium zur historischen Geographie des Altertums 2 (1984) and 3 (1987),* edited by E. Olshausen and H. Sonnabend, pp. 203–58. Bonn.

———. 1992. "Agriculture and Country Life in Classical Attica." In *Agriculture in Ancient Greece*, edited by B. Wells, pp. 29–57. Stockholm.

Loomis, W. T. 1997. "A Standard Athenian Wage?" Presentation to New England Ancient History Colloquium, Brown University, March 3.

———. 1998. *Wages, Welfare Costs and Inflation in Classical Athens.* Ann Arbor.

Loraux, N. 1974. "Socrate contrepoison de l'oraison funèbre. Enjeu et signification du Ménexène." *L'Antiquité classique* 43: 172–211.

———. 1978. "Sur la transparence démocratique." *Raison présente* 49: 3–13.

———. 1979. "L'autochtonie: Une topique athénienne. Le mythe dans l'espace civique." *Annales (economies, sociétés, civilisations)* 34: 1–26.

———. [1981] 1986. *The Invention of Athens: The Funeral Oration in the Classical City.* Cambridge, Mass. 1993. Originally published as *L'invention d'Athènes: Histoire de l'oraison funèbre dans la "cité classique."* Paris.

———. [1984] 1993. *The Children of Athena: Athenian Ideas about Citizenship and the Division between the Sexes.* Translated by C. Levine. Princeton. Originally published as *Les enfants d'Athéna: Idées athéniennes sur la citoyenneté et la division des sexes.* Paris.

———. [1989] 1995. *The Experiences of Tiresias: The Feminine and the Greek Man.* Princeton. Originally published as *Les expériences de Tirésias: Le féminin et l'homme grec.* Paris.

———. 1996. *Né de la terre: Mythe et politique à Athènes.* Paris.

Lord, C. trans. 1984. *Aristotle: The Politics.* Chicago.

———. 1991a. Introduction. In Lord and O'Connor 1991, pp. 1–10.

———. 1991b. "Aristotle's Anthropology." In Lord and O'Connor 1991, pp. 49–73.

Lord, C., and D. K. O'Connor, eds. 1991. *Essays on the Foundations of Aristotelian Political Science.* Berkeley.

Lotze, D. 1981. "Zwischen Politen und Metöken: Pasivbürger im klassischen Athen?" *Klio* 63: 159–78.

———. 1990–92. "Die sogenannte Polis." *Acta Antiqua* 33: 237–42.

Lowry, S. T. 1987. *The Archaeology of Economic Ideas: The Classical Greek Tradition.* Durham, N.C.

Luhmann, N. 1982. *The Differentiation of Society.* Translated by S. T. Holmes and C. Larsmore. New York.

Luzzi, G. 1980. "I nuovi cittadini di Clistene." *Annali della Scuola Normale Superiore di Pisa* 10: 71–78.

MacDowell, D. M., ed. 1962. *Andokides: On the Mysteries.* Oxford.

———. 1971. "The Chronology of Athenian Speeches and Legal Innovations in 401–398 B.C." *Revue internationale des droits de l'antiquité* 18: 267–73.

———. 1976a. "*Hubris* in Athens." *Greece & Rome* 23: 14–31.

———. 1976b. "Bastards as Athenian Citizens." *Classical Quarterly* 26: 88–91.

———. 1978. *The Law in Classical Athens.* London.

———. 1985. Review of M. J. Osborne 1981–83. *Classical Review* 35: 317–20.

———. 1989. "The *Oikos* in Athenian Law." *Classical Quarterly* 39: 10–21.

MacDowell, D. M., ed. 1990. *Demosthenes: Against Meidias*. Oxford.

———. 1994. "The Case of the Rude Soldier (Lysias 9)." In *Symposion 1993*, edited by G. Thür, pp. 153–64. Cologne.

———. 1995. *Aristophanes and Athens*. Oxford.

MacIntyre, A. 1981. *After Virtue: A Study in Moral Theory*. South Bend, Ind.

———. 1989. *Relativism: Interpretation and Confrontation*. Edited by M. Krausz. South Bend, Ind.

Macleod, C. 1983. *Collected Essays*. Oxford.

Maffi, A. 1971. "La capacità di diritto privato dei meteci nel mondo greco classico." In *Studi in onore di Gaetano Scherillo*, edited by A. Biscardi, 1: 177–200. Milan.

———. 1973. "'Strateuesthai meta Athenaion'—contributo allo studio dell' isoteleia." *Rendiconti del' reale Istituto Lombardo di Scienze e Lettere* 107: 939–64.

Malkin, I., ed. Forthcoming. *Ancient Perceptions of Greek Ethnicity*.

Manville, P. 1990. *The Origins of Citizenship in Ancient Athens*. Princeton.

———. 1994. "Toward a New Paradigm of Athenian Citizenship." In Boegehold and Scafuro 1994, pp. 21–33. Baltimore.

Marmor, A. 1992. *Interpretation and Legal Theory*. Oxford.

Marx, K. 1970–72. *Capital*. 3 vols. London. Translation of *Das Kapital*. Berlin, 1951.

Mathieu, G., and E. Brémond, eds. [1929–42] 1963. *Isocrate*. Collection des Universitès de France. 4 vols. Paris.

Maurizio, L. 1995. "Anthropology and Spirit Possession: A Reconsideration of the Pythia's Role at Delphi." *Journal of Hellenic Studies* 115: 69–86.

———. 1998. "The Panathenaia: Processing Athenian Notions of Status and Identity."In *Democracy, Empire and the Arts in Fifth-Century Athens*, edited by D. Boedeker and K. Raaflaub, 297–317. Cambridge, Mass.

Mauss, M. 1923–24. "Essai sur le don. Forme et raison de l'échange dans les sociétés archaïques." *L'Année sociologique*, n.s., 1: 30–186.

McCabe D. F. 1981. *The Prose-Rhythm of Demosthenes*. New York.

McClees, H. 1920. *A Study of Women in the Attic Inscriptions*. Ph.D. dissertation, Columbia University.

McDonald, R. A. 1991. "Independent Economic Production by Slaves on Antebellum Louisiana Sugar Plantations." In Berlin and Morgan 1991, pp. 182–208.

McGinn, T.A.J. 1989. "The Taxation of Roman Prostitutes." *Helios* 16:79–111 Reprinted in McGinn 1998, chapter 7.

———. 1990. "Ne serva prostituatur: Restrictive Covenants in the Sale of Slaves." *Zeitschrift der Savigny-Stiftung für Rechtsgeschichte, Romanist. Abt.* 107: 315–53. Reprinted in McGinn 1998, chapter 8.

———. 1998. *Prostitution, Sexuality, and the Law in Ancient Rome*. Oxford.

———. Forthcoming. *Prostitution and Roman Society*. Ann Arbor.

McGregor, M. F. 1973. "Athenian Policy at Home and Abroad." In *Lectures in Memory of Louise Taft Semple*, pp. 53–66. Norman, Okla.

McInerney, J. Forthcoming a. *The Folds of Parnassos: Land and Ethnicity in Ancient Phokis*.

———. Forthcoming b. "Ethnicity and *Altertumswissenschaft*." In *Political Economy in the Ancient World*, edited by D. Tandy.

McIntosh, M. 1978. "Who Needs Prostitutes? The Ideology of Male Sexual Needs." In *Women, Sexuality and Social Control*, edited by C. Smart and B. Smart, pp. 53–64. London.

McKechnie, P. 1989. *Outsiders in the Greek Cities in the Fourth Century* B.C. London.

Meier, C. 1984. *Introduction à l'anthropologie politique de l'antiquité classique*. Translated by Pierre Blanchaud. Paris.

Meiggs, R. 1972. *The Athenian Empire*. Oxford. Reprinted with corrections, Oxford, 1975.

Meiggs, R. 1973. *Roman Ostia.* 2d ed. Oxford.

Meiggs, R., and D. M. Lewis, eds. 1988. *A Selection of Greek Historical Inscriptions.* Rev. ed. Oxford.

Meikle, S. 1995a. *Aristotle's Economic Thought.* Oxford.

———. 1995b. "Modernism, Economics, and the Ancient Economy." *Proceedings of the Cambridge Philological Society* 41: 174–91.

———. 1996. "Aristotle on Business." *Classical Quarterly* 46: 138–51.

Meillassoux, C., ed. 1975. *L'esclavage en Afrique précoloniale.* Paris.

———. 1991. *The Anthropology of Slavery: The Womb of Iron and Gold.* Chicago. Originally published as *Anthropologie de l'esclavage: Le ventre de fer et d'argent.* Paris, 1986.

Méridier, L., ed. 1964. *Platon.* Vol. 5. Paris.

Meritt, B. D., and J. S. Traill 1974. *Inscriptions: The Athenian Councillors.* Athenian Agora 15. Princeton.

Meritt, B. D., H. T. Wade-Gery, and M. F. McGregor. 1939–53. *The Athenian Tribute Lists.* 4 vols. Princeton.

Mette, H. J. 1982–85. "Euripides: Die Bruchstücke." *Lustrum* 23; 25: 5–14; 27: 23–26.

Metzger, H. 1976. "Athéna soulevant de terre le nouveau-né. Du geste au mythe." In *Mélanges P. Collart*, pp. 295–303. Lausanne.

Meyer, E. 1993. "Epitaphs and Citizenship in Classical Athens." *Journal of Hellenic Studies* 113: 99–121.

Miers, S., and I. Kopytoff, eds. 1977. *Slavery in Africa.* Madison, Wis.

Migeotte, L. 1995. Review of E. Cohen 1992. *L'Antiquité classique* 64: 461–62.

———. Forthcoming. "Quelques aspects légaux et juridiques de l'affermage des taxes en Grèce ancienne. In *Symposion 1997.* Cologne.

Miller, D. 1995. *On Nationality.* Oxford.

Miller, F. D., Jr. 1974. "The State and the Community in Aristotle's *Politics." Reason Papers* 1: 61–69.

———. 1995. *Nature, Justice, and Rights in Aristotle's "Politics."* Oxford.

Miller, M. J. 1983. "The Athenian Autochthonous Heroes from the Classical to the Hellenistic Period." Ph.D. dissertation, Harvard University.

Millett P. 1983. "Maritime Loans and the Structure of Credit in Fourth-Century Athens." In *Trade in the Ancient Economy*, edited by P. Garnsey, K. Hopkins, and C. R. Whittaker, pp. 36–52. Berkeley.

———. 1991. *Lending and Borrowing in Ancient Athens.* Cambridge.

———. 1998. "Encounters in the Agora." In Cartledge, Millett, and von Reden 1998, pp. 203–28.

Mills, S. 1997. *Theseus, Tragedy and the Athenian Empire.* Oxford.

Mirhady, D. 1996. "Torture and Rhetoric in Athens." *Journal of Hellenic Studies* 116: 119–31.

Missiou, A. 1992. *The Subversive Oratory of Andokides.* Cambridge.

Mitteis, L. 1908. *Römisches Privatrecht bis auf die Zeit Diokletians.* Vol. 1. Leipzig.

Momigliano, A. 1930. "Il Menesseno." *Rivista di filologia e d'istruzione* 58: 40–53.

———. 1974. "Historicism Revisited." *Mededelingen der Koninklijke Nederlandse Akademie van Wetenschappen*, Afd. Letterkunde, n.s., 37, no. 3: 63–70. Reprinted in *Essays in Ancient and Modern Historiography.* Oxford, 1977.

Montanari, E. 1981. *Il mito dell'auctonia: Linee di una dinamica mitico-politica ateniese.* Rome.

Montepaone, C. 1990. "Bendis: Tracia ad Atene." *Annali. Sezione di archeologia e storia antica* 12: 103–21.

Montuori, M. 1976. "Su fedone di elide." *Atti dell'Accademia Pontaniana,* n.s., 25: 1–14.

Moore, J. M. 1986. *Aristotle and Xenophon on Democracy and Oligarchy.* Berkeley.

Moretti, L. 1962. *Ricerche sulle leghe greche.* Rome.

Morgan, C. 1991. "Ethnicity and Early Greek States: Historical and Material Perspectives." *Proceedings of the Cambridge Philological Society* 37: 131–63.

———. 1996. "Ethnicity." In *Oxford Classical Dictionary,* 3d ed., edited by S. Hornblower and A. H. Spawforth, pp. 558–59.

Morgan, C., and J. Hall. 1996. "Achaian *Poleis* and Achaian Colonisation." In *Introduction to an Inventory of Poleis*, edited by M. H. Hansen, pp. 164–232. Copenhagen.

Morris, I. 1987. *Burial and Ancient Society: The Rise of the Greek City-State.* Cambridge.

———. 1992. *Death-Ritual and Social Structure in Classical Antiquity.* Cambridge.

———. 1994. "The Athenian Economy Twenty Years after the *Ancient Economy.*" *Classical Philology* 89: 351–66.

Morrow, G. R. 1939. *Plato's Law of Slavery in Its Relation to Greek Law.* Urbana, Ill.

———. [1960] 1993. *Plato's Cretan City: A Historical Interpretation of the Laws*. Princeton.

Mossé, C. [1962] 1979. *La fin de la démocratie athénienne*. Paris.

———. 1967. "La conception du citoyen dans la *Politique* d'Aristote." *Eirene* 6: 17–22.

———. 1972. "La vie économique d'Athènes au IVème siècle. Crise ou renouveau?" In *Praelectiones Patavinae,* edited by F. Sartori, pp. 135–44. Rome.

———. 1973. *Athens in Decline: 404–86.* London.

———. 1979. "Citoyens actifs et citoyens 'passifs' dans les cités grecques: Une approche théorique du problème." *Revue des études anciennes* 81: 241–49.

———. [1985] 1988. "*Astè kai Politis*. La dénomination de la femme athénienne dans les plaidoyers démosthénienne." *Ktéma* 10: 77–80.

———. 1986. "La démocratie athénienne." In *La Grèce ancienne*, edited by C. Mossé and the staff of *L'histoire*, pp. 115–29. Paris.

———. 1989. *L'antiquité dans la révolution française*. Paris.

———. 1995. *Politique et société en Grèce ancienne: Le "modèle" athénien.* Paris.

Mossé, C., and R. di Donato. 1983. "Status e/o funzione. Aspetti della condizione della donna-cittadina nelle orazioni civili di Demostene." *Quaderni di storia* 17: 151–59.

Mukhopadhyay, B. [1876] 1969. "Svapnalabdha bhrāratbarser ithās" (in Hindi). In *Bhūdeb racanā sambhār*, edited by P. Bisi, pp. 341–74. Calcutta.

Mulgan, R. G. 1977. *Aristotle's Political Theory.* Oxford.

Müller, O. 1899. "Untersuchungen zur Geschichte des attischen Bürger- und Eherechts." *Jahrbücher für klassische philologie,* suppl. 25: 661–866.

Muller, R. 1993. "La logique de la liberté dans la Politique." In *Aristote Politique: Études sur la Politique d'Aristote,* edited by P. Aubenquel, pp. 185–208. Paris.

Munn, M., and M. L. Zimmermann-Munn. 1989. "Studies on the Attic-Boiotian Frontier: The Stanford Skourta Project, 1985." In *Boeotia Antiqua*, vol. 1, edited by J. Fossey. Amsterdam.

———. 1990. "On the Frontiers of Attica and Boeotia: The Results of the Stanford Skourta Plain Project." In *Essays in the Topography, History and Culture of Boeotia*, edited by A. Schachter, pp. 33–40. Montreal.

Murdock, G. P. 1967. "Ethnographic Atlas: A Summary." *Ethnology* 6: 109–236.

Murnaghan, S. 1988. "How a Woman Can Be More Like a Man: The Dialogue between Ischomachus and His Wife in Xenophon's Oeconomicus." *Helios* 15: 9–22.

Murray, O. 1990a. "Cities of Reason." In Murray, O. and S. Price eds. 1990, pp. 1–25. Oxford. Originally published in *Archives européennes de sociologie—European Journal of Sociology* 28 (1987): 325–46.

———. 1990b. "The Solonian Law of Hubris." In *Nomos: Essays in Athenian Law, Politics and Society,* edited by P. Cartledge, P. Millett, and S. Todd, pp. 139–45. Cambridge.

———. 1993. "*Polis* and *Politeia* in Aristotle." In *The Ancient Greek City-State*, edited by M. H. Hansen, 197–210. Copenhagen.

Murray, O., and S. Price, eds. 1990. *The Greek City from Homer to Alexander.* Oxford.

Nash, M. 1989. *The Cauldron of Ethnicity in the Modern World.* Chicago.

Nestle, W. 1940. *Vom Mythos zum Logos.* Stuttgart.

Netting, R., R. R. Wilk, and E. J. Arnould. 1984. *Households: Comparative and Historical Studies of the Domestic Group.* Berkeley.

Newman, W. L. 1887–1902. *The Politics of Aristotle.* 4 vols. Oxford.

Nicholas, B. 1962. *An Introduction to Roman Law.* Oxford.

Nielsen, T. H. 1995. "Was Eutaia a *Polis*? A Note on Xenophon's Use of the Term *Polis* in the *Hellenika*." In Hansen and Raaflaub 1995, pp. 83–102. Stuttgart.

———. 1996a. "Arkadia. City-Ethnics and Tribalism." In *Introduction to an Inventory of Poleis*, edited by M. H. Hansen, pp. 117–63. Copenhagen.

———. 1996b. "Was There an Arkadian Confederacy in the Fifth Century B.C.?" In Hansen and Raaflaub 1996, pp. 39–61.

———. 1996c. "A Survey of Dependent *Poleis* in Classical Arkadia." In Hansen and Raaflaub 1996, pp. 63–106.

———. Forthcoming. *Triphylia: An Experiment in Ethnic Construction and Political Organization.*

Nightingale, A. 1998. "Aristotle on the 'Liberal' and 'Illiberal' Arts. *Proceedings of the Boston Area Colloquium in Ancient Philosophy* 12 (1996): 29–70.

Nilsson, M. P. 1951. *Cults, Myths, Oracles and Politics in Ancient Greece.* Lund.

Nippel, W. 1985. "'Reading the Riot Act': The Discourse of Law Enforcement in 18th Century England." *History and Anthropology* 1: 401–26.

Nixon, L., and S. Price. 1990. "The Size and Resources of Greek Cities." In Murray and Price 1990, pp. 146–70.

Nouhaud, M. 1982. *L'utilisation de l'histoire par les orateurs attiques.* Paris.

O'Callaghan, S. 1961. *The Slave Trade Today.* New York.

Ober, J. 1989. *Mass and Elite in Democratic Athens.* Princeton.

———. 1991. "Aristotle's Political Sociology: Class, Status, and Order in the *Politics*." In *Essays on the Foundations of Aristotelian Political Science*, edited by C. Lord and D. K. O'Connor, pp. 112–35. Berkeley.

———. 1993. "The Polis as a Society. Aristotle, John Rawls and the Athenian Social Contract." In M. H. Hansen 1993, pp. 129–60.

Ober, S., and C. Hedrick, eds. 1996. *Dēmokratia: A Conversation on Democracies, Ancient and Modern.* Princeton.

Oertel, F. 1928. Review of J. Hasebroek, *Staat und Handel im alten Griechenland, Deutsche Literaturzeitung* 49: 1618–29.

Ogden, D. 1996. *Greek Bastardy in the Classical and the Hellenistic Periods.* Oxford.

Oikonomakos, M. 1990. "Χρονικά." Ἀρχαιολογικὸν Δελτίον 45: 77–78.

Oikonomidēs, B. D. 1981. Βιβλίο της Χρονίας. 3d ed. Athens.

Oliver, G. J. 1995. "The Athenian State under Threat: Politics and Food Supply, 307 to 229 B.C." D. Phil. thesis. Oxford.

Oppenheimer, K. 1933. *Zwei attische Epitaphien.* Berlin.

Osborne, M. J. 1972. "Attic Citizenship Decrees: A Note." *Annual of the British School at Athens* 67: 128–58.

———. 1981. "Entertainment in the Prytaneion at Athens." *Zeitschrift für Papyrologie und Epigraphik*: 153–70.

———. 1981–83. *Naturalization in Athens.* 4 vols. Brussels.

Osborne, M. J., and S. G. Byrne, eds. 1994. *A Lexicon of Greek Personal Names. II. Attica.* Oxford.

Osborne, R. G. 1985a. *Demos: The Discovery of Classical Attika.* Cambridge.

———. 1985b. "Buildings and Residence on the Land in Classical and Hellenistic Greece: The Contribution of Epigraphy." *Annual of the British School at Athens* 80: 119–28.

———. 1987. *Classical Landscape with Figures: The Ancient Greek City and Its Countryside.* London.

———. 1988. "Social and Economic Implications of the Leasing of Land and Property in Classical and Hellenistic Greece." *Chiron* 18: 279–323.

———. 1990. "The Demos and Its Divisions in Classical Athens." In Murray and Price 1990, pp. 265–93.

Osborne, R. G. 1991. "The Potential Mobility of Human Populations." *Oxford Journal of Archaeology* 10, no. 2: 231–50.

———. 1992. "'Is it a farm?' The Definition of Agricultural Sites and Settlements in Ancient Greece." In *Agriculture in Ancient Greece*, edited by B. Wells, pp. 21–27. Stockholm.

———. 1995. "The Economics and Politics of Slavery at Athens." In *The Greek World*, edited by A. Powell, pp. 27–43. London.

Østergård, U. 1992. "What Is National and Ethnic Identity?" In Bilde et al. 1992, pp. 16–38.

Ostwald, M. 1969. *Nomos and the Beginnings of the Athenian Democracy*. Oxford.

———. 1996. "Shares and Rights: 'Citizenship' Greek Style and American Style." In Ober and Hedrick 1996, pp. 49–61.

Owen, A. S., ed. 1939. *Euripides*. Oxford.

Oxford Classical Dictionary. 1996. 3d ed. Edited by S. Hornblower and A. Spawforth. Oxford.

Padel, R. 1983. "Women: Model for Possession by Greek Daemons." In *Images of Women in Antiquity*, edited by A. Cameron and A. Kuhrt, pp. 3–19. Detroit.

Paley, F. A., and J. E. Sandys. [1896–98] 1979. *Select Private Orations of Demosthenes*. 3d ed. 2 vols. Cambridge.

Palmer, R. R. 1953. "Notes on the Use of the Word 'Democracy' 1789–1799." *Political Science Quarterly* 68: 203–26.

Palmer, S., and J. A. Humphrey. 1990. *Deviant Behavior: Patterns, Sources, and Control*. New York.

Paoli, U. E. [1930] 1974. *Studi di diritto attico*. Milan.

———. 1936. "L'ἀγχιστεία nel diritto successorio attico." *Studia et Documenta Historiae et Iuris* 2: 77–119.

———. 1976. *Altri studi di diritto greco e romano*. Milan.

Paradiso, A. 1988. "L'agrégation du nouveau-né au foyer familial: Les Amphidromies." *Dialogues d'histoire ancienne* 14: 203–18.

Parke, H. W. 1977. *Festivals of the Athenians*. London.

Parker, H. 1937. *The Cult of Antiquity and the French Revolutionaries: A Study in the Development of the Revolutionary Spirit*. Chicago.

Parker, R. 1987. "Myths of Early Athens." In *Interpretations of Greek Mythology*, edited by J. Bremmer, pp. 187–214. London.

———. 1996. *Athenian Religion: A History*. Oxford.

———. 1998. *Cleomenes on the Acropolis*. Oxford.

Parsons, T. [1944] 1951. *The Social System*. Chicago.

Partsch, J. 1909. *Griechisches Bürgschaftsrecht*. Leipzig.

Pateman, C. 1988. *The Sexual Contract*. Cambridge.

Paton, J. M., ed. 1927. *The Erechtheum*. Cambridge, Mass.

Patrianakou-Iliaki, A. 1989. "Αρχαιολογικές έρευνες στο δήμο Αχαρνών." *Á Συμπόσιο Ἱστορίας—Λαογραφίας Βορείου Αττικής*, pp. 241–86. Akharnai.

Patterson, C. 1981. *Pericles' Citizenship Law of 451–50 B.C.* New York.

———. 1985. "'Not Worth the Rearing': The Causes of Infant Exposure in Ancient Greece." *Transactions of the American Philological Association* 115: 103–23.

———. 1986. "*Hai Attikai*: The Other Athenians." *Helios* 13, no. 2: 49–67.

———. 1990. "Those Athenian Bastards." *Classical Antiquity* 9: 40–73.

———. 1991. "Marriage and the Married Woman in Athenian Law." In *Women's History and Ancient History*, ed. S. B. Pomeroy, pp. 48–72. Chapel Hill, N.C.

Patterson, C. 1994. "The Case against Neaira and the Public Ideology of the Athenian Family." In Boegehold and Scafuro 1994, pp. 199–216.

———. Forthcoming. "The Athenian Metic in Court." In *Law and Status*, edited by J. Edmonson and V. Hunter. Oxford.

Patterson, O. 1982. *Slavery and Social Death: A Comparative Study.* Cambridge, Mass.

Patteson, A. J. 1978. "Commentary on [Demosthenes] LIX: *Against Neaera.*" Ph.D. dissertation, University of Pennsylvania.

Pauly-Wissowa, G., ed. 1894–1972. *Real-Encyclopädie der klassischen Altertumswissenschaft.* Rev. G. Wissowa et al. Stuttgart.

Pavan, E. 1980. "Police des moeurs, société et politique à Venise à la fin du Moyen âge." *Revue historique* 264, no. 536: 241–88.

Pearson, L. 1966. "Apollodorus, the Eleventh Attic Orator." In *The Classical Tradition: Literary and Historical Studies in Honor of H. Caplan*, edited by L. Wallach, pp. 347–59 . Ithaca, N.Y. Reprinted in Pearson 1983, pp. 211–23.

———. 1969. "Demosthenes, or Pseudo-Demosthenes, xlv." *Antichthon* 3: 18–26. Reprinted in Pearson 1983, pp. 224–32.

———. 1972. *Demosthenes: Six Private Speeches.* Norman, Okla.

Pečirka, J. 1966. *The Formula for the Grant of Enktesis in Attic Inscriptions.* Prague.

———. 1973. "Homestead Farms in Classical and Hellenistic Hellas." In *Problèmes de la terre en Grèce ancienne,* edited by M. I. Finley, pp. 113–47. Paris.

———. 1975. "Die athenische Demokratie und das athenische Reich." *Clio* 57, no. 2: 307–11.

———. 1976. "The Crisis of the Athenian Polis in the Fourth Century B.C." *Eirene* 14: 5–29.

Perlman, P. 1995. "ΘΕΩΡΟΔΟΚΟΥΝΤΕΣ ΕΝ ΤΑΙΣ ΠΟΛΕΣΙΝ: Panhellenic *Epangelia* and Political Status." In Hansen 1995d, pp. 113–64.

Perotti, E. 1974. "Esclaves ΧΩΡΙΣ ΟΙΚΟΥΝΤΕΣ." In *Actes du Colloque d'histoire sociale 1972 sur l'esclavage,* pp. 47–56. Paris. Originally published as "Una categoria particolare di schiavi attici, i χωρὶς οἰκοῦντες." *Rendiconti del reale Istituto Lombardo di Scienze e Lettere* 106 (1972): 375–88.

Peschel, I. 1987. *Die Hetäre bei Symposion und Komos in der attisch-rotfigurigen Vasenmalerei des 6–4 Jahrhunderts vor Christus.* Frankfurt.

Petropoulakou, M., E. Tsimbidis, and E. Pendazos. 1973. Αττική, Οικιστικά Στοιχεία—Πρώτη Εκθεση. Athens.

Petropoulos, G. 1939. Πάπυροι τῆς ἐν Ἀθήναις Ἀρχαιολογικῆς Ἑταιρείας. Athens.

Phillips, W. D., Jr. 1985. *Slavery from Roman Times to the Early Transatlantic Trade.* Manchester.

Pleket, H. W. 1964. *Epigraphica: Texts on the Economic History of the Greek World.* Leiden.

Pohlenz, M. 1948. "Zu den attischen Reden auf die Gefallenen." *Symbolae Osloenses* 20: 46–74.

Polanyi, K. 1944. *Origins of Our Time: The Great Transformation.* New York.

Polanyi, K., M. Arensberg, and H. W. Pearson, eds. 1957. *Trade and Markets in the Early Empires.* New York.

Polignac, F. de. 1995. *Cults, Territory and the Origins of the Greek City-State.* Chicago. Originally published as *La naissance de la cité grecque.* Paris, 1984.

Pollitt, J. J. 1961. *Hesperia* 30: 293–97, no. 1 (*S.E.G.* 21.542).

Pomeroy, S. 1975. *Goddesses, Whores, Wives and Slaves: Women in Classical Antiquity.* New York.

———. 1994. *Xenophon Oeconomicus: A Social and Historical Commentary.* Cambridge.

———. 1997. *Families in Classical and Hellenistic Greece: Representations and Realities.* Oxford.

Popper, K. R. 1950. *The Open Society and Its Enemies.* Princeton.

Posner, R. A. 1992. *Sex and Reason.* Cambridge, Mass.

———. 1995. *Overcoming Law.* Cambridge, Mass.

Powell, J. E. 1938. *A Lexicon to Herodotus.* Cambridge.

Price, M. J. 1968. "Early Greek Bronze Coinage." In *Essays in Greek Coinage Presented to Stanley Robinson*, edited by C. M. Kraay and G. K. Jenkins, pp. 90–104. Oxford.

———. 1979. "The Function of Early Greek Bronze Coinage." *Atti del VI Convegno del Centro Internazionale di Studi Numismatici: Napoli 17–22 aprile 1977.* Supplement to *Atti dell'Istituto italiano di numismatica* 25: 351–65.

Pringsheim, F. 1955. "The Transition from Witnessed to Written Transactions in Athens." In *Aequitas und Bona Fides: Festgabe für A. Simonius*, pp. 287–97. Basel.

Pritchett, W. K. 1971–91. *The Greek State at War.* 5 vols. Berkeley.

Pritchett, W. K., D. A. Amyx, and A. Pippin. 1953. "The Attic *Stelai*. Part 1." *Hesperia* 22: 225–99.

———. 1956. "The Attic Stelai. Part 2." *Hesperia* 25: 178–317.

Purpura, G. 1987. "Ricerche in tema di prestito marittimo." *Annali del Seminario Giuridico dell' Università di Palermo* 39: 189–337.

Raaflaub, K. A. 1980. "Des freien Bürgers Recht der freien Rede: Ein Beitrag zur Begriffs- und Sozialgeschichte der athenischen Demokratie." In *Studien zur Antiken Sozialgeschichte: Festschrift F. Vittinghoff*, edited by W. Eck et al., pp. 7–57. Kölner historische Abhandlungen 28, Cologne.

———. 1983. "Democracy, Oligarchy, and the Concept of the 'Free Citizen' in Late Fifth-Century Athens." *Political Theory* 11: 517–44.

———. 1993. "City-State, Territory, and Empire in Classical Antiquity." In *City-States in Classical Antiquity and Medieval Italy*, edited by A. Molho, K. Raaflaub, and J. Emlen, pp. 565–88. Ann Arbor.

———. 1994. "Democracy, Power, and Imperialism in Fifth-Century Athens." In *Athenian Political Thought and the Reconstruction of American Democracy*, edited by J. P. Euben, J. R. Wallach, and J. Ober, pp. 103–46. Ithaca, N.Y.

Rahe, P. A. [1992] 1994. *Republics Ancient and Modern: The Ancien Régime in Classical Greece.* Chapel Hill.

Rahn, P. 1986. "Funeral Memorials of the First Priestess of Athena Nike." *Annual of the British School at Athens* 81: 195–207.

Rainer, J. M. 1986. "Zum Problem der Atimie als Verlust der bürgerlichen Rechte insbesondere bei männlichen homosexuellen Prostituierten." *Revue internationale des droits de l'antiquité*, 3d ser., 33: 89–114.

Randall, R. H., Jr. 1953. "The Erechtheum Workmen." *American Journal of Archaeology* 57: 199–210.

Raubitschek, A. E. 1948. "The Case against Alcibiades (Andocides iv)." *Transactions of the American Philological Association* 79: 191ff.

Reger, G. 1993. "The Public Purchase of Grain on Independent Delos." *Classical Antiquity* 12: 299–334.

Reinsberg, C. 1989. *Ehe, Hetärentum und Knabenliebe im antiken Griechenland.* Munich.

Report of the United Nations International Labor Organization. 1998. *The Sex Sector: The Economic and Social Bases of Prostitution in Southeast Asia.* Geneva.

Rhodes, P. J. 1972. "The Five Thousand in the Athenian Revolutions of 411 B.C." *Journal of Hellenic Studies* 92: 115–27.

———. 1979. "*Eisangelia* in Athens." *Journal of Hellenic Studies* 99: 103–14.

———. 1981. *A Commentary on the Aristotelian Athenaion Politeia.* Oxford.

———. 1993. "The Greek *Poleis*: Demes, Cities and Leagues." In Hansen 1993, pp. 161–82. Copenhagen.

———. 1995. "Epigraphical Evidence: Laws and Decrees." In Hansen 1995d, pp. 91–112.

———. 1996. "Federal States." In *Oxford Classical Dictionary*, 3d ed., pp. 591–92. Oxford.

Richards, D.A.J. 1982. *Sex, Drugs, Death and the Law: An Essay on Human Rights and Decriminalization.* Totowa, N.J.

Richter, G. 1961. *Archaic Gravestones of Attica.* London.

Riedel, M. 1975. *Metaphysik und Metapolitik: Studien zu Aristoteles und zur politischen Sprache der neuzeitlichen Philosophie.* Frankfurt.

Ritter, J. 1961. *Naturrecht bei Aristoteles.* Stuttgart.

Roberts, J. 1996. "Athenian Equality: A Constant Surrounded by Flux." In Ober and Hedrick 1996, pp. 187–202.

Robertson, M. 1975. *A History of Greek Art.* Vols. 1–2. Cambridge.

Robertson, N. 1985. "The Origin of the Panathenaea." *Rheinisches Museum für Philologie* 128: 231–95.

Robinson, R. [1962] 1995. *Aristotle: Politics Books III and IV.* Oxford.

Robinson, T. M. 1981. Review of Dover [1978] 1989. In *Phoenix* 35:160–63.

Rocchi, G. Daverio. 1993. *Città-Stato e stati federali della Grecia classica.* Milan.

Roesch, P. 1965. *Thespies et la confédération béotienne.* Paris.

Romanucci-Ross, L., and G. A. de Vos. 1995. Preface. In *Ethnic Identity: Creation, Conflict, and Accommodation*, edited by L. Romanucci-Ross and G. de Vos, pp. 11–14. Walnut Creek, Calif.

Rosen, M. 1996. Review of Sandel 1996. In *Times Literary Supplement,* October 18, 1996, p. 14.

Rosen, R. 1982. *The Lost Sisterhood: Prostitution in America, 1900–1918.* Baltimore.

Rosivach, V. 1987. "Autochthony and the Athenians." *Classical Quarterly* 37: 294–306.

———. 1989. "*Talassiourgoi* and *Paidia* in IG ii^2 1553–78: A Note on Athenian Social History." *Historia* 38: 365–70.

Ross, W. D. 1949. *Aristotle.* London.

Rossiaud, J. 1982. "Prostitution, sexualité, société dans les villes françaises au XVe siècle." *Communications* 35: 68–84.

———. 1988. *Medieval Prostitution.* Translated by L. G. Cochrane. Oxford. Originally published as *La prostituzione nel Medioevo.* 1984. Rome.

Roussel, D. 1976. *Tribu et cité: Études sur les groupes sociaux dans les cités grecques aux époques archaïque et classique.* Paris.

Roy, J. 1997. "An Alternative Sexual Morality for Classical Athens." *Greece & Rome* 44: 11–22.

———. 1998. "The Threat from the Piraeus." In Cartledge, Millett, and von Reden 1998, pp. 191–202.

Royce, A. P. 1982. *Ethnic Identity.* Bloomington, Ind.

Rubinstein, L. 1993. *Adoption in IV. Century Athens.* Copenhagen.

Rudhardt, J. 1958. *Notions fondamentales de la pensée religieuse et les actes constitutifs du culte dans la Grèce classique.* Caen.

———. 1962. "La reconnaissance de la paternité: Sa nature et portée dans la société athénienne." *Museum Helveticum* 19: 39–64.

Rueschemeyer, D. 1984. "Theoretical Generalization and Historical Perspective in the Comparative Sociology of Reinhard Bendix." In *Vision and Method in Historical Sociology*, edited by T. Skocpol, pp. 129–69. Cambridge.

Runciman, W. G. 1990. "Doomed to Extinction: The *Polis,* an Evolutionary Dead-End." In Murray and Price 1990, pp. 347–67.

Ruschenbusch, E. 1965. "*Hybreos Graphe*: Ein Fremdkörper in athenischen Recht des 4. Jahrhunderts v. Chr." *Zeitschrift der Savigny-Stiftung für Rechtsgeschichte. Romanistische Abteilung* 82: 302–9.

———. 1978. *Untersuchungen zu Staat und Politik in Griechenland vom 7.–4. Jh. v. Chr.* Bamberg.

———. 1979. *Athenische Innenpolitik im 5 Jahrhundert v. Chr.: Ideologie oder Pragmatismus?* Bamberg.

———. 1981. "Noch Einmal die Bürgerzahl Athens um 330 v. Chr." *Zeitschrift für Papyrologie und Epigraphik* 44: 110–12.

———. 1984. "Die Bevölkerungszahl Griechenlands im 5. und 4. Jh. v. Chr." *Zeitschrift für Papyrologie und Epigraphik* 56: 55–57.

———. 1985. "Die Zahl der griechischen Staaten und Arealgrösse und Bürgerzahl der 'Normalpolis.'" *Zeitschrift für Papyrologie und Epigraphik* 59: 253–63.

Rustow, D. 1967. *A World of Nations*. Washington, D.C.

Rutter, N. K. 1981. "Early Greek Coinage and the Influence of the Athenian State." In *Coinage and Society in Britain and Gaul: Some Current Problems*, edited by B. Cunliffe, pp. 1–9. London.

Rydberg-Cox, J. 1998. *The Rhetoric of Myth in the Isocratean Corpus*. Ph.D. dissertation. Chicago.

Sagan, E. 1991. *The Honey and the Hemlock: Democracy and Paranoia in Ancient Athens and Modern America*. New York.

Sakellariou, A. 1989. *The Polis-State: Definitions and Origin*. Athens.

Salkever, S. G. 1991. "Aristotle's Social Science." In Lord and O'Connor 1991, pp. 11–48.

Sallares, R. 1991. *The Ecology of the Ancient Greek World*. Ithaca, N.Y.

Saller, R. 1986. "Patria Potestas and the Stereotype of the Roman Family." *Continuity and Change* 1: 6–22.

———. 1987. "Men's Age at Marriage and Its Consequences in the Roman Family." *Classical Philology* 82: 21–34.

Salmon, P. 1978. *Etude sur la confédération béotienne (447/6–386)*. Brussels.

———. 1985. "Droits et devoirs des cités dans la confédération béotienne (447/6–386)." In *La Béotie antique*, edited by G. Argoud and P. Roesch, pp. 301–6. Paris.

Sandel, M. 1982. *Liberalism and the Limits of Justice*. Cambridge.

———. 1984. "The Procedural Republic and the Unencumbered Self." *Political Theory* 12: 81–96.

———. 1996. *Discontent: America in Search of a Public Philosophy*. Cambridge, Mass.

Sandys, J. E. [1912] 1966. *Aristotle's Constitution of Athens*. London.

Saunders, T. J. 1972. *Notes on the Laws of Plato*. Bulletin of the Institute of Classical Studies, suppl. 28. London.

———. 1995. *Aristotle: Politics, Books 1 and 2*. Oxford.

Saxonhouse, A. W. 1986. "Myths and the Origins of Cities: Reflections on the Autochthony Theme in Euripides' *Ion*." In *Greek Tragedy and Political Theory*, edited by J. P. Euben, pp. 252–73. Berkeley.

———. 1991. "Aristotle: Defective Males, Hierarchy, and the Limits of Politics." In *Feminist Interpretations and Political Theory*, edited by M. L. Shanley and C. Pateman, pp. 32–52. University Park, Pa.

———. 1996. *Athenian Democracy: Modern Mythmakers and Ancient Theorists*. Notre Dame.

Schäfer, A. [1885–87] 1979. *Demosthenes und seine Zeit*. 3 vols. 2d ed. New York.

Scafuro, A. 1994. "Witnessing and False Witnessing: Proving Citizenship and Kin Identity in Fourth-Century Athens." In Boegehold and Scafuro 1994, pp. 156–98. Baltimore.

———. 1997. *The Forensic Stage: Settling Disputes in Graeco-Roman New Comedy*. Cambridge.

Scarborough, W. K. 1976. "Slavery—The White Man's Burden." In *Perspectives and Irony in Americn Slavery*, edited by H. P. Owens, pp. 103–35. Jackson, Miss.

Schama, S. 1987. *The Embarrassment of Riches: An Interpretation of Dutch Culture in the Golden Age*. London.

Schaps, D. M. 1979. *Economic Rights of Women in Ancient Greece*. Edinburgh.

———. 1998a. Review of D. Tandy, *Warriors into Traders: The Power of the Market in Early Greece*. *Bryn Mawr Classical Review*, November 1: 1–13. An e-journal at owner_bmcr_l@brynmawr.edu.

Schaps, D. M. 1998b. "What Was Free about a Free Athenian Woman?" *Transactions of the American Philological Association* 128: 161–88.

Scheidel, W. 1998. Addendum to chapter 11. In Garnsey 1998, pp. 195–200.

Schenkl, H. 1880. "De metoecis atticis." *Wiener Studien* 2: 161–225.

Scherling, K. 1898. *Quibus rebus singulorum Atticae pagorum incolae operam dederint*. Leipziger Studien zur klassischen Philologie 18.

Schlotterbeck, J. T. 1991. "The Internal Economy of Slavery in Rural Piedmont Virginia." In Berlin and Morgan 1991, pp. 170–81.

Schmid, W. 1955. "Zu Thukydides I 22.1 und 2." *Philologus* 99: 220–33.

Schmitt, H., ed. 1969. *Die Staatsverträge der antiken Welt.* Vol. 3. Munich.

Schmitt-Pantel, P. 1987. "Les pratiques collectives et le politique dans la cité grecque." In *Sociabilité, pouvoirs et societé*, pp. 279–88. Actes du colloque de Rouen, 24–26 November 1983. Rouen.

———. 1990. "Collective Activities and the Political in the Greek City." In Murray and Price 1990, pp. 199–214. Oxford.

Schmitz, W. 1988. *Wirtschaftliche Prosperität, soziale Integration und Seebundpolitik Athens: Die Wirkung der Erfahrungen aus dem ersten attischen Seebund auf die Aussenpolitik in der ersten Hälfte des 4. Jahrhunderts v. Chr.* Munich.

Schneider, H. 1912. *Untersuchungen über die Staatsbegräbnisse und den Aufbau der öffentlichen Leichenreden bei den Athenern in der klassischen Zeit.* Diss. Berne.

Schoeffer, V. von. 1903. "Demoi." In Pauly-Wissowa 1894–1972, 5.1: cols. 1–131.

Scholl, N. 1957. *Der platonische Menexenos*. Diss. Frankfurt.

Schonbeck, H.-P. 1981. *Beiträge zur Interpretation der plautinischen "Bacchides."* Düsseldorf.

Schuller, W. 1985. *Frauen in der griechischen Geschichte.* Konstanz.

———. 1995. "Poleis im Ersten Attischen Seebund." In Hansen 1995d, pp. 165–70.

Schütrumpf, E. 1991. *Aristoteles, Politik.* 2 vols. Berlin.

Schwimmer, E. 1990. "La genèse du discours nationaliste chez les Maoris." *Culture* 10: 23–34.

———. 1992. "La spirale dédoublée et l'identité nationale: L'art abstrait traditionnel maori a-t-il une signification?" *Anthropologie et sociétés* 16: 59–72.

Seaford, R. 1994. *Reciprocity and Ritual.* Oxford.

———. 1998. Introduction. In Gill, Postlethwaite, and Seaford 1998, pp. 1–11.

Seager, R. 1966. "Lysias and the Corn-dealers." *Historia* 15:172–84.

Sealey, R. 1960. "Who Was Aristogeiton?" *Bulletin of the Institute of Classical Studies* 7: 33–43.

———. 1984. "On Lawful Concubinage in Athens." *Classical Antiquity* 3: 111–33.

———. 1987. *The Athenian Republic: Democracy or the Rule of Law?* University Park, Pa.

———. 1990. *Women and Law in Classical Greece*. Chapel Hill, N.C.

Segrè, A. 1947. "Note sull' economia di Atene nel IV secolo av. Cr." *Studi italiani di filologia classica* 22: 133–63.

Seton-Watson, H. 1977. *Nations and States*. Boulder, Colo.

Shapiro, H. A. 1992. "Theseus in Kimonian Athens." *Mediterranean Historical Review* 7, no. 1: 29–49.

Shennan, S. 1989. Introduction to *Archaeological Approaches to Cultural Identity*, edited by S. Shennan, pp. 1–32. London.

Sherk, R. 1990. "The Eponymous Officials of Greek Cities." *Zeitschrift für Papyrologie und Epigraphik* 83: 249–88.

Shorter, E. 1977. *The Making of the Modern Family.* New York.

Shulsky, A. N. 1991. "The 'Infrastructure' of Aristotle's *Politics*: Aristotle on Economics and Politics." In Lord and O'Connor 1991, pp. 74–111.

Sicari, A. 1991. *Prostituzione e tutela giuridica della schiava: Un problema di politica legislativa nell' impero romano*. Bari.

Sieg, J. 1873. "Der Verfasser neun angeblich von Demosthenes für Apollodor geschriebener Reden." *Jahrbücher für classische Philologie,* suppl. 6: 395–434.

Silver, M. 1995. *Economic Structures of Antiquity.* Westport, Conn.

Simms, R. R. 1988. "The Cult of the Thracian Goddess Bendis in Athens and Attica." *Ancient World* 18: 59–76.

Simon, E. 1996. "Theseus and Athenian Festivals." In *Worshipping Athena: Panathenaia and Parthenon,* edited by J. Neils, pp. 9–26. Madison.

Sinclair, R. K. 1988. *Democracy and Participation in Athens.* Cambridge.

Sissa, G. 1986. "La famille dans la cité grecque (V–IV siècle avant J.-C.)." In *Histoire de la famille*, edited by A. Burguière et al., pp. 163–94. Paris.

Skinner, M. 1997. "Introduction: Quod multo fit aliter in Graecia." In *Roman Sexualities*, edited by J. Hallett and M. Skinner, pp. 3–25. Princeton.

Smith, A. D. 1981. *The Ethnic Revival in the Modern World.* Cambridge.

———. 1986. *The Ethnic Origins of Nations.* Oxford.

———. 1991. *National Identity.* London.

Smith, J. M. 1964. "Group Selection and Kin Selection." *Nature* 201, no. 4924: 1145–47.

Smith, M. 1960. *The Ancient Greeks.* Ithaca, N.Y.

Sokala, A. 1993. "The Effectiveness of the 'Ne Prostituatur' Clauses in Roman Law." *Eos* 81: 97–100.

Sommer, F. 1948. *Zur Geschichte der griechischen Nominalkomposita.* Munich.

Sommerstein, A. H. 1990. *Lysistrata.* Warminster.

Sourvinou-Inwood, C. 1987. "*Antigone* 904–920: A Reading." *Archeologia e storia antica.* Annali. Istituto Universitario Orientale, Napoli, Dipartimeno del mondo classico e del mediterraneo antico 9–10: 19–35.

———. 1990. "What Is *Polis* Religion?" In Murray and Price 1990, pp. 295–322.

———. 1994. "Something to Do with Athens: Tragedy and Ritual." In *Ritual, Finance, Politics: Athenian Democratic Accounts Presented to David Lewis*, edited by R. Osborne and S. Hornblower, pp. 269–90. Oxford.

———. 1995. "Male and Female, Public and Private, Ancient and Modern." In *Pandora: Women in Classical Greece*, edited by E. D. Reeder, pp. 111–20. Princeton.

———. Forthcoming. *Women, Religion and Tragedy: Readings in Drama and the Polis Discourse.*

Spelman, E. V. 1994. "Hairy Cobblers and Philosopher-Queens." In *Feminist Interpretations of Plato*, edited by N. Tuana, pp. 87–107. University Park, Pa.

Stahl, M. 1987. *Aristokraten und Tyrannen im archaischen Athen.* Stuttgart.

Stancomb, W. 1993. "Arrowheads, Dolphins and Cast Coins in the Black Sea Region." *Classical Numismatic Review* 18, no. 3: 5.

Stanton, G. R. 1984. "Some Attic Inscriptions." *Annual of the British School at Athens* 79: 289–306.

———. 1994. "The Rural Demes and Athenian Politics." In *The Archaeology of Athens and Attica under the Democracy*, edited by W.D.E. Coulson, O. Palagia, T. L. Shear Jr., H. A. Shapiro, and F. J. Frost, pp. 217–24. Oxford.

Ste. Croix, G.E.M. de. 1953. "Demosthenes' Timema and the Athenian Eisphora in the Fourth Century." *Classica et Mediaevalia* 14: 30–70.

———. 1966. "The Estate of Phaenippus (Ps.-Dem., xlii)." In *Ancient Society and Institutes: Studies Presented to Victor Ehrenberg,* edited by E. Badian, pp. 109–14. Oxford.

———. 1970. Review of A.R.W. Harrison, *The Laws of Athens. I.* (Oxford, 1968). *Classical Review,* n.s., 20: 387–90.

———. 1972. *Origins of the Peloponnesian War.* London.

———. 1974. "Ancient Greek and Roman Maritime Loans." In *Debits, Credits, Finance and Profits,* edited by H. Edey and B. S. Yamey, pp. 41–59. London.

———. 1981. *The Class Struggle in the Ancient Greek World.* London.

Ste. Croix, G.E.M. de. 1988. "Slavery and Other Forms of Unfree Labour." In *Slavery and Other Forms of Unfree Labour*, edited by L. J. Archer, pp. 19–32. London.

Starr, C. G. 1958. "An Overdose of Slavery." *Journal of Economic History* 18: 17–32.

Steinberg, J. 1976. *Why Switzerland?* Cambridge.

Steiner, D. T. 1994. *The Tyrant's Writ.* Princeton.

Steinhower, G. 1994. "Παρατηρήσεις στην οικιστική μορφή των αττικών δήμων." In *The Archaeology of Athens and Attica under the Democracy*, edited by W.D.E. Coulson, O. Palagia, T. L. Shear Jr., H. A. Shapiro, and F. J. Frost, pp. 175–89. Oxford.

Steltzer, E. 1971. Untersuchungen zur Enktesis im attischen Recht. Dissertation. Munich.

Stengel, P. 1958. "Amphidromia." In Pauly-Wissowa 1894–1972, 1.1: cols. 1901–2.

Stewart, A. F. 1990. *Greek Sculpture.* New Haven.

Stirbois, M. F. 1990. "Discussion du projet de loi Jean-Claude Gayssot tendant à réprimer tout acte raciste, antisémite ou xénophobe." *Journal officiel de la République française*, May 3, pp. 907–11.

Stockton, D. 1990. *The Classical Athenian Democracy.* Oxford.

Strauss, B. S. 1987. *Athens after the Peloponnesian War: Class, Faction, and Policy, 403–386 B.C.* Ithaca, N.Y.

———. 1993. *Fathers and Sons in Athens: Ideology and Society in the Era of the Peloponnesian War.* Princeton.

Stroud, R. 1974a. "Three Attic Decrees." *California Studies in Classical Antiquity* 7: 279–98.

———. 1974b. "An Athenian Law on Silver Coinage." *Hesperia* 43: 157–88.

———. 1998. *The Athenian Grain-Tax Law of 374/3 B.C. Hesperia* suppl. 29. Princeton.

Stupperich, R. 1977. "Staatsbegräbnis und Privatgrabmal im klassischen Athen." Dissertation. Munich.

Swanson, J. A. 1992. *The Public and the Private in Aristotle's Political Philosophy.* Ithaca, N.Y.

Swoboda, H. 1924. "Κώμη." *RE* Suppl. Band 4, edited by W. Kroll, pp. 950–76.

Sykutris, J. 1928. "Der demosthenische Epitaphios." *Hermes* 63: 241–53.

Taillardat, J. 1962. *Les images d'Aristophane. Etudes de langue et de style.* Lyon.

Tambiah, S. J. 1989. "Ethnic Conflict in the World Today." *American Ethnologist* 16: 335–49.

Tandy, D. W. 1997. *Warriors into Traders: The Power of the Market in Early Greece.* Berkeley.

Taylor, A. E. 1952. *Plato: The Man and His Work.* 6th ed. New York.

Thomas, R. 1989. *Oral Tradition and Written Record in Classical Athens.* Cambridge Studies in Oral and Literate Culture 18. Cambridge.

———. 1992. *Literacy and Orality in Ancient Greece.* Cambridge.

Thompson, H. A. 1982. "The *Pnyx* in Models" In *Studies in Attic Epigraphy, History and Topography Presented to Eugene Vanderpool. Hesperia* suppl. 19, pp. 133–47.

Thompson, H. A., and R. L. Scranton. 1943. "Stoas and City Walls on the Pnyx." *Hesperia* 12: 269–83.

Thompson, H. A., and R. E. Wycherley. 1972. *The Agora of Athens.* Athenian Agora 14. Princeton.

Thompson, T. 1992. *Early History of the Israelite People from the Written and Archaeological Sources.* Leiden.

Thompson, W. E. 1968. "An Interpretation of the 'Demotionid' Decrees." *Symbolae Osloenses* 42: 51–68.

———. 1971. "The Deme in Kleisthenes' Reforms." *Symbolae Osloenses* 46: 72–79.

———. 1976. *De Hagniae Hereditate: An Athenian Inheritance Case. Mnemosyne,* suppl. 44. Leyden.

———. 1979. "A View of Athenian Banking." *Museum Helveticum* 36: 224–41.

———. 1980. "An Athenian Commercial Case: Demosthenes 34." *Tidjschrift voor Rechtsgeschiedenis* 48: 137–49.

———. 1981a. "Apollodoros v. Phormion: The Computation of Damages." *Revue internationale des droits de l'antiquité,* 3d ser., 28: 83–94.

———. 1981b. "Athenian Attitudes toward Wills." *Prudentia* 13, no. 1: 13–23.

———. 1983. "The Athenian Entrepreneur." *L'Antiquité classique* 51: 53–85.

Thomsen, R. 1964. *Eisphora*. Copenhagen.

Thornton, B. S. 1997. *Eros: The Myth of Ancient Greek Sexuality.* Boulder, Colo.

Thür, G. 1977. *Beweisführung vor den Schwurgerichtshöfen Athens: die Proklesis zur Basanon.* Vienna.

———. 1989. "Wo wohnen die Metöken?" In *Demokratie und Architektur: Die hippodamische Städtebau und die Entstehung der Demokratie,* edited by W. Schuller, W. Hoepfner, and E. L. Schwandner, pp. 117–21. Munich.

Todd, S. 1990. "The Purpose of Evidence in Athenian Courts." In *Nomos: Essays in Athenian Law, Politics and Society,* edited by P. Cartledge, P. Millett, and S. Todd, pp. 19–39. Cambridge.

———. 1993. *The Shape of Athenian Law.* Oxford.

Todd, S. 1994. "Status and Contract in Fourth-Century Athens." In *Symposion 1993*, edited by G. Thür, pp. 125–40. Cologne.

———. 1997. "Status and Gender in Athenian Public Records." In *Symposion 1995*, edited by G. Thür and J. Vélissaropoulos-Karakostas, pp. 113–24. Cologne.

Todd, S., and P. Millett. 1990. "Law, Society and Athens." In *Nomos: Essays in Athenian Law, Politics and Society,* edited by P. Cartledge, P. Millett, and S. Todd, pp. 1–18. Cambridge.

Tonkin, E., M. McDonald, and N. Canon. 1989. Introduction to *History and Ethnicity,* edited by E. Tonkin et al., pp. 1–21. London.

Touchais, G. 1985. "Chronique des fouilles et découvertes archéologiques en Grèce en 1984." *Bulletin de correspondance hellénique* 109: 768 and fig. 17.

Traill, J. S. 1975. *The Political Organization of Attica*. Princeton.

———. 1982. "An Interpretation of Six Rock-Cut Inscriptions in the Attic Demes of Lamptrai." In *Studies in Attic Epigraphy, History and Topography Presented to E. Vanderpool,* pp. 162–71. *Hesperia,* suppl. 19. Princeton.

———. 1986. *Demos and Trittys: Epigraphical and Topographical Studies in the Organization of Attica.* Toronto.

Travlos, J. 1988. *Bildlexikon zur Topographie des antiken Attika.* Tübingen.

Treves, P. 1937. "Note sulla guerra corinzia." *Rivista di filologia e di istruzione classica* 65: 113–40.

Trevett, J. 1992. *Apollodoros the Son of Pasion*. Oxford.

Trexler, R. C. 1981. "La prostitution florentine au XVe siècle: patronages et clientèles." *Annales (économies, sociétés, civilisations)* 6: 983–1015.

Tsitsidiris, S. 1998. *Platons Menexenos: Einleitung, Text und Kommentar.* Stuttgart.

Turner, E. R. 1911. *The Negro in Pennsylvania.* Washington, D.C.

Turner, F. M. 1981. *The Greek Heritage in Victorian Britain.* New Haven.

Turner, J. A. 1983. "Hiereiai: Acquisition of Feminine Priesthoods in Ancient Greece." Ph.D. dissertation, University of California at Santa Barbara.

Twersky, I. 1972. *A Maimonides Reader*. Philadelphia.

Tyrrell, W. B., and F. S. Brown. 1991. *Athenian Myths and Institutions: Words in Action.* Oxford.

Uchendo, V. C. 1995. "The Dilemma of Ethnicity and Polity Primacy in Black Africa." In Romanucci-Ross and de Vos 1995, pp. 125–35.

Van den Berghe, P. 1978. "Race and Ethnicity: A Sociobiological Perspective." *Ethnic and Racial Studies* 1, no. 4.

van Effenterre, H. 1985. *La cité grecque*. Paris.

van Groningen, B. A. 1953. *In the Grip of the Past.* Leiden.

van Wees, H. 1992. *Status Warriors: War, Violence and Society in Homer and History.* Amsterdam.

Vatin, C. 1984. *Citoyens et non-citoyens dans le monde grec*. Paris.

Vélissaropoulos, J. 1980. *Les nauclères grecs*. Geneva.

Vernant, J.-P. 1980. *Myth and Society in Ancient Greece.* Sussex. Originally published as *Mythe et société en Grèce ancienne*. Paris, 1974.

———. 1986. *Mythe et pensée chez les Grecs.* 3d ed. Paris.

Verrall, A. W. 1895. *Euripides the Rationalist.* Cambridge.

Vestergaard, T., M. H. Hansen, L. Rubinstein, L. Bjertrup, and T. H. Nielsen. 1992. "The Age-Structure of Athenian Citizens Commemorated in Sepulchral Inscriptions." *Classica et Mediaevalia* 43: 5–21.

Veyne, P. 1971. *Comment on écrit l'histoire, essai d'épistémologie.* Paris.

———. 1988. *Did the Greeks Believe in Their Myths?* Chicago. Originally published as *Les Grecs ont-ils cru à leurs mythes?* Paris 1983.

———. 1995. *Le quotidien et l'intéressant.* Paris.

Vian, F. 1963. *Les origines de Thèbes: Cadmos et les Spartes.* Paris.

Vickers, M. 1985. "Early Greek Coinage: A Reassessment." *Numismatic Chronicle* 45: 108–28.

Vidal-Naquet, P. 1986. *The Black Hunter: Forms of Thought and Forms of Society in the Greek World.* Baltimore. Originally published as *Le chasseur noir: Formes de pensées et formes de société dans le monde grec.* Paris, 1981.

———. 1990. *La démocratie grecque vue d'ailleurs.* Paris.

Vollgraff, W. 1952. *L'oraison funèbre de Gorgias.* Leiden.

von Loewenclau, I. 1961. *Der platonische Menexenos.* Stuttgart.

von Reden, S. 1992. "Arbeit und Zivilisation. Kriterien der Selbstdefinition im antiken Athen." *Münstersche Beiträge z. antiken Handelsgeschichte* 11: 1–31.

———. 1995. *Exchange in Ancient Greece.* London.

———. 1997. "Money, Law and Exchange: Coinage in the Greek Polis." *Journal of Hellenic Studies* 117: 154–76.

———. 1998. "The Commodification of Symbols: Reciprocity and Its Perversions in Menander." In Gill, Postlethwaite, and Seaford 1998, pp. 255–78.

Wade-Gery, H. T. 1958. *Essays in Greek History.* Oxford.

Wagner, H. 1967. "Zur Freiheitserteilung in den einem Generalpfandnexus unterliegenden Sklaven." *Studia et Documenta Historiae et Iuris* 33: 163–88.

Walbank, F. W. [1967] 1985. "Speeches in Greek Historians." In *Selected Papers*, pp. 242–61. Cambridge. Originally published as Third Myres Memorial Lecture. Oxford.

Waldstein, W. 1986. *Operae Libertorum: Untersuchungen zur Dienstpflicht freigelassener Sklaven.* Stuttgart.

Walker, H. J. 1995. *Theseus and Athens.* Oxford.

Wallace, R. 1994. "The Athenian Laws against Slander." In *Symposion 1993*, edited by G. Thür, pp. 109–24. Cologne.

Walsh G. 1978. "The Rhetoric of Birthright and Race in Euripides' *Ion.*" *Hermes* 106: 301–15.

Walters, J. 1997. "Invading the Roman Body: Manliness and Impenetrability in Roman Thought." In *Roman Sexualities*, edited by J. Hallett and M. Skinner, pp. 29–43. Princeton.

Walters, K. R. 1983. "Perikles' Citizenship Law." *Classical Antiquity* 2: 314–36.

Waltz, J. 1936. *Der lysianische Epitaphios. Philologus,* suppl. 29.

Washburn, P. C. 1982. *Political Sociology: Approaches, Concepts, Hypotheses.* Englewood Cliffs, N.J.

Watson, A. 1987. *Roman Slave Law.* Baltimore.

Weber, M. [1909] 1924. *Agrarverhältnisse im Altertum.* Tübingen. Translated as *The Agrarian Sociology of Ancient Civilizations.* London, 1976.

———. 1921. "Die Stadt." *Archiv für Sozialwissenschaft* 47: 621–772. Reprinted in *Wirtschaft und Gesellschaft.* Tübingen, 1922; translation, *The City*, translated and edited by D. Martindale and G. Neuwirth. Glencoe, Ill., 1958.

———. [1922] 1968. *Wirtschaft und Gesellschaft.* Tübingen 1922. Translated as *Economy and Society.* New York, 1968.

Webster, T.B.L. 1973. *Potter and Patron in Classical Athens.* London.

Weil, R. 1960. *Aristote et l'histoire: Essai sur la Politique.* Études et Commentaires 36. Paris.

Weiss, E. 1923. *Griechisches Privatrecht auf rechtsvergleichender Grundlage.* Leipzig.

Welskopf, E. C. 1985. *Soziale Typenbegriffe im alten Griechenland und ihr Fortleben in den Sprachen der Welt, I. Belegstellenverzeichnis altgriechischer sozialer Typenbegriffe von Homer bis Aristoteles.* Berlin.

Welwei, K.-W. 1967. "Der 'Diapsephismos' nach dem Sturz der Peisistratiden." *Gymnasium* 74: 423–37.

———. 1974. *Unfreie im Antiken Kriegsdienst.* Vol. I. Wiesbaden.

———. [1983] 1998. *Die griechische Polis.* Stuttgart.

———. 1992a. *Athen: Vom neolithischen Siedlungsplatz zur archaischen Grosspolis.* Darmstadt.

———. 1992b. "Polisbildung, Hetairos-Gruppen und Hetairien." *Gymnasium* 99: 481–500.

Wenger, L. 1906. *Stellvertretung im Rechte der Papyri.* Leipzig.

Wesenberg, B. 1981. "Zur Baugeschichte des Niketempels." *Jahrbuch des Deutschen Archäologischen Instituts* 96: 28–54.

West, S. 1988. "The Transmission of the Text." In *A Commentary on Homer's Odyssey,* by A. Heubeck, S. West, and J. B. Hainsworth, Oxford.

Westermann, W. E. 1955. *The Slave Systems of Greek and Roman Antiquity.* Philadelphia.

Whitby, M. Forthcoming. "The Grain Trade of Athens in the Fourth Century B.C." In *Trade, Traders and the Ancient City.* London.

Whitehead, D. 1977. *The Ideology of the Athenian Metic.* Cambridge.

———. 1984. "Immigrant Communities in the Classical Polis: Some Principles for a Synoptic Treatment." *L'Antiquité classique* 53: 47–59.

———. 1986a. *The Demes of Attica 508/7-ca. 250 B.C.: A Political and Social Study.* Princeton.

———. 1986b. "Women and Naturalisation in Fourth-Century Athens: The Case of Archippe." *Classical Quarterly* 36: 109–14.

———. 1993. "Norms of Citizenship in Ancient Greece." In *City-States in Classical Antiquity and Medieval Italy,* edited by A. Molho, K. Raaflaub, and J. Emlen, pp. 135–54. Ann Arbor.

———, ed. 1994. *From Political Architecture to Stephanus Byzantius. Historia,* Einzelshriften, 87. Stuttgart.

———. 1996. "Polis-Toponyms as Personal Entities." *Museum Helveticum* 53: 1–11.

Whitelam, K. 1996. *The Invention of "Ancient Israel": The Silencing of Palestinian History.* London.

Wiedemann, T. 1987. *Slavery.* Oxford.

Wilamowitz-Moellendorff, U. von. 1887. "Demotika der attischen Metoeken." *Hermes* 22: 107–28, 211–59.

———. 1893. *Aristoteles und Athen.* 2 vols. Berlin.

Will, E. 1954. "Sur l'évolution des rapports entre colonies et métropoles en Grèce à partir du VIe siècle." *La nouvelle Clio* 6: 413–60.

———. 1972. *Le monde grec et l'Orient. I: Le V*[e] siècle (510–403). Paris.

Willemsen, F., and S. Brenne. 1991. "Verzeichnis der Kerameikos-Ostraka." *Mitteilungen des Deutschen Archäologischen Instituts* 106: 147–56.

Wilson, F. W. 1935. "Studies in the Social and Economic History of Ostia: Part I." *Papers of the British School at Rome* 13: 41–68.

Wilson, J. 1982. "What Does Thucydides Claim for His Speeches?" *Phoenix* 36: 95–103.

Winkler, J. J. 1990a. "Laying Down the Law: The Oversight of Men's Sexual Behavior in Classical Athens." In *Before Sexuality: The Construction of Erotic Experience in the Ancient Greek World,* edited by D. M. Halperin, J. J. Winkler, F. I. Zeitlin, pp. 171–209. Princeton.

———. 1990b. *The Constraints of Desire: The Anthropology of Sex and Gender in Ancient Greece.* New York.

Wohl, V. 1996. "εὐσεβείας ἕνεκα καὶ φιλοτιμίας: Hegemony and Democracy at the Panathenaia." *Classica et Mediaevalia* 47: 25–88.

———. 1998. *Intimate Commerce: Exchange, Gender, and Subjectivity in Greek Tragedy.* Austin.

Wolff, H. J. 1944. "Marriage Law and Family Organization in Ancient Athens." *Traditio* 2: 43–95. Reprinted in *Beiträge zur Rechtsgeschichte Altgriechenlands und des hellenistisch-römischen Ägypten,* pp. 155–242. Weimar, 1961.

———. 1966. *Die Attische Paragraphe.* Weimar.

Wollstonecraft, M. [1790] 1983. "A Vindication of the Rights of Men." In *A Mary Wollstonecraft Reader,* edited by B. H. Solomon and P. S. Berggren. New York.

Wolters, P. 1913. "Eine Darstellung des athenischen Staatfriedhofs." *Sitzungsberichte der Königlich Bayerischen Akademie der Wissenschaften: 5 Abhandlung.* Munich.

Wood, E. M. 1983. "Agricultural Slavery in Classical Athens." *American Journal of Ancient History* 8, no. 1: 1–47.

———. 1988. *Peasant-Citizen and Slave: The Foundations of Athenian Democracy.* London.

Wood, E. M. 1996. "Demos versus 'We, the People': Freedom and Democracy Ancient and Modern." In Ober and Hedrick 1996, pp. 121–37.

Woodward, C. Vann, ed. 1981. *Mary Chesnut's Civil War.* New Haven.

Worthington, I. 1992. *A Historical Commentary on Dinarchus: Rhetoric and Conspiracy in Later Fourth-Century Athens.* Ann Arbor.

———. 1994. "The Canon of the Ten Attic Orators." In *Persuasion: Greek Rhetoric in Action,* edited by I. Worthington, pp. 244–63. London.

Wright, F. A. [1923] 1969. *Feminism in Greek Literature: From Homer to Aristotle.* Port Washington, N.Y.

Wyse, W. [1904] 1967. *The Speeches of Isaeus.* Cambridge.

Yack, B. 1993. *The Problems of a Political Animal: Community, Justice and Conflict in Aristotelian Political Thought.* Berkeley.

Yiannopoulou-Konsolakē, E. 1990. Γλυφάδα: Ἱστορικό Παρελθόν καί Μνημεία. Athens.

Young, J. H. 1956. "Studies in South Attica. Country Estates at Sounion." *Hesperia* 25: 122–46.

Zeitlin, F. 1993. Foreword. In Loraux [1984] 1993, pp. xi–xvii.

———. 1996. "Mysteries of Identity and Designs of the Self in Euripides' *Ion.*" In *Playing the Other: Gender and Society in Classical Greek Literature,* pp. 185–338. Chicago.

Zimmern, A. 1911. *The Greek Commonwealth.* Oxford.

Ziolkowski, J. 1981. *Thucydides and the Tradition of Funeral Speeches at Athens.* New York.

✦ GENERAL INDEX ✦

INDEX OF PASSAGES CITED